Constitutional Coup

Constitutional Coup

Privatization's Threat to the American Republic

Jon D. Michaels

Harvard University Press

Cambridge, Massachusetts & London, England

2017

Copyright © 2017 by the President and Fellows of Harvard College
All rights reserved
Printed in the United States of America

First printing

Library of Congress Cataloging-in-Publication Data
Names: Michaels, Jon D., author.
Title: Constitutional coup : privatization's threat to the American republic/Jon D. Michaels.
Description: Cambridge, Massachusetts : Harvard University Press, 2017. |
Includes bibliographical references and index.
Identifiers: LCCN 2017015512 | ISBN 9780674737730
Subjects: LCSH: Privatization—United States—History. | Welfare state—United States—
History. | Constitutional law—United States. | United States—Politics and government.
Classification: LCC HD3850 .M53 2017 | DDC 338.973/05—dc23
LC record available at https://lccn.loc.gov/2017015512

To Mom and Dad

CONTENTS

Introduction

If men were angels, no government would be necessary. If angels
were to govern men, neither external nor internal controls on government would be necessary. In framing a government which is to
be administered by men over men, the great difficulty lies in this:
you must first enable the government to control the governed; and
in the next place oblige it to control itself.

—JAMES MADISON, *THE FEDERALIST 51* (1788)

The administrative process is . . . our generation's answer to the
inadequacy of the judicial and the legislative processes. . . . The
creation of administrative power . . . though it may seem in theo-
retic violation of the doctrine of the separation of power . . . [is]
the means for the preservation of the content of that doctrine.

—JAMES M. LANDIS, *THE ADMINISTRATIVE PROCESS* (1938)

I'm going to get good contractors and push the hell out of them.

—DONALD J. TRUMP, *NEW YORK TIMES* (1986)

In 1986, President Ronald Reagan proclaimed that "the nine most terrifying words in the English language are: 'I'm from the Government, and
I'm here to help.'"[1] We as a nation had come a long way from the fireside
chats of the Great Depression. Back then, Franklin Roosevelt regularly
took to the airwaves, assuring a downtrodden people that Washington was
the answer to America's economic and social maladies. We had even come
a long way from the heady days of the 1960s, Camelot, and the Great
Society. Taking government's virtue for granted, a newly inaugurated John
F. Kennedy famously called upon us to do more: to "ask not what your

country can do for you—ask what you can do for your country."² Many answered that call. A new generation of whiz kids entered government service, determined to combat poverty, end discrimination, extend the franchise, export democracy, and send a man to the Moon.

But soon enough the tide turned. We labored through the 1970s, a decade marked by civil unrest, Vietnam, Watergate, forced busing, oil embargoes, stagflation, and the Iranian hostage crisis. *Malaise,* to use Jimmy Carter's term, set in as a string of perceived failures, some rightly and others unfairly ascribed to Washington, made it easy for critics to depict government as a fading Midas; suddenly, everything the feds touched turned to ruin. Indeed, in his "terrifying words" speech, Reagan attributed all of America's problems to government—effectively pitting a torpid, bumbling bureaucracy against a just, dynamic, rational, and above all free market.

By the 1980s, the pitchforks were out in force. Pundits, legislators, and newly politicized business and religious leaders joined Reagan in railing against the American version of what Margaret Thatcher derisively called the Nanny State. For supporters of the expansive welfare state of FDR and LBJ—and, yes, Eisenhower and Nixon, too—the end seemed nigh.

But a funny thing happened on the way to the gallows. The mob got cold feet. The torch and pitchfork crowd realized they really, really liked government programs—*at least the ones that benefited them directly.* They liked their pensions, tax credits, health care, subsidies, licenses, and housing and education loans. They liked their clean air and water. They liked their safe workplaces. And they liked the fact that they could trust the food, drugs, consumer products, and financial services and instruments they purchased. What they really disliked, they decided, was the government itself—its people, its procedures, and its institutional and organizational architecture.

And so, over the past thirty-odd years, elected officials across the political spectrum have acted accordingly, simultaneously indulging and deceiving the American public by disassociating government goods and services from the government, at least as it has been traditionally conceived and staffed. Though these efforts have been framed, quite pointedly, in terms of decreasing the size, reach, and power of government, what's really happening is that the government is being transformed. There is no denying that the State today is bigger and more potent than ever before. It just happens to look very different—a consequence of it being privatized, marketized, and generally reconfigured along decidedly businesslike lines. In short, Reagan didn't, and couldn't, kill the Nanny State. But he did replace our old familiar nanny with a commercial upstart, a nanny corporation as it were.

Mary Poppins, Inc.

Consider just some of the ways the privatized, businesslike State comports itself today. Private contractors now number in the millions. These contractors have taken leading roles in fighting our wars in Afghanistan and Iraq; running prisons and immigration detention facilities; facilitating domestic surveillance and counterterrorism operations; drafting major rules; shaping energy, transportation, health care, and environmental policy; rendering public benefits decisions; collecting taxes; and monitoring and enforcing regulatory compliance across the vast administrative expanse. The stated justification for such privatization is, very often, that contractors are more efficient than their government counterparts—driven, we're told, by market competition to provide higher-quality and lower-cost services.[3]

At the same time, government agencies are privatizing from within, radically overhauling their in-house employment practices to better match what we generally find in the private sector. Among other things, hundreds of thousands of tenured civil servants have been reclassified as at-will employees, subject to summary termination just as they would be if they were working for McDonald's. The Trump administration is pushing further still, promising to strip the rest of the career federal workforce of its legal protections. The stated justification for this overhaul—this *marketization of the bureaucracy*—is substantially the same: to make government workers internalize the pressures, demands, and incentives of the competitive private labor market.

Government contracting and marketizing the bureaucracy represent the biggest, most consequential manifestations of the contemporary businesslike government movement. But those seeking to remake the State have experimented further. They've created an array of intra-governmental venture capital and IT firms; transformed essential bureaucratic offices into for-profit revenue centers; converted our storied space program into something akin to a galactic Uber; established charitable trusts, allowing wealthy individuals and powerful corporations to finance and effectively direct State programs and initiatives; and created VIP prisons, posh accommodations for those able and willing to pay a hefty price to buy their way out of gen pop.[4]

This is, for better or worse, the moment we find ourselves in. Americans are still (grudging) enthusiasts of government goods and services, still deeply allergic to government instruments and instrumentalities, and still very much captivated by the lures of the Market. This book is a meditation on this moment, its ironies, paradoxes, wonders, and shortcomings. But it is also a far more expansive effort to understand how we got here and where we should be going.

Specifically, this book takes us back in time to explore the project of twentieth-century administrative governance as a normatively and constitutionally virtuous one. It describes the almost evangelical denunciation of that project, as evidenced by what is now a multigenerational campaign to refashion public governance in the image of a Fortune 500 company, if not now something straight out of the new gig economy. And it explains how dangerous, distorting, and destructive this campaign has been—and why the operational challenges and democratic imperatives of the twenty-first century compel us to redeem that original, and long beleaguered, administrative project.

Needless to say, mine is hardly the first account of contemporary businesslike government and its transformative effects. Others have looked at particular aspects of businesslike government or confronted this businesslike turn from economic, political, and even sociological and philosophical perspectives. But this is the first account to take in the entirety of businesslike government and understand it as a constitutional phenomenon— weighty in its own right and rendered all the more meaningful and fraught once mapped onto a legally, normatively, and historically textured set of landscapes from 1787 onward.

My argument, in brief, is that the State cannot be separated from its people, practices, and infrastructure without doing considerable violence to our constitutional order. For it is these very (and very distinctive) people, practices, and infrastructure—and the interplay among them—that legitimate the State and validate State exercises of sovereign, coercive, and moral force. And it is these distinctive actors, procedures, and institutions that infuse liberal democratic governance with the necessary admixture of normative politics, civic engagement, professional expertise, financial disinterest, and fidelity to the rule of law. Indeed, a State shorn of these constitutive people, practices, and infrastructure is perhaps better described as part gated community, part corporate conglomerate.

To be sure, gated communities and corporate conglomerates have their charms. And so does businesslike government. It promises to be faster, more innovative, cheaper, and more "customer" friendly—and that no doubt sounds appealing to any number of us who have endured long lines at the DMV or who have otherwise experienced wasteful, sclerotic, or simply apathetic government. But even assuming that those promises can be kept (*a big if*), there is good reason not to embrace privatized, commercialized government.

Government's force, and ultimately its favor, turns on it being decidedly unlike IBM or Walmart or Facebook. This book explains why government is—and very much ought to remain—a fundamentally different enterprise. Businesslike government is all about embracing the logic and discipline of the Market. But the Market, at least in its pure, idealized state, is not democratic, deliberative, or juridical. Nor need it be. It is the world of Schumpeter and Coase, not Montesquieu or Madison.

We can tolerate, even admire, corporate hierarchy, leanness, and efficiency. We can do so because those organizations have (or are presumed to have) a single, objective mission: to maximize shareholder value. We can tolerate, even admire, the unforgiving laws of capitalism. We can do so because only in the rarest of circumstances does the single-mindedness of individual businesses endanger our economic or national security. And we can tolerate, even admire, the rising cult of all-powerful CEOs. We can do so because, generally speaking, their word is not law, their fiefdoms are bounded, and rarely can they exert real coercive force.

This isn't to say, of course, that all firms invariably act in the single-minded manner just described. But the businesslike government crowd is eyeing a particular type of firm: blue chip, publicly traded companies understood to have little time, interest, or discretion to do anything other than maximize profits.

None of the seemingly celebrated market norms, practices, or fiduciary and legal duties translates well into the liberal democratic arena, and certainly not into our constitutional realm. For starters, there is no such thing as a single public goal or truth to pursue. We have no magic commonweal formula, certainly none that's the political equivalent to the maximization of shareholder value. Some of us surely prize national economic growth above all else, and those who do might be the closest approximation of corporate shareholders. But many do not. Instead, we privilege the plight of the poor and disenfranchised. We prioritize social justice or environmental causes or consider the best government to be as unobtrusive as possible. Interests in military hegemony, reproductive rights, and religious freedom throw yet more, often incommensurable, variables into the mix. As such, we cannot readily reduce the goal of government to a single, undifferentiated objective; nor can we readily aggregate or harmonize our interests and channel them through one political leader, an inside-the-Beltway version of a Steve Jobs or Henry Ford. Rather, we need multiple voices, amplified by multiple platforms, constantly speaking to a multiplicity of decisionmakers scattered across multiple branches of government. This isn't efficient or orderly. But it is democratic, pluralistic, inclusive, and deliberative.

What's more, even if we somehow could effectively aggregate, rank, or harmonize our interests and direct a single leader to implement the public's will, we still should resist the temptation to do so. We should resist for two reasons. First, absolute power corrupts, and a renegade sovereign that chooses to deviate from the public's charge poses infinitely greater danger than does a rogue or simply tone-deaf corporate CEO. Second, and more importantly, even if we could effectively aggregate the public's interests *and* ensure the selection of a faithful leader, there still is the very real possibility of tyranny by the majority. That is to say, a dominant faction, or cluster of factions, might settle on a course of action that stigmatizes or oppresses broad classes of minorities. In either case, we want, indeed need, a heterogeneous, overlapping, and cross-checking government to limit the possibility of myopic or abusive exercises of State power.

Sovereign power, unlike most (but of course not all) expressions of corporate power, is intentionally and necessarily morally inflected and coercive. As such, so long as men and women—*rather than angels*—govern, that sovereign power must be subject to checks and balances, even if such checks and balances are messy, time-consuming, and very much lend themselves to what market actors consider waste and obstinacy.

It is for this reason that the United States is founded in large part upon a simple structural commitment: the separation of powers. Separation prevents tyranny, promotes liberty, and helps enrich public policy. Separation gives voice and venue to any number of important but conflicting values and provides procedures and pathways for those values to collectively inform American public law and governance.

This simple structural commitment, and all that it enables, animated the framers' constitutional architecture. But it didn't stop there. This commitment carried forward into the twentieth century, ultimately structuring (and legitimating) our modern welfare state. Now, however, that dynamic commitment—a commitment to separation of powers *all the way forward*—is very much threatened by the instant movement to render the American government more like a business—and a politicized one at that.

The Constitutional Era

Let's start at the beginning. The framers were revolutionaries, but cautious ones at that. Understanding the concentration of sovereign power as "the very definition of tyranny," those convening in Philadelphia's Independence Hall divided a proposed federal government among legislative, executive, and judicial branches. For James Madison, the Constitution's leading architect, "the great security against a gradual concentration of the several powers in the same department consists in giving those who administer each department the necessary constitutional means and personal motives to resist encroachments of the others."[5] Accordingly, no one branch, on its own, could monopolize federal power.

Of course, the framers didn't just divide State power among any three groups. Each of these groups was specially chosen for its distinctive dispositional and institutional characteristics. The president, members of the House and Senate, and federal judges were each made answerable to different constituencies and subject to different temporal and occupational demands. These differences ensured that the branches would regularly clash. And such clashing was good. It was good for the prevention of tyranny and for the corresponding promotion of liberty. It was good, too, for the refinement and enlargement of public policy. After all, actions undertaken by this new national government required broad buy-in from the very differently situated and naturally rivalrous president, House, Senate, and, at least implicitly, judiciary.

Madison and his fellow framers disaggregated government power along other dimensions, too—most notably between the feds and the several states. Though further testament to the constitutional commitment to separating, checking, and balancing, federalism must necessarily be treated only parenthetically so as not to distract us from our central and overriding inquiry into the ongoing formulation, expression, and (normative) legitimation of *federal* power.[6]

The Administrative Era

In time, however, the framers' initial architecture came to be seen as outdated. A regime that relied on several hundred legislators and a single, unitary executive was simply not up to the twentieth-century task of nourishing and housing the poor, protecting workers and consumers, busting trusts, steering monetary policy, regulating the financial sector, stabilizing a volatile economy, and readying a nation for war. Indeed, the social, economic, and geostrategic dislocations associated with modernity called out for a more capacious and interventionist federal government. Congress responded principally by creating a phalanx of agencies, equipping those agencies with legislative, executive, and judicial powers, and directing them to design and administer immensely important programs. In short order, the power and reach of the federal government expanded exponentially, with agency administrators—*bureaucrats!*—supplanting legislators, presidents, and federal judges as the dominant figures directing and overseeing the modern American welfare state.

For many, the rise of administrative agencies signaled the death knell of the constitutional separation of powers. Suddenly these agencies were making rules that carried with them the force of law, enforcing those rules, and ultimately adjudicating alleged violations of those rules. Justice Robert Jackson, a New Deal loyalist, was just one in a long line of jurists, policymakers, and scholars who sounded the alarm over a Leviathan-like administrative state that, in his words, "deranged" our constitutional system.[7]

Concerns over the concentration of legislative, executive, and judicial power—powers the framers took great pains to disaggregate—perdure. Contemporary scholars, even those, like Justice Jackson, generally friendly to progressive government regulation, continue to underscore how much "we have struggled to describe our regulatory government as the legitimate child of constitutional democracy."[8] Other, less sympathetic commentators are even less sparing. They declare agencies "unlawful"[9] and "unconstitutional,"[10] and go so far as to characterize the rise of the Administrative Era as "a bloodless constitutional revolution."[11]

To be sure, most of us have made our peace with administrative agencies.[12] But it remains an uneasy, awkward peace, particularly for those troubled by the fact that the separation of powers—what Chief Justice Warren Burger called our "finely wrought" system—seemingly fell by the wayside.[13]

By my reckoning, the price of such peace isn't nearly so dear. Through a variety of measures and a good bit of serendipity, the nascent administrative architecture of the 1930s and 1940s was refashioned and made to resemble the framers' tripartite scheme. In quick order and with the help of a pair of "superstatutes," initially concentrated administrative power was itself divided, triangulated among presidentially appointed agency heads, career civil servants insulated from political pressures, and the public writ large authorized to engage meaningfully and directly in most administrative matters. Under this newly reconfigured system of *administrative separation of powers,* it was as if James Madison and Franklin Roosevelt had joined forces: we combined modern architecture, sturdy and sophisticated enough to confront twentieth-century socioeconomic challenges, with an interior design styled to make the tyranny-fearing framers feel very much at home.

Specifically, within the administrative arena, agency leaders stood in for the president, taking on the president's political, agenda-setting role; the tenured, expert civil service acted the part of our independent and largely apolitical federal judiciary, insisting on reasoned explanations and an intra-agency commitment to the rule of law; and the public writ large (what I call civil society) re-created Congress's populist, pluralistic, and cacophonic deliberative role, bringing new and diverse opinions and sentiments into the administrative polis.

We of course know that federal legislative action is rendered constitutional by the meaningful interplay of the three great branches. That is the essence of our democratic republic. The same became true with respect to federal administrative action once that realm cobbled together its own system of separated and checked powers. Indeed, if we were to classify the architecture of administrative tripartitism, we would undoubtedly call it *constitutional revivalism,* with civil servants, presidential deputies, and members of civil society well positioned to approximate the rivalrous, contentious, and competitive engagement we associate with the (framers') three great branches. Yet to this day, constitutional revivalism—that is, this inventive and constitutionally validating administrative design—has remained overlooked, underappreciated, and misunderstood.

This misunderstanding matters. It matters for three reasons. First, there is a resurgent conservative legal movement whose adherents are increasingly hostile to the administrative state on constitutional grounds. As D.C. Circuit Judge Douglas Ginsburg puts it, it was the New Deal era when the constitutional "wheels began to come off,"[14] and the Constitution went into "exile."[15] To the extent that the conservative concern is rooted in principles of checks and balances (and not just rote constitutional formalism),[16] the realization of an administrative separation of powers should be welcome news—underscoring, as it does, the disaggregation and fragmentation of State power in ways that reprise and redeem the original tripartite scheme.

Second, there are those who assume that the advent of administrative agencies problematically displaced the framers' separation of powers but nonetheless accept the new world order of American administrative governance. For many years, this sizable group of scholars, lawyers, and jurists didn't need a theory of administrative separation of powers. But now they do.

They need a theory now to respond to the recently emboldened constitutional conservatives. And they need a theory now to distinguish administrative governance from the new upstart: privatized governance. Simply stated, so long as many scholars, lawyers, and jurists remain troubled by what they see as the administrative state's ignoble origin story, they cannot rightly object—at least not on constitutional grounds—to further reconstructions and reformulations of State power similarly disconnected from Madison's intentionally triangulated scheme. The constitutional transgression happened, so their thinking goes, with Franklin Roosevelt and the New Deal Congresses, not Ronald Reagan and others who later took up the privatization mantle. Mindful of the "glass houses" adage, if the New Dealers first crossed the constitutional Rubicon, the subsequent, instant (and quite disconcerting) jump from administrative agencies to privatized and marketized entities cannot provoke much constitutional controversy.

Here is where the theory of administrative separation of powers does a good deal of its work. The truth of the matter is that, for the reasons this book describes, the existence of an administrative separation of powers belies any claim that the administrative state is a constitutional glass house—and we thus can and should be willing to throw a few stones when sufficiently provoked, as we are today by businesslike government. Otherwise, we cede too much legal and moral ground and risk leaving the fate of twenty-first century constitutional government in the hands of dickering pundits and policy analysts who debate whether privatization is efficient and cost-effective.

Third, this misunderstanding skews such punditry and policy analysis. Those who correctly see administrative agencies as internally divided and contentious—*but assign no constitutional significance to those divisions*—are apt to be especially welcoming of a cleaner, seemingly more efficient businesslike alternative. In short, if the inner workings of fractured, fragmented administrative agencies are seen, as they almost invariably are, as nothing more than misguided and wasteful, if not organizationally pathological, then it only follows that we should quickly and warmly embrace the logic and discipline of markets. We should, that is, privatize, corporatize, and commercialize as much as we can. After all, those who deem the administrative state's tripartite architecture a clumsy mess have little reason to do anything but bulldoze over it.

The Privatized Era

And bulldoze they have. Today's administrative state is being reconfigured along businesslike lines. To date, few have grasped the depth, breadth, and texture of businesslike government in its variegated forms. (Even a seemingly straightforward exercise like a simple head count of the number of federal service contractors has proven alarmingly elusive.) And even fewer appreciate what's actually going on.

For starters, many are quick to equate privatized government with cost savings and greater efficiencies. They emphasize outsourcing and other forms of businesslike government as apolitical, technocratic tools used to promote smarter, sounder government. That's certainly what drives the "make or buy" decision in the private sector, as explained long ago in Ronald Coase's *The Nature of the Firm*.[17] Here, however, we're talking about *The Nature of the State*—a market-oriented State, but a State nonetheless. And, within a State, political power remains the coin of the realm. We thus need to assess privatization as a political phenomenon, and a particularly beguiling one at that.

Many are, furthermore, quick to equate privatized government with smaller government. This quite popular gloss gives false comfort to libertarians and conservatives who believe, with Bill Clinton, that the "era of big government is over."[18] And this gloss—conceit, really—throws red herrings in the air for those distraught, unreconstructed New Deal and Great Society types, who took Bill Clinton's businesslike proclamation at face value, all the while obscuring the constitutional calamity staring them— *and us*—in the face.

This constitutional calamity is privatization's evisceration of the administrative separation of powers—again, the often overlooked but nevertheless undeniable architecture that effectively constitutionalized twentieth-century administrative governance, restoring and renewing the framers' commitment to separating and checking power through a mixture of democratic and juridical actors. In brief, today's fusion of market and political power—this running government like a *politicized* business—has the effect of sidelining or defanging otherwise independent, expert, and truly mandarin civil servants and marginalizing the populist contributions of an otherwise empowered and diverse civil society. The fusion also has the effect, quite often, of funneling government responsibilities through private or essentially privatized corridors, far away from public scrutiny and legal constraints. All told, sovereign power is being concentrated in the hands of presidentially appointed agency heads and the private actors paid to do their bidding. The end result is an unprecedentedly potent and potentially abusive State, led by a largely unfettered executive capable of wielding concentrated sovereign power in a hyperpartisan or crassly commercialized fashion.

For those distressed by this recent turn of events, the framers' commitment to checks and balances provided, and still provides, an answer.

It provided an answer to constrain not only the First Congress but also the alphabet agencies arising out of the New Deal and World War II. That same commitment needs to be renewed today, to address the State-aggrandizing, power-concentrating challenges posed by twenty-first-century privatization.

Today is the operative word. One is reminded of the hopeful yet chilly words of Benjamin Franklin, when asked by an inquisitive Philadelphian what form of government the framers concocted: "A republic, if you can keep it." Generations past have done their best to *keep it*. Now that it is our turn, the instant challenge is privatization. If we wait much longer, we're certain to reach a tipping point, at which time reversing the privatization trend will prove next to impossible. This is true on legal, pragmatic, and even psychological levels.

Legally, the more privatization is allowed to continue apace without muscular constitutional pushback, the harder it will be for the courts to take late-arriving challenges seriously. Even if those challenges prove compelling, the courts' hands may very well be tied as the federal landscape continues to be drastically and possibly inexorably altered by the forces of privatization and as a host of sticky cultural norms, instances of congressional acquiescence, and years of historical gloss render the privatized State constitutional by default.

Pragmatically, we will have hollowed out the government sector to such an extent that we may well lack the capacity, infrastructure, and know-how to reclaim that which has increasingly been outsourced or marketized. Indeed, there is seemingly no other explanation for the State Department's recent practice of renewing contracts with the notorious Blackwater firm after the Obama administration sanctioned Blackwater for illicit arms smuggling, after federal prosecutors brought murder charges against Blackwater employees, and after the American-backed governments in Baghdad and Kabul designated Blackwater employees as personae non gratae. Apparently, the United States had no viable in-house alternative.[19]

And, psychologically, we will have done such a good job disassociating the public services we like from the government itself—and will have been doing that job for so long—that we'll risk altogether forgetting the State's sovereign, democratic mission.[20] Indeed, the more we indulge the fiction of governmentless government, and the longer we enable those who demonize government workers, the harder it becomes to generate support, or even respect, for the actual public sphere and its role in the political economy.

Consider, for example, President Barack Obama's now-infamous "you didn't build that" speech. In a 2012 campaign stop in Roanoke, Virginia, Obama chided his audience, urging them not to forget how much the government has done to facilitate economic growth and entrepreneurial opportunities. Seemingly innocently enough, Obama mentioned government's role in educating the nation's youth, building roads and bridges, awarding student scholarships, and investing in the arts and sciences. These public contributions, the president insisted, were critical to the success of America's businessmen and women.[21] Yet the public outcry was deafening—*how dare the president say I didn't build my business!*[22] And even though Obama could have doubled down, reminding his critics of further government support in the form of limited corporate liability, liberal bankruptcy laws, unemployment insurance, workers' compensation, domestic policing, and national defense, the president blinked. Within days, he started to backpedal, placating an unjustifiably offended public by insisting his words were misconstrued.[23]

Our evidently growing distance from this simple, irrefutable truth may make it increasingly challenging to conceive of the State as anything other than transactional, if not entirely parasitic. Many today would no doubt insist that they built their businesses *notwithstanding* the burdens of government taxes and regulations. As this impression—what Jacob Hacker and Paul Pierson call "American Amnesia"[24]—hardens into gospel, even if we could repudiate privatization at some later date and resurrect the administrative separation of powers, it would be a Pyrrhic victory. We'd have the right structure, but the spirit of liberal democratic, contentious, redistributive, and, yes, business-facilitating government would be all but extinguished. So too would any passion for public service.

It is therefore imperative to reverse course now: to "insource" State responsibilities that have long been privatized, to redeem the constitutionally legitimating project of the administrative separation of powers, and to make clear that government's legality and efficacy turn on it being a manifestly unbusinesslike institution. This is how we carry the commitment to separation of powers all the way forward.

The timing of a book of this sort appears particularly propitious. Nothing epitomizes today's constitutional zeitgeist better than the Donald Trump presidency. Leaving aside (as best one can) the new president's alarming mendacity and crass nativism, Trump represents the apotheosis of the businesslike government movement. He pays no fealty to the State. Quite the opposite: he promises to "drain the swamp," meaning the Washington bureaucracy—and to govern the United States like he ran his real estate and entertainment empire.

Trump celebrates his lack of government experience. Half-Barnum, half-Bourbon, Trump insists he'll deal with officials from the Mexican government like he dealt with cranky building-trade vendors: sticking them with the bill for his infamous border wall. He insists he'll deal with civil servants like he dealt with strong-willed contestants on TV's *The Apprentice:* dismissing them with his signature "you're fired!" And he insists that there is no conflict in his retaining his vast business holdings while serving his term as leader of the free world. The corporate mogul turned populist president is, in short, our CEO *Rex.*

Bear in mind that, as I said above, the businesslike government movement has been a long time in the works. We'd be continuing to lurch, if not flat-out race, in this direction regardless whether Donald Trump won or lost. For decades, the two most powerful trends in administrative governance have been the rise of what Elena Kagan calls presidential administration and the pivot to privatization. And, over that span of time, these two trends have been converging, even fusing—hence running the government like a *politicized* business.

Still, President Trump deserves special attention. He deserves special attention not just because he's our sitting president but also because he promises to be a transformative president, one way or the other. Will he be a Joshua to Reagan's Moses, completing the anti-government constitutional moment that the Gipper started? Or will he be the last (and least) of the Reaganites, on whose unsteady watch businesslike government finally jumps the shark?

Our generation's challenge—our turn, that is, as guardians of Dr. Franklin's precarious republic—is to tip the scales. This book, clearly, favors repudiation of the Privatization Revolution. This book rejects businesslike government as antithetical to a dynamic separation of powers—and to the values which give that enduring, evolving structural commitment its meaning and purpose. And this book prescribes a redemptive path forward, allowing us to proudly reclaim and improve upon the virtuous features of twentieth-century public administration while lancing the various warts and malignancies that afflicted and ultimately doomed the first go-around.

This book proceeds as follows. Chapter 1 addresses the history of privatized and businesslike government. By commencing our inquiry here, I am able to furnish necessary background. The early American Republic boasted fleets of naval privateers, private jailers, Pinkerton detectives, and zealous tax farmers. It was against this colorful and, by contemporary lights, highly irregular backdrop that modern administrative governance emerged.

That said, I have a secondary reason for starting with this quick jaunt through the eighteenth and nineteenth centuries. One of the more resonant claims about today's turn to the Market is that such a turn is hardly new—and that greater sensitivity to privatization's long, rich history should serve to allay contemporary agita over businesslike government.

Not so, I argue. While it is true that private and commercialized actors carrying out State responsibilities have been around since before the Founding, any comparison between those folks and the ones we encounter today is entirely inapt. The comparison is inapt because back then there was not much of a difference between public and privatized government, if only because public administrators of the eighteenth and nineteenth centuries were themselves not very democratically or legally accountable. In short, the choice between public and private administrators wasn't a very momentous one.

Now, of course, the political and legal gap between public and private actors has widened considerably. Thus the choice is a tremendously consequential one today. In the twentieth century, voting rights extended to previously disenfranchised women, people of color, and those who could not afford to pay a poll tax. As a result, the modern electorate is more inclusive, more diverse, and more fully empowered—and thus far better positioned to hold public officials (but still not private contractors) politically accountable. At the same time, legal remedies proliferated, equipping modern-day Americans with more and better opportunities to sue state actors (but, again, not private contractors) deemed arbitrary or abusive.

In all, it is my contention that appeals to history by privatization's proponents actually backfire. Revisiting early privatization and examining such practices against the rather impoverished public law backdrop of eighteenth- and nineteenth-century America serves only to underscore how far the State has come as a democratic, deliberative, and professional institution—and thus makes plain why we should be so especially alarmed by the resurgence of privatized practices against the far richer public law backdrop of today.

Chapter 2 endeavors to document the twentieth-century development of that far richer public law backdrop. It is here where I explain that the architects of the modern administrative state made a decisive turn away from the often shabby administrative practices of the eighteenth and nineteenth centuries, practices employed by government and private actors alike. These architects banished many of the private actors, phased out the politicized and hackish government workers who were a product of the old spoils system, and established a merit-based civil service in its stead. These efforts took some time, of course, but ultimately produced a professional, deliberative, and legally accountable public bureaucracy.

And, as if the personnel overhaul wasn't sufficiently momentous, these architects also broadened the government's regulatory powers, substantially increased opportunities for public participation, and fleshed out what we today know of as administrative law to handle the new challenges and new material, legal, and dignitarian demands of modernity. I refer to this period as *pax administrativa*—so labeled to connote the remarkable growth, stability, rigor, and broad public and legal acceptance of this twentieth-century American administrative achievement.

In Chapter 3, I build on the foundation laid in the previous two chapters and explain *pax administrativa* in explicitly constitutional terms. I show how the rise of a large and rangy administrative state initially posed a very real threat to the constitutional separation of powers. After all, the assignment of legislative, executive, and judicial powers to single agencies appeared to do great violence to Madison's unmistakably disaggregated federal scheme. Though many lamented and, to this day, continue to lament that apparent concentration of federal power, I argue that they have overlooked something quite important. They have overlooked the fact that mid-twentieth-century administrative lawyers redeemed that constitutional commitment to separating and checking State powers—and did so by triangulating administrative power among the presidentially appointed agency leaders, politically insulated civil servants, and the general public given the means to engage directly in most facets of administrative policy design and implementation.

The redemption operates on two levels. As a threshold matter, the simple, mechanical triangulation of administrative power does important work in limiting the potential for abusive, even tyrannous acts by an otherwise unfettered, monolithic bureaucracy—run either by the political agency heads or the mandarins themselves. More trenchantly, there is something special about these three administrative players in particular. Individually and collectively, they channel the dispositional characteristics and institutional obligations of the three great constitutional branches. Again, agency heads stand in for the president. Tenured, expert civil servants committed to reason-giving and fidelity to professional norms and to the rule of law are naturally, if not obviously, the jurists of the administrative domain. And the diverse, inclusive, and non-hierarchical public serves as a truly plenary legislative assembly, voicing varied opinions in an effort to shape administrative policy. All told, the rivalrous interplay of these three administrative actors helps ensure that a wide range of interests are fully incorporated into agency deliberations, thus enriching administrative policymaking, balancing arid expertise with passionate populism, and lowering the risk of abuse or overreach.

This chapter's characterization of an administrative separation of powers illuminates our past—and our future. Specifically, the administrative separation of powers connects us to the framers' constitutional architecture. Though early twentieth-century administrative governance initially collapsed that original tripartite scheme, the eventual engendering of an administrative separation of powers was an act of constitutional restoration. The administrative separation of powers anchored otherwise unnervingly concentrated administrative agencies firmly within the constitutional tradition of employing rivalrous institutional counterweights to promote good governance, political accountability, and compliance with the rule of law. Again, it reconciled Madison with modernity and set the terms for twentieth-century constitutional administrative governance.

Additionally, the theory and reality of an administrative separation of powers exposes the true dangers of today's turn to privatized government. The lessons of an enduring, evolving commitment to separating and checking power that carried forward into the Administrative Era (and arena) teach us that privatization is anything but a *sui generis* phenomenon. Instead, privatization's fusion of State and commercial power represents simply the latest and perhaps greatest threat to that fundamental constitutional commitment. Specific instances of consolidated, privatized power may look quite novel or at least quite different. They are certainly treated as such. But the underlying challenges privatization poses are the same ones we have encountered before: to marshal the grammar, devices, and doctrines related to the constitutional separation of powers and insist upon the continued relevance of separating and checking State power in whatever form that power happens to take.

Before mastering and then implementing those lessons, however, much ground still needs to be covered. Among other things, we need to understand the late-twentieth-century decline of *pax administrativa* and the corresponding rise of our current, if still nascent, Privatized Era. That bridging work begins in Chapter 4. Here I capture burgeoning disenchantment with *pax administrativa*—specifically, the emergence and, in time, convergence of academic, legal, business, and political forces intent on dismantling the twentieth-century administrative state. Looping in neoliberal economists, big business lobbyists, and disillusioned lunchpail Reagan Democrats, I describe how these varied and sundry critics of the administrative state rallied around the Market, which they celebrated as a more rational, virtuous alternative to (what they saw as) a bloated, untrustworthy, and perhaps still constitutionally suspect public bureaucracy; and I show how these critics managed to spark what would become a full-fledged Privatization Revolution.

Chapter 5 follows that revolution's progression. Here I demonstrate how the momentum built during the Reagan presidency carried forward into the

Bush *père*, Clinton, and Bush *fils* years. If anything, the revolution picked up steam in the 1990s and 2000s. It was during these decades when privatization became at once more mainstream and more politically charged, redefining the State's relationship to the Market, reframing how we thought about and practiced American administrative law, and reconfiguring many agencies and programs along businesslike lines.

Among other things, privatization not only began to reach deeper into more sensitive policy areas (such as military and intelligence operations, prison management, and welfare administration), it also began to take many new, different, and hardly recognizable forms. What was initially largely a push to privatize via government contractors—and thus involved private sector workers hired to replace government civil servants—became infinitely more varied and, again, more political. This new millennial privatization included the crowdsourcing of public responsibilities; the offering of bounties to secure private assistance; the acquisition of "private" equity to regulate corporate behavior; the creation of in-house venture capital firms; the stripping of civil service tenure protections (thereby effectively privatizing the government workforce from within); and countless more creative and legally vexing combinations of sovereign and commercial power.

Chapter 6 takes stock of this new millennial privatization and zeros in on its constitutional implications. Here I challenge the dominant contemporary understandings of privatization as incomplete, if not inapposite. Most treatments of modern privatization focus on questions of economic efficiency to the exclusion of political expediency—that is, using the levers of businesslike government to concentrate political power. They do so even though most agency heads are apt to prize political expediency over (the possibility of) marginal cost savings. Furthermore, most treatments of modern privatization assume that the turn to businesslike government entails the abdication, not aggrandizement, of sovereign power. They do so even though any measure of the government's true size and scope must include both the exclusively public sector and the rangy, varied hybrid quasi-public, quasi-private sector that is increasingly carrying out State functions, big and small alike.

These dominant contemporary understandings of privatization have led us astray, distracting us—and thus keeping us—from exploring privatization's effects on constitutional governance—specifically, on the administrative separation of powers. Simply put, privatization in its various forms tends to supplant or defang the federal civil service and marginalize or co-opt members of civil society otherwise authorized to participate in most administrative matters. As a result, State power is *aggrandized* at the expense of private autonomy and private social and economic ordering. And State power is *concentrated* in the hands of federal agency heads—the president's proxies—at the expense of civil servants and the public writ large. This commercially inflected and politically and legally unrivaled federal executive is apt to wield its aggrandized and concentrated power in hyperpartisan, parochial, and potentially abusive ways.

Chapter 6 therefore recasts privatization as posing an existential threat to the American constitutional system, one remade and redeemed by the instantiation of an administrative separation of powers.

The chapters that follow seek a path forward, a way to rededicate ourselves to a new and improved, second *pax administrativa*. In some respects, the original *pax administrativa* never got a fair chance. Its logic, architecture, and legal bona fides were never truly appreciated—and thus these chapters serve as much as a first, if long overdue, defense as they do as a surreply.

Chapter 7 begins by explaining the continuing importance of the separation of powers. In recent years, the framers' separation of powers has often been derided as antiquated, unnecessary, or ineffectual. There has been, during this time, a certain wistfulness for a more unitary, parliamentary system of government. What's more, pressures to collapse various other constitutionally relevant lines of separation—for example, federal-state, church-State, civilian-military—now abound. I devote this initial reconstructive chapter to doubling down as it were on the separation of powers. It is my contention here that, if anything, the separation of powers (broadly conceived) matters more today than ever before—and thus there is good reason to insist upon a recommitment to the vintage framework popularized by the likes of Montesquieu and Madison and redeemed by the twentieth-century engineers of administrative law. And it is my further contention that a separation of powers *within the administrative arena* is in many respects even more important than is a separation of powers within the traditional constitutional arena.

Chapters 8–10 do the heavy lifting of reconstructing a government once again committed to an administrative separation of powers—and to a second *pax administrativa*. All too often during the mid-twentieth-century golden age of modern administrative governance, Congress and the president destabilized the administrative separation of powers. At times, such destabilizing interventions were intentional: the political branches sought to dominate administrative proceedings in service of some programmatic, partisan, or institutional end. At other times, such destabilizing interventions were unwitting and inadvertent, reflecting a lack of appreciation for the constitutional significance of this triangulated administrative scheme.

Still, it isn't clear that the political branches would have acted differently had they been advised of the legitimating aspects of administrative tripartitism. Thus for a new, twenty-first-century administrative separation of powers to truly work, to merit greater and more explicit popular, normative, and legal respect, and to prove more resilient, all three constitutional branches need to act as custodians, nurturing and protecting (rather than exploiting) a well-functioning system of administrative rivalries. Chapter 8 explains the conceptual reorientation necessary for the constitutional branches to recognize and, ideally, embrace this custodial role.

Chapter 9 concentrates on judicial custodialism, underscoring how courts (the branch least inclined to act exploitatively) can use their existing tools and cultivate new doctrines to promote a well-functioning administrative separation of powers—and compel the likely more reluctant political branches to do the same. Here I advance a jurisprudential theory called *reinforcing rivalrous administration*. A takeoff on John Hart Ely's famed "reinforcing representative democracy," reinforcing rivalrous administration obligates judges to ensure that agency actions are forged in the crucible of competition, as evidenced by the rivalrous interplay of agency heads, civil servants, and civil society. Under this theory, courts would be expected to invalidate agency actions that fall short of those participatory and deliberative goals, leaving it to the political branches (whether they like it or not) to address identified shortcomings and prescribe corrections that promote a well-functioning administrative separation of powers.

Chapter 10 turns to legislative custodialism, exploring ways in which Congress can meet its custodial constitutional obligations and likewise promote a well-functioning administrative separation of powers. Among other things, Congress needs to provide considerably more support for the currently beleaguered and oft-marginalized civil service; increase the level and quality of public participation in administrative proceedings; and minimize bad-faith obstructionism by any and all of the administrative rivals. The combined effect of these legislative solutions would be to enrich administrative actors, sharpen administrative rivalries, and, again, help usher in a second *pax administrativa* that is not only more in keeping with our constitutional commitments but also far more capable of parrying political critiques and fending off programmatic attacks.

I conclude by way of a brief Epilogue that celebrates government's rivalrous, clunky contentiousness as constitutionally necessary and appropriate given the special—and, quite often, sacred—obligations under which the State operates.

PART I

PAX ADMINISTRATIVA'S RISE

Modern Public Administration and the
Administrative Separation of Powers

The first part of this book captures the rise and reign of *pax administrativa*—an era of great administrative growth, stability, and achievement in the realms of social and economic welfare, civil rights, business regulation, and national security. Over the course of the following three chapters, I explain how a special combination of people, practices, and institutions lent credence to and ultimately constitutionalized this twentieth-century administrative enterprise.

Chapter 1 kicks things off by exploring the early and often irregular administrative arrangements that dotted the eighteenth- and nineteenth-century American landscape. Here I introduce bounty hunters, railroad cops, and tax ferrets. A deep, if quick, dive into this roguish premodern administrative realm is illuminating in its own right. Indeed, one might fault Twain himself for not having mined this very subject for picaresque gold.

Such a dive has considerable instrumental value as well. Understanding the premodern administrative realm helps us make better sense of the twentieth-century administrative state that succeeded it. Specifically, *pax administrativa* is more rejection than refinement—as signature features of the administrative separation of powers act as antibodies, effectuating immune-like responses to the unprofessional, profit-seeking, and undemocratic components of that earlier era.

In addition, understanding the premodern administrative state helps us make better sense of today's turn to privatization and businesslike government. Present-day proponents of privatization casually avert to this earlier period when private or commercially oriented actors carried out many government responsibilities. Our inquiry in Chapter 1 reveals that history actually cuts against any claim that privatization has a long and legitimate American lineage—and that, by virtue of that long and legitimate lineage, today's businesslike manifestations ought to be grandfathered in. Simply put, too much has changed in the interim, thus breaking that lineal line; and many of those points of disruption reflect intentional and constitutionally resonant disavowals of businesslike practices.

Chapter 2 then examines the modern administrative state, cataloging its characteristics, dimensions, and accomplishments. I associate the *pax administrativa* era with remarkable innovation, expansion, and legitimation—and this chapter depicts how quickly and precipitously the federal administrative infrastructure grew; how federal administration became far more professionalized and public, sweeping aside both political hacks (hired under the old spoils system) and private deputies; how federal administration became more procedurally robust, inclusive, and regularized; and how federal administration effectively supplanted the constitutional branches as the epicenter of national policy design, implementation, and adjudication.

Chapter 3 completes our first troika of chapters. In it, I explain the principles underlying the administrative separation of powers and connect *pax administrativa*'s tripartite structural architecture with the institutional designs employed by the framers. Indeed, in rejecting the forms and practices of premodern administrative governance, the modern administrative state established its constitutional bona fides, redeeming (while refashioning) Madisonian separation of powers and tethering twentieth-century public administration to the larger project of American liberal republicanism.

1

Historic Privatization and the Premodern Administrative State

L ike most of us living in the age of social media, privatization has an inescapable past. Historians thus do a great service when they insist that the Jeremiahs of contemporary outsourcing take a deep breath and appreciate that a good deal of what we are seeing today isn't new. To the contrary, it looks remarkably similar to what happened in the first hundred or so years of the Republic.

Surely scholars of present-day constitutional and administrative law should not gloss over that history. History does matter. At the same time, we must be careful to avoid placing too much emphasis on what happened in eighteenth- and nineteenth-century America, a legally, politically, and culturally different—almost foreign—land from the one we occupy today. Appeals to history run the risk of giving contemporary audiences the wrong idea, conveying a sense of timeless normalcy to a practice that—like medieval barbers playing doctor—ought to offend modern sensibilities notwithstanding its uncontroversial or ubiquitous past.

The point of this chapter is to flip the historical claims on their head— and thus further underscore why today's (re)embrace of privatization is so jarring. Far from linking eras, a legally textured historical inquiry exposes the contradictions and discontinuities, establishing how different past and present really are, illuminating how much more portentous the decision to privatize is today, and revealing how much more constitutionally offensive the contemporary strain of businesslike government is.

This chapter proceeds as follows. I first provide a brief tour of eighteenth- and nineteenth-century privatization in America. This tour makes many of the major stops, highlights key incidents and examples, and above all provides a flavor for the rich and complicated set of practices that contributed to the roguish early decades of our nascent Republic.

Second, I put these early practices into some perspective. I do so by giving them a backhanded compliment. I explain how privatization fit right in, albeit with what was a relatively unprofessional, un-juridical, and undemocratic public infrastructure—a scoundrel among scoundrels, as it were.

Third, I detail, also briefly, how and why those privatization practices fell out of favor. The story of the rise, legitimation, and constitutionalization of twentieth-century American public administration will be the focus of the succeeding chapters. Nevertheless, a quick preview of that story is necessary here to bring our account of privatization's early history to a close.

I end this chapter with a simple but consequential claim: Even assuming that the eighteenth- and nineteenth-century version of privatization is exactly the same as the contemporary manifestation, the radical changes that transformed practically every other facet of American constitutional law and administrative governance cast today's privatization in an entirely different, and far less favorable, light. Privatization today might be the same old (and perhaps still reckless) Falstaff. But we as a State, like young Prince Hal, matured. Just as the newly crowned King Henry had little need or use for his erstwhile drinking buddy, we have outgrown the privatization of our nation's insouciant youth.

Historical Governmental Reliance on Private Actors

What I am calling *privatization* isn't new. We have been down this road before. Even leaving aside Old World precedents and analogs as too distant, the history of the United States is itself replete with private actors tasked with carrying out sundry State functions. Part of this story of premodern privatization is one of necessity. We were a fledgling nation, with limited resources, limited expectations placed on the government, and therefore little capacity or reason to hire, train, and dispatch government employees, especially to the far-flung, sparsely populated places that only a small number of Americans were just beginning to settle.

And part of this story is cultural. We were a people who profoundly distrusted government—certainly the old British monarchy, but our own infant Republic as well. Hence there were politically strategic reasons for keeping government's footprint as small and shallow as possible and relying instead on private actors to advance State interests.

Let me provide a few examples. Perhaps most notable of all were naval privateers. Substituting for a standing Navy, these enterprising swashbucklers—*and swashbuckling entrepreneurs*[1]—seized and plundered enemy ships in both the Revolutionary War and the War of 1812. In the former conflict, the Continental Congress commissioned some 792 privateers, whose militarized ships captured or destroyed around 600 British vessels. By comparison, the Continental forces boasted only forty-seven regular war ships and a supplemental fleet of sixty-four. What is more, the Continental fleet had less than one-tenth the number of guns and swivels as the private armada.[2]

In the latter conflict, there was, again, far greater reliance on privateers than on our still meager Navy. More than 500 private vessels manned by private crews overshadowed the Navy's fleet of twenty-two.[3] Indeed, privateers' presence in American public law and life was important enough, not to mention acceptable enough, to merit explicit inclusion in the first Article of the Constitution, which grants Congress the power to "grant Letters of Marque and Reprisal."[4] After all, it was a professional military, not pillaging privateers, who were seen as the greater threat to the Republic.[5] And had it not been for the American colonists' recent battles with untold numbers of Hessian mercenaries in the employ of the British crown, perhaps we might have had greater enthusiasm for private soldiering as well. Instead, we tended to rely on locally conscripted militiamen, pulled from the fields, shops, and quite often the taverns, to provide for our early national defense.[6]

On the domestic front, surely the most iconic image of nineteenth-century law enforcement is that of the steely and fearsome bounty hunter. These Boba Fetts of the Wild West were charged with bringing to justice suspected criminals and escaped prisoners. As anyone who has watched old Westerns knows, bounty hunters were often paid whether they returned their fugitive *dead or alive*. Bounty hunters, along with other private actors—think ragtag, hastily deputized posses—supported a fragile, uneven, and skeletal system of what passed for public law enforcement, particularly in parts of the country without the resources, need, or desire for anything approximating a permanent police force. Like the naval privateers, bounty hunters too had a moment in the constitutional sun: In the 1873 case *Taylor v. Taintor,* the Supreme Court acknowledged the bounty hunters' sweeping powers "to go beyond the limits of the State."[7]

Though bounty hunters stand out in legend and lore, privatized policing of a more mundane, urban stripe was far more pervasive and no doubt consequential. As David Sklansky has written, colonial American towns "relied on the medieval institutions of the constable, the night watch, and the hue and cry—institutions that drew no clear line between public and private."[8] Such reliance on private policing did not change considerably in the decades that followed Independence and constitutional ratification. Instead, there remained substantial dependence on a mix of citizen patrols, individuals hired by members of that patrol to take their place (a form of subcontracting, as it were), and supplemental security details hired by, for example, groups of merchants.[9] Though some of our largest cities began establishing truly public metropolitan police forces in the late antebellum period—New York City's originated in 1853—more modest municipalities continued to rely on various forms of private policing well into the late nineteenth century.[10]

So, too, did the federal government. Throughout much of the latter half of the nineteenth century, private security agents—often drawn from the notorious Pinkerton Agency—handled a considerable number of federal investigative and policing responsibilities. Allan Pinkerton himself warned Abraham Lincoln of a southern conspiracy to assassinate the then president-elect en route to his inauguration. Pinkerton quickly rearranged Lincoln's travel itinerary and personally escorted him as they switched trains to elude the conspirators. (Adding to the theatrics, rumor has it that Pinkerton dressed Honest Abe in women's clothes to further confuse his would-be assailants.) Later, Pinkerton conducted spy operations for the Union Army and also did contract work for the Treasury Department, the State Department, and the Post Office.[11]

Lastly, there were so-called company police forces. These forces were under the direct employ of railroads and other business concerns. The private police forces existed ostensibly to counter criminal threats such as train robberies. But they were regularly used as a tool of industrial relations, tasked with monitoring employees and busting union activity.[12] What makes them relevant to this story—and distinguishes them from the robber baron equivalent of the feckless Mall Cop—is that state legislatures granted these private forces all the public powers to question, detain, and arrest.[13] For example, the Coal and Iron Police, private detectives operating with permission of the Pennsylvania state legislature, conducted extensive surveillance of mine employees and brought charges against dozens of miners (who were then criminally prosecuted by the coal companies' own private attorneys).[14] And the Carnegie Steel Company hired 300 Pinkerton agents to infiltrate and arrest more than 3,800 striking steel workers, a campaign that cost the lives of ten strikers.[15] So much for the State's monopoly power over the use of force.

Outside of the policing context, the United States Post Office—the fore-runner to today's fully corporatized United States Postal Service—also reg-ularly relied on private actors.[16] It wasn't just federal employees who endured snow, rain, heat, and gloom of night to ensure "swift completion of their appointed rounds."[17] Private stagecoach drivers, independent cou-riers (including the famed Pony Express), crews aboard commercial steam-boats, and employees of America's privately owned railroads likewise braved the elements to bring your great-great-grandparents news from the Old Country, updates from their congressman, and, eventually, their first Sears catalog.[18]

Shifting from dogs' nemesis—that is, the postal worker—to mankind's, we encounter yet more privatized government in the form of tax collectors and lawyers. In the nineteenth century, states, localities, and even the fed-eral government contracted with legions of aptly named tax ferrets. These private contractors were tasked with collecting revenue owed to various government agencies.[19] Iowa, among other states, even had its own Association of Tax Ferrets, an appellation its members evidently bore proudly.[20] At the same time, private lawyers were standing in for the gov-ernment in civil suits[21] and, as alluded to above, to prosecute the criminally accused.[22] Incredibly enough, then prairie lawyer Abraham Lincoln served as an occasional private prosecutor.[23] (And, as evidence that the public–private divide was traversed in both directions, Roger Taney, future author of the vile *Dred Scott* opinion, maintained an active private law practice while serving as Attorney General of the United States.[24]) Those convicted might then find themselves incarcerated in privately maintained prisons and jails.[25]

Early Government Was Relatively Small Government

This is just a short and relatively breezy list—but perhaps not as artificially truncated as one might think. Remember: our governments—and by that I mean our local, state, and federal governments—were very limited ones. Rugged individualism and a perhaps problematic dose of benign neglect of society's most vulnerable and often disenfranchised ruled the day. Our governments simply weren't as extensively involved in day-to-day social, economic, or domestic affairs as they are now.

Indeed, the domains discussed in this section—namely, national defense, public safety, tax collection, and mail delivery—were among the principal (and, in places, the *only*) services the nascent American state pro-vided.[26] Jerry Mashaw, lately a keen historian of early American public administration, is right to note other services, including the regulation of steamboats and the management and dispensation of federal lands.[27] Still, by contemporary lights, what Mashaw calls "the lost hundred years of American administrative law" remained at best a proto-administrative state where roads were quite often privately financed and maintained;[28] welfare services, meager as they were, were the purview of religious and other charitably minded civic groups;[29] and, to the extent persons suffered environmental or workplace injuries or were cheated in a business dealing, those persons by and large prevailed upon the courts for help (and did so, to be sure, with limited success).

In keeping with one of Alexis de Tocqueville's penetrating observations, "[s]carcely any political question ar[ose] in the United States that [wa]s not resolved, sooner or later, into a judicial question."[30] We were, to sharpen the French chronicler's point, a government of common law judges, not agency administrators.[31] Today, of course, we have the Environmental Protection Agency and the Departments of Labor, Transportation, Agriculture, Housing and Urban Development, Education, and Health and Human Services—and their state and often municipal or county equivalents—doing this work of protecting health and public welfare.

In addition to government's shallow programmatic footprint was its narrow spatial one. Like a child's sock that barely can be stretched beyond the toes of her parent's foot, the early American administrative infrastructure covered only a fraction of the vast physical expanse. In fairness, much of the country beyond the populated eastern seaboard wasn't densely settled. Whatever government responsibilities needed to be attended to in the hinterlands were not regular or demanding enough to justify full-time employees. Hence there was considerable reliance on folks already out there—farmers, tradesmen, and shopkeepers—who could do a little work for the government on the side.

Of some note, out in the backcountry, often the only true representatives of the federal government to speak of were judges, and even they famously and no doubt uncomfortably rode circuit—traveling from town to town to preside over cases. Early on, Congress tried to add some of the federal government's few administrative responsibilities—notably, veterans' pensions—to the judiciary's workload. But in a seminal opinion, *Hayburn's Case,* the Supreme Court deemed this administrative assignment unconstitutional. The justices understood Article III of the Constitution to authorize judges to decide only cases or controversies.[32] This restriction on judges' ability to act as de facto administrators placed only greater pressure on Congress to find and finance other—and, by default, often private—personnel to carry out necessary tasks.

Early Government Was Not Very Governmental

All in all, private actors were very much a part of the first hundred or so years of American administrative governance. During this period, there seemed to be few objections to private service providers. This tolerance ought not be confused with anything like a self-conscious championing of the Market over the State, at least not in the way we now think about such neoliberal preferences.[33] Claims to the contrary seem misplaced, if not altogether anachronistic. Instead, such tolerance likely reflected the public's understandable indifference. After all, at that time, there wasn't a dime's worth of difference between contractors and government employees. And what we today term as the "make or buy" privatization decision—that is, the decision whether to assign State responsibilities to federal civil servants or commercial service contractors—had few, if any, of the political, fiscal, legal, or sociocultural implications that the choice now has.

Let me explain. First, like their private sector counterparts, many government employees worked only part time for the State.[34] So if you were someone troubled by conflicts of interest, both nominally public and categorically private officials had them in spades. And if you were instead someone who fretted over distracted, moonlighting administrators, presumably both sets of workers had other jobs that tugged at their time and blurred their focus.

Second, neither workforce was especially professional. Throughout this premodern period, there was not much in the way of professional technocrats hired on the basis of their educational achievements or because they aced a civil service exam. Instead, many government employees were duly rewarded party loyalists. They secured their jobs because they were helpful on the hustings or wily in the wards—thereby earning the gratitude of powerful political patrons.[35] Compounding their lack of professionalism was their admittedly rational disinclination to develop substantive expertise. After all, these employees knew that their careers in government turned more than anything else on their bosses' successes at the polls. Thus, rather than invest in further education or deeper study of the programs they were administering, the better use of their time was spent knocking off early from work to help with party politicking.[36] For this reason, too, irregular contractors and other private deputies did not seem outclassed or unsophisticated when compared to their government counterparts.

Third, a sizable number of government workers in this premodern era were not regularly salaried employees. These government employees were, instead, much more like today's private contractors. As legal historian Nicholas Parrillo has documented, government personnel conferring licenses, grants, and other awards of legal or material value often received "facilitative payments" directly from those benefiting from the services rendered. Thus, government immigration and land office officials received, and by law were allowed to receive, additional sums in exchange for particularly expedient or generous dispensation. Tempted as many of us might today be to slip one of the DMV minotaurs a $20 bill to move us quickly through those labyrinthine lines, it is precisely the audacity of any such system where government employees act like smarmy maitre d's that brings into relief how foreign this once entrenched system of commercialized public administration now seems.

The same story of profit-driven government service played out, Parrillo tells us, where government personnel worked in more adversarial positions. Personnel seeking to compel individuals or firms to do something, such as pay fines or taxes, regularly received a portion of whatever was ultimately recovered from the targeted scofflaws.[37] Given this eat-what-you-kill compensation scheme, there was little to distinguish bounty-seeking government employees from plundering privateers or private prosecutors paid by the conviction.

Lastly, though there was an important (albeit often overlooked) internal set of laws, rules, and regularized practices guiding and constraining federal administrative departments,[38] many of the government employees of the eighteenth and nineteenth centuries were not very accountable to the public. Sure, it is possible that poor service by rank-and-file employees would have had a trickle-up effect, resulting in the electoral defeat of those employees' patrons. But other than that highly indirect, and improbable, effect, there were few political avenues open to dissatisfied benefit seekers or wrongly accused transgressors. Thus there was no obvious political reason to draw sharp lines of distinction between government employees and their commercial counterparts.

The same was true when it came to legal accountability. Administrative practice at that time was largely governed by writs of injunction and mandamus that were—particularly by today's lights—extremely limited.[39] Suits, assuming they could be brought at all, generally alleged violations of the common law. Because these claims against the government were not unlike those brought against private contractors or deputies, there was, again, little basis for preferring public over commercial provision.[40]

In short, what I am getting at here is that premodern government employees were not very governmental, at least not in the ways we have come to understand that critical workforce. Instead, government employees looked, acted, and were compensated in a substantially similar fashion to contractors and other private deputies. For these reasons, the eighteenth- and nineteenth-century choice between in-house and contracted-out State service provision does not appear to have been a very consequential one—and perhaps that too helps explain why extensive privatization was not then an especially vexing phenomenon (as it is, or at least ought to be, today).

Rising Demand for Big Government

Over time, the eighteenth- and nineteenth-century model of limited government that could get by offering few services and employing a small number of nonprofessional personnel (public and private alike) became outdated—and, with it, the nation's deep-rooted aversion to big, interventionist government softened. Recurring bouts of economic dislocation, punctuated by a pair of all-consuming world wars, helped many government skeptics find religion. (And those who didn't were in any event increasingly outvoted by newly enfranchised political classes more acutely affected by economic and military hardships.)

That religion enabled the engendering of a large and rangy administrative state at home, one capable of dispersing an ever-expanding suite of cash and in-kind benefits; of protecting an ever-broadening array of consumers, workers, children, and even businesses; of funding, coordinating, and directing increasing numbers of monumental public projects involving the energy, education, and transportation sectors; and of providing credible assurances of economic security.[41]

That religion also enabled the buildup of an unprecedentedly large and mobilized military. Though the United States had a long and conspicuous history of beating its swords into ploughshares, after a while the public got tired of having to convert those ploughshares back into swords. After two world wars and the ever-present threat of a third, mid-twentieth-century Americans heeded President Dwight Eisenhower's warning that "now we can no longer risk emergency improvisation of national defense."[42] As a result, in addition to the development of a massive domestic welfare state, we created a large standing military and built up a correspondingly large civilian bureaucracy to support it. (Ironically enough, in our rush to assume the role of global superpower, we didn't heed Eisenhower's other, far more memorable warning. Instead, we countenanced and opportunistically supported the concomitant and, in Ike's words, "disastrous" rise of a military-industrial complex that in many respects presaged today's even more disastrous Privatization Revolution. But, for now, that story will have to wait.)

Rising Demand for Good Government

Big government does not necessarily mean good government. Yet that too would come. Beginning in the late nineteenth century, a growing number expressed dissatisfaction with the old ways, including with the rough and irregular qualities of the premodern administrative workforce. Good government groups cropped up across the country.[43] These elite societies, along with cohorts of frustrated ordinary citizens, increasingly viewed private actors as corrupt and unprofessional—and disparaged them as hired guns. Scandals involving unethical tax ferrets and abusive Pinkerton detectives more interested in fighting labor than crime made these unfavorable impressions that much more concrete. Indeed, Congress finally responded to labor concerns regarding what Sklansky calls "America's de facto national law enforcement agency."[44] In 1893, Congress passed the Anti-Pinkerton Act, barring Pinkerton and similar such organizations from working for the federal government.[45]

To be sure, critics of the status quo also disliked the old guard of government workers. This makes sense insofar as, per my claim, there wasn't a dime's worth of difference between nineteenth-century contractors and government workers. It was around this time that, as Parrillo tells us, elected officials at the federal, state, and local levels prohibited facilitative payments and bonuses—systems that smacked of legalized corruption and even public racketeering—and adopted more regular, impartial, salaried compensation schemes.[46]

In addition, these elected officials instituted a series of civil service reforms that thinned the ranks of party hacks and replaced ward heelers with professional technocrats who earned their government jobs through merit examinations and kept them by dint of their good work.[47] The engendering of civil service reforms was no mean feat. Since at least the presidency of Andrew Jackson, the spoils system—which elevated political patronage to an art form—had come to dominate nineteenth-century party politics and, with it, nineteenth-century public administration. But, by the end of that century, patronage jobs were rapidly being phased out. And, by the early twentieth century, new contingents of professional technocrats began receiving tenure.

Tenure insulated rank-and-file government workers from the vagaries and indelicacies of politics. In conjunction with anti-politicking laws,
such as the Hatch Act of 1939, tenure enabled government officials to
operate as professional lawyers, engineers, inspectors, analysts, social
workers, scientists, and economists serving the interests of the State rather
than the particular partisan agenda of any one incumbent presidential
administration.[48]

The Emergence of Big, Good, and Distinctive Government

All of this is to say that, by the middle of the twentieth century, a public
workforce largely purged of its original sins of partisanship, privatization,
and profit-seeking came into its own. Federal civilian employment rose
from approximately 250,000 in 1900 to well over 3 million during World
War II and then settled in just north of 2 million for much of the post-war
period. What's more, by the 1950s, over 90 percent of the federal civilian
workforce was now part of the civil service.[49] On the national defense side,
concerted recruitment efforts coupled with the adoption and continuation
of peacetime drafts perpetuated a large standing military.

The corresponding effect on contractors and other private deputies ought
to be apparent: their role in American public life was reduced to the margins. Contractors did not altogether disappear, and new and important
forms of privatization continued to crop up. But those contractors who
remained and those who newly emerged held themselves out as similarly, if
not exceptionally or extraordinarily, professional.[50] Indeed, those contractors—think Manhattan Project physicists and Rand analysts—were primarily tasked with scientific, engineering, energy, and weapons development responsibilities[51]—vital areas to be sure, but ones far removed from
the lawmaking and policymaking processes. More generally, the State and
the Market seemed increasingly distinct, divided, and adversarial, as evidenced by the growing regulation of business—and by the growing opposition of the business community to those State regulatory initiatives.[52]

Contemporary Challenges to Big, Good,
and Distinctive Government

This big, good, and distinctive government had a great mid-twentieth-
century run. But, of late, support has waned considerably. Over the past
few decades, what I call *pax administrativa* and associate with a dominant,

prosperous era of federal administrative governance, has been questioned, challenged, and battered. As Chapter 5 will show, private military contractors, tax collectors, prison administrators, police officers, and lawyers have all reemerged as major players. In addition to those familiar faces, we now have a new and novel vanguard of private environmental inspectors, welfare administrators, and transportation personnel doing practically every job within agencies. Indeed, we now have, to use Paul Light's term, a "shadow" workforce of private actors and private deputies who outnumber the regular, federal civil servants.[53]

The modern administrative state isn't just being reprivatized through outsourcing. It is also being newly hollowed out from within. Some of the landmark achievements of modern American public administration mentioned briefly above—including, most prominently and importantly, merit hiring, tenure, and salarization—are being rolled back. As Chapters 5 and 6 will show, across all levels of government, we are witnessing a reversion to at-will employment, performance-based pay, and far more casualized, part-time government work. Seemingly, our instant infatuation with the Market—and, increasingly, with the highly flexible gig economy in particular—has made us look upon, and treat, the federal bureaucracy with contempt and even revulsion. The end result—the marketization of the bureaucracy—represents a direct assault on *pax administrativa*. Among other things, marketization (once again) narrows the gap between public and private provision. After all, a twenty-first-century marketized employee stripped of tenure and compensated partly by bonuses shares more in common with private contractors (of today and, perhaps, the nineteenth century) than she does with her mid- to late-twentieth-century government counterparts, who were salaried and insulated from undue political influence.

Does History Matter?

Having taken a quick romp through the history of American privatization and an even quicker peek forward at what has been happening in the early twenty-first century, let's return to the claim with which this chapter began: Some of privatization's proponents insist that what we are seeing today is not new and, often, not that remarkable. At times, these champions press further, suggesting that extensive privatization, marketization of the bureaucracy, and a general commitment to businesslike government reflect the normal state of affairs—and that the mid-twentieth-century *pax administrativa* was an anomaly. That is to say, instead of talking about contemporary businesslike government as the avulsive change, we should be treating today's Privatization Revolution as restorative—returning us to the traditional and longstanding customs and practices of American law and politics.

These are not idle claims. Nor are they claims relegated to the periphery of contemporary discourse. Instead, we see arguments of this sort shaping debates within agencies, on the floors of legislative assemblies, on the hustings, and in the courts of law.

I have two, related responses, both of which are central to this project and which will be better and more fully articulated in the chapters to come. But, for starters, consider the following:

My first response is a normative, ahistorical one. Even assuming that there once was a traditional preference for private or otherwise commercialized government service provision, that preference was repudiated in the twentieth century. For my money, that repudiation was the right and quite likely constitutionally necessary move. An administrative state with a salaried, tenured public workforce is better and more legitimate for all the reasons it was created and then some. (I will explain as much in later chapters.) The State must be in a position to handle the exceedingly great and sophisticated demands placed upon it—and to handle those demands impartially, professionally, and consistently with our democratic values and the rule of law. That is a tall order, and the best way the State can satisfy that order is with the help of a permanent, well-qualified, and legally accountable workforce, not swayed by politics or profits.

Public bureaucracy, once professionalized through merit exams, scrubbed of opportunities for self-dealing, and depoliticized through the adoption of a tenure system, is simply more reliable and constitutionally legitimate. This isn't to say that such an independent, salaried public workforce is perfect. It can be costly, slow, and at times frustratingly obstinate. But that is the price we must pay for a deliberative, procedurally robust, and expert bureaucracy that has neither financial nor political incentives to deviate from sound scientific, sociological, or legal judgments.

My second response is an apples-to-oranges one. History does matter, but we need to look at historical dynamics more broadly. Even if privatization yesterday looks like the privatization that is on the upswing today (and, in some respects, it certainly does), the fact is that yesterday and today represent otherwise very different moments. Throughout the first hundred or so years of the American Republic, the admittedly widespread, nonchalant blending of public and private spheres was considerably less significant than it is today. The blending was less significant if only because the public sphere was not very *public,* and the private sphere was not nearly as *private.*

Consider the public sphere first. As alluded to above, for much of our history, the right to vote was jealously guarded, extending to new groups at a glacial pace.[54] Rights to sue the government were also less than robust. This was a time when sovereign immunity (barring suits against the government) had far fewer exceptions;[55] before Congress passed the landmark Civil Rights Act of 1871 that authorized lawsuits against state actors for constitutional violations;[56] before Congress enacted the Federal Tort Claims Act of 1946;[57] and before the Supreme Court, in 1971, recognized *Bivens* suits for constitutional violations committed by federal officials.[58] It was also a time before passage of the Administrative Procedure Act of 1946 ("APA") and before decisions such as *ADAPSO v. Camp,* in 1970, which empowered a far broader range of people to bring a far broader set of claims challenging the legality or even the reasonableness of agency actions or inactions.[59] And it was a time before the courts recognized that individuals may have a constitutionally protected interest in so-called new property—notably, government entitlements—and thus are empowered under the Due Process Clause to challenge wrongful deprivations or denials of many welfare benefits.[60]

During such an era, would it really matter to the average, effectively disenfranchised person (that is, someone with not only limited democratic rights but also few opportunities for legal redress) whether policy was carried out by a New Jersey state corrections officer or an employee of Yokel Brothers Jail, Inc.? Would it matter to a nineteenth-century sharecropper whether a federal employee or a contractor denied his application for a government land grant? In terms of electoral influence or legal effect, the choice between public and private was, for many, often meaningless, perhaps not much different from a choice between the Church and the Crown to, say, a seventeenth-century French peasant holding sway over neither.

Today, by contrast, public exercises of power are extensively regulated through elections and administrative lawsuits, ensuring the opportunity to apply political and legal pressure on potentially abusive agents of the State—but not necessarily on similarly abusive private contractors who regularly evade political scrutiny, not to mention legal liability.

Add to that unpromising view of unresponsive, unaccountable premodern government the fact that many importantly positioned government workers were mini franchisees, mixing service to the State with financial self-dealing. What relief or comfort would you, a mid-nineteenth-century petitioner, draw from the fact that you were not just legally permitted but fully expected to grease the palms of government agents who controlled access to valuable, perhaps essential, licenses, benefits, and property? All of this is to say that we would be ill advised to idealize early American public administration and hard pressed to find much space between those public administrators and their private counterparts.[61]

Today, of course, the gap between professional civil servants and government contractors could hardly be wider—such that the choice between the two really matters in a way that simply was not true back in the day. As it happens, the two groups now regularly find themselves working side-by-side across any number of federal programs. Like a unified squad of, say, South and North Korean soccer players, the combination of civil servants and contractors onto a single "team" both papers over and accentuates those differences.

Turn next to the private. "Public" corporations were, quite often, more public-regarding in the eighteenth and nineteenth centuries than they are today. (I focus here on publicly traded corporations because these entities are the mainstay of modern contracting—think multinational behemoths like Lockheed Martin, Booz Allen Hamilton, and SAIC, which today combine to transact billions of dollars a year in business with the federal government.) In the premodern era, states granted corporate charters principally to firms understood to promote public interests such as roads and transportation facilities.[62]

Today, the designation of a corporation as public is a nominal, perhaps misleading, formality, at least in the United States.[63] This is especially true given contemporary demands, expectations, and understandings that corporations advance a singular objective: the maximization of shareholder value. As Kent Greenfield has written: "The nineteenth century conception of the [corporation], as a historical matter, included a much stronger nod toward the public purpose of the firm than does the modern view."[64] And, as Justice John Paul Stevens reminded us in the pivotal *Citizens United* case: "Corporations were [originally] created, supervised, and conceptualized as quasi-public entities, 'designed to serve a social function for the state.'"[65]

Thus, historically speaking, the private sphere was not as hermetically private (that is, self-interested) as it is now in an era when the pursuit of profits is the overriding imperative. Even assuming it is true that private entities of yesteryear were socially useful and public-regarding in the ways Greenfield and Stevens suggest, that's not what we can expect from the firms of today.

Accordingly, in many respects, the history just described, however rich, is not *our* history. Like a Connecticut Yankee in King Arthur's Court, even if privatization today is the same as it always was, everything else has changed. We have constructed a much thicker, more comprehensive public legal regime that constrains and disciplines public civil servants. And we have relieved private firms of many of the public-regarding charges we previously expected them to fulfill, allowing businesses to instead focus entirely and unapologetically on profit maximization. That divide between public and private—which, again, has widened considerably since the nineteenth century—ought to give us pause about the use of history in this space. History's relevance, if any, is in illuminating how much more momentous the "make or buy" decision (between public and private employment) is today.

2

The Rise and Reign of
Pax Administrativa

The previous chapter described an early period of extensively (and often nonchalantly) privatized American administration. Hired guns, naval privateers, and tax ferrets played large and critical roles in the first hundred years of our Republic. So did tip-grubbing and bounty-seeking government employees. Indeed, it might be better to classify this early period as ancient rather than simply historic because there was such an abrupt break between it and the Privatized Era of today. That abrupt break, which I previewed above, took the form of the modern, twentieth-century administrative state, one that effectively demolished the heavily privatized, commercialized, and marketized administrative architecture of the late eighteenth and nineteenth centuries.

If Chapter 1 captured the prehistory of American public administration, this chapter introduces the start of *our* history. Like anthropologists looking back to the time of the Neanderthals, we can marvel at contemporary similarities and commonalities with nineteenth-century governance while still marking that early era as different from and largely noncontinuous with our own. The evolutionary ruptures between the nineteenth and twentieth centuries are indeed profound: the bounty hunters of the Wild West and the swashbuckling privateers of the high seas must have seemed as remote to, say, the New Deal brain trust and Kennedy–Johnson whiz kids as cavemen were to the Greeks and Romans of antiquity.

This chapter will necessarily be another quick and stylized jaunt through a complicated and fascinating period. Still, there is much we can and need to accomplish in this short space, some historical material to foreground and some novel inquiries to tee up. We need to do so in order to fully appreciate that which is currently under siege. It is this twentieth-century public, professional administrative state that I argue is itself now being unmade.

With that in mind, I first traverse the historical. Here I cover the transition from premodern to modern administrative governance, showing specifically how changes in law, culture, and personnel reshaped American public administration and ushered in a period of *pax administrativa*. This *pax administrativa* is characterized by a large, wide-reaching, and meaningfully public State bureaucratic infrastructure, thick legal webs constraining and guiding administrative exercises of State power, and broad (but, as we now know, ultimately fleeting) popular support.

It then falls to the next chapter to take up the novel. It isn't enough for me simply to assert that the modern administrative state is *the* standard against which to measure and assess today's Privatization Revolution, even though that is certainly true and, for many, reason enough. *Pax administrativa* is more than our near legacy, good or bad. It is a virtuous one. Showing why the twentieth-century administrative state is indeed something to celebrate has special urgency today for two reasons: because its luster has been lost and largely forgotten; and because, again, there is a new and very formidable challenger seeking to finish the job of demolition and delegitimation.

Accordingly, Chapter 3 provides a heretofore unarticulated defense of the normative and constitutional underpinnings of *pax administrativa*—a defense that centers on the recognition and valorization of what I call the administrative separation of powers. Responding to still lingering constitutional questions surrounding administrative governance and increasingly loud laments that our public bureaucracy is woefully inefficient, my theory of administrative separation of powers places the modern American administrative state on terra firma.

The administrative separation of powers lends new and richer constitutional gloss to the twentieth-century administrative state, redeeming and extending the framers' commitment to checks and balances in a way that even the stoutest defenders of modern welfare and regulatory programs have overlooked or ignored. What's more, the administrative separation of powers provides an explanation as to why today's push to run government like a business is so disconcerting, even in cases where businesslike government's cost savings are apparent and where there is no whiff of contractor waste, fraud, or abuse. That is, once we appreciate what is good and necessary about the twentieth-century administrative state, we can then understand why the instant Privatization Revolution is a problem of constitutional proportions.

Big, public government of the twentieth century was no doubt inspired and propelled forward by the maturation and democratization of the American Republic. Late-nineteenth- and early-twentieth-century industrialization produced major socioeconomic shocks. These were hardly Americans' first experiences with poverty, dangerous working conditions, or injustice. But industrialization concentrated and exacerbated such problems, and an increasingly inclusive and mobilized public was, seemingly for the first time, able to assert political influence. And assert it they did. Voters demanded greater protection from the vagaries, deceptions, and dangers of the marketplace; they petitioned for a broader array of benefits and services; and they clamored for a more regular and immediate State role in any number of heretofore unregulated private affairs.

A State newly tasked with these weighty and extensive responsibilities (and newly attuned to the disciplining effects of a more demanding, empowered, and diverse electorate) could no longer get away with being small or amateurish. Staffing couldn't be comprised of private irregulars or ward heelers. Nor could the State countenance greedy government employees seeking to profit by overly indulging benefit seekers or by overzealously prosecuting regulatory miscreants. Likewise, administrative procedures could no longer be opaque or ad hoc. Instead, a bold, large government had to be above reproach as it intervened aggressively in the national economy, combated social and economic injustice, and provided the necessary domestic and overseas support befitting an emerging global superpower.

This modern administrative state—the very embodiment of big, public government—was revolutionary in all respects. It ballooned in size. Its professionalism rose by leaps and bounds. Its operating procedures became far more rigorous and transparent. And newfound opportunities for public participation and legal redress transformed the relationship between the citizen and the State. All of these exciting gains (or—as some saw them—unfortunate encrustations) crowded out privatized or marketized administration and other forms of private self-help that individuals previously had to rely on for protection from unfair and harmful businesses or for the basic provision of food, medicine, and shelter.

The Size of the Twentieth-Century
Administrative State

It would be hard to overstate the exponential growth of federal administrative power in the twentieth century. To be sure, we long had federal officials doing important work. As mentioned in Chapter 1, customs officials, postal personnel, veterans' benefits administrators, land officers, and the like dotted the early federal landscape. But even after factoring in the panoply of private deputies then working for or with the government, the premodern federal footprint was, again, small and faint.

This all changed in the twentieth century. At the beginning of the century, federal civilian employment was approximately 250,000.[1] Over the next few decades, employment more than tripled, nearing 850,000 during the mid-to-late 1930s,[2] and then skyrocketing again during World War II, when federal civilian employment approached 3.8 million.[3] For decades afterward, employment hovered around 2 million, eventually peaking at slightly over 3 million in the late 1980s and early 1990s—a far cry from the modestly sized staff present at the creation of the modern administrative state.[4]

The institutional architecture supporting these millions of new workers grew in turn. From the dawn of the Republic to the close of the Civil War, a smattering of key agencies handled the bulk of federal responsibilities. Then another handful or so were created between 1865 and 1900. It was only in the twentieth century when we witnessed rapid and exponential growth. The first wave of modern agencies were products of the Progressive Era. They included the Federal Trade Commission, the Federal Reserve, and the initially combined Department of Commerce and Labor. Second came Franklin Roosevelt's dizzying menagerie of New Deal alphabet agencies. Soon enough, a third wave was upon us, as 1940s Washington made way for the arrival of massive (and permanent) military and intelligence bureaucracies. A fourth, particularly expansive period spanned the mid-1960s to mid-1970s, when the Department of Housing and Urban Development, the Department of Transportation, the Department of Energy, the Environmental Protection Agency, and the Consumer Product Safety Commission all came into existence. Looking back over those decades, one may be excused for being overwhelmed by all the acronyms, let alone by the tremendous growth they symbolized as new—*and newly expanded*—agencies, departments, bureaus, and government corporations squeezed into and concomitantly reshaped an increasingly crowded federal landscape.[5]

The Funding of the Twentieth-Century
Administrative State

Expenditures offer another way to gauge the State's—and, specifically, the administrative state's—importance and power. Scholars and budget officials chart rather flat and low real per capita expenditures during the nineteenth century and contrast those modest numbers with the steady and continual growth in federal expenditures throughout the twentieth century. Indeed, expenditures rose steadily even during the 1920s, a decade commonly associated with laissez-faire retrenchment and the small government policies of the Harding, Coolidge, and Hoover administrations.[6] Moreover, these steady increases occurred independently of the major military buildups associated with the two world wars.[7]

One useful indicator of government growth is federal spending as a percentage of America's gross domestic product (GDP). Reliable federal data dates back only to 1930. Between 1930 and the mid-1980s, federal expenditures grew from approximately 3.5 percent of national GDP to around 20 percent.[8] This story of secular growth and expansion is corroborated by any number of more nuanced analyses, the specifics of which need not distract us from this basic, undisputed, and powerful lesson.[9]

The Professionalization of the Twentieth-Century
Administrative State

Government became bigger in all the ways just described. It also became more professional. I previewed some of this story in the previous chapter. I return to it here to explain what I mean by *more professional* and to underscore professionalization's significance in shaping the modern administrative state and in distinguishing *pax administrativa* from what preceded it.

Civil service reforms of the late nineteenth and early twentieth centuries transformed the government bureaucracy, its norms, and its staffing protocols. Exam scores, not political favoritism, dictated new hires and placements.[10] Tenure protections—including, most notably, legal assurances of continued employment absent a showing of cause—provided government employees with considerable job security; encouraged these employees to acquire significant expertise; insulated them from the partisan pressures of presidential politics; and allowed agencies to develop stronger, richer institutional cultures in ways that simply weren't possible given the hackishness, lackeyism, and high turnover associated with the old spoils system.

By the mid-twentieth century, practically all federal civilian employees enjoyed these protections.[11] They were now far more likely to make a career out of serving the State rather than spend just a few years serving the party machine—and a particular president.[12]

The salarization of government employees lent further professionalism to the federal workforce. As Nicholas Parrillo explains, by eliminating financial incentives for government workers to be overly generous to benefit seekers or overly punitive in their dealings with regulated parties, salarization rendered government officials more impartial.[13] Indeed, it would be difficult to make the case that many nineteenth-century government workers—at least those whose compensation was tethered to bribes and bounties—could have served as truly honest brokers.

Lastly, the cause of professionalism was advanced by a series of laws prohibiting federal employees from engaging in, being drawn into, or drawing others into partisan politicking.[14] These bans distanced the federal workforce from the rough-and-tumble of the campaign trail and from the machinations of smoke-filled backrooms—and reduced the pressure politically appointed agency heads could exert in the administrative arena. As the Supreme Court recognized, such anti-politicking laws helped make sure that "employment and advancement in the Government service [did] not depend on political performance"[15] and relieved government workers of any expectation to "perform political chores in order to curry favor with their superiors."[16] Thus the rank-and-file were able to focus on being competent, independent civil servants in ways that furthered "the great end of Government—the impartial execution of laws."[17]

Whether one is more likely to think of the *ancien régime*'s administrative staffing protocols in terms of Jacksonian populism or Tammany corruption, the fact remains that the twentieth-century turn in the direction of a more permanent, depoliticized, financially disinterested government workforce represented a sea change in American public administration. Public administration could now be more stable because employees retained their jobs across presidential administrations. Public administration could now be more expert because politically insulated employees had the incentive and opportunity to learn more about the programs they were administering and the communities they were serving. Public administration could now be more esteemed, taken more seriously because those who secured jobs did so as engineers, lawyers, scientists, social workers, inspectors, and clerks who aced an exam and drew a regular salary for their service to the State. It was, not coincidentally, during the heyday of *pax administrativa* when the phrase "good enough for government work" first entered the American English lexicon. Jarring as it may seem to contemporary

audiences—who instantly associate the saying with scornful, sarcastic critiques of the State—the mid-twentieth-century phrase reflected earnest
admiration for the federal bureaucracy and its exacting standards. "Good
enough for government work" signified high-quality work of the sort that
might earn even the U.S. government's stamp of approval.[18]

Perhaps most importantly, public administration could now be more
balanced, incorporating and harmonizing the political interests of the
agency leaders (still, as the Constitution prescribes, appointed by the president) and the technocratic, apolitical expertise of the career staff. After
all, the tenured, secure, and esteemed civil servants now had the legal
authority and institutional impetus to resist partisan overreaching by
impatient, imprudent, or myopic agency leaders and also to challenge foot
dragging by presidential administrations ideologically hostile to regulatory
initiatives or benefits programs.

One might go further and say that the professionalization of the workforce had the effect of fueling government expansion. Those committed to
government service as a vocation likely believed in the mission and capacity
of the State to solve problems. And those with responsibilities over government programs may have wanted to enlarge their portfolios and expand
their organizations. But it is not necessarily true that these professionalized
workers, even if we stipulate that they were indeed sympathetic to the
government enterprise, were any more enthusiastic about government
growth than were the nineteenth-century elected officials who no doubt
viewed the government workforce as, if nothing else, fertile ground for the
accrual and payment of political debts. Nor is it necessarily true that these
professionalized workers were more enthusiastic about government
growth than are today's government contractors who are financially
dependent on an activist State and who stand to profit from a bigger,
rangier government. I will take up some of these considerations more fully
in later chapters.

The Procedural Legalism of the Twentieth-Century Administrative State

Turning from personnel to procedures, it is important to stress, again, that
premodern administrative law was not a barren wasteland. The excavating
work of Jerry Mashaw attests to that. But it also was not very fecund. As
even Mashaw's illuminating interventions suggest, the law at that time was

splotchy and uncertain, covering only select sets of actors or select sets of circumstances and thus leaving any number of gaps across the administrative terrain.[19]

This too was all to change in the twentieth century. Acts of Congress, White House directives, and judicial opinions helped fill in and smooth out the previously patchy administrative landscape. This flurry of legal and regulatory activity culminated in the passage of the Administrative Procedure Act. According to the Supreme Court, Congress enacted the APA "to introduce greater uniformity of procedure and standardization of administrative practice among diverse agencies whose customs had departed widely from one another."[20] The Court's understanding resonates with that of then Attorney General Tom Clark. Clark argued that the APA was needed to "deal horizontally with the subject of administrative procedure, so as to overcome the confusion which inevitably has resulted from leaving to basic agency statutes the prescription of the procedures to be followed, or in many instances delegation of authority to agencies to prescribe their own procedures."[21] Scholars concur. They too emphasize the pro-standardization purpose and effect of the APA. Specifically, "the APA transformed federal administrative law from a loose assortment of constitutional and common law doctrines into a body of law that centered on a single, overarching statute [and] established a general statutory framework [for] the procedures agencies must follow and the availability and scope of judicial review of agency decisions."[22]

I don't want to overstate the APA's effect or understate its historical antecedents.[23] Nor do I want to downplay the subsequent work by the agencies and the courts to thicken and strengthen the 1946 legislation.[24] Nevertheless, it is safe to say that the APA represented a momentous legislative achievement, in then Professor Antonin Scalia's words, "a sort of superstatute," worthy of special constitutional solicitude.[25]

Among other things, the APA rationalized and standardized the two principal means of public administrative engagement—rulemaking and adjudication—and made those processes relatively uniform across the various agencies. (Compounding this standardization story, most states, in turn, have created their own, baby APAs.[26]) Rules are generally applicable statements of agency policy that have the force of law. They are, in appearance and effect, agency-made *laws*. Before agencies may promulgate these powerful directives, they first have to give notice of a proposed rule, provide opportunities for the public to comment on the proposed rule, and then publish a final rule accompanied by a concise general statement explaining their decisionmaking process, how and why the final version of the rule differed from that which was initially and provisionally proposed, and what comments it relied upon (and disregarded)—and why.[27] Afterward, persons alleging injury may sue the agency, challenging the adequacy of the procedures employed or the reasonableness of the final rule.[28]

This rulemaking process—often called *informal rulemaking* (for reasons that need not distract us) and actually only fully utilized starting in the 1960s and 1970s—represents a huge delegation of lawmaking power from Congress to the personnel leading and staffing federal agencies. But it doesn't necessarily follow that the delegation engenders a democracy deficit.[29] After all, the rulemaking process is itself highly democratic, transparent, and inclusive, allowing for presidential surrogates, nonpartisan experts, and members of the public writ large to contribute to the shaping of the final rule.[30] Kenneth Culp Davis called rulemaking "one of the greatest inventions of modern government."[31] Cass Sunstein, reflecting on his experiences as both legal scholar and federal regulator, calls the rulemaking process "immensely important and very substantive"—and insists that the public's role is crucial in helping to shape and formulate final rules.[32]

To be sure, in earlier times, those with political or financial clout could always bend the ear of administrators and find ways to influence administrative policy. After the APA was enacted, those heavyweights were, not surprisingly, still ever present. But they would now have to make room at the table for everybody else. Thus, when an agency contemplates what foods qualify for inclusion in the federal school lunch program, nutritionists, parents, and school administrators can weigh in alongside agribusinesses and Big Food lobbyists. And when decisions have to be made about the regulation of workplaces, agencies must entertain input from laborers, physical therapists, and customers—and not just from the big shots in the unions, the National Association of Manufacturers, and the Chamber of Commerce.

Likewise, the APA helps frame how agencies adjudicate disputes. Those disputes often center on whether a particular person was wrongfully denied a government benefit or whether an individual or entity has in fact run afoul of an act of Congress or an administrative rule. Pursuant to the APA and the requirements of constitutional due process, agency adjudications are often trial-like, in large part to ensure the integrity and impartiality of the decisionmaking process.[33] As with rulemaking, parties may seek judicial redress for practically any injury resulting from an administrative adjudicator's inattentiveness to the statutorily or constitutionally required procedures[34] or from the unreasonableness of an agency's final order.[35]

The thick statutory laws and constitutional imperatives governing agency adjudications further rationalized and professionalized administrative governance, making agencies truly the go-to adjudicatory bodies for twentieth-century Americans. Indeed, earlier I referenced Tocqueville and his observation about nineteenth-century Americans' penchant for litigiousness. Had one of his great-grandkids repeated the French aristocrat's study, she would have probably drawn a similar conclusion. One difference she would have discerned, however, would be in venue. For reasons of convenience and efficiency—and because government regulators became more centrally involved in the lives and relationships of all Americans—twentieth-century disputes were increasingly reconciled in the corridors of agencies rather than in the courtrooms of our common law judges.[36]

The Hegemony of the Twentieth-Century Administrative State

Perhaps most importantly, the impact of the twentieth-century federal administrative state can be gauged by reference both to its objectively broad political support and to its effective marginalizing or supplanting of most other forms of social and economic ordering.

First, the New Deal-Great Society coalitions effectively controlled the federal agenda for forty-some-odd years, from 1933 through the early 1970s. Throughout this time, *pax administrativa* remained strong and largely unquestioned. Even on the two occasions when Republicans managed to capture the White House, things pretty much remained business as usual. Presidents Dwight Eisenhower and Richard Nixon were centrist, big government types, who tolerated and quite frequently expanded the groundbreaking programs we associate with Democrats Franklin Roosevelt, Harry Truman, and Lyndon Johnson. President Eisenhower, it is important to remember, wrested the Republican nomination away from then Senator Robert Taft, a true foe of the administrative state. Eisenhower's was thus a nomination that further signaled mainstream Republican acceptance of the welfare state and the bureaucratic infrastructure undergirding it.[37]

And President Nixon, for all his conservative bluster, presided over the creation of the Environmental Protection Agency, the Occupational Safety and Health Administration, and the Consumer Product Safety Commission, all the while championing a guaranteed basic income for all Americans and "health care reforms way to the left of the Clinton or Obama health plans."[38]

All told, as political scientist James Kurth explains, every Republican presidential nominee during this mid-century period, with the notable exception of Barry Goldwater, was "in favor of some kind of large role for the federal government in many sectors of society." The political convergence, indeed consensus, in favor of a far-reaching federal administrative state thus "caused many political commentators to refer to the Republicans as the 'me-too' party."[39]

Second, this was a period in which the federal administrative state displaced most other forms of social and economic ordering. Eighteenth- and nineteenth-century federal administrative governance left plenty of room for direct congressional efforts to shape private behavior and for state and local governments to do the same; for nongovernmental regulation and self-help, including private contract and norm enforcement, industry self-governance, private risk pooling, and charitable giving through extended families and churches; and for the courts to draw upon state common law and doctrines of equity to help settle what today we see as quintessentially federal regulatory disputes. Indeed, by the 1980s and 1990s, scholars were marveling at the throwback, self-regulating practices of Shasta County ranchers[40] and Maine lobster gangs[41] who, like lost tribes in the Amazon, remained aloof from the ever-expanding orbit of Beltway bureaucracy.

In short, the administrative state of the eighteenth and nineteenth centuries was often not the only or even the primary game in town. But that all changed in the twentieth century. By then, states and municipalities began recognizing that many problems were national in scope and effect—and thus looked to Washington for guidance, direction, and funding. And in Washington, Congress became all too aware of its institutional limitations—its lack of technical sophistication and its meager staff support—and thus delegated vast amounts of authority to expert agencies.

Private self-help continued, of course, but was increasingly pushed to the sidelines by more powerful, more reliable, and more legitimate forms of government regulation, insurance schemes, and benefit programs. For example, systemic economic shocks exposed the frailties of privately organized pools for voluntary, charitable giving. When communities are socially cohesive and flush, it is easy to be charitable. But more people need assistance in less prosperous times—the very moment when voluntary charitable giving also dries up. Indeed, what happens when that uncle whom you are counting on to float you a loan is also out of work? What's more, any number of private contracts and other market-based governance regimes were deemed unreliable, unconscionable, or monopolistic in light of widespread information asymmetries and the unequal bargaining power between and among the parties.[42]

Lastly, the common law yielded to an age of statutes and rules.[43] In the late nineteenth and early twentieth centuries, courts were asked to apply any number of vintage, even crusty, precedents to the very different, technologically challenging, and often highly acute problems associated with industrialization. By the mid-twentieth century, agencies relieved courts of much of that burden. Armed with fresh tools, newly minted legal authorities, and well-trained staffs, these burgeoning administrative juggernauts were ready to combat the societal ills of the day.[44]

Truly we were in the midst of a *pax administrativa,* in which agencies were seen as credible, capable, and accessible. These agencies were, during this time, so popular that some, notably Bruce Ackerman, understood the New Deal as engendering a "constitutional moment" in which *We the People* effectively ratified the big, activist, intrusive, redistributive federal administrative apparatus.[45] Agencies were hardly perfect, of course. Nor were their tools or personnel. There were plenty of things agencies could have done better, more carefully, or with greater attention to the needs and interests of regulated parties and beneficiaries alike. But they nevertheless were dominant and, again, objectively the go-to instruments of the State and civil society, both of which were rapidly maturing and trying to navigate the dangerous waters between unfettered capitalism and full-blown socialism—the Scylla and Charybdis of twentieth-century life not just in the United States but around the world.

As later chapters will show, the very characteristics that define this Administrative Era—size, professionalism, democratic inclusiveness, legalism, and dominance—are now proving to be its undoing. But before addressing the contemporary backlash against *pax administrativa,* more needs to be said about the modern administrative state, about its structure, architecture, and constitutional foundations. Only by understanding *pax administrativa* on this deeper level can we truly appreciate what is at stake in the instant Privatization Revolution—and why we should care.

3

The Constitutional and Normative Underpinnings of the Twentieth-Century Administrative State

Twentieth-century American public administration didn't just supplant the prior regime, such as it was—like Henry IV seizing the throne from the similarly despotic Richard II or Michael Corleone bumping off the equally corrupt Moe Greene to consolidate his control over Las Vegas. Twentieth-century public administration did what the young Godfather promised but never delivered. It went legitimate.

The last chapter cataloged the ingredients of *pax administrativa* and explained how that regime cast aside the irregularities of premodern administration. But there is still the question whether our administrative state, irregular or not, is constitutionally grounded. Though many—indeed most—understand the modern American administrative state to be lawful and just, those are characteristics I need to show, not simply assert. After all, some well-placed jurists, lawmakers, and scholars continue to profess doubts over the constitutionality of the administrative state. What's more, while those influential critics appear to be winning over new converts every day, the pro-administrative state camp has done little to stem the tide. Supporters of administrative governance often prove vague or seem put upon when pressed to explain our regulatory regime in explicitly constitutional terms. Quite possibly, it is this inability or reluctance to defend the modern administrative state that has left *pax administrativa* so vulnerable to contemporary critiques and challenges.

Here I address the modern American administrative state's constitutional and normative underpinnings. It is the often overlooked and underappreciated architecture of *pax administrativa*—specifically, the administrative separation of powers—that gives the administrative state its constitutional moorings. Disaggregation and triangulation of administrative power bespeak fidelity to an enduring, evolving commitment to the separation of powers and thus reconcile modern agencies with the framers' original tripartite scheme.

Ironically, it is these legitimating, constitutionalizing qualities that awaken and incite yet another group of critics: the privatization crowd. Whereas the constitutional skeptics blast what they see as the structural and procedural inadequacies of a way-too-unfettered administrative state, proponents of privatization have the converse beef—that the administrative state, far from lacking in such legal and institutional safeguards, is too thoroughly constrained (and should be run more like a business). In this respect, the theory of administrative separation of powers exhibits a bit of a Goldilocks quality, explaining how *pax administrativa* is neither too unfettered nor too hamstrung—but rather just right.

Breaking the Constitutional Mold

The pressures and demands of modernity required a big, sophisticated, and expedient administrative apparatus. Our tripartite system of constitutional governance might have been well tailored to our preindustrial, libertarian, and patrician early Republic. Under those circumstances, the federal government could afford to be led by unhurried generalists working across the three branches. But now the onerous requirements for constitutional lawmaking—passage through both houses of Congress and presentment to the president—seemed, in the words of future Justice William O. Douglas, "our great public futility."[1]

As calls for more interventionist, responsive, redistributive government rang louder and louder, our elected leaders answered. They answered not by overhauling or streamlining the original constitutional system itself. Rather, they worked around it. The growth and expansion of federal agencies detailed in the previous chapter represented an indirect assault on the framers' finely wrought, but often painfully ponderous, tripartite system. Agencies combined that which the Constitution so carefully separated. The heretofore separated powers—legislative, executive, and judicial— were consolidated. They were brought under one roof, enabling administrative government to act without the cross-institutional rivalries and hassles associated with governing across three great and, by design, contentious branches. In Judge Richard Posner's words, the imperatives of modernity demanded that "the constitutional mold had to be broken and the administrative state invented."[2]

These new agencies made rules (that, again, had substantially the same effect as laws passed by Congress) often faster and with far greater technical competence than could Congress. After all, legislators were not experts in most regulatory realms, had minimal staff support, and had to constantly compromise, water down, horse trade, and log roll in order to get anything accomplished amid strong partisan, regional, and institutional divisions in the House and Senate.[3]

In addition, agencies directly enforced the rules they promulgated—again eliminating many of the interbranch costs and obstacles that inhibit and ultimately limit congressional–presidential cooperation. Even duly enacted legislation may regularly go unenforced or, at least, under-enforced when the president deems those laws to be unimportant, unlawful, or retrograde. Such presidential nonenforcement was most recently on display in the immigration context, as federal agents in the Obama administration were instructed not to deport certain classes of undocumented persons notwithstanding federal laws directing their removal. The same had been true with respect to the nonenforcement of certain marijuana crimes.[4] Though explicit and ostentatious defiance of Congress might draw the ire of the courts, as happened with President Obama's immigration directive,[5] there is little, if anything, that can be done when it comes to subtle, implicit acts of under-enforcement or nonenforcement. This gap between congressional lawmaking and executive law enforcing is a central and purposeful design feature of the framers' constitutional system. Yet it all but disappears in the administrative realm where the same body that's making rules is also in charge of enforcing them.

Lastly, just as agencies combined lawmaking and law enforcing powers, they also fused law enforcing and adjudicatory powers. This dual prosecutorial/adjudicatory capacity thus spares agencies from having to rely on the federal courts. Instead, agencies can identify opportune disputes and bring enforcement proceedings against suspected transgressors in certain sequential patterns to shape and advance agency policies in a way that the federal courts—which may hear only the cases brought to them—lack the power and often the incentive to do.

For all these reasons, the mechanics and architecture of modern administration amplified federal power and eliminated slack and interbranch veto points to an unmatched degree.[6] The administrative state was, indeed, in Lawrence Friedman's words, a "Leviathan."[7] As mentioned above, the twentieth-century agencies were numerous, their powers expansive, and their efficiencies unprecedented. These agencies could act fast and decisively even if—and perhaps particularly when—two or all three constitutional branches were at loggerheads.[8]

The Constitutional Uncertainty

All of this seemed great to those, like William Douglas, who appreciated that "[t]he relentless pressures of modern times demanded that government do a streamlined job,"[9] and to another future justice, Felix Frankfurter, who argued that government was finally on the right track, capable of meeting the "needs of society at once the most complicated and fundamental."[10] For these enthusiasts, administrative agencies were nothing short of a godsend.

For others, big, public administration was a sign of the apocalypse. Hyperbole aside, modern federal agencies didn't so much as supplement the framers' constitutional system, as was the case with the more modest nineteenth-century agencies. Rather, they collapsed it. Modern agencies largely crowded out Congress, albeit at Congress's express instruction (given the federal legislature's role in creating, empowering, and funding agencies). This radical toppling of the framers' tripartite system was nothing short of an act of constitutional apostasy. After all, the cross-branch rivalries specified in the first three articles of the Constitution weren't an accident of legal drafting. Nor were they a shameful feature like the horrid three-fifths rule, forced down the throats of our more enlightened but still eminently practical delegates who recognized the imperative to secure the assent of the southern colonies.[11] They weren't even an expedient but normatively contestable compromise, such as the Connecticut Compromise, incorporated to balance the representational interests of the lesser and more populous states.

Instead, the constitutional separation of powers was deliberate and generally celebrated, a source of security, and perhaps the document's chief selling point to a founding generation so scarred by the powerful, centralized government of King George III and so apprehensive about popular rule. Knowing that men, not angels, would govern, James Madison characterized the concentration of power—*even democratic power*—as "the very definition of tyranny."[12] His antidote, of course, was rivalrous separation in which ambition would counteract ambition,[13] a scheme that Justice Antonin Scalia, writing almost exactly two hundred years after Madison, called "the absolutely central guarantee of a just government."[14]

Needless to say, many of the earliest examples of modern administrative governance—undertaken without the benefit of a fully realized professional, tenured civil service and without expansive opportunities for public participation—comported none too well with the framers' constitutional commitment to separating and checking State power. To be sure, premodern administrative governance also didn't sit well with the framers' constitutional commitment. But we must remember that the administrative state of the eighteenth and nineteenth centuries was a smaller, more peripheral actor. With limited legislative and adjudicative powers, premodern administrative government was a fly in the ointment, not a bull in a china shop.[15]

Not surprisingly, therefore, early modern agencies of the 1930s equipped with sweeping powers and granted expansive jurisdictional reach were ripe for challenging. As with many plaintiffs, those attacking the nascent modern administrative architecture were not offended on constitutional principle alone. When it came to the rending of clothes, Wall Street silk, rather than campus tweed, was the fabric of choice. Mourning the collapsing of Madisonian tripartitism most acutely were captains of industry and finance who resented aggressive regulation and longed for the days when the constitutional separation of powers increased the odds that federal measures to break up trusts, improve labor conditions, and eliminate deceptive business practices would never see the light of day.[16]

Still, motives aside, their constitutional arguments were compelling ones: Even assuming that efforts to govern across the three great and rivalrous constitutional branches were stymying, supercharged, unencumbered agencies led by presidential appointees presented the converse problem. Relatively speaking, they were unconstrained vehicles of government intervention, procedurally and structurally unfettered, highly partisan, and potentially intemperate.[17]

In due time, the courts weighed in. After some shots across the bow— and a couple of direct hits that sunk key pieces of Franklin Roosevelt's so-called First New Deal—the Court blinked and made its peace with the administrative juggernaut. The basis for this constitutional blessing was, and remains, somewhat vague and slippery. The Court seemed to rely on such touchstones as what it called "an intelligible principle" and on the corresponding legal fiction that agencies weren't actually making laws.[18]

For these reasons, among others, though the constitutional battle over delegations of federal power to administrative agencies was quickly and decisively won, many of the combatants weren't fully satisfied with the outcome—or, at the very least, with the Court's underlying reasoning. To this day we hear leading scholars and jurists insisting that the administrative state is a constitutionally tenuous proposition.[19] One recent and widely debated book published by Philip Hamburger asks (and answers in the affirmative) whether the administrative state is in fact unlawful.[20] Though criticized by many colleagues—Harvard's Adrian Vermeule pointedly titled his review of the book *No*[21]—Hamburger's work resonates with key members of the federal judiciary. In 2015, Justice Clarence Thomas, in a concurring opinion broadly challenging the constitutionality of the modern administrative state, cited Hamburger approvingly.[22] Just a few years earlier, Chief Justice John Roberts voiced similar concerns when he himself seemed to question the very foundation of what I'm calling *pax administrativa*. Roberts wrote: "The Framers could hardly have envisioned today's vast and varied federal bureaucracy and the authority administrative agencies now hold. . . . The administrative state with its reams of regulations would leave them rubbing their eyes."[23] Newest Justice Neil Gorsuch seems to agree. In a provocative and much-discussed 2016 circuit court opinion, then Judge Gorsuch worried that the courts have allowed "bureaucracies to swallow huge amounts of core judicial and legislative power and concentrate federal power in a way that seems more than a little difficult to square with the Constitution of the framers' design."[24] For Gorsuch, who likewise cited Hamburger, the time had "come to face the behemoth."[25]

Why is all of this important? Even if we assume that Chief Justice Roberts and Justices Thomas and Gorsuch are serious in their opposition, they remain in the minority. (They've also just lost fellow traveler and influential D.C. Circuit Judge Janice Rogers Brown, who retired in August 2017. Judge Brown, for her part, memorably characterized the New Deal as "our own socialist revolution."[26]) Still, the dissenting broadsides and revanchist critiques matter if for no other reason than they keep open a second front in the attack on administrative governance. Would-be champions of *pax administrativa* must remain on the defensive, responding to those pushing to run government like a business (the focus of the chapters that follow) from a position of ostensible constitutional weakness. A strong and confident administrative state would be far better positioned to resist the challenges posed by privatization. But an uncertain, defensive, even apologetic administrative state—such as ours still at times struggling to shore up its constitutional bona fides—is no match for the Privatization Revolution already under way, and the sharks, vultures, and neighborhood bullies all know this.

Indeed, today's self-described champions of the administrative state cede much ground. They engage in appeasement tactics, notably by mimicking privatization from within. And they quibble on the margins, taking exception less with privatization writ large than with some of privatization's puffery, contending (not incorrectly) that privatization's claims of efficien-cies and cost savings are exaggerated. All of this is to say that—going back to my earlier analogies to one king or mobster toppling another—who really cares if one questionable practice today is seeking to supplant a sim-ilarly questionable one?

But this is wrong. The modern administrative state needs a Churchill, not a Chamberlain. Deep down, the modern administrative state is strong, just, and above all constitutional—and constitutional precisely because of the administrative separation of powers. And it is time to claim the virtue in what others have persuaded us are vices. Once we peel away layers of doubt and restore *pax administrativa*'s constitutional luster, we begin to see that the modern administrative state purged itself of whatever original sins it bore in infancy, quieting, one hopes, the again revanchist impulses of the Thomas/Roberts/Gorsuch/Brown/Hamburger variety.

And once we recast *pax administrativa* as intentionally and constitu-tionally necessarily rivalrous and fragmented, we can explain to the other, newer set of critics that today's purported administrative inefficiencies are not bugs in the American public law system. Rather, they are essential features of the constitutional and administrative design.[27] In short, only through understanding and appreciating *pax administrativa* as constitu-tionally grounded can we see privatization the way Hamlet came to see his uncle: as a false and illegitimate usurper.

The Administrative Separation of Powers as Constitutional Redemption

Even if most scholars, lawyers, and jurists are now willing to recognize the constitutionality of the administrative state (as they surely are, albeit under varied, competing theories), they continue to struggle with how such con-centrated administrative power folds into our constitutional canon.[28] After all, agencies combined and centralized powers that the framers had sepa-rated across three great branches. Technocrat Georganne may have replaced Tyrant George III, but the concerns of absolute power carry forward.

Such concerns are, however, misplaced. Instead of thinking about the initial collapsing of the constitutional separation of powers, what really matters is what happened soon afterward. Like many tales of youthful rebellion, the modern American administrative story is ultimately one of redemption. The administrative powers that started off so dangerously consolidated and unchecked soon became disaggregated—and, with it, the initially collapsed framers' checks and balances were restored and refashioned to function within the administrative realm. As a result, even some of the clunkiness characteristic of the constitutional separation of powers returned.

It is for this reason that the administrative state gets hit from both sides. On the one hand, the administrative state is attacked by those who do not look past the initial and admittedly disconcerting consolidation of administrative power. And, on the other hand, the administrative state is criticized by privatization hawks who seemingly recognize latter-day administrative fragmentation and bristle at the inefficiencies associated with a disaggregated architecture to which they assign no constitutional significance.

Nevertheless, it is the administrative separation of powers that redeems constitutional governance in the Administrative Era. Redemption and restoration occurred somewhat serendipitously, even haphazardly. Perhaps that's why the administrative separation of powers remains to this day often overlooked or unappreciated. Plus, like Andrew Jackson's victory at New Orleans, it came a little late. The Supreme Court had already made its peace with the administrative state, albeit hastily and somewhat politically expediently. (Recall that the Court endorsed a flabby "intelligible principle" standard and propagated the fiction that Congress isn't actually delegating legislative power to agencies.[29])

Again, what ultimately made administrative power kosher was the eventual re-creation and refashioning of the framers' tripartite scheme. This administrative scaffolding is a necessary part of constitutional construction; it provides the specific institutional support we need, in Jack Balkin's words, to "fulfill constitutional purposes."[30] Like the constitutional separation of powers, the administrative separation of powers triangulates power among three sets of competing administrative actors. This administrative trio resembles the three great branches—and situates the modern administrative state squarely within the constitutional tradition of pitting rivalrous, diverse institutional counterweights against one another to protect liberty, promote pluralistic, democratic governance, and assure fidelity to the rule of law. The wages of that necessary constitutional corrective are, ironically enough, a rejection of the unfettered, streamlined, and concentrated powers that made the initial turn to agencies so wildly attractive to generations of Progressives and New Dealers—and that drove constitutional conservatives batty. But they are wages well spent even if, today, they draw the ire of privatization's proponents.

The Mechanics of the Administrative Separation of Powers

Let me explain first what I mean by the administrative separation of powers. We often think of agencies as unitary and monolithic—hence we worry about highly concentrated power. Though that worry persists to a bizarre degree (particularly given, again, loud complaints from the businesslike government crowd that the administrative state is woefully fractured and inefficient),[31] modern public administrative power has long been divided among three sets of rivals: presidentially appointed agency heads who direct the administrative agenda, politically insulated civil servants who carry out most of the agency's day-to-day responsibilities, and the general public authorized and empowered to participate broadly and meaningfully in the development and implementation of agency policies and programs.

Agency Leaders. Agency leaders are the presidentially appointed, statutorily responsible agenda setters and decisionmakers. They include George W. Bush's Condoleezza Rice, Bill Clinton's Donna Shalala, and FDR's Harold Ickes. They also include scores of deputy, under, and assistant secretaries and sundry high-ranking administrators, all of whom serve at the pleasure of the president. These agency leaders propose and promulgate rules, decide what responsibilities to prioritize, allocate appropriated funds, and set expectations regarding what they hope the agency will accomplish.

Generally speaking, these top officials are the administrative standard-bearers for the president. This is because the president usually appoints only those who share her political commitments and policy goals.[32] (There are exceptions, of course. A president could opt for a Lincoln-esque Team of Rivals, but modern history suggests that presidents make at most a couple of token appointments of nonloyalists.[33]) Once selected, these agency officials are expected to remain enthusiastic, energetic, and loyal to the president and her agenda. Those who stray risk political marginalization, if not summary dismissal.[34]

Agency leaders aligned with the White House have reason to skirt procedurally or substantively burdensome congressional directives—directives that happen to be a staple of *pax administrativa*. They also have reason to bypass other agency personnel, notably civil servants, who may insist upon adherence to those directives or who otherwise resist the president's initiatives on policy grounds. Remember, term-limited presidents have only a short window within which to enact their preferred policies. Thus there is an inherent tension between achieving the president's goals and complying with procedurally lengthy and substantively constraining congressional mandates. As such, we can presume that agency leaders will feel pressure to advance the president's agenda even, at times, at the expense of rational, legalistic, inclusive, or procedurally robust public administration. My understanding here tracks that of Bruce Ackerman. Ackerman describes modern presidents as "tempted to achieve [their] objectives by politicizing the administration," placing "political partisans in charge," and encouraging them "to bend the law to fulfill the administration's program." It is therefore "no surprise that some presidential loyalists" are indeed "tempted to take the law into their own hands."[35]

Were these agency leaders to operate unilaterally—that is, were all administrative power concentrated in agency leaders—federal regulatory programs would either be politically supercharged or, if the president is of an anti-regulatory mindset, steadfastly inert. Either way, the wielders of such unrivaled power would be dangerously potent and constitutionally suspect, precisely because they'd be operating outside of the constitutional structural imperatives of separating and checking power. But again, agency leaders are anything but unfettered. They're consistently, sometimes maddeningly, checked by civil servants and the public writ large.

Civil Servants. Modern administrative agency tasks and responsibilities are diverse, complex, and numerous, so much so that agency leaders cannot and do not run agencies all by themselves. Instead, the relatively small (and often relatively inexperienced) coterie of presidential appointees necessarily rely on lower-level government officials to research, design, promulgate, implement, and enforce compliance with administrative programs.[36]

Most of these lower-level government officials are career civil servants.[37] Civil servants are below the agency leaders on every agency "org chart." And many leading scholarly and judicial accounts treat civil servants as if they were straight subordinates of the agency leadership. But notwithstanding these spatial depictions and common characterizations, the fact of the matter is that civil servants are legally, culturally, and practically independent—and cannot be fired, demoted, or promoted based on political considerations.[38] Thus unlike nineteenth-century at-will government employees who often owed their jobs to political patrons, modern civil servants have the opportunity, responsibility, and independent authority to question agency leaders on programmatic and procedural grounds.[39]

Specifically, civil servants shape agency policy by conducting research and by writing reports that frame, justify, strengthen, or discredit government interventions. They also make policy when administering programs on the ground. When it comes to regulatory oversight and enforcement, civil servants have broad discretion whether to inspect, where to inspect, and whether to counsel, admonish, or prosecute those who fail inspections. Likewise, on the public benefits front, civil servants have considerable leeway when advising benefit seekers and determining their eligibility for grants and assistance programs.[40]

In addition, civil servants influence policy by resisting agency leaders' efforts to implement unreasonable or simply hyperpartisan programs.[41] Resistance can take the form of lethargic and half-hearted administration, selective leaking, back-channeling to allies on Capitol Hill, and, of late, "rogue" tweeting. Resistance can also take the form of outright defiance and opposition. Numerous studies attest to civil servants largely seeing themselves as professional public servants. That is, they take pride in their professional roles as engineers, chemists, biologists, attorneys, social workers, inspectors, accountants, and the like. As David Lewis says, these civil servants "often feel bound by legal, moral, or professional norms to certain courses of action and these courses of action may be at variance with the president's agenda."[42] This commitment to professionalism, Harold Bruff adds, positions civil servants as "an often unappreciated bulwark to the rule of law."[43]

For the reasons just described, the politically responsive agency leaders and politically insulated civil servants can be seen as rivals with conflicting interests, competing commitments, and different sources of accountability.[44] The civil servants are not true subordinates but potentially formidable counterweights, quite capable of shaping administrative policy. Indeed, unlike their nineteenth-century predecessors—recall the menagerie of party hacks, contractors, and part-timers—the legally independent civil servants are true experts. They're neither pawns of the president nor hired guns. Rather, they are servants of the State, having secured their placements on the basis of academic and professional achievement. Thus, as Peter Strauss has remarked, prudent agency heads recognize that the civil service's "cooperation must be won to achieve any desired outcome."[45]

Already we should be beginning to see the restaging of Madison's dramatic production of ambition countering ambition, as political agency heads and expert bureaucrats with overlapping responsibilities duke it out. But like the constitutional scheme, the administrative realm is a triangulated one. Hence we need to consider a third combatant.

Civil Society. Enter civil society. I recognize that the term *civil society* is often a freighted one. But my use of it is rather straightforward. It refers to the broad and broadly inclusive public at large: individuals, groups,

organizations, corporations, and the like. Through the APA and subsequent acts of Congress, judicial decisions, and evolving customs and practices, members of the public enjoy the legal authority to, among other
things, obtain agency information,[46] petition for a new rule or for a change
to an existing rule,[47] intervene in adjudicatory proceedings,[48] and comment
on a pending rule.[49] Aggrieved members of the public may, moreover, seek
judicial redress, challenging agency officials for failing to properly attend
to public requests[50] or comments[51] or for acting in a procedurally impoverished, substantively unreasonable, or legally erroneous fashion.[52]

Scholars who appreciate the powerful role civil society plays in administrative governance liken public participants to hammers that "pound agencies."[53] While that characterization is both accurate and vivid, it is also
incomplete. The public doesn't just pound on agency heads and civil servants. Its members are also constructive participants, helping set the
administrative agenda by conferring with agency officials, engaging in
media strategies to bring attention to their causes, proposing new rules,
and commenting on and thus shaping already proposed ones. Research
shows that members of the public, including those we might refer to as lay
people, play a significant role in getting proposed rules on the administrative agenda and then massaging those and other rules' substantive content
during the open comment period.[54] Agency heads and civil servants who
fail to take seriously petitions for rules or who disregard material comments on already proposed rules risk judicial sanction.[55]

The incentive for members of the public to put forward their own
agendas and to challenge those of agency heads and civil servants ought to
be plain enough. The public comprises a vast and diverse universe of individuals and groups, any one of which is bound to be adversely affected by
any change (or non-change) in administrative policy. Someone, somewhere
will always be using formal legal channels and any available political conduits to constrain, prod, or redirect agency officials.[56]

Before turning to consider how *pax administrativa*'s administrative separation of powers legitimates administrative governance, a couple of clari-
fying notes are in order. First, modern administrative power didn't become
truly disaggregated in this triangulated fashion until the mid-twentieth
century. Specifically, it took decades before the civil service was fully tenured. The landmark Pendleton Act, ushering in a skeletal federal civil service, itself provided no protection against at-will terminations.[57] It wasn't
until the 1940s and 1950s when tenure blanketed the overwhelming
majority of federal civilian employees.[58] So, for much of the early modern

Administrative Era, the government workforce wasn't really capable of being a rivalrous counterweight to an overzealous leadership or to a politically powerful set of special interest groups. Likewise, opportunities for meaningful and truly democratic public participation became a legal reality only after the passage of the APA in 1946—if not later, amid the subsequent judicially led reformation that fleshed out and expanded upon the APA's commitment to robust public engagement.[59]

Second, I concede that the depiction I just offered of the three rivalrous entities is a rosy one. There is, of course, no guarantee that the three sets of partisans will always act energetically and in the rivalrous ways instantly characterized. But I aim to underscore a nagging fear and an enduring hope. The fear is of insular, unilateral agency control, by overly politicized agency leaders, insufficiently democratic mandarin technocrats, or selfishly myopic special interest groups. And the hope is that the interplay of these three rivals will not only militate against exercises of unilateral control that are potentially abusive and corrupt but also engender constructive, productive engagement that reflects broad, inclusive buy-in by important and diverse stakeholders.

I hasten to add that any critique of my hopeful characterization of the sharpness of administrative rivalries ought to apply with equal force to Madison, his fellow framers, and their understanding of the rivalrous constitutional separation of powers. At various times, Congress, the judiciary, and even the president have not been up to the task of checking and counteracting one another. But such lapses, as troubling as they are, ought not cast too dark a shadow over a system that for the most part has lived up to its founding hype. Still, I take these real and anticipated administrative lapses seriously. I thus devote much of Part Three of this book to defending my faith in an enduring, evolving separation of powers and to devising jurisprudential and legislative strategies for further strengthening and sharpening the administrative rivalries.

The Administrative Separation of Powers as a Constitutional and Normative Enterprise

I've just shown that administrative power isn't concentrated in the way constitutional critics fear. That power is subject to its own version of intra-administrative checks and balances. But the disaggregation of power, by itself, is still not enough to render the modern administrative state constitutionally or normatively legitimate. Squabbling warlords might be highly effective checks on one another, ensuring that no one gains too much turf or acts too abusively. But such a system cannot be called legitimate. Warlords achieve and maintain power through violence and payoffs rather than through demonstrations of expertise, shows of reasoned deliberation, or evidence of popular support.

In the remaining sections of this chapter, I explain how our particular web of regulatory rivalries has over time rendered administrative power compatible with, coextensive with, and in some respects even superior to the premodern constitutional baseline of governing across the three great branches. What's more, this administrative design helps promote and harmonize the competing, conflicting values generally understood to animate and inform public administration. Once we understand the modern administrative state's deeper ties to the Constitution, its structures, its forms of political and legal accountability, and its normative aspirations, we will have newfound reasons and newfound capacity to defend and champion *pax administrativa* against would-be usurpers.

First, the three administrative rivals aren't just blustering, whimsical titans like Athena, Apollo, and Poseidon battling over the fate of Troy and achieving little more than a bloody impasse. Instead our Olympians are ready, if imperfect, stand-ins for the three constitutional branches. These administrative alter egos carry into the regulatory arena certain dispositional characteristics and commitments that also happen to be central to the identities and agendas of the president, Congress, and the courts. Like understudies in a play, the agency leadership assumes the president's political agenda-setting role; the civil service re-creates the independent judiciary's reason-giving and rule-of-law-promoting role; and civil society takes up Congress's pluralistic, populist deliberative role. What this means is that there is something special and constitutionally salient about this particular trio of administrative actors, essentially reprising the separation of powers drama long performed on the grand constitutional stage.

Second, the administrative separation of powers provides a jurisprudential answer to those continuing to question the constitutionality of the modern administrative state. Theories of constitutional construction teach us to implement the *constitution-in-practice,* and that is precisely what the administrative separation of powers does. It disaggregates initially concentrated administrative power, thereby reconciling federal administrative agencies with the Constitution's underlying and transcendent structural commitments. In short, the administrative separation of powers constitutionalizes *pax administrativa,* domesticates the administrative state, and turns what otherwise would be a jarringly incongruous imposition on the constitutional landscape—a garish McMansion on a block of Craftsman-style bungalows—into a logical and worthy complement and heir to the framers' original scheme.

Separately and distinct from the constitutional construction analysis, the administrative separation of powers benefits from the constitutional anchoring of a pair of superstatutes. Following theorists ranging from Charles Beard to William Eskridge and John Ferejohn, the salient, transformative, and ultimately entrenched Pendleton Act and APA both merit quasi-constitutional status. And that status is important to us because those two laws happen to be the very ones that, along with Article II of the Constitution, lay the constitutional foundation for our tripartite administrative structure.

Third, the administrative separation of powers helps resolve otherwise intractable debates about the normative underpinnings of American public administration. Critics are quick to say that the American administrative state doesn't do enough to promote expertise *or* civic participation *or* presidential control. But what those critics often fail to appreciate is that expertise, civic participation, *and* presidentialism are in conflict with one another. It would therefore be impossible for an administrative state to simultaneously promote all three values. So, in the absence of a clear consensus as to which value to prioritize (and there is no such consensus), the best we can hope for is precisely what the administrative separation of powers provides: a structure that helps harmonize, accommodate, and cycle among leading, but conflicting, administrative values.

The ability of this system of administrative separation of powers to, first, channel and roughly reproduce the constitutional rivalries in the administrative realm, second, tether administrative government to the underlying constitutional order, and, third, promote the fair contestation of competing, conflicting visions of public administration writ large combine to cement *pax administrativa*'s constitutional and normative bona fides. Accordingly, the legitimating effects of the administrative separation of powers cast our long beleaguered administrative state in a different, more nuanced, and far more celebratory light.

The Administrative Separation of Powers and Constitutional Isomorphism

No doubt some will quibble with the connections I am about to draw between constitutional and administrative actors. They will suggest, with reason, that the analogies aren't tight enough. Let me therefore start by conceding the point. I am neither striving for nor insisting upon a perfect translation between the constitutional and administrative. And that's okay. For what I care about is that the kinds of legal, democratic, and professional interests, commitments, and approaches that Madison and his colleagues pitted against one another in the constitutional arena are revived and restaged as an administrative scrum. *West Side Story* gets the Bard's tale of star-crossed lovers basically right—and, again somewhat serendipitously, the same is true for the administrative separation of powers and its fidelity to the original constitutional design.

With that concession out of the way, let us proceed to the analogies in question. Recall that the framers' tripartite system comprises a unitary executive body operating pursuant to a national political mandate—this is, of course, the presidency; a popular, diverse, and often cantankerous deliberative body, which we call Congress; and a politically independent body—the judiciary—dedicated to promoting the rule of law and whose currency is impartiality and reason-giving. It is my argument, again, that our administrative trinity plays substantially similar roles to those of the president, Congress, and the courts.[60] This reproduction helps mark the administrative state as a constitutionally coextensive, legitimate, and worthy enterprise, one that redeems, refashions, and arguably upgrades the framers' central structure and casting choices even as State power extends beyond the boundaries of its 1787 architecture.

Agency Leaders: The Administrative State's "President." This is the most straightforward affinity and can be addressed with the greatest brevity. Agency leaders play a substantially similar role within the administrative separation of powers to that played by the president within the constitutional separation of powers. Like the president, agency leaders have significant managerial responsibilities, including authority to shape agency policy, dictate agency priorities, and allocate agency resources.

What's more, agency leaders are reliable presidential proxies. These leaders are selected and appointed by the president, and, with the exception of independent commissioners (whom I will consider at length in Chapter 9), they serve only at the president's pleasure. For these reasons, agency leaders can generally be expected to internalize and champion the White House's political and programmatic agenda.

Civil Servants: The Administrative State's "Judiciary." Less obvious is the connection between civil servants and federal judges. To be sure, civil servants and judges perform very different tasks. But, again, I am stressing dispositional linkages. And, as a dispositional matter, the civil service has emerged as the administrative trinity's rule-of-law "bulwark"—not unlike the position judges occupy within the constitutional separation of powers. As explained earlier in this chapter, tenured civil servants design studies, draft reports, write rules, grant or deny welfare benefits, and prosecute (or simply admonish) regulatory scofflaws. Both senior and field-level civil servants are legally well situated and institutionally and even culturally inclined to counter political overreaching, promote reasoned approaches to decisionmaking, and provide intergenerational stability[61] in ways not unlike the unelected federal judiciary in its interactions with Congress and the president.[62]

Let me draw this out a little further. Both federal judges and civil servants are ostensibly nonpartisan, insulated from political pressure by virtue of custom and job tenure. Both groups are committed to upholding and promoting the rule of law and their professional codes of conduct. Indeed, judges and civil servants operate within similar cultural milieus that prize analytical rigor and pooh-pooh politicking.

Yet both groups must, invariably, wade into countless political thickets, causing no shortage of headaches, tricky balancing acts, and crises of legitimacy. (Indeed, it is not coincidental that federal judges and civil servants find themselves in each other's company as the two groups often draw the lion share of President Trump's ire.) Judges and civil servants cannot stand truly aloof, simply calling "balls and strikes," as Chief Justice John Roberts once characterized his role. Instead, they are regularly obligated to render decisions of great political consequence. When doing so, they can and often do take pains to demonstrate their fidelity to congressional dictates and professional norms. They also highlight their commitment to rationality, employing reason-giving processes to explain and legitimate their at times countermajoritarian interventions.[63]

To be sure, judges and civil servants usually abide by what the president or agency head wants and does. Yet they still shape policies in crucial ways. Their very presence deters partisan overreaching or procedural shortcuts. And, when deterrence fails, both groups are well suited to resist or reconfigure initiatives that, however popular, seem lawless or unreasonable.[64]

It is, of course, possible that partisanship gets the better of civil servants. But even when civil servants let partisanship or ideology influence their work, they do so in ways quite similar to federal judges.[65] No judge or career civil servant can fully suppress all of her political instincts or commitments. Nevertheless, the diffusion of responsibility among the many federal judges— just like the diffusion of responsibility among the many, many civil servants— dilutes the effects of any one individual's politicized actions or decisions.[66]

Again, I am endeavoring here to show how the administrative separation of powers can operate. I recognize that today's civil service may fall short of these lofty expectations. Though this stylized, even idealized, sketch will have to suffice for now, I will return to the civil service in later chapters, first to detail the ways in which the civil service has in recent years been side-lined and debased and then to proffer strategies for reviving the civil service and restoring it to its rightful place as a formidable administrative rival.

Civil Society: The Administrative State's "Congress." In our administrative revival of the great constitutional drama, civil society takes up the part of Congress. Here too there are obvious differences between Congress's sweeping lawmaking, budgetary, and investigatory powers and the considerably more modest ones that the public enjoys in the administrative arena. As a matter of disposition, however, the comparison is far more meaningful.

Like Congress, civil society is internally heterogeneous, encompassing wide-ranging views, voicing various popular and oddball sentiments, articulating local concerns as well as cohering around national priorities, and mixing self-interest with civic regard—all in furtherance of expressing the People's will on matters of public import. And just as constitutional legislation is the product of diverse engagement by senators and representatives from across the country, agency rules are, to a not-insignificant extent, shaped by the broad array of public comments.

On occasion, civil society will no doubt deviate from both majoritarian and deliberative ideals, with moneyed, corporate interests crowding out would-be public participants.[67] But, regrettably, this only underscores the connection between Congress and civil society: our friends in Congress are themselves all too likely to be swayed by big donors who bankroll their campaigns.[68]

As with the civil service, we need to appreciate the legal and institutional frameworks that enable robust public engagement while also acknowledging that civil society does not always live up to its billing. I will not dwell here on civil society's instant shortcomings. Instead, I underscore the modern administrative state's receptivity to public participation, leaving for later chapters my proposals for a stronger, more democratically inclusive civil society.

The Administrative Separation of Powers and Constitutional Foundations

The administrative state's constitutional bona fides are, at once, patently obvious and, in practically the same breadth, a source of considerable consternation. As noted, most jurists, lawyers, and scholars accept the modern administrative state—and do not see the framers' specific three-branch design as foreclosing institutional innovation of the sort that modernity demanded. As the Supreme Court held in *Mistretta v. United States*, "[O]ur jurisprudence has been driven by a practical understanding that in our increasingly complex society, replete with ever changing and more technical problems, Congress simply cannot do its job absent an ability to delegate power under broad general directives."[69] Yet despite wide acceptance, the theories supporting the constitutionality of the administrative state—for example, living constitutionalism of the sort *Mistretta* seems to embody,[70] historical glosses attesting to the long, slow accretion of administrative power that dates back to the Founding,[71] Bruce Ackerman's "constitutional moment,"[72] and even those claiming kinship to originalism[73]—remain varied and contested. Such uncertainty matters. As discussed above, it has emboldened critics, while rendering those sympathetic to the administrative state somewhat sheepish about the project's origins.

One important source of this sheepishness is the apparent disconnect between the initially conceived modern administrative state and the preexisting constitutional order. That is to say, even if we accept that the administrative state is technically constitutional—via, perhaps, historical gloss, living constitutionalism, the ratifying effects of a constitutional moment, or some convenient legal fiction that agencies do not exercise legislative authority—there is still the residual question of constitutional compatibility. Specifically, how do we jibe the seeming (again initial) concentration of administrative powers with our underlying constitutional traditions, culture, and architecture, all of which reflect a transcendent commitment to separation of powers?

For some, no such reconciliation is necessary. The New Deal changed, so one story goes, everything, including our slavish fidelity to the separation of powers. But for those who think separation of powers endures—and should endure notwithstanding the need for a modern, sophisticated welfare state (more on this in Chapter 7)—more work needs to be done. We have to make the administrative state fit neatly within our constitutional order, as a welcome kinsman rather than as a rowdy and disruptive gate crasher. That is, after all, the project of constitutional construction, the work of implementing and applying what Jack Balkin calls the "Constitution in practice."[74] We turn, as Balkin suggests, to construction "when we need to create laws or build institutions to fulfill constitutional purposes."[75]

And this is precisely where the administrative separation of powers comes in, as *the institution* that effectively constrains and domesticates the initially unfettered administrative juggernaut. Though the administrative separation of powers has been regularly overlooked, it is this fragmented, tripartite scheme that serves as a constitutional salve, taking some of the sting out of otherwise unitary (and thus hyperpotent and unchecked) agencies. It serves as a constitutional adhesive, binding the burgeoning administrative state to the preexisting, paradigmatically fragmented and triangulated system prescribed by the framers. And it serves as a constitutional emulsifier, mixing the administrative regime into what Thomas Merrill calls an overarching separation of powers doctrine that is "more than the sum of the specific clauses that govern relations among the branches."[76] Thus if State power morphs and evolves (as it does)—and if State power is allowed to flow through instruments new and different from those expressly mentioned in the first three articles of the Constitution (as it seemingly is)—one means of ensuring constitutional fidelity between the old and the new is to insist that the new instruments are themselves democratically informed and subject to substantially similar institutional checks and balances.

Such an enduring, evolving understanding of separation of powers *all the way forward* is very much consonant with the administrative ecosystem I've been describing. Taken as a whole, agency leaders, the civil service, and civil society share many of the individual and collective characteristics and dispositional attributes of the three constitutional branches. In both the constitutional and administrative domains, we encounter two popular institutions (one singular and decisive, the other diverse and speaking with many voices) and one apolitical, mandarin, and at times countermajoritarian counterweight all duking it out. This faithful restaging is, therefore, essential to the constitutionalization of the administrative state, disaggregating concentrated administrative powers and thus reconciling them with the structures, personalities, and substantive content of our constitutional separation of powers.[77]

The constitutional foundations of the administrative separation of powers run deeper still.[78] The tripartite administrative scheme enjoys additional anchoring by virtue of a pair of powerful superstatutes. The pathbreaking Pendleton Act of 1883 laid the groundwork for an independent, professional civil service capable of playing a central, rivalrous, and durable role in modern administrative governance. And the landmark APA did very much the same thing for civil society, guaranteeing the public meaningful and extensive opportunities to help shape modern welfare and regulatory policy.

What do I mean by superstatutes? Superstatute theory, popularized by William Eskridge and John Ferejohn, assigns quasi-constitutional status to legislation that "successfully penetrate[s] public normative and institutional culture in a deep way."[79] Superstatutes fundamentally alter the underlying legal and political status quo; come about only after extensive public deliberation; become, in time, entrenched, garnering support or at least acceptance across the political aisle; and are extended or expanded upon by subsequent generations.[80]

Eskridge and Ferejohn focus intently on many substantive administrative laws, classifying legislation pertaining to securities regulation, collective bargaining, food and drug safety, and environmental protection as superstatutes.[81] In doing so, they largely leave to the side those framework statutes that define the basic structures of modern administrative governance. This strikes me as a missed opportunity: the Pendleton Act and the APA both seem to readily qualify as superstatutes.[82] First, both acts dramatically altered their respective political and legal landscapes. The Pendleton Act marked a sharp turn away from premodern public employment, sweeping away the longstanding spoils system and, with it, layers upon layers of administrative hackery. The APA had a similarly heroic arc. According to Cass Sunstein and Adrian Vermeule, the APA constituted an "organizing charter for the administrative state,"[83] a new, comprehensive, and transsubstantive blueprint for procedural rigor and extensive and inclusive public engagement.

Second, each statute was the subject of considerable elite and popular debate. Civil service reform was a major issue in good governance circles for years[84]—and the movement took on singular significance in the wake of President James Garfield's assassination by a disgruntled spoils seeker.[85] The APA, though not nearly as popularly resonant, was itself the culmination of a series of high-profile, blue-ribbon commissions aimed at reforming and standardizing federal administrative governance.[86] To put it bluntly, both statutes were very big deals.

Third, both the Pendleton Act and the APA have proven remarkably resilient and generative. The Pendleton Act was, as mentioned above, a decisive first step. Modest in reach, the Pendleton Act nevertheless set the tone and agenda for future Congresses and presidents to extend coverage to more and more federal employees and to thicken the protections enjoyed by all civil servants, new and old alike.[87] (Theodore Roosevelt, for instance, was a lifelong champion of the civil service. His early years in public office included stints as a member of the New York Civil Service Reform Association and then atop the federal Civil Service Commission.) The APA was likewise a crystallizing legislative achievement, the effects of which are far broader today as a result of post-enactment congressional amendments and capacious judicial interpretations, many of which have been in service of broadening and facilitating public participation.

It bears further mention that the Pendleton Act and the APA comport well with Charles Beard's far earlier treatment of superstatutes. Writing in 1917, the historian better known for his controversial economic interpretation of the Constitution suggested that statutes relating to (and specifying) government's "fundamental organization" take on quasi-constitutional significance.[88] Consistent with Beard's formulation, the Pendleton Act and the APA merit constitutional solicitude because they undergird two of the three pillars of our administrative edifice: the civil service and civil society. Together—and in conjunction with the Constitution's Appointments Clause (which provides for the president to appoint and, implicitly, to remove agency heads)[89]—the two statutes help define the administrative governing structure and specify the basic rules of tripartite rivalrous administrative engagement.

It is, once more, the Pendleton Act that jumpstarted the movement to engender and empower an independent, expert, and politically insulated administrative workforce. And it is the APA that assured civil society a seat at the administrative table. Without these two superstatutes, the structure of administrative governance would look very different. Most importantly, the president would be far better positioned to exercise monopolistic control over regulatory and welfare programs. In effect, then, these two complementary and mutually reinforcing superstatutes validate (and in turn are validated by) the constructive, constitutionalizing project of the administrative separation of powers.

The Administrative Separation of Powers and Value Harmonization

Just as lingering constitutional doubts have, I'd argue, haunted the modern administrative state, so too has normative confusion. Administrative legitimacy (again, of the normative variety) is generally tied to theories of process or substance. Different scholars, policymakers, and jurists understand administrative legitimacy in terms of expertise,[90] nonarbitrariness,[91] rationality,[92] efficiency,[93] civic republicanism,[94] interest-group representation,[95] or presidential accountability.[96] These broadly recognized values are, without doubt, of immense importance. But they are also normatively contested, empirically challenged, and, above all, often at odds with one another.[97]

Consider just a few examples. Prioritizing expertise will regularly come at the expense of popular democracy—and vice versa. Shall we be ruled by the mandarins or the masses? Choices far less stark prove just as vexing.

Take the choice between presidential administration and civic republicanism. Both visions of administrative governance are democratic, yet there is a world of difference between the two. The former understands political accountability as best expressed through the leadership of a nationally elected (and intensely scrutinized) chief executive. Put concretely, the president should direct the administrative state. The latter vision, flatter and more fluid, seeks to amplify the voices of individuals and groups, including those who may fall outside of the president's governing coalition. Under a civic republican model of public administration, these individuals and groups need not rely on a friendly White House or even an influential congressional representative. Instead, they can register their interests directly via the administrative process, setting and shaping the regulatory agenda by petitioning for new rules or for the rescission of old rules, filing comments, and participating in hearings and adjudications.

Even the seemingly anodyne vision of administrative efficiency is a fraught one, likely to undercut any number of other celebrated values. Efficiency conflicts with, among other things, civic republicanism. Flatter, more inclusive, and highly deliberative public engagement requires a commitment of considerable time and resources. Rarely has anyone left a contentious town hall meeting saying, "well, that was efficient!" But, of course, that's not the point. Efficiency may likewise conflict with visions of mandarin bureaucracy. Painstakingly researched and expertly crafted reports are often essential in establishing the utility and fairness of a rule or program. But, to efficiency hawks, these reports may seem wasteful and tedious. Such a clash between efficiency, on the one hand, and public hearings and expert deliberation, on the other, brings to mind every administrative law professor's favorite example: the FDA's generation of a 7,700-page record in service of deciding whether products labeled "peanut butter" must consist of 87.5 percent or 90 percent peanuts.[98]

Some administrative systems clearly and unambiguously privilege one—and only one—of these values. Ours, however, does not. Hence, at first blush, our system looks like a mess—a babel of inconsistent structures, practices, and policies that are partially expert, partially civic republican, partially presidentialist, and only somewhat efficient. Critics seize upon that apparent mess, viewing it is a sign of incoherence and as further reason not to defend, let alone valorize, the modern administrative state.

Nevertheless, that mess is a true testament to the success of the administrative separation of powers in accommodating fickle masters, namely an

American political and legal community deeply conflicted over what values should predominate. The lesson to be drawn from these deep and long-standing conflicts is an important one: our administrative state isn't about value maximization or regulatory optimization. It is about amplification, contestation, and, ultimately, harmonization of pluralistic values.

Indeed, precisely because there is no consensus view on which value or values should predominate, the best, and perhaps only, way to proceed is via a structural system of separating, checking, and balancing that tries to give at least some meaning, effect, and voice to all of those values.[99] This is, of course, what we see at the constitutional level, too. We're not a nation committed to, say, parliamentary sovereignty, the divine right of kings, aristocracy, or some sort of scripturally informed caliphate. We reject the absolutisms of *any* political system, and that's one of the reasons why the constitutional separation of powers is so fundamentally crucial above and apart from the fear of State tyranny. The tripartite constitutional scheme is itself not a blueprint for value maximization but rather for accommodation and for balancing the conflicting commitments to majoritarianism, federalism, limited government, and the rule of law.

Absent a vibrant system of administrative separation of powers, one of the three administrative rivals might well go unchecked. That was my precise argument earlier in this chapter, cast again principally in terms of tyranny, abuse, and myopic policy development. But there's more: Each of the rivals is likely to embody a particular value—such as efficiency, technocratic expertise, or civic republicanism—that informs our understanding of normatively legitimate, constitutionally sound public administration. Thus the administrative separation of powers holds the promise that none of these often competing values dominates to the point of crowding out the others.

For example, if the civil service (whose stock in trade is apolitical expertise) unilaterally controlled administrative proceedings, administrative action would likely be an arid technocratic endeavor, very much insulated from presidential politics and populist, civic participation. If instead the politically appointed agency leaders reigned supreme over administrative proceedings, agencies would parrot the president's interests, albeit likely at the expense of such administrative values as apolitical expertise, reason-giving, and civic republicanism. And if civil society dominated, administrative governance would reflect a strong nod to civic republicanism, possibly leaving little room for apolitical expertise or presidential leadership to shape agency decisionmaking. In short, if the political appointees, the civil servants, or members of civil society were to operate outside of a system of checks and balances, they would not only run roughshod over their administrative rivals but also marginalize the values most closely associated with those vanquished rivals. Hence the concentration of administrative power (in agency leaders, civil servants, or civil society) does far more than invite government abuse and narrow policymaking perspectives. The concentration also impoverishes the normative enterprise of administrative governance by suppressing a range of highly prized administrative values and voices.

Fortunately, the administrative separation of powers does exist. And its existence enables multiple administrative values to flourish. At any given moment, different, seemingly contradictory substantive values are each ascendant in various pockets of the administrative state. Critically, in none of these pockets are the other, non-ascendant values completely silent— nor is the current ordering of values, or positioning of rivals, necessarily a stable one. So long as the somewhat subordinated values and rivals remain in the game—which a robust system of administrative separation of powers ensures—they may "cycle" among themselves in such ways that no one administrative value or rival consistently trumps or is trumped. Instead, they all have their respective moments to shine.[100] Such cycling is especially helpful in contexts like this one, where the political and legal community holds dear a particular set of conflicting or incompatible values but cannot or does not want to choose among them.[101] As Heather Gerken argues, "cycling thus signals a reluctance to indulge in absolutes, a recognition of the variety of normative commitments that undergird any democratic system, and an acknowledgment that our identities are multiple and complex."[102]

All told, the administrative separation of powers accommodates central but conflicting values. This essential accommodation goes a long way in validating American public administration and marking it as a worthy extension of and successor to the framers' governance scheme—a scheme itself celebrated for its anti-absolutist balancing of conflicting normative commitments.

Looking Forward

This chapter's three claims about the legality and legitimacy of the modern administrative state—claims which I call constitutional isomorphism, constitutional foundations, and value harmonization—rest on a theory of public governance that embraces and endorses expressions of State power that are the product of rivalrous, heterogeneous, and inclusive engagement. In short, mine is a theory of separation of powers *all the way forward*[103]— from the constitutional to the administrative domain and, perhaps, to wherever else State power flows or will be funneled. While it is true that the administrative state was conceived largely to bypass the conflicts and inefficiencies of the constitutional separation of powers, what ultimately, and again ironically, legitimated the otherwise menacingly consolidated administrative state was the reaffirmation and renewal of the framers' tripartite scheme and the substantive and procedural values that support it.

This understanding of *pax administrativa* places critiques of modern administrative governance in an entirely different light. Today's jeremiads against unchecked, unaccountable administrative power—or against administrative power untethered to its constitutional progenitors—seem oddly anachronistic. It is true that executive, legislative, and judicial power is delegated en masse to administrative agencies in ways that challenge our constitutional order. But thanks to the construction of the administrative separation of powers, those agencies often cannot act—*just like legislation cannot be passed, signed, enforced, and withstand judicial scrutiny*—without significant voluntary buy-in from rivalrous groups with conflicting political, legal, institutional, and technocratic commitments.

That brings us to the second, almost polar opposite, line of criticism: that the administrative state has become too constrained, too costly, and too inefficient. Those leveling such charges—namely, the champions of more streamlined, businesslike government—must surely, if only implicitly, sense the workings of the administrative separation of powers. They must do so at least to the extent that they rail against the hamstringing effects of tenured civil servants, boisterous members of civil society, and a panoply of legal and institutional safeguards that they characterize as "red tape." Yet like newly arriving tenants who tear down an unsightly wall without first investigating whether that wall was a structural necessity, the businesslike government crowd blusters along, endeavoring to collapse the administrative separation of powers without considering the constitutional weight-bearing work that tripartite system does.

The next few chapters focus on frustrations with the modern administrative state—and on how those frustrations have spurred initiatives to run government like a business. As I will show, the businesslike government crowd has taken the offensive all too frequently. Thus the complaints these critics voice are often treated as presumptively valid before anyone gets the chance to refute them.

So it is important here to use this extended discussion of the administrative separation of powers to flip the script and preemptively set the record straight. The internally rivalrous administrative state in its mature, constitutionally valid form isn't meant to be a model of efficiency or cost-consciousness (though, even on those counts, it is generally an improvement over the framers' original governing scheme if for no other reasons than agencies' comparative expertise and their capacity to specialize). The administrative separation of powers is meant, instead, to reproduce in basic form the types of procedural safeguards, pluralistic and democratic inputs, and substantive rivalries that legitimate expressions and exercises of State power at the constitutional level. None of that comes cheap or fast.

As much as we still, understandably and laudably, aspire to greater efficiencies, we must again recognize that efficiency is just one of many values central to our constitutional culture and commitments. For sure, fewer axes of administrative separation and fewer opportunities for checking and balancing would speed up the administrative process and make government run more like a lean business. But such streamlining may well require the categorical rejection of broad democratic, legalistic, and expert input. Because we prize such input, we necessarily insist on structures that promote inclusive, rivalrous decisionmaking. Such insistence on separating and checking means accommodation, resistance, and untidiness of the sort that is missing from more efficient, more unitary, but also more constitutionally suspect exercises of State power.

Honoring such a clunky system as the administrative separation of powers might look odd to those who instead endorse a unitary executive model of administrative governance, a Weberian administrative ideal, or a businesslike approach to public administration. It might also look odd to those who have no truck for theory but simply want things accomplished faster, cheaper, or "smarter," whatever that last term may mean. But odd as it might look and undesirable as it might seem, the administrative separation of powers is in keeping with a constitutional vision that rejects unrivaled expressions of State power in favor of expressions that are the product of contentious, multipolar engagement.[104]

It is perhaps only through this lens that we can truly appreciate the modern American administrative state. The pervasive failure to understand this enterprise, its strengths and weaknesses, and its constitutional pedigree has turned good-faith champions of the administrative state into apologists and appeasers for too long. But once we understand the administrative separation of powers, we can celebrate administrative clunkiness as a necessary component of our rivalrous public administration. Only then are we truly ready to take on the challenge posed by privatization and the broader forces of businesslike government.

PART II

THE PRIVATIZATION REVOLUTION

Privatization, Businesslike Government, and
the Collapsing of the Administrative
Separation of Powers

The second part of this book captures the decline and fall of *pax administrativa* and the corresponding rise of privatized, businesslike government. Over the next three chapters, I describe how various constituencies came to resent, and ultimately reject, the modern welfare state—*but not the welfare programs themselves*—and how elected officials and policymakers turned to the Market, looking to its people, practices, and institutions for help in addressing the public's confusing, dissonant mandate.

This turn to the Market, pitched largely in technocratic, apolitical terms, had the effect, if not also the intent, of increasing the size and scope of the State. It also had the effect, and seemingly the implicit intent, of weakening the administrative separation of powers. For these reasons, privatized, businesslike government must not be considered, as it often is, primarily a topic of political or economic concern. It must, first and foremost, be recognized as a constitutionally significant—and constitutionally fraught— project, one that challenges our most basic and central legal and normative commitments.

Chapter 4 starts things off by transporting us to a period of growing disenchantment with *pax administrativa*. Here we encounter a new generation of libertarian scholars employing powerful tools, models, and rhetoric to decry the pathologies of bureaucracy and celebrate the rationality of markets; we find business executives, surprisingly slumberous during the mid-twentieth-century reign of *pax administrativa*, rise up and challenge an administrative state that, as they saw it, threatened to tax and regulate them into oblivion; and, perhaps most jarringly, we confront disillusionment and cleavage within the broad New Deal coalition—as many previously supportive of the Rooseveltian welfare state abandon faith in a government that, by their lights, lost the war on poverty, lied and cheated on matters of war and politics, and deeded the country years of stagflation and despair.

In time, these powerful constituencies changed the nation's political discourse and discovered their champion in the form of a fiery yet folksy Ronald Reagan. Reagan came to Washington prepared to tear it down. But he soon realized that even the staunchest anti-*pax administrativa* crusaders were unwilling to give up on the federal programs that benefited them. Reagan and his allies thus found themselves in a difficult situation: the American people hated the welfare state in toto but liked (their) welfare.

The solution they eventually arrived at—*a magic bullet of sorts*—was privatization. Wholesale outsourcing, the reliance on private actors to carry out public responsibilities, would seemingly satisfy everyone. It would lead to the nominal shrinking of the federal bureaucracy, an anticipated reduction in federal expenditures (under the theory that private, market actors were more efficient—and thus cheaper—than lethargic or procedurally encumbered bureaucrats), and the quiet preservation of cherished programs.

Privatization would indeed become a revolutionary sensation. But it hardly happened overnight. Indeed, privatization didn't really become a dominant force in national public affairs until the 1990s, during the Bill Clinton presidency. This is where Chapter 5 begins. In this chapter, I first describe how privatization under President Clinton lost—or rather appeared to lose—much of its ideological edge and became an instrument of choice for politicians across the political spectrum. I then show how deeply privatization insinuated itself, philosophically, into the American political psyche and, concretely, into some of the federal government's most sensitive, important, and discretion-laden policymaking and policy-implementing domains. Lastly, I posit that privatization is now a truly big-tent phenomenon, catalog a multitude of forms that privatization currently takes, and consider privatization's instant impact on core civil servants, members of the armed services, and even public school teachers.

Chapter 6 rounds out the *Privatization Revolution* trilogy. It is here that I unpack the constitutional implications of this popular, powerful, and increasingly variegated movement. I start by insisting that most of the contemporary discussions of privatization are economic, political, or logistical in nature—and often miss the mark. By and large, these discussions either offer false comfort or introduce red herrings, while obscuring the true, even existential, dangers that sound in constitutional law and liberal democratic theory. What we should be attending to, I argue, is the ways in which privatization systematically undermines the administrative separation of powers and, with it, the entire constitutional foundation upon which the modern welfare state is built.

Specifically, and perhaps counterintuitively, privatization aggrandizes, rather than siphons, State power—and concentrates it, strengthening agency leaders at the expense of the civil service and civil society. Privatization does so, first, either by directly replacing independent, rivalrous civil servants with for-profit (and politically compliant) contractors; or by marketizing—in effect, defanging—the career workforce, converting tenured civil servants into at-will (and thus far more compliant) employees. Privatization does so, second, by shifting the physical locus of State power out of traditional government corridors, thereby making it much more difficult for members of civil society to participate regularly and robustly in administrative affairs.

At the end of the day, privatization cannot be considered a neutral, technocratic endeavor. Rather, it is a practice of immense normative consequence. What's critical is the way privatization aggrandizes and concentrates sovereign authority, disables the administrative separation of powers, destroys our *pax administrativa,* and ushers us into new, uncharted spaces where the routine, almost nonchalant, fusion of market and State power threatens our constitutional order.

Understanding privatization for what it is (and for what it is not) positions us for the work ahead. Part Three of this book develops a richer, more comprehensive constitutional theory of administrative governance, repudiates the Privatization Revolution, and sketches a corresponding blueprint for the construction of a second, stronger *pax administrativa.*

4

The Beginning of the End

Disenchantment with *Pax Administrativa*
and the Pivot to Privatization

P *ax administrativa* was not destined to perdure. Those contesting the
constitutionality of the modern administrative state—who, again,
either failed to see or ascribed little value to the fragmented nature of
administrative power—continued to grumble. But they were not very
effective critics and, until quite recently, their complaints fell on deaf ears
in Congress and the courts.

The successful challenges came from the opposite direction. They came
from those seemingly quite sensitive to the administrative separation of
powers and to the unique brand of bureaucratic governance that system
promoted. Thus unlike the constitutional critics, these challengers realized
that the administrative state wasn't dangerously unencumbered. To the
contrary, it was far too encumbered. *Pax administrativa* meant inefficient,
distorted, even pathological government.

Specifically, those claiming the modern administrative state was too
encumbered railed against agency capture, bureaucratic empire building,
and organizational torpor; against red tape; and, often, against the regulatory and benefits programs themselves. But they could hardly champion a
return to the insularity, amateurism, and legalized corruption of the premodern administrative state. Nor would they want to. The world of
bounty hunters, tax ferrets, and Tammany toadies was, after all, more bad
disco than old-time rock 'n' roll. Furthermore, these challengers could not,
and ultimately did not, get very far calling for an end to government

programs, the vast majority of which proved remarkably resilient. So instead they leveraged Cold War politics, the specter of communism, the rise of neoclassical economics, and the nation's rekindled romance with free enterprise to hammer home their position that government should, in essence, run more like a business. Explicitly, they were celebrating markets over bureaucracy and entrepreneurism over collectivism. But make no mistake: these challengers were implicitly attacking the specialness of government and the constitutional architecture of *pax administrativa*.

Firms, of a certain, stylized sort, were held up as the ideal. What America's leading businesses had going for them—and what those seeking to run government like a business hoped agencies would adopt—were unitary organizational structures; employment arrangements that used the lures of monetary bonuses and the threats of summary termination to maximize worker fealty and productivity; and a more transactional relationship with the public that admitted far fewer opportunities for civic "meddling" in corporate decisionmaking. All of those quintessential features of modern American corporate governance would, they presumed, make public administration far more efficient, innovative, responsive, and lean. Quite possibly lurking in the background was the hope that such an altered, retooled, and businesslike government would also be more sympathetic to what they saw as the plight of extensively regulated and highly taxed American entrepreneurs—and thus would ease up on federal regulatory and spending programs.

This chapter, like Chapter 2, serves as a bridge. It takes us from the heights of mid-twentieth-century *pax administrativa* to today's highly privatized, commercialized, and businesslike reality. The history we need to traverse is rich and contested. Still, I resist the temptation to go down the historical wormhole and instead provide a more readily digestible account of how various groups of market-oriented scholars and political activists regained their footing (after being knocked to the ropes by the forces of *pax administrativa*), while other opponents of modern administrative governance cropped up anew. Combined, these constituencies marshaled the intellectual, political, financial, and cultural resources necessary to mount a veritable revolution. This revolution began not with a bang but a series of whimpers reverberating out from Hyde Park, Sacramento, Richmond, and even London and Saigon. Soon enough, we would find ourselves enamored with a new wave of politicians dedicated to tearing down the architecture of the administrative separation of powers. These politicians brought with them to Washington (and to their respective state capitals) legions of private contractors, private deputies, and commercialized government workers—foot soldiers in the war against *pax administrativa*.

Into the Wilderness—and Back

By the middle of the twentieth century, *pax administrativa* vanquished most of its foes. Professional, respected civil servants represented over 90 percent of the federal civilian workforce, and opportunities for meaningful public participation in administrative governance were widespread. At the same time, substantive administrative power surged. Congress continued to create new agencies and expand existing agencies' reach, resources, and authority, directing them to tackle more and more socioeconomic problems. Agencies, in turn, drew upon a broader range of tools to carry out their missions.[1]

During this time, those critical of *pax administrativa* took a big reputational hit. Libertarian and conservative economists, political scientists, and legal scholars were pushed to the academic fringe.[2] (Tellingly, in 1950, *Road to Serfdom* author and future Nobel Laureate Friedrich Hayek secured an appointment at the University of Chicago—but only after a right-wing foundation promised to cover his salary for the next ten years.[3])

The same was true, of course, with respect to politicians. New Dealers trounced, won over, or silenced big, public government skeptics. Indeed, Franklin Roosevelt quickly amassed supermajority support in the House and Senate and repudiated the laissez-faire policies of his predecessors, including Calvin Coolidge, whom later generations would lampoon for his insistence that the business of America is business. Mid-century Republicans left standing fell into line, too, with a series of presidential candidates— Landon, Wilkie, Dewey, Eisenhower, and Nixon—all more or less accepting the New Deal consensus.[4] Decades passed before a true champion of the free market emerged on the national scene. Running in 1964 against Lyndon Johnson and his expansive Great Society platform, Barry Goldwater was clobbered. As the *New York Times* reported: "Barry Goldwater not only lost the presidential election yesterday but the conservative cause as well."[5] In short, throughout the 1930s, 1940s, 1950s, and 1960s, those who viewed big, public government as an imposition "lost" their credibility and seemed "obsolete and quaint,"[6] if not, as in Goldwater's case, downright mad.[7]

Businesses too appeared cooperative. Part of the reason for their cooporation was strategic. Those businesses benefited from many of the large federal spending programs. What's more, business executives recognized that outright opposition or even dissent would have placed them well outside of the then prevailing political mainstream.[8]

Beyond those strategic, expedient reasons lay earnest enthusiasm for the State and its dynamic, helpful role in the political economy. Many corporate officers and executives struggled during the Depression, served in government during World War II, and continued to work with the feds during the immediate aftermath of the war. Those who were folded into the wartime military and civilian bureaucracies realized that government agencies worked really well, often better than their own commercial outfits.[9] If anything (and recalling the original, complimentary meaning of "good enough for government work"), the popular move at that time was to render businesses more like government bureaucracies—not the other way around.

That thinking would not last. The time critics of the welfare state spent relegated to the periphery of political, commercial, and academic engagement was time well spent. Like MacArthur triumphantly returning to the Philippines, libertarian and conservative scholars, politicians, and corporate executives reemerged more powerful than ever before. In time, they would regain positions of influence—doing so by outlining a strong, promarket alternative to American administrative governance, forming strategic alliances, and taking advantage of the public's growing disillusionment with a post-Vietnam, post-Watergate government suddenly viewed as ineffective, wasteful, unjust, and mendacious.

Professors at the Gate

The scholars were among the first to reemerge. After a couple of decades of academic marginalization, conservative and libertarian professors began raising forceful and sophisticated challenges to *pax administrativa*. Many of these challenges were rooted in economics and public choice theory. Milton Friedman, James Buchanan, and Gordon Tullock, among others, posited that government officials were no different from other rational, self-interested economic actors. The problem, however, was that unlike other rational, self-interested economic actors, government officials were forced to operate within a torturous bureaucracy. According to these scholars, the civil service was demoralizing and self-defeating. It deprived government workers of necessary incentives—carrots to strive for excellence and sticks to ward off apathy, mediocrity, and outright failure.[10]

The civil service's combined systems of job tenure and strict salarization meant that government employees (*qua* rational economic actors) had little to gain or lose. In the absence of opportunities to maximize personal wealth, government officials would—so these academics argued—choose to maximize something else. They might maximize their leisure, slacking off on the taxpayers' dime. Or they might engage in empire building, asserting greater jurisdictional reach and engorging their staffs as a means of signaling their importance.[11]

According to these critics, government workers' liberation from the disciplining effects of the Market was empowering in all the wrong ways: It left these workers unhinged, rendering them a threat to the public fisc and a menace to all those who came into contact with the State. After all, empire-building officials had to prove their worth, quite likely by excessive meddling in private industry. Alternatively, this liberation from the Market might push government employees in an entirely different direction, inviting them to cozy up with the industries they were supposed to regulate, if for no other reason than to increase their chance of a big payday upon leaving the bureaucracy.

Agencies themselves were likewise viewed as organizationally perverse. Unlike commercial firms operating in a crowded marketplace—and thus forced to sink or swim—agencies faced no competitive pressures. They were also wholly underwritten by Congress. As such, the academic critics accused agencies of functioning like the worst sort of monopolies. Insulated from the harsh realities of industry competition, from the risk of bankruptcy, and from the stresses of having to raise money through debt and equity markets, agencies had little reason to innovate, attend to public needs, or act in a fiscally responsible fashion.

Perhaps recognizing that government could not—or would not—abandon its welfare and regulatory responsibilities, the academics argued that government should either reconstruct itself along businesslike lines or turn over the levers of administrative control to private individuals and firms accustomed to operating in competitive environments. This pivot from outright deregulation to privatization was a critical one. In proposing new and varied approaches to public administration, the scholars provided the intellectual brief and operational blueprint to upend *pax administrativa*.

Public Discontent

The public at large was slower to turn against the *pax administrativa* consensus. Support for the big, modern administrative state remained high throughout the 1950s and 1960s. Painful memories of the Depression coupled with fond remembrances of the magic of Roosevelt's first hundred days and the successful prosecution of World War II were still fresh in the minds of many. So too were the rousing days of Camelot. These warm and fuzzy feelings displaced, at least for a few decades, the American public's legendary distrust of government.[12]

Soon enough, however, that distrust resurfaced: Between 1964 and 1974, faith in government plummeted from its perch of 75 percent down to 34 percent.[13] By 1980, it had dropped further still, down to 26 percent.[14] In a generation's time, we went from JFK's stirring cry for public service, "ask what you can do for your country," to Ronald Reagan's outright denunciation of the State: "Government is not the solution to our problem, government is the problem." By 1996, with trust in government still languishing in the mid-20s,[15] Bill Clinton would confirm the bipartisan nature of the Reagan reversal, receiving thunderous applause for assuring the American people that, indeed, "the era of big government is over." With the benefit of hindsight, it became clear that the early 1930s to the early 1970s represented the high-water mark of federal administrative government.

What changed? Why did that once strong love affair between the American people and big government prove no more than a fling? Voters weren't making pilgrimages to the lecture halls of the University of Chicago. They weren't modeling the comparative efficiencies of markets over bureaucracy. And they certainly weren't pondering the virtues and vices of the administrative separation of powers.

Some, to be sure, might have been reading William F. Buckley's biting critiques in the *National Review* of the post-war, big government consensus; some too were surely reading the objectivist novels of Ayn Rand.[16] But mostly their disillusionment was much more visceral: the marriage of the American people to big government foundered on the rocks of political turmoil, economic dislocation, and changing mores.

In fairness to the restive public, a lot happened to remind the American people why they had long been wary of government. First, there was a sense that government was reaching too far. The new regulatory initiatives of the late 1960s and early 1970s included major expansions in welfare services and programming to address workplace, education, and housing discrimination as well as environmental, occupational, and consumer safety issues. Some traditional supporters of the New Deal viewed this second wave of progressive initiatives as too radical—advancing, as they did, the rights and interests of women and people of color—or simply as injurious to the financial security of America's working class.[17] These soon-to-be-called Reagan Democrats became a key swing constituency aggressively courted by both major parties.

Second, there was decreased faith in the efficacy of government. Even when the public believed in the causes Washington was lately championing, the fact of the matter was that the feds had an increasingly poor track record of success.[18] As political scientist Jeffrey Henig puts it:

> The "can do" atmosphere of the Kennedy/Johnson years had been displaced by a somewhat dispirited resignation to the fact that poverty and other social and racial problems were deeply ingrained and that efforts to use government

to redress inequities would entail cost and conflict. There was a sense that the national government through the various Great Society programs had given its best shot and that it had failed.[19]

For some, such failures could be traced back to the thickening of administrative procedural safeguards. Consider, for instance, the landmark welfare case, *Goldberg v. Kelly*. Justice Hugo Black—a staunch New Deal Democrat—dissented from the 1970 decision guaranteeing the continuation of welfare benefits to those appealing the government's determination of ineligibility.[20] Though the Court deemed the continuation of welfare benefits constitutionally necessary in order to sustain those seeking to appeal, Black viewed this guarantee of post-termination assistance as indicative of process run amok. According to Black, the *Goldberg* decision would divert funds away from those truly deserving and instead subsidize those quite likely scamming the government.[21]

It was against this backdrop of programmatic failure and perceived procedural indulgences that William Simon, Treasury secretary to Presidents Richard Nixon and Gerald Ford, emphasized how "little progress seems to have been made in solving national problems."[22] Once again, it was Reagan who best captured the prevailing zeitgeist, placing the blame squarely on government's shoulders and quipping that "[w]e waged a war on poverty, and poverty won."[23]

Third, the economy foundered. In the mid-1970s, the country experienced stagflation, a brutal mix of slow or declining growth, persistently high unemployment, and inflation;[24] major cities, including New York, teetered on the brink of bankruptcy;[25] and recurring energy crises (and concurrent gas rationing) symbolized a crippled and scared economy.[26] By the 1980s, many lamented what they saw as America being eclipsed as an economic superpower by the likes of Japan[27] and possibly West Germany.[28] These fiscal fears fueled tax revolts[29]—notably California's transformative Proposition 13[30]—calls for deregulation,[31] and generally inflamed anti-government feelings.[32]

Fourth, government at this time was spectacularly mendacious and malfeasant. Among the lies and criminality surrounding what came to be known as Watergate,[33] it became increasingly difficult to trust government institutions and personalities.[34]

And then there was Vietnam. Vietnam represented a perfect storm of all the problems just mentioned, broadcast nightly to an American public glued to their TVs. Vietnam constituted an audacious and dangerous overreach, particularly as fighting spilled into neighboring countries and threatened to embroil China and the Soviets. It was, by most accounts, a largely unsuccessful campaign, exposing the frailties of the world's supposedly invincible superpower.[35] It had an awful effect on our nation's economy, contributing mightily to the aforementioned stagflation that came to define the mid-1970s.[36] And, of course, the war was premised on a series of half-truths, lies, and acts of duplicity, including the seeming overreaction to the Gulf of Tonkin incident, the secret expansion of the conflict into Laos and Cambodia,[37] and the covert surveillance and sabotage operations waged against domestic anti-war groups throughout the United States.[38] Of considerable consequence, among those most disenchanted were liberals—a group we'd ordinarily expect (and rely upon) to strongly support big government.

In President Jimmy Carter's words, these various experiences and events sparked "a crisis of confidence."[39] Seemingly conceding defeat (and previewing some of Reagan's thunder), Carter announced: "Government cannot eliminate poverty or provide a bountiful economy or reduce inflation or save our cities or cure illiteracy or provide energy."[40] In short, frustrations and failures conspired against the big government consensus of the mid-twentieth century, opening the door to politicians who never fully believed in the modern administrative state and who now had a seeming mandate to scale back the size and scope of government. Once again, the Market served as the knight in shining armor, a muscular, virtuous alternative to big, feckless, and perfidious government.

Big Business Awakens from Its Slumber

In an era such as ours in which big business is virtually synonymous with immense and outsized political influence—think the Koch brothers, Walmart, Goldman Sachs, or Halliburton—it is almost impossible to fathom that just a generation or two ago, the American business community was unsophisticated in the ways of Washington. But unsophisticated it was, as evidenced by a 1971 memo drafted by a corporate lawyer in Richmond, Virginia, named Lewis F. Powell, Jr. The memo, titled "Attack on America's Free Enterprise System," is in many ways surprisingly primitive both in form and content, further testament to the callowness of America's titans of industry. A rousing call—if not shrill shout—to arms, the Powell Memo explained how businesses can and should enter the political fray, principally to ease their regulatory and tax burdens but also to disabuse wayward youth reared to loathe the free enterprise system. Soon enough, Powell would be named to the United States Supreme Court, and the businesses he stirred would be ready to wage war on the American welfare state.

Powell attacked not only government regulators but also the forces in society alleged to be fueling the push for greater regulation and bigger government. One such antagonist mentioned by name was Ralph Nader, whom Powell credited with successfully pressing the federal government to enact highly stringent safety, welfare, and health laws and regulations. Powell suggested that Nader and his confederates were corrupting promising students, who then "end up in regulatory agencies or governmental departments with large authority over the business system they do not believe in."[41]

Here in this thirty-four-page memo, written for the Chamber of Commerce (and widely circulated within the business community), there aren't many traces of the measured tones characteristic of Powell's careful, centrist judicial opinions. Instead, this was Powell the polemicist, insisting that we were in the throes of an existential struggle: "what we call the free enterprise system, and all that this means for the strength and prosperity of America" was imperiled. Powell's prescriptions were rangy. He urged the business community to sponsor and publicize the writings and lectures of free market scholars; prepare critiques rebutting prominent left-leaning authors and activists; design pro-market classes and distribute course materials for secondary, college, and graduate students; and cultivate better relations with the (liberal) mainstream media. Most importantly, Powell underscored the importance of the business community beefing up its political and judicial activism. Again in terms almost unfathomable to a twenty-first-century reader, Powell decried the weakness of corporate America in its efforts to influence Congress, state legislatures, and the courts.[42]

Scholars and pundits point to the memo as defining, galvanizing, and mobilizing the business community.[43] The memo certainly packed a powerful one-two punch of rhetoric and action plan. Equal parts bloody shirt and marching orders, the memo set forth the *casus belli* and laid out a comprehensive blueprint for capitalism's revanchism.

Though it is difficult to gauge with any precision how effective or influential the memo has been,[44] it suffices for our purposes that Powell's missive at the very least captures the business community's nascent activism after decades of political drowsiness. What followed the Powell Memo, or at least coincided with it, is, by now, familiar history.

First, in the 1970s, corporate donors poured money into new conservative and libertarian organizations such as the Heritage Foundation and the Cato Institute (originally called the Charles Koch Foundation) as well as into older entities like the American Enterprise Institute, deemed by many to have lost its way after the Goldwater shellacking in 1964.[45] Those think tanks became the intellectual breeding ground for the conservative resurgence of the 1970s and 1980s—and served as de facto farm teams for the Reagan White House.[46]

Second, right-wing legal advocacy groups were likewise buoyed as big business bankrolled innovative litigation shops such as the Pacific Legal Foundation "to counter public-interest law firms and represent the interests of business and private property holders."[47] Over the past four decades, these firms have racked up a most impressive string of business-friendly court victories.[48]

Third, legal advocacy groups like Pacific Legal have been especially aided by the intellectual contributions of the John M. Olin Foundation. Long moribund, the Olin Foundation leaped into action in the early 1970s, sponsoring the nascent and powerfully influential law-and-economics movement that celebrated free market capitalism, looked skeptically at big, public government, and—most significantly—supplied the legal vocabulary, methodology, and skilled disciples to challenge the logic and efficacy of many business regulations and tort liabilities.[49]

Fourth, during this same period of awakening, businesses took direct action, involving themselves more fully in electoral politics, lobbying, and litigation. Business-affiliated political action committees (PACs) skyrocketed in number and influence. In the mid-1970s, corporate executives were lectured that if they didn't set up PACs, they were "apathetic, unintelligent, or [had] a death wish."[50] Clearly the executives took such advice to heart. In 1974, there were just 89 corporate PACs. By 1978, that number had jumped to 821.[51] Corporate PAC growth continued well into the 1980s, when the tally exceeded 1200. Not surprisingly, total expenditures surged as well, as overall corporate PAC spending during the span of a decade increased more than 600 percent.[52]

Fifth, business trade associations likewise stepped up their game. Specifically, umbrella outfits such as the Chamber of Commerce, the Business Roundtable, the National Federation of Independent Business, and the National Association of Manufacturers began pressing agencies, legislatures, and the courts—and did so with remarkable success.[53]

Staring Them in the Face the Whole Time

By the late 1970s, the undeniable strains of stagflation, the reemergence of popular distrust of government, and the stirrings of a business community now willing to flex its muscles helped shape and support a new generation of political leaders. This new generation, the spiritual children and grandchildren of those Franklin Roosevelt and Lyndon Johnson so easily vanquished, effectively ran *against* government. Outside candidates of both political parties were elected to go to Washington to fight Washington. And fight Washington they did.

Recall that as late as 1972, the seemingly conservative and highly polarizing Richard Nixon was instrumental in the creation of new agencies to protect the environment, consumers, and workers.[54] He was also trumpeting a guaranteed minimum income for America's poor,[55] effectuating wage and price controls,[56] and pushing Congress to enact progressive health care reforms.[57]

Soon, though, the tide turned. It was, tellingly, a Democrat from Plains, Georgia, peanut farmer Jimmy Carter, who first rode this new wave. By the end of the 1970s, Carter implemented a policy of federal fiscal austerity, began to deregulate important industrial sectors, and devolved significant federal responsibilities to the states.[58] Ronald Reagan succeeded Carter in office, expressly running on an even more aggressively anti-government platform. (Carter was also outflanked on the left. Ted Kennedy mounted a powerful but ultimately unsuccessful primary challenge that turned on the Massachusetts senator's commitment to continuing and expanding the programs and policies of the modern welfare state.) Reagan sought to scale back the administrative state and to govern according to a theory of supply-side economics that joined low tax rates with expectations that a less regulated, less heavily taxed market economy would empower all Americans, including our most downtrodden.[59]

Yet Washington and a surprising band of allies fought back. Notwithstanding an apparent mandate to tear government down to size, even the most popular of reformers—*and President Reagan was popular*—found the administrative state a formidable opponent. When push came to shove, many hardliners softened their anti-government positions, insisting that *their* programs—that is, the particular programs that benefited them or their constituents—remain unmolested. Thus long entrenched entitlement programs like Social Security and even newer ones such as Medicare were safeguarded by their legions of beneficiaries. So too was nearly every little niche regulatory and welfare program, whether it advantaged rich CEOs, chocolate milk peddlers, or friends of the spotted owl.[60]

As a result, the Reagan administration got only so far with deregulation and efforts to reduce spending. The public by and large still demanded the full suite of benefits and regulatory protections big government afforded and therefore resisted the administration's efforts to curtail or repeal substantive programs.[61] Such popular resistance led to the preservation and at least partial strengthening of the Clean Air Act,[62] to the rejection of the White House's plan to "mine more, drill more, cut more timber,"[63] and to the expansion of federal welfare and education programs that Reagan routinely attacked.[64] Civilian federal employment during this time also rose by over 200,000.[65]

Given these developments, it should come as no surprise that the federal government ran huge deficits throughout the 1980s. And deficit spending can last only so long before prompting a major budgetary crisis (especially given Reagan's unapologetically profligate military spending and unbending commitment to low taxes).

Enter, or rather reenter, privatization, albeit seemingly as a fallback option. During the *pax administrativa* years, private actors carrying out government responsibilities spent their own time in the wilderness, pushed to the margins by the expansion of the full-time, salaried federal civil service. Contractors were never banished, just somewhat limited in the roles they could play. Often they were confined to handling tasks that were primarily commercial in nature.[66]

Wholesale government service contracting started to reemerge in the 1960s and 1970s, and it did so first at the local level.[67] City and county governments were far riper for contracting for several reasons. First, localities hadn't gone as far as the feds or even the states in constructing a fully professionalized bureaucracy. The psychic, practical, and legal gaps between contractors and government workers were therefore not such big ones to close.

Second, the services cities and counties offered were, for the most part, less politically charged than those we find at the federal and state levels. As famed New York City Mayor Fiorello LaGuardia once said, "There is no Republican or Democratic way to pick up the garbage." He was, of course, right. Outsourcing garbage collection, sewage treatment, or park maintenance work—the bread and butter of local government—tends to spark fewer political and philosophical questions about democratic governance, the exercise of coercive sovereign force, or the architecture of the State than would be the case were the government using private actors to draft environmental rules, adjudicate welfare eligibility, or interrogate enemy combatants. And, indeed, what marks local contracting during this time was its very banality. Local contracting really did concentrate in such eminently practical and apolitical domains as janitorial and clerical work.[68] As even further proof of contracting's low profile during the heights of *pax administrativa,* in some locations, notably California, contracting was really an extended exercise in keeping it in the family. Postage-stamp-sized California cities, too small to support their own municipal infrastructure, contracted with bigger neighboring cities. Those bigger cities would then, for a fee, send their employees across municipal lines to serve communities likely altogether unaware of the underlying contractual arrangements.[69]

Third, the imperative to cut costs was much greater at the local level. Across the country, many localities were hard hit by the economic downturn of the mid-1970s—a downturn that was only made worse by the so-called white flight that marked this tumultuous period.[70] Municipal tax bases shriveled, the demand for social services swelled, budgets had to be balanced, and these local governments did not have the same capacity as the feds to pool risk, raise revenue, or fall back on deficit spending. So they turned to contracting.[71]

Contracting provided, at least in theory, better services at lower prices.[72] According to privatization's proponents, contractors who operate in a competitive market must find ways to offer high-quality services at low rates. Otherwise they won't be able to stay in business. Public agencies and employees face few, if any, of those competitive pressures. They therefore are viewed as less efficient and less cost-conscious. Hence, if cities and counties can replace inefficient civil servants with highly efficient contractors, those jurisdictions are apt to save money.

What's more, even if the contractors aren't more efficient, they may nevertheless be more cost-effective. That is, they may simply do the same job, at the same speed, for less money or fewer benefits. Most rank-and-file government workers receive (or are understood to receive) higher compensation than their private sector counterparts. Above-market compensation has historically reflected a deliberate effort on the part of political communities to support *rather than squeeze* their workforces. In many places, a government job was the surest gateway to the middle class—stable work, decent pay, good benefits, and a pension upon retirement.

This is precisely how Daniel Patrick Moynihan viewed government work. In 1966, Moynihan argued that Post Office jobs constituted a form of welfare. For a fraction of the cost of federal means-tested programs, such as the heavily criticized Aid to Families with Dependent Children, the Post Office could hire a letter carrier "who raises a family, pays his taxes . . . and delivers the mail."[73] The extra expense, Moynihan added, should not be seen as a form of waste or even as a cost attributable to a spendthrift Post Office. Rather, the extra expense should be understood as the price of stabilizing struggling communities.[74]

As important as these stabilizing measures no doubt were, it is not hard to imagine cash-strapped communities contracting around "expensive" city and county employees, preferring instead private contractors paid lower—that is, non-subsidized—wages.

A last explanation for the popularity of contracting among local governments sounds in economies of scale. Simply stated, if a single firm is able to provide services for a number of adjacent cities and counties, it can realize economies of scale that no one small political jurisdiction enjoys. Consider, for example, the possibility that each of three adjoining cities needs to purchase, maintain, and staff at least one fire truck—and thus hires its own firefighters, paramedics, dispatchers, mechanics, etc. But if Acme Fire Company has a contract with all three cities, it might need a combined fleet of only two trucks, under the theory that fires are highly unlikely to rage in all three cities simultaneously. Furthermore, Acme might need just one team of centrally located dispatchers and mechanics (rather than, again, three) and perhaps only one or two teams of firefighters and paramedics.

Somewhat surprisingly, the Reaganites didn't appear to cotton to contracting right away, nor fully realize it was already robustly practiced across the United States. As late as 1983, a highly anticipated presidential report touted the novelty of federal government outsourcing. Though it explains that privatization "had been applied successfully at the state and local levels," the report nevertheless presents contracting as "a relatively new concept" for the administration to try.[75]

Also somewhat curiously, Team Reagan seemingly failed to follow the lead of at least one senior member of the administration: Housing official E. S. Savas. Savas spent the 1970s shuttling between municipal government and the ivory tower.[76] During this time, he penned for *Harper's* one of the most influential articles on early modern privatization.[77] Savas joined the Reagan administration in 1981 and continued to write. Indeed, the book he published in 1982, while still at the Department of Housing and Urban Development, has a title that says it all: *Privatizing the Public Sector.*[78] Savas left government in 1983 and to this day still authors widely read and frequently cited articles and books on the virtues of outsourcing. Yet for years the administration looked past local governments, including those in Reagan's own California, where contracting was prevalent; the administration also evidently looked past the writings of Savas and other intellectuals championing contracting. (One such article, published in the conservative periodical, *Policy Review,* was not-so-subtly titled *The Privatization Revolution: What Washington Can Learn from State and Local Government.*[79]) Instead, the administration fixed its gaze elsewhere, overseas to Jolly Old England.

The choice to zero in on the United Kingdom is not an entirely unreasonable one. The governing British Conservative Party provided inspiration, rhetoric, and concrete policy ideas to like-minded Americans, and Prime Minister Margaret Thatcher was doing in Britain what Reagan aspired to do in the United States. She was trying to wean the Brits off of what she derisively called the Nanny State—the UK's big welfare programs and infrastructure.[80] "We should not," Thatcher insisted, "expect the State to appear in the guise of an extravagant good fairy at every christening, a loquacious and tedious companion at every stage of life's journey, the unknown mourner at every funeral."[81] As it turns out, Thatcher was weaning the Brits in large part through a massive privatization program.

But there was a problem in the translation. Like the word *football* to a Manchester United as opposed to a Dallas Cowboys enthusiast, privatization has a different meaning on that side of the pond. Privatization in the UK (and throughout much of the rest of the world) refers to the sale of State-owned assets. The United Kingdom owned, among other things, luxury car companies, including Jaguar and Rolls-Royce. It owned British Telecom, the nation's primary telecommunications firm; a world-class airline, British Airways; a world-class defense and civil aviation firm, British Aerospace; various energy companies, including British Gas, British Petroleum, and Britoil; and even a sugar company.[82] From the late 1970s to the late 1980s, Thatcher's Tory government sold all of those major assets, providing a huge (though short-lived) windfall to the Exchequer and forever recalibrating the balance between public and private power in that nation.

Looking overseas to his British doppelganger, Reagan contemplated the same thing at home. But the United States didn't own nearly the quantity or quality of assets that Her Majesty's government possessed.[83] A privatization auction in the United Kingdom was like a shopping spree in Mayfair. A similar sale held by the United States government would have had the feel of a picked-over flea market. While the Brits were peddling Rolls-Royce and British Aerospace, the best we could offer was the only recently nationalized (and struggling) Conrail freight system,[84] a dairy farm outside of Annapolis, Maryland,[85] and assorted weather satellites.[86]

It was, seemingly, only then, after unsuccessfully trying to slash government programs and sell State assets, that the administration turned in earnest to government contracting, the solution staring them in the face the whole time. (It was during this time too that reliance on vouchers, tradable credits, and other programs that encourage market transactions also took off, thereby laying the foundation for additional strands of contemporary businesslike government.)

Perhaps I am being uncharitable. Perhaps only with the benefit of hindsight does it seem somewhat incredible that contracting out wasn't a more obvious, immediate, and central element of the Reaganite game plan. We know today that outsourcing is completely and utterly ubiquitous—and still gaining speed. After all, and as Reagan confidants eventually impressed upon the president, privatization was almost too good to be true.

Yet this isn't what President Reagan initially wanted. Reagan wanted more: to end (not simply mask) big federal spending and regulatory programs. But *that* revolution—call it the *aspirational* Reagan Revolution—was stopped dead in its tracks. However much the American public said it wanted to downsize government, we refused to let go of pretty much all of our welfare and regulatory programs.

So Reagan nimbly pivoted. The second-best solution was outsourcing. This distinctively American version of privatization held out the promise of providing the same services for less money and less bureaucracy. Americans cared about their clean water and their Social Security checks. But they did not necessarily care for (or even like) the administrators of those programs. Privatization thus provided a double windfall; the big, popular programs could be preserved and run more cheaply, without the distrusted and sometimes despised agency personnel. To the extent that this American brand of privatization caught on—and it most certainly did—its power of disassociation was celebrated as a wonder drug, a cure for Carter's malaise and a tonic for Reagan's scaled-down fury.[87]

Seemingly a seminal work that connected the academic preference for markets over bureaucracy and the political imperative to shrink the size of government, lower costs, and maintain services was Stuart Butler's *Mandate for Leadership II: Continuing the Conservative Revolution*. The effects of this widely circulated report are largely underappreciated.[88] Indeed, the report itself isn't well known even in scholarly circles. But *Mandate II* remains the stuff of legend within the conservative movement. As a testament to its importance, *Mandate II* was reportedly placed on the chair of every cabinet member before the president convened the first meeting of his second term of office.[89]

Butler, a longtime heavyweight in the world of Beltway think tanks, stressed that privatization of government services should be the centerpiece of Reagan's second term. Specifically, Butler wrote:

> The central theme of the Second Reagan Administration's approach to budget cutting must be privatization—shifting government functions to the private sector. During its first four years, the Reagan Administration met with defeat after defeat in Congress on budget votes because it took the position that the only way to reduce government spending was to reduce services. It is not the only way. Private firms, for instance, can provide many government services—either under contract or completely within the private sector—much less expensively than federal workers. The Reagan Administration thus must offer

the American people the alternative prospect of a reduction in spending with the same, or even better, levels of service. By taking this position, the Administration would not be forced into the position of denying that certain essential or useful services should be provided.[90]

Even after the circulation of Butler's report, the Reagan administration proceeded slowly and modestly. The president directed more studies and convened more commissions.[91] But relatively little happened on the ground; the outsourcing that was undertaken under Reagan and even under his successor, George H. W. Bush, centered principally on mundane and ministerial responsibilities.[92] It thus would be another decade or so before outsourcing became a truly transformative phenomenon—sizable, influential, and expansive, weaving its way into increasingly sensitive domains. This was achieved during the Bill Clinton presidency, which aggressively promoted privatization. Indeed, one of Vice President Al Gore's most important briefs was, quite plainly, to "reinvent government."[93] For Clinton and Gore, reinventing government was part of a new, Third Way politics. It involved running the government more like a business while for the most part preserving the mid-twentieth-century regulatory and social welfare programs.[94]

So how then might we think about the 1970s and 1980s? Maybe Reagan's achievement was similar to that of Christopher Columbus. In some ways it is silly to say that Columbus "discovered" America, a place already intimately known to its millions of inhabitants and to those intrepid Vikings who visited centuries before Columbus set sail from Spain. It is in that vein that Reagan "discovered" contracting, a practice that had chugged along in relative but not complete obscurity throughout the golden age of *pax administrativa*. Still, Columbus's achievement as a discoverer of record put America on the map and encouraged generations of further explorers and settlers. Reagan seemingly did the same with privatization. He laid the groundwork for the Privatization Revolution to come.

5

The Mainstreaming of Privatization

An Agenda for All Seasons and All Responsibilities

We're all privatizers now. What started out as an apparent fallback option for a deeply partisan and surprisingly thwarted president has become the signature reform movement of the late twentieth- and early-twenty-first centuries. Along the way, privatization has shed much of its ideological baggage, gained adherents across the political spectrum, and evolved, morphed, and simply intensified, reaching deeper and more broadly into sensitive State domains.

Privatization stands today as the latest and no doubt greatest threat to *pax administrativa* and to the administrative and constitutional separations of powers that undergird it. Yet the practice remains a bit of a cipher. Proponents and opponents alike project their wishes, preferences, and fears onto privatization—albeit in ways that do not always ring true.

This chapter tells the story of privatization's emergence as a central, pivotal tool of contemporary American governance. Here I explain how privatization grew into a mainstream, bipartisan, and avowedly nonideological movement; how it took new forms; how it supplanted, demoralized, and defanged the federal civil service; and how it co-opted some parts of civil society (while marginalizing others).

This is, again, the true legacy of the Reagan Revolution. Stymied by the American people's refusal to give up their government goodies and thus unable to fully realize a libertarian constitutional realignment, President Reagan and his fellow travelers deftly pivoted. In the process, they set in motion forces that would batter and, in time, destabilize *pax administrativa*, the apotheosis of twentieth-century constitutional governance. They did so, most plainly, by a (re)turn to privatization.

I start therefore where Reagan and his immediate successor, President George H. W. Bush, left off, with what I call the curious Clinton Continuity: the furtherance of the privatization agenda by President Bill Clinton and other similarly centrist and center-left governors and mayors during times far more prosperous than those that fueled the initial backlash against *pax administrativa* and propelled Reagan into office. It was during the post-Reagan period that, like sabermetrics or originalism, the once outré privatization agenda entered the political and cultural mainstream and showed itself to be an inexorable force in American law and public policy.

I next turn to the years following the Clinton Continuity—those of the new millennium. Here I introduce and catalog a wide array of novel and expansive privatization initiatives (far broader than the original, straightforward contracting-out model), show how these initiatives are changing the way we govern, and select two particularly potent strains of new millennial privatization for more rigorous examination.

In all, the explorations that follow immediately below set the stage for the work of Chapter 6, where I explain how the Privatization Revolution, in its sundry forms and guises, represents a direct assault on *pax administrativa* and the legal and normative architecture of the administrative separation of powers.

The Curious Clinton Continuity

Privatization—chiefly in the form of outsourcing government services to private contractors—really picked up in the 1990s, during the Bill Clinton presidency. Unfortunately, we lack good, hard numbers detailing exactly how rapidly privatization surged. As John Donahue notes, the best way to "get a precise fix on privatization's impact [is] by simply comparing trends in actual spending on traditional versus privatized government spending." Yet such a comparison, Donahue laments, is "impossible." The data simply do not exist.[1] Alternatively, we might hope for an accurate headcount by the folks doing the hiring or writing the checks. Alas, no such luck. As the Director of the Congressional Budget Office (CBO) advises us, "[r]egrettably, CBO is unaware of any comprehensive information about the size of the federal government's contracted workforce."[2]

That can't be good. Worse still, the unofficial accountings that do exist are of limited utility, at least for our purposes. For example, some studies zero in on government expenditures. They therefore tally all the costs of contracting, including for big-ticket acquisitions of submarines and jet fighters. These hardware expenditures completely overwhelm and obscure government payments to service contractors.[3]

Other studies concern themselves with the overall size of government. These findings likewise do not meaningfully separate out contractors involved in the manufacturing, maintenance, and marketing of goods the State procures.[4] Such lumping is unfortunate. Contractors not tasked with discretion-laden policymaking or policy-implementing responsibilities are of little relevance to us.

With respect to our particular—though let me stress hardly esoteric—inquiry, we are left out in the empirical cold. As a leading government watchdog organization concludes, "[t]here is currently no way to quantify the actual number of contractor employees who perform government functions at a particular department or agency at a given time."[5] Thus we must settle for anecdotes, impressions, and estimates, all of which point squarely in the direction of a federal service contracting boom in the 1990s that has carried into the 2000s and 2010s.[6] And we must draw upon the flurry of new laws, regulations, executive orders, and government reports promoting and directing greater federal service contracting as further indicative of a political and legal cultural commitment to privatizing State responsibilities.[7] In short, we might not be able to measure how fast the wind is gusting, but there is no doubt which direction it is blowing.

The Mainstreaming of Privatization's Ideology

In many respects, Bill Clinton and his contemporaries were surprising heirs to Ronald Reagan, and the 1990s was a surprising decade to carry the Privatization Revolution forward. For starters, Clinton seemed to differ from Reagan along every relevant dimension. Clinton was a center-left Democrat, whereas Reagan was a rock-ribbed Republican. Clinton was a Rhodes Scholar and Yale-trained lawyer, whereas Reagan was a C student and B actor. On the hustings, Clinton was empathetic and (passably) hip, whereas Reagan was homespun yet steely. And Clinton was a child of the very big government liberalism of 1960s and 1970s against which Reagan built his political fortune. Yet here was Clinton advancing the Reagan agenda, announcing, celebrating, and not unjustifiably taking credit for bringing about an end to big government.[8]

Clinton did so substantively by helping to eliminate the basic entitlement to welfare and by supporting the deregulation of the telecommunications and financial industries.[9] And he did so operationally by, among other things, cutting the number of federal civilian jobs *every* single year of

his presidency[10] while presiding over the wholesale privatization and commercialization of many key government services and functions. These
were achievements that Reagan, who thundered against welfare queens,
government largesse, and excessive regulatory burdens, fell far short of
realizing.

In addition to the outsourcing of government service responsibilities,
Clinton reorganized and then sold off what became known as the U.S.
Enrichment Corporation, an outfit tasked with collecting and converting
overseas military-grade uranium for use in domestic power plants.[11] He
cleaved off and commercialized some of the CIA's internal R&D responsibilities, entrusting them instead to a venture capital firm charged with
seeding technologies of use to both the intelligence community and commercial enterprises.[12] And he spun off what became known as United
States Investigations Services,[13] the privatized security apparatus later
sternly rebuked for its perfunctory background check of, among others,
one Edward Snowden.[14] Reports indicate that Clinton even seriously considered "privatizing" Social Security—and that only the Monica Lewinsky
scandal, not a change of heart, derailed his plans.[15]

So what explains how a Democratic president who came of age idolizing
JFK, protesting Vietnam, and stumping for McGovern[16] ended up out-
Gippering the Gipper—altering the topography of the American State and
changing the words and inflections we use to describe it? Occam's razor
might point us to the simple conclusion that Clinton was himself a closet
conservative. Perhaps, but that does little to account for the fact that
Clinton was hardly alone. Similarly self-described moderate governors and
mayors were, like Clinton, quick to demonize big government and embrace
private sector solutions to public problems. Indeed, stalwart Democrats
such as Ed Rendell, who served as mayor of Philadelphia, governor of
Pennsylvania, and chairman of the Democratic National Committee
(DNC), was a big enthusiast of contracting out, as was Mayor Richard
Daley of Chicago.[17] Daley reportedly urged his successor, Rahm Emanuel,
to "privatize everything you can."[18] Dyed-in-the-wool Democrats Kurt
Schmoke, mayor of Baltimore, and Thomas Menino, mayor of Boston,
likewise championed privatization.[19]

On a smaller stage, the 1990s witnessed Weston, Florida transforming
itself into a full-fledged contract city. The sizable Miami suburb, incorporated as a city in 1996, started out with just three full-time city employees—
and increased to nine only a decade later. These employees managed hundreds of contracts and oversaw gaggles of contractors carrying out
practically all of the municipality's responsibilities.[20] Lest one assume that
Weston was a bastion of anti-government libertarianism, recent DNC

Chair and Democratic Congresswoman Debbie Wasserman Schultz calls Weston home. What's more, Weston has overwhelmingly voted Democratic in every presidential election since its incorporation. Bill Clinton, Al Gore, John Kerry, Barack Obama, and Hillary Clinton all received around two-thirds of all votes cast from this almost completely privatized community.[21] Weston has, not surprisingly, inspired others to throw off what they too see as the shackles of government bureaucracy. Most notable among them is Sandy Springs, Georgia, population 90,000.[22] In 2005, Sandy Springs seceded from Fulton County with the goal of reconstituting itself as a contract city. Sandy Springs employs only seven full-time employees. Even its municipal judge—whom the New York Times dismisses as a "legal temp"—works on a $100/hour contract.[23]

Pundits and scholars likewise carried the privatization torch in the 1990s. Best-selling books such as David Osborne and Ted Gaebler's Reinventing Government called for greater government reliance on market instruments and market practices.[24] Considered deeply influential "within government circles"[25] and labeled the "leading theorists of the Clinton–Gore reforms,"[26] Osborne and Gaebler preached the gospel of businesslike government. As political scientist B. Guy Peters explained at the time, "the current Zeitgeist of reform in government is to use the market and to accept the assumption that private-sector methods for managing activities (regardless of what they are) are almost inherently superior to the methods of the traditional public sector."[27] Perhaps not surprisingly, Osborne himself joined the Clinton–Gore White House, ultimately drafting Gore's groundbreaking National Performance Review.[28]

So, either this new cadre of privatizers were all secretly conservative (or libertarian) or the Privatization Revolution—and underlying disillusionment with pax administrativa—had become very much mainstream. The latter explanation seems to make more sense, both in terms of the flurry of centrists, Democrats, and the like advancing privatization in word or deed and in terms of privatization being spun as a decidedly technocratic endeavor.[29] These new champions of privatization proudly proclaimed that they were policy wonks, not political ideologues—and had no broader agenda or ulterior motives. (Osborne and Gaebler, for instance, argued that "what government should do, and for whom [are] secondary" considerations, distinct from those that center on how government should "operate."[30]) In short, by insisting that they sought only to make government leaner and more responsive, these self-professed tinkerers largely succeeded in defusing the revolution of its political charge. Anti-government sentiment was recast as smart government—and with that change in affect and tone, we could all be privatizers now.

But make no mistake, privatization remained a normatively freighted enterprise. Technocratic government was—and remains—a worldview expressed in scientific, neutral terms. After all, who isn't in favor of smarter government? (We hear similar arguments from those who trumpet cost–benefit analysis in government regulation as if it likewise lacks an ideological hue.[31]) Part of my project is to explain why indeed there is a considerable political and legal valence to privatization and why, notwithstanding privatization's popularity, we should resist this seemingly unstoppable force. That will be the work of Chapter 6. For now, however, let us simply recognize that the purportedly neutral and limited ambitions of privatized administration disarmed and ultimately won over would-be critics. Perhaps more importantly, this bipartisan, smart-government consensus lulled us into a sense of false comfort, desensitizing us to the deeper, more drastic constitutional and administrative challenges that were about to come.

The Mainstreaming of Privatization's Political Economy

The second surprising aspect of the Clinton Continuity has to do with the 1990s being a very prosperous period—quite unlike the anemic 1970s that sparked the Reagan insurgency and informed his patented brand of Reaganomics. The 1990s were a time of placidity, optimism, and remarkable political and economic strides. The Cold War ended, with the United States emerging as the world's lone superpower and enjoying the fruits of a sizable "peace dividend."[32] Mideast peace seemed, for a time at least, finally within reach, as Yasir Arafat and Yitzhak Rabin gathered at the White House to sign the Oslo Accords.

Even more pertinently, the U.S. economy soared. America's chief economic rivals of the 1980s—Japan and Germany—struggled mightily.[33] Oil prices plummeted, weakening previously potent petrostates.[34] The United States, meanwhile, pulled far ahead. America took full advantage of the opening of new markets in the developing and post-communist worlds.[35] And it reaped the benefits of Silicon Valley's huge technological leap forward.[36] Indeed, during this decade, the United States enjoyed what was then the longest continuous period of economic expansion in its history. As the *Washington Post* reported in 2000, the decade-long boom "lifted the nation's production of goods and services by more than a third and created millions of new jobs and vast new wealth, with inflation coming down to boot."[37] Yet, and again curiously, privatization marched apace.

What explains this push to continue privatizing at a time of great prosperity? Why didn't such a healthy political economy temper anti-government sentiments? The answer is not immediately apparent, but one might think about the very ascendancy of American economic power as sustaining rather than stanching the Reagan Revolution. The 1990s were perhaps a period in which opportunity rather than desperation could account for the strong preference for markets over bureaucracy. Everyone likes to follow a winner. Why not emulate America's businesses that, more so than America's public institutions, were the envy of the world? This was especially true at this particular moment in our history, amid the rise of celebrity CEOs.

Previous generations elevated public servants to the status of celebrity: the Roosevelts, Dwight Eisenhower, Douglas MacArthur, Adlai Stevenson, Nelson Rockefeller, and, of course, the Kennedys. Now it was the scores of dot-com wizards who, practically overnight, went from college dropouts to mega millionaires. It was also celebrity real estate moguls like Donald Trump and entertainers such as Oprah Winfrey, lauded as much for her gargantuan business empire as for her fluffy daytime talk show. These entrepreneurs were an entirely different breed from both the faceless corporate suits of the 1950s, 1960s, and 1970s and from their own contemporaries in government employ. Indeed, the entrepreneurs were (or at least portrayed themselves as) larger than their companies—and often exercised complete and charismatic control over business operations. They got things done in ways that those working within the webs of *pax administrativa* simply couldn't.

Unsurprisingly, mayors, governors, and federal agency heads wanted that type of executive control, too—and privatization and other business-like reforms seemed to offer public officials the power and flexibility they were looking for, again under the neutral guise of smart government. But even assuming, for argument's sake, that hierarchical, CEO-like control is a politically neutral managerial choice in the corporate world, it is anything but neutral in the public sphere. This is a claim I'll circle back to in Chapter 6.

New Millennial (Big Tent) Privatization

In the 1990s, privatization took a great leap forward. Yet that leap paled in comparison to what was to follow. Twenty-first-century privatization represented the next, more intense phase of the Privatization Revolution, taking on new and counterintuitive guises, penetrating deeper into core government domains, and posing an existential threat to *pax administra-tiva*, its purposeful but clunky architecture, and the administrative rivalries that legitimate this constitutional project.

I define privatization broadly.[38] By my lights, privatization involves government reliance on private actors to carry out State responsibilities; government utilization of private tools or pathways to carry out State responsibilities; or government "marketization" of the bureaucracy, converting civil servants into effectively privatized, commercialized versions of their former selves and relying on them to carry out State responsibilities.

I appreciate that my big tent definition will not be to everyone's liking. A crisper, narrower definition—one that splits rather than lumps—is no doubt easier to defend. What's more, adopting a narrower, more literal definition is by far the safer move and a sufficient one here. I have no pressing need to quarrel with those who prefer splitting. And, of much greater significance, no part of my constitutional or normative theory depends on a catholic understanding of privatization. Still, I favor a capacious definition here for several reasons: to suggest that a range of seemingly *sui generis*, one-off, or simply unrelated and isolated practices share a common origin and inspiration; to signal how the Privatization Revolution has progressed, expanded, and even mutated in ways that defy ready identification, analysis, and synthesis; and to underscore why we need a regulatory solution more philosophically ambitious and constitutionally resonant than might appear to be necessary were we sure that the Privatization Revolution confined itself within the four corners of traditional government contracting.

Among some of the newer and more intriguing privatization practices that commingle State and commercial power beyond the simple—though still central—practice of contracting out, consider the following:

Private Standard Setting. Most federal agencies encourage and endorse private standard setting as a substitute for notice-and-comment agency rulemaking. By last count, federal agencies have incorporated approximately 10,000 such standards privately formulated by various trade groups, nongovernmental organizations, and business, consumer, or professional associations.[39] Needless to say, participation by the civil service and by many members of civil society is often considerably narrowed when private groups, rather than agency officials, take the lead in setting standards.

Private Accreditation and Administration. Many agencies team up with private accreditation organizations that then devise and administer nominally federal policies. For example, the private Financial Industry

Regulatory Authority (FINRA) "oversees approximately 4380 brokerage firms, and 633,000 registered securities representatives."[40] Just a decade old and already about the size of the Securities and Exchange Commission, FINRA supervises 80 percent of all equity trading in the United States, makes and enforces membership rules, arbitrates disputes between and among members and customers, oversees compliance with federal securities laws, conducts disciplinary hearings, and imposes fines.[41] Thus, in all practical senses, FINRA constitutes a private arm of the State.

Marketization of the Bureaucracy. Many federal agencies are internalizing the norms and practices of the Market, refashioning their own workforces along businesslike lines. What I call the "marketization of the bureaucracy" and will discuss in considerable detail below involves the conversion of tenured civil servants into at-will employees. These newly reclassified (and almost invariably downgraded) employees enjoy the same job security—or *lack thereof*—accorded to most private sector workers.

Deputization. Intelligence and law-enforcement agencies rely heavily on private deputies, both big corporations and small-fry truck drivers, cable and Internet technicians, and apartment doormen to serve as the government's eyes and ears. Behemoth companies such as AT&T, Verizon, Google, Facebook, Yahoo, Microsoft, and Apple have at times provided ready (and legally questionable) access to their customers' telephone conversations, email correspondence, text messages, Internet searches, and the like.[42] (AT&T employees got so caught up in helping the feds that they referred to themselves as part of "TEAM USA," proposed and engineered technical and legal shortcuts to enable faster and less judicially reviewable collection of personal data, and even took the lead in conducting their own counterterrorism analysis, bringing to the FBI's attention "very interesting" patterns, and recommending that the FBI investigate further.[43])

Ordinary Joes, for their part, have been dragooned into any number of counterterrorism initiatives as they interact with potential suspects in the course of delivering packages, installing and repairing telephone, cable, and Internet equipment, selling retail goods, and providing concierge and building maintenance services.[44]

Combined, these corporate and individual deputies act, first, as force multipliers, extending the government's reach in untold directions. Second, they act as covert operatives; assuming technicians, couriers, and doormen to be ordinary employees of ordinary businesses, surveillance targets are likely to lower their guard and grant these deputies considerable access (far more than those targets would ever voluntarily afford to known government agents). Third, these deputies act relatively unencumbered by the laws that more stringently regulate government agents. This arbitraging opportunity comes about because Congress and the courts have long (and sensibly) presumed that State power is more potent and coercive than private power—and that government officials would be the exclusive stewards of State power.

Crowdsourcing. Just as commercial firms increasingly crowdsource advertising and R&D—*who doesn't love Frito-Lay's customer contests to design the next great potato chip?*[45]—so too is the government beginning to crowdsource some of its responsibilities. Reminiscent, perhaps, of Tom Sawyer convincing his friends of the joys of whitewashing Aunt Polly's fence, federal agencies draw on the public's enthusiasm, ingenuity, and free labor to help with the design and administration of homeland security,[46] workplace safety,[47] and fair labor policies.[48] One instance of government crowdsourcing can be found in the Department of Labor's effective marshaling of citizen-consumers. Smartphone apps now combine Yelp consumer reviews with government data regarding workplace health, safety, and wage violations. Fusing commercial and regulatory reviews enables and encourages would-be shoppers, diners, and lodgers to effectively boycott and thus privately "punish" businesses tagged as having alleged labor and health violations.[49] Government reliance on, and encouragement of, private forms of punishment enables the State to reach broader and deeper—and to do so in circumstances where agencies may lack the resources, political support, or (most alarmingly) sufficient evidence to initiate prosecutions and collect the fines levied.[50]

Patriotic Philanthropy. Complementing crowdsourcing is crowdfunding. Crowdfunding, known in government circles as patriotic philanthropy, constitutes a privatized supplement—or, in some cases, alternative—to general taxes and user fees. The National Park Service, among other federal entities, has set up a private trust through which corporations and individuals may donate funds.[51] The Park Service uses those funds to develop new programs, improve existing ones, and generally lessen reliance on congressional appropriations and on its own civil servants. (At times, the private trust—and, more specifically, its big donors—may exert undue influence on Park Service policy, but I leave that issue to the side here.[52])

Solicitation of such private funding is increasingly common at the state and local levels, too. Private individuals and firms bankroll special litigation funds for state attorneys general—funds that have enabled state lawyers to challenge, among other things, the Affordable Care Act and federal immigration laws and policies.[53] Such private giving is particularly important in jurisdictions where state legislatures are disinclined to fund such suits (perhaps because the legislators and the governor support the federal programs in question). Private funds are also being used to support failing school districts. Most famously, Mark Zuckerberg granted $100 million to the Newark schools.[54] That grant came with considerable strings attached, including the requirement that Newark share authority over the design of class curricula and over personnel decisions with the Facebook chief's charitable foundation.

Because patriotic philanthropy, like other forms of charitable giving, is tax deductible, it has the effect of lowering donors' taxable income. Unlike other forms of charitable giving, which simply siphon off government revenue, patriotic philanthropy shifts government money around—removing it from the general coffers and earmarking it for special projects as the donors see fit. As such, this targeted government giving reflects yet another modality of privatization: it allows government to effectively auction off policies and programs that otherwise might not be pursued (or pursued in the manner so directed).

Venture Capital. Some agencies—including the CIA, the Department of Energy, and the Army—have gone so far as to create their own venture capital outfits to promote and shepherd the development of technologies that are both useful to the government and commercially profitable.[55] Among other things, In-Q-Tel, the CIA's venture capital firm, is responsible for the development of the fantastically profitable product that has come to be known as Google Earth.[56] The venture capital model of public administration is particularly interesting as it exhibits some characteristics of traditional government contracting and some that are more in keeping with the marketization of the bureaucracy, in which government units—and not just personnel—are converted into de facto businesses.

Social Impact Bonds. Some federal agencies have decided to create quasi-private markets for the provision of social services such as education, welfare, and criminal rehabilitation. Rather than simply administer programs in-house, contract directly with private providers, or issue vouchers, the government offers a large bounty, payable if and only when a private provider proves successful (according to some prearranged benchmark). These arrangements—called social impact bonds—encourage private financial institutions to "invest" in private social service providers, underwriting the expense of the service provision, helping to monitor the private provider, bearing the costs if the private provider fails, and reaping a windfall if the provider succeeds.[57]

State Ventriloquism. Federal officials have struck backroom deals with TV networks, secretly relieving broadcasters of their formal regulatory responsibilities on the condition that those broadcasters incorporate government-approved, anti-drug themes into the plotlines of some of their most popular shows.[58] This was a particularly big deal in the late 1990s and early 2000s, amid a federal push to curtail drug use, particularly among teens and twentysomethings. *ER* and *Beverly Hills 90210*, among others, "filled their episodes with anti-drug pitches to cash in on a complex government advertising subsidy."[59] In essence, government provided regulatory relief in exchange for the networks' willingness to amplify government messaging—while making that messaging seem authentically private and therefore less paternalistic and preachy.

Equity Investing and Backdoor Regulation. Amid the global financial collapse of 2008 and 2009, the Department of Treasury became equity partners in some of America's failing investment banks, insurance firms, and carmakers. Treasury leveraged its ownership stake (newly acquired in exchange for federal relief) to direct corporate policies—and did so without having to engage in the normal administrative rulemaking process that would necessarily involve extensive participation by (and likely pushback from) civil servants and members of the public.[60] The government urged, among other things, that the bailed-out companies cap the level of executive compensation, that the automakers expand their fleets of fuel-efficient cars, and that the same automakers cancel plans to move jobs overseas. Though many might characterize the federal bailout as a form of nationalization—and therefore as the converse of privatization—I see no such reason to treat nationalization as categorically different from rather than as an extension of today's broader privatization agenda. After all, the government is *buying* rather than *legislating* compliance, eschewing the thickly constrained sovereign regulatory tools of constitutional and administrative governance for the more nimble, forceful commercial instruments that Treasury paid dearly to wield.

This is, as I said, a dizzyingly eclectic list—one that reflects just a few of the many forms and patterns new millennial privatization takes. My goal here is not definitional precision or a comprehensive mapping, typology, or numerical accounting. Rather, I am surveying initiatives that rely on the participation of private actors or their functional equivalents (i.e., marketized government workers) to carry out State policymaking or policy-implementing responsibilities; that vest discretionary authority in private actors or, again, their functional equivalents, at the expense of civil servants; and that shift the physical locus of State power such that it is logistically and legally more difficult for the rest of civil society to participate meaningfully in policy development and execution.

For simplicity's sake, the remainder of this chapter focuses on only two privatization practices. Both practices stand out for their ubiquity, durability, and transsubstantive reach. In what follows, I describe these two practices—*deep service contracting* and the *marketization of the bureaucracy.* Chapter 6 builds on these two detailed case studies to show how each enables the evasion of legal and political checks across a wide range of federal policy domains. Such evasions compromise, if not altogether subvert, a well-functioning administrative separation of powers and thus imperil the constitutional project of *pax administrativa.*

Deep Service Contracting

Just a few short decades ago, service contracting was largely confined to the most ministerial and vanilla of government functions. Now, of course, contracting knows no such bounds. Everywhere we look, the federal government is engaged in *deep service contracting*: the outsourcing of sensitive policy design and policy-implementing responsibilities.

As often happens, with familiarity comes acceptance, even complaisance. For this reason, if for no other, we need to go back and kick the tires. That is my aim here—to examine deep service contracting with fresh eyes. As with other case studies and treatments in this book, my aim isn't to be exhaustive or encyclopedic but rather illustrative.

Policy Design and Administration. Agency leaders are not sufficiently numerous to do most of the work researching, preparing, and even writing rules, guidance documents, and policy statements. They lack the time, range, and, quite often, expertise. Thus much of this important, often inescapably political, and invariably highly discretionary work necessarily falls to the rank-and-file who constitute the bulk of the agency workforce. During the high-water decades of *pax administrativa,* the rank-and-file were overwhelmingly members of the civil service.

Today, service contracting is crowding out even those civil servants with significant policymaking and policy-implementing responsibilities. New millennial contractors, working for practically every federal agency, draft legal memoranda for the agency leadership, produce economic and scientific studies critical to the rulemaking process, design government license

and benefit applications, run public hearings, ghost-write publicly dissem-
inated policy statements, produce agency guidance documents (including
those on how to contract), provide legal services, and author parts of final
rules promulgated in the Code of Federal Regulations.[61] They are also
tasked with the outright design of cooperative federalism programs pertaining to criminal justice, welfare, and public health.[62] Again, actual numbers are just about impossible to come by. But nary a soul disputes that
contracting has intensified over the past twenty or so years, reaching
wider, deeper, and more conspicuously into highly sensitive, discretionary
domains.[63]

Policy Implementation and Counseling. Further down in the administrative trenches lie those officials directly and personally interacting with program beneficiaries and regulated parties. For much of the American public,
it is these street-level officials—not the political leaders who sit in the president's cabinet or the most senior career personnel—who are the faces and
voices of the agency. They are the ones who counsel, cajole, assist,
encourage, or alienate benefit seekers and regulated parties. They are likewise the ones who judge and, ultimately, approve or deny requests for
government licenses, variances, waivers, and the like.

Such interpersonal dealings occur in the manifold areas of public benefits: welfare, housing, disability, health care, veterans' services, and student
loans to name just a few. Such dealings occur too in thickly regulated commercial contexts such as construction, pharmaceuticals, agriculture, manufacturing, and sales, investments, and marketing. This is where businesses, states, and local governments come face-to-face with their frenemies
from the IRS, the EPA, the FDA, OSHA, and the Departments of Energy,
Treasury, Education, Justice, and Transportation.

There is, of course, considerable discretion exercised by on-the-ground
officials. These officials can—*and often must*—determine for themselves
whether laws apply. And, even where the law is more or less settled, on-the-
ground civil servants still have to determine whether to give a regulated
party a second chance, provide technical support to an individual or firm
attempting to meet federal standards, or immediately bring an enforcement action.

Discretion is also a signature feature in the public benefits arena.
Notwithstanding guidance provided by Congress, by agency leaders, and
even by senior civil servants, the implementation and administration of
welfare and anti-discrimination programs require street-level officials to
make many judgment calls. Personnel decide how much advice to dispense
(or withhold), how much assistance to offer (or withhold), and whether to

believe an applicant's story, help that applicant substantiate her story, or initiate an investigation. Even officials' often unconscious choice whether to be friendly or unwelcoming is of considerable consequence: rudeness or aloofness can be a tool of diverting, shaming, and dissuading would-be benefit seekers.[64] Needless to add, because many benefit seekers tend to be less sophisticated than managers of regulated firms and more dependent on the good graces of government, the subtle power of benefits administrators cannot be underestimated. The continuation of government support is, for many, a life-or-death proposition.[65]

Again, what we find today are contractors replacing civil servants and assuming all of the highly discretionary, policy-sensitive responsibilities mentioned above. This regular and routine reliance on private actors represents a sea change in the way government operates.[66] While no shortage of scholars and policymakers have confronted what I'm calling deep contracting, they've done so largely from an anti-fraud, anti-corruption, or anti-abuse perspective. For them, the fear is one of wayward, careless, or cruel contractors and the indolent, hapless agency heads they fleece. As Chapter 6 will show, the real—that is, the constitutionally salient—fear should be the converse one: dutiful contractors overly solicitous of the canny and cunning agency leadership.

The Special (and Related) Case of Military Privatization. Military privatization, like domestic regulatory privatization, is part of our new normal. During the long wars in Iraq and Afghanistan, contractors were—and some still remain—everywhere, doing everything. From peeling potatoes to piloting drones,[67] contractors operate on the very tip of the proverbial spear and along all points of its shaft. They detain and interrogate prisoners, including those infamously brutalized and humiliated at the Abu Ghriab prison in Iraq.[68] They protect visiting civilian government officials and manage and defend U.S. and allied bases.[69] And they design operational plans, maintain hardware, lead caravans transporting materiel, and routinely patrol areas teeming with insurgents.[70]

Working with the CIA, government contractors "rendered" high-value detainees to secret black site prisons in places such as Egypt, Morocco, Syria, and Poland.[71] Perhaps of greatest significance, contractors participated in armed commando raids described by the *New York Times* as occurring "virtually nightly" and involving "hundreds of guys . . . rotating in and out over a period of several years."[72] For much of the invasion, occupation, and counterinsurgency campaigns in Iraq and Afghanistan, military contractors rivaled and often exceeded the number of regular, uniformed U.S. troops.[73]

Again, as with domestic outsourcing, military contracting is relatively new, or at least newly renewed. Historic reliance on military contracting—largely confined in the United States at least to naval letters of marque—fell out of favor by the time of the Mexican-American War.[74] Throughout the nineteenth and twentieth centuries, military contracting was subject to any number of international rebukes and bans.[75] It was during this long period between the late 1840s and mid-1990s[76] that the United States (and most other nations) drew principally on combinations of enlistees and conscripted personnel. This left rogue states, teetering banana republics, and mercurial bands of rebels as the primary purchasers of private military services.[77]

In the 1990s, the military privatization freeze began to thaw. The Clinton administration discreetly deployed small units of contractors to support the War on Drugs in Colombia. Contractors were prized in that particular conflict because they didn't count against the congressionally imposed cap on U.S. troop involvement. In addition, President Clinton orchestrated the deployment of American-based contractors to the troubled, disintegrating Balkans, primarily to help beleaguered Bosnian and Croatian forces in their struggles with the Serbs. Here contractors enabled the United States and its allies to work around international arms embargoes.

It wasn't until the 2000s when the military privatization floodgates opened. Recall that hostilities broke out first against al-Qaeda and the Taliban in Afghanistan, then against Saddam Hussein's regime, and, still later, against the Iraqi insurgents who filled the power vacuum left by the ousted Baathists. Contractors played a central role in every phase of the planning and prosecution of those various military campaigns. Still, the aggressive turn to contractors caught most commentators and policy-makers entirely off guard. Consider, for example, the fact that scholars writing at least somewhat sympathetically about U.S. domestic contracting in the early 2000s were nevertheless quick to insist that military outsourcing remained unthinkable.[78] Yet here we were already fighting what would become the longest continuous wars in American history and already heavily reliant on hundreds of thousands of contractors—and countless numbers of foreign subcontractors such as Afghan warlords and Nepalese Gurkhas. Now, during the long wind-down, contractors are almost all that is left in Afghanistan, far outnumbering U.S. troops.[79] And the smart money is on contractors playing a central role if and when the United States intensifies its campaign against the Islamic State.[80]

Marketization of the Bureaucracy

Much of the enthusiasm for service contracting turns on various forms of labor arbitrage. It is widely believed that most civil servants receive higher levels of compensation than do their private sector counterparts.[81] And most civil servants enjoy stronger collective bargaining protections than those commonly found in the private sector.[82] Of perhaps greatest importance of all, unlike most private sector workers, civil servants generally cannot be fired absent a showing of cause.[83]

As mentioned above, over the past few decades, those frustrated with what they view as an expensive and obstinate government workforce have championed government service contracting.[84] It was, after all, easier for such critics to contract around government labor policy than to directly confront the then still entrenched civil servants.[85]

Easy in some ways, but hard in others. Let's not kid ourselves. Contracting is expensive. A good deal of time and resources must be devoted to soliciting bids for prospective contracts, evaluating those bids, and then drafting the precise language of those contracts. Then there is all the follow-up: the monitoring, oversight, and evaluation. Before you know it, the term of the contract is set to expire, and agency officials must decide whether to renew, seek new bids, or attempt to insource the work.[86] This is precisely why those who are skeptical of contracting's supposed cost savings and dubious of contracting's purported leanness harp on the hidden overhead costs associated with designing government contracts and then managing the contractors.[87] Taking this overhead into account (which few studies of contractor performance do), the truth of the matter is that contractors might well have to outperform government employees by more than 20 percent to generate any appreciable savings.[88]

Today of course the civil service is no longer untouchable. After decades of incessant anti-government political messaging, the civil service no longer needs to be treated with kid gloves. A powerful coalition of free market enthusiasts and frustrated taxpayers (who cannot understand, for example, why a federal letter carrier earns significantly more than her FedEx counterpart) has opened the door to more direct attacks. Politicians, TV talking heads, and newspaper editorial boards across the ideological spectrum now take direct aim at those they pejoratively call bureaucrats[89]—so much so that, as the *Washington Post* reported, contemporary "politicians talk about government employees . . . with the kind of umbrage ordinarily aimed at Wall Street financiers and convenience store bandits."[90] Indeed, dislike for government workers runs so high that, in 2011, a significant segment of Congress tried to defeat entirely symbolic legislation honoring federal civilian workers killed in the line of duty. One critic of the bill explained that the conferral of any such honor would be misplaced, if not offensive. It would, this pundit insisted, "become[] just another trapping of power from the federal government available to all those people in the ever expanding federal bureaucracy."[91]

With the tide clearly turning against the civil service, elected officials have pounced, reducing civil servants' salaries, cutting benefits, renegotiating pensions, and limiting and weakening public employee unions.[92] Most drastically, they are altogether reclassifying swaths of civil servants as at-will employees, no longer insulated from politically motivated hiring and firing decisions.[93]

So far, marketization has been considerably more pronounced at the state and local levels. Governors such as Wisconsin's Scott Walker have made marketization a signature issue.[94] But the feds are quickly catching up. Well before President Trump vowed, as he put it, to "drain the swamp" and made clear his intentions to do away with the entirety of the federal civil service,[95] federal marketization was already a reality for hundreds of thousands of federal civil servants, including many charged with exercising judgment and discretion at the policymaking and implementation stages.[96] Indeed, it was during the Obama years when Congress sought to convert all members of the Senior Executive Service—the top, and arguably most important, stratum of the career civil service—into at-will employees.[97] And, it was President Obama's own Office of Personnel Management that advanced a rule authorizing White House officials to reclassify as at-will employees all civil servants with responsibilities pertaining to national or homeland security, critical physical or electronic infrastructure, or the safeguarding, maintenance, or disposal of hazardous materials or natural resources.[98] Many of these designated responsibilities reach well beyond the conventionally conceived national security infrastructure (which has always stood somewhat outside of the strictures of administrative law) and extend so far as to cover employees in such core domestic outfits as the EPA and the Departments of Health and Human Services, Energy, Treasury, Interior, and Transportation.[99]

Scholars are just now beginning to appreciate this wholesale privatization of the public workforce from within. They are recognizing that the "public sector is conforming more and more to the normal disciplines of the private sector."[100] And they are realizing that "many public servants today work in settings that are not too different from their private sector counterparts."[101] Marketization, in short, provides much of what privatization's proponents have been seeking via outsourcing without the concomitant hassles of contracts and contract management. Like a film buff who rearranges her living room to resemble a movie theater (sans sticky floors and overpriced popcorn), agency heads can now carry out the privatization agenda without leaving the comfort of their homes.

The Special (and Related) Case of Teacher Tenure. Marketization of the bureaucracy has, as suggested, attracted very little attention—far less, indeed, than a seemingly closely related set of initiatives aimed at transforming the way we hire, promote, fire, and compensate public school teachers. Today, various groups are railing against the power of teachers' unions, decrying districts' inability to summarily fire allegedly apathetic or underachieving teachers, and lamenting the fact that our best and brightest eschew careers in teaching for more remunerative vocations. Over the past decade or so—a period that roughly corresponds with the marketization of bureaucracy movement—these groups have had considerable success, making inroads in California, Wisconsin, New York, and North Carolina, among other places.[102]

I loop in teachers for several reasons. First, schools, like administrative agencies, are a place being broadly reinvented along businesslike lines. This businesslike turn is reflected in the emphatic embrace of standardized performance evaluations (for students and teachers alike, the latter of whom often feel compelled to *teach to the test*); in efforts to award bonuses for high-scoring teachers and to fire those whose students underperform; and in the increasing privatization of education through charter schools (which *Forbes* of all periodicals calls "a backdoor for corporate profit"[103]), public vouchers to parochial schools, and the literal contracting out of public school administration.[104] With an ardent supporter of school privatization, Betsy DeVos, newly installed as President Trump's education secretary, one can only expect this businesslike overhaul to intensify.

Second, the popularity of the anti-teacher-tenure movement, like the movement to marketize the bureaucracy, transcends traditional political dividing lines.[105] Famed liberal law professor Laurence Tribe and Democratic super-litigator David Boies are among those spearheading legal challenges to teacher tenure.[106] They seemingly enjoyed the support of senior members of the Obama administration,[107] as well as many leading Democratic governors, mayors, and members of Congress.[108]

Third, the justifications for tenure are not unrelated in the two realms. Teacher tenure matters for academic freedom, even at the primary and secondary levels. Such freedom isn't just an intellectual indulgence, a soapbox in every classroom as it were. It is also a means of empowering teachers to speak truth to power; to teach evolution in creationist towns, distressingly a conversation as fresh in some locales today as it was in 1925 during the Scopes Monkey Trial; to teach sexual education, history, and cultural studies without fear of reprisal; and to support and mentor student journalists, political activists, artists, and those children facing various forms of discrimination. In these respects, teacher tenure is a close cousin of bureaucratic tenure. Job security provides teachers and civil servants with the professional discretion and legal protection to question prevailing popular sentiments. Civil servants are well positioned to act as rivalrous counterweights to agency heads and particularly potent segments of civil society. Tenured teachers, in turn, may play a similar role vis-à-vis school administrators, elected officials, community leaders, and, of course, helicopter parents.

6

Privatization as a Constitutional—
and Constitutionally Fraught—Project

We wouldn't expect an observer ill-informed about czarist Russia to comprehend the Bolshevik Revolution, nor would we expect someone unschooled in the Hollywood classics to appreciate the satirical brilliance of *Young Frankenstein* or *Blazing Saddles*. The same is invariably true about privatization. Context is everything. And it is context that we've been missing. Because we never fully grasped the essence of the modern administrative state, it is only natural that we have misconstrued the Privatization Revolution that threatens to supplant it. But now that I have recast the administrative state as constitutional precisely because of its structural recommitment to the separation of powers, we can, perhaps for the first time, truly appreciate privatization and the special threat it poses.

Specifically, today's privatization must be understood as it maps onto a rich and varied set of architectural and legal landscapes that date back to the Founding. This more contextual framing reveals how privatization aggrandizes, not dissipates, State power; (further) politicizes, rather than makes more technocratic, government welfare and regulatory programs; and consolidates, rather than fragments, presidential control over government policymaking and policy implementation. Viewed with these understandings in mind, privatization looks far less like a *sui generis* phenomenon than as the latest threat to an enduring, evolving commitment to separating and checking State power.

The previous chapter introduced and described various privatization practices, with special attention paid to deep service contracting and the marketization of the bureaucracy. This chapter takes the inquiry further, examining those two dominant practices through the lens of constitutional and administrative law. In what follows, I present the prevailing arguments in favor of and against modern privatization. I challenge those arguments—both pro and con—and call instead for privatization to be understood in terms of structural constitutional law, power politics, and the underappreciated nexus between political expediency and economic efficiency. For too long we have been focusing on greedy contractors and anemic agency leaders. In truth, the constitutionally more salient (and more dangerous) dynamic is the converse one: the tandem of compliant contractors and the cagey agency leaders who hire them. This powerful, mutually beneficial pairing subverts the administrative separation of powers. And while agency leaders gain a firmer grip on administrative power, their private, for-profit facilitators get rich.

Once this relationship between privatization and the administrative separation of powers comes into focus, we can derive a fuller, sharper constitutional theory of the Privatization Revolution and draft a corresponding judicial and legislative blueprint for confronting the existential challenge privatization poses to American liberal democracy. That is the work of Part Three.

The Prevailing Understandings

Prevailing accounts of contemporary privatization coalesce around a couple of basic claims: First, the emerging privatized State of the twenty-first century is smaller and less potent, as a result of the literal offloading of government responsibilities onto the private sector. Second, this privatized regime is more efficient, precisely because it abides by the logic of the Market rather than that of the polis or the bureaucracy.[1] Beyond those basic claims, consensus quickly breaks down. There is, after all, little agreement on whether the pivot to privatization—and all that such a pivot entails—is a good or bad thing.

Privatization's proponents hail the arrival of cadres of contractors and other privatized agents, celebrating what they see as the end of big, unresponsive government and a corresponding boon to individual liberty, technocratic governance, fiscal discipline, and the free market system. By contrast, critics treat the Privatization Revolution as a national tragedy in which the Lear-like State is being cannibalized, marginalized, and tossed asunder by its hastily chosen and disingenuous heirs.

These competing narratives are powerful, as evidenced by their prominent place in popular and academic discourse. But they are also quite limited, often overly simplified, and insufficiently attuned to constitutional structures and administrative processes and personalities. Below I examine and then question these accounts, ultimately concluding that both champions and critics have missed the mark. Specifically, I break down the conventional arguments in favor of and against privatization into three constituent parts, showing how debates over the *size, efficiency,* and *legality* of the increasingly privatized State are incomplete, misleading, and obscure more than they illuminate.

Efficiency Debates. First and undoubtedly most saliently are the discussions about privatization's promised efficiencies. As addressed in Chapter 4, privatization's enthusiasts have long considered government agencies wasteful and government employees indolent. By their reckoning, bureaucracies are insufficiently motivated to provide the highest quality services, goods, or counsel at the lowest possible cost. Hence the allure of markets and market practices.

For many, the billion-dollar question—yes, that's what the feds spend annually on service contractors—is whether market actors and practices are indeed more efficient than their bureaucratic counterparts. Disagreements are principally empirical: Is privatization delivering the promised benefits? Is the government really as slothful as critics claim? Nuance is added when such conversations consider the government's overhead costs associated with drafting really good contracts, the existence or absence of a competitive market of would-be contractors (such that contractors actually, and not just theoretically, feel pressure to keep costs low and service quality high), and the capacity of government units to monitor and evaluate the private or marketized workers.[2]

These considerations are all well and good. But it seems as if neither side is asking the right questions. Those skeptical of privatization's promise of efficiencies often fixate on the dangers of wayward contractors. Accounts of contractor fraud, abuse, and venality are catnip to an American public reared on gotcha politics—and often serve to knock the wind out of the sails of those reflexively drawn to market solutions. There is thus much to be said for exposing evidence of contractor wrongdoing and for disputing privatization's purported cost savings. Yet there are several problems with focusing on the existence or absence of contractor efficiencies.

First, focusing on waste, fraud, and abuse provides little insight into the majority of contracting or marketized arrangements that show no such infirmities. Does that mean many, if not most, privatized arrangements are *prima facie* acceptable? If so, then there is little reason to oppose privatization in principle.

Second, even where fraud, corruption, or waste seems evident, we must remember that private or otherwise commercialized actors hardly have a monopoly on acting venally or irresponsibly. Recently, the General Services Administration, the Secret Service, the National Security Agency, the Air Force, and the Department of Veterans Affairs have all been embroiled in major scandals involving the misuse of appropriated funds, the abuse of State power for personal or political gain, or the dereliction of duty.[3]

And, third, a focus on comparative market efficiencies gives us little basis for distinguishing between the contracting out of sanitation duties and those of, say, diplomacy. At the risk of straying a bit afield, I think it is fair to conclude that many would be willing to outsource garbage collection even if the turn to the Market promised only marginal cost savings. By contrast, just as many, if not more, would resist privatizing diplomacy notwithstanding assurances of considerable budgetary savings.

To be sure, privatization's cheerleaders seem to have it wrong, too. At the most basic level, even if they are right as an empirical matter that the Market is generally more efficient, they assume without explaining why economic efficiency is an unalloyed good or why it translates well into the public arena. Specifically, they fail to reconcile this celebration of efficiency with an underlying constitutional culture that is decidedly skeptical of efficiency arguments. As Chief Justice Warren Burger put it, "convenience and efficiency are not the primary objectives—or the hallmarks—of democratic government,"[4] let alone *our* democratic government in which separated, triangulated power (and the inefficiencies separation and triangulation engender) is a purposeful feature rather than a bug in the design. Going further back in time, Justice Louis Brandeis reminded us that "separation of powers was adopted by the Convention of 1787, not to promote efficiency but to preclude the exercise of arbitrary power. The purpose was, not to avoid friction, but, by means of the inevitable friction incident to the distribution of the governmental powers among three departments, to save the people from autocracy."[5] At the very least then, we need a theory of what types of efficiencies are constitutionally compatible—and what types are anathema.

Beyond that big, conceptual challenge, those insisting that privatization is indeed efficient often fail to distinguish efforts in which privatization represents a true efficiency gain from those that simply reflect successful labor or regulatory arbitrage. This is where technocratic and political arguments get jumbled. Is a turn to the Market really more efficient in the true, economic sense of the term if the cost savings are entirely attributable to contracting firms either paying their employees lower wages or having to comply with fewer regulatory responsibilities? That is to say, is the cost savings a convenient albeit insidious and hardly politically neutral means of circumventing public law commitments sounding in economic and procedural justice?

By way of comparison, an American textile plant might move from Santa Monica, California to Tupelo, Mississippi and, within weeks, experience a spike in profits. The spike may well be a function of Mississippian ingenuity. More likely, it is a function of the latter locale having a lower minimum wage, weaker labor laws, and fewer environmental and occupational safety standards. Thus, as common as the focus on efficiency is, the debate is an incomplete one. It either fails to prove much of anything or relies on a series of normative stipulations that are at best contestable and, quite possibly, wrong.

Size-of-Government Debates. Another front in the privatization wars is privatization's supposed transformation of the public and private sectors. The conventional story is that privatization in its various forms limits the size, scope, and reach of the State. Many conservatives and libertarians welcome privatization precisely because they see the businesslike turn as effectuating a shrinking and weakening of the bureaucratic Leviathan— and a corresponding expansion of private rights, commercial activity, and market autonomy. By contrast, many progressives rue what they see as a State all too willing to abdicate its sovereign powers.

Here too it seems as if both sides are thinking about privatization too narrowly. For example, what would privatization hawks say about the marketization of the bureaucracy, in which the size of the government sector does not change at all? Would they be arch-formalists and thus not credit the fact that such privatization from within has practically the same effect as conventional outsourcing? Or would they applaud marketization, notwithstanding the fact that the total number of federal employees remains the same? Similarly, would defenders of *pax administrativa* cheer marketization as job preserving or bemoan marketization because it hollows out and effectively privatizes the State?

More generally, those focusing on size are often just chasing their own tails. Conservatives and libertarians should and, in fairness, increasingly do realize that a heavily privatized State enables only the fiction of smallness, with contractors playing the role of the public sector's *Shabbos goy.* Government isn't shrinking. It is switching out ID badges, masking FTEs, and shifting costs from one budgetary line to another.[6] As Paul Light emphasizes, the "true size of government" must account for the many, many contractors and other deputies advancing any number of federal programs.[7] Indeed, if anything, this switcheroo is likely to allow further expansion of the State, as contractors can be discreetly hired while politicians boast a nominally shrinking civilian and military federal workforce.[8] This switcheroo is also apt to enable especially aggressive State interventions—doing so for reasons I'll describe below.

Meanwhile, the criticisms voiced by those deploring privatization as a form of government abdication are overblown—and likely misplaced. One would be hard pressed to show that the federal government is in retreat as a result of the privatization of government services. Again, Light's work on the "true size of government" is instructive, as is John DiIulio's. The latter, a political scientist and veteran of the George W. Bush administration, spotlights what he calls "government by proxy"—the giant shadow workforce of private actors supporting government operations and initiatives.[9] Even if the official government workforce is declining, such a numerical decline is more than offset by the correspondingly precipitous rise in contractors, private standard setters, deputies, and the like. Look no further than the substantive domains where privatization is most obviously surging. I doubt a credible claim could be made that the federal government is doing anything but accreting power in the areas of national defense, homeland security, and intelligence—three domains absolutely flooded with private actors of various sorts. The same has been true in the public health arena, given the pivotal role contractors and other private deputies have played in designing and implementing the Affordable Care Act.

To be sure, there are the occasional contractor frolics and detours, when private actors seize, divert, or squander State power. These frolics and detours are especially likely to occur when contractors are awarded long-term contracts, have no real market competitors, or possess expertise that far outstrips the government's. There are also the rare cases when government officials see some political advantage in turning over near-complete control of State responsibilities to private actors. But, by and large, these are the exceptions. Most contractors and other privatized actors are instead simply, if imperfectly, amplifying the power and influence of the feds.

More to the point, private contractors, especially if they live up to their billing as rational economic actors, are apt to press, lobby, and create opportunities for the State to more fully commit to federal programs. They are likely to do so if for no other reason than that expansive State programming is good for business: government contractors do well when there are lots of contracts to be won—and that happens only when the State is big, rangy, and intrusive.

Recasting contractors as rationally unabashed champions of big government is hardly a radical pivot. We've long feared the military and prison-industrial complexes—and their ballooning effects on America's defense and carceral policies. Generations have understood defense contractors to be skillful and at times reckless champions of a hawkish foreign policy and of a correspondingly large, well-equipped military. They've likewise appreciated the influence of the private prison lobby, known to urge legislators to build more detention facilities, criminalize more behavior, and set longer and stiffer sentences.[10]

Of course, contractor lobbying and cheerleading might give us reason to think that, at least on this score, privatization is good for ensuring a big, albeit highly reconfigured, welfare state. Take, for example, Lockheed Martin and Maximus Inc., two powerful providers of, among other things, government welfare services. These major corporations are better funded and likely more effective advocates of extensive benefits and liberal eligibility standards than are either government social workers or the poor recipients themselves.

Legal Debates. Lastly, there are legal debates. Here too the discussions are robust but uneven and a bit superficial. Rarely, for instance, are efforts made to situate privatization within the broader context of modern administrative law. And even when privatization discussions are capacious and nuanced enough to include consideration of administrative law, there is nevertheless scant recognition of anything approximating the administrative separation of powers and its structural constitutional significance.

Privatization's proponents point to the rich, though uncritically examined, history of extensive and quite matter-of-fact federal reliance on private actors; decades of congressional acquiescence (if not outright support) of privatization; and longstanding judicial acceptance of the practice. Perhaps conceding the point, privatization's challengers have not confronted those historical claims directly. Instead, these challengers endeavor to tether privatization to specific constitutional or statutory prohibitions, the thinness of which simply cannot be stretched to cover twenty-first-century political-commercial operations. (Paul Verkuil has admitted as much, reminding us that "[t]he only reference in the Constitution arguably relevant to delegation to private parties is the Marque and Reprisal Clause."[11]) Thus in the absence of clear, prohibitory language, courts have largely continued giving privatization a free pass. Specifically, courts have generally declined to treat contractors, deputies, and the like as the true recipients of delegated powers—and thus subject to the doctrinal bar on private delegations.[12] And they've generally avoided treating contractors, deputies, and the like as so-called *state actors* and thus accountable for any constitutional violations they may commit.[13]

What's altogether missing from the legal discussions is recognition of the constitutional project of administrative separation of powers and how it disrupted those historical and, by extension, legal narratives. A less static treatment of history would reveal the inaptness of the premodern precedents, for reasons I articulated in Chapter 1. A less static treatment would also free those lawyers challenging privatization from having to rely on often reedy legal text or on confused doctrines that hardened well before the advent of the contemporary privatization movement. Instead, those advocates could draw upon the administrative separation of powers, invoking thicker, more dynamically resonant structural constitutional principles in efforts to regulate if not altogether invalidate today's privatization initiatives.

Recasting the Debate: Privatization as Power

As important and vibrant as these privatization debates have been, they have led us astray, tripping false alarms while distracting us from the more vexing and constitutionally salient challenges that privatization actually poses. Simply stated, the fusion of State and market power is not what it commonly seems.

First, privatization—at least when it implicates policymaking or policy-implementing responsibilities—is not a neutral exercise in smarter or leaner government. Rather, it is a normatively inflected endeavor that does considerable violence to a system that is not accidentally clunky but purposely (and necessarily) so. Cleaning up that clunkiness is not a little botox under the eyes. It is, for better or worse, a full-blown lobotomy.

Second, privatization of, again, the sensitive policymaking and policy-implementing sort, is unlikely to sap or dissipate State power. Instead, this commingling of government and market forces enables the accretion of State power at the expense of the private sector, *threatening to destabilize the liberal democratic order*. Further, this commingling enables the accretion of political executive power at the expense of Congress and the civil service, *threatening the constitutional and administrative separations of powers*.

It is wrong to think about the increasingly privatized State as smaller, more modest, or more technocratic. When the federal government hired hundreds of thousands of contractors to serve in Iraq and Afghanistan, the presence of this contracting force allowed the Pentagon to conduct larger, longer, and more unilaterally directed campaigns—far more than would be the case were the government reliant only on American servicemen and women. In this example, the official government footprint is technically smaller. But make no mistake: the State has expanded its reach as a matter of raw numbers and raw power. And once we recognize that privatization has an emboldening, empowering effect on the State, we begin to see how freighted a term like *efficiency* actually is.

Consider contractors working for the EPA, HHS, or the Department of Labor. Maybe these contractors save the taxpayers some money. And maybe they end up skimming off the top. Either way, these contractors might please agency heads who prefer a privatized workforce to independent and potentially cantankerous civil servants better situated and more inclined to question and possibly resist the administration's agenda. Indeed, the Nixon administration so distrusted civil servants and so feared their capacity to undermine White House policy that officials often raged against agency heads showing even the slightest inclination of "going native"— that is, being swayed by the bureaucracy to adopt positions contrary to those of the president.[14] The same tensions seem to be surfacing today, as reports suggest that President Trump's EPA Administrator is being pressed to bypass the civil service, hiring contractors in its stead to draft rules relaxing or altogether rescinding highly protective environmental regulations. The reason for this personnel workaround ought to be clear enough: the Trump administration is worried that the career civil servants will contest and resist the deregulatory directives.[15]

But even under significantly less adversarial circumstances, agency leaders may think of efficiency in terms of political expediency and thus may be willing to pay more money for the luxury of replacing rivalrous, possibly headstrong civil servants with contractors who owe their jobs and thus their loyalty to the agency leaders who hired them. Like the MasterCard ads used to say, perhaps circumventing the administrative separation of powers is, for agency heads, priceless.

Justice Antonin Scalia, no apologist for the welfare state, appreciated the politicized nature of contracting better than most. Contemplating the purported market efficiencies of prison privatization, Scalia struck a note of incredulity:

> It is fanciful to speak of the consequences of "market" pressures in a regime where public officials are the only purchaser, and [taxpayer] money the medium of payment. Ultimately, one [contractor] will be selected to replace

another . . . only if a decision is made by some *political* official not to renew the contract. This is a government decision, not a market choice. If state officers turn out to be more strict in reviewing the cost and performance of privately managed prisons than of publically managed ones, it will only be because they have *chosen* to be so. The process can come to resemble a market choice only to the extent that political actors *will* such resemblance—that is, to the extent that political actors . . . are willing to place considerations of cost and quality of service ahead of such political considerations.[16]

Again, we have largely missed this political dynamic (in which cost may or may not be a priority). Why? Perhaps we are easily seduced by assurances of technocratic governance and promises of smarter, businesslike government. Perhaps we are swayed instead by splashy and stunning accounts of contractor misdeeds and hence are quick to cast blame on the agents (that is, the venal contractors) rather than the goodly government principals who hired them—*even though privatization is often premised in part on a profound distrust of government officials and their motives.* Perhaps we, more so than Justice Scalia, too readily forget that agency heads may care more about accreting political authority and discretion than cutting costs or operating more economically efficiently—*even though privatization is further premised on the presumption that government personnel are insufficiently attentive to fiscal considerations.* And perhaps we have heretofore been insensitive to the legal and political implications of fragmented and internally rivalrous administrative power.

But once we comprehend *pax administrativa* and appreciate its architectural underpinnings—and once we recognize that agency heads (and their boss in the Oval Office) may talk the talk of cost savings but care principally about political expediency—we can see why, how, and to what effect the forces of privatization are marshaled. Specifically, we can see how those forces help consolidate, homogenize, and aggrandize that which has been disaggregated, diversified, and hamstrung. To the extent that such disaggregating, diversifying, and hamstringing was, and remains, constitutionally and normatively necessary, the present-day privatization of policy-making and policy-implementing powers represents a major challenge to our liberal democratic order.

For these reasons, our focus should be less on renegade contractors than on compliant contractors—and, even more critically, on the canny agency heads who hire them. The bigger, more constitutionally resonant risk that privatization poses is that private actors or their functional equivalents are brought in precisely because they are apt to be "yes" men and women. They are apt to be "yes" men and women precisely because, unlike the tenured civil servants, they serve at the pleasure of the agency heads. This is of course why I draw a tight connection between contractors and marketized (at-will) government employees. Simply put, privatization *qua* contracting or *qua* marketization weakens the administrative separation of powers, subduing if not supplanting the rivalrous, independent civil service and thereby concentrating control more fully in the hands of presidentially appointed agency leaders. And this is true regardless whether the agency heads are grand schemers or stumbled, like Woody Allen's Fielding Mellish, into the Privatization Revolution.

Note that this recasting of privatization's challenges and dangers has practical implications as well. Our current tools of oversight and control are all directed at deterring and corralling renegade contractors. Indeed, everyone—agency heads, government auditors, journalists, and even employees of contracting firms themselves—is on high alert for contractor fraud and corruption. And everyone presumably already has an incentive to curb such abuses. (I include employees of contracting firms as having such incentives because they may bring *qui tam* suits against their bosses for defrauding the government. Bringing such suits is not at all improbable given that the plaintiffs in *qui tam* cases stand to profit handsomely, receiving a hefty percentage of whatever monies the government recovers.[17])

By contrast, who is scrutinizing compliant service contractors? Who is questioning whether they are too dutiful? "Yes" men and women by definition tend not to stick out, and certainly agency leaders—best positioned to observe obsequiousness—have no reason to discipline those contractors who are helping the president's appointees consolidate previously fragmented administrative power. (Perhaps the remaining civil servants could, assuming that they're close enough and adroit enough to truly monitor. But even if the civil servants were sufficiently well perched—a big if, as I will explain below—their objections would likely fall on deaf ears. Given that contractors so clearly endanger the livelihood of civil servants, complaints by the career workforce would no doubt be dismissed as sour grapes.)

We thus must appreciate the limited effectiveness of our conventional tools of contract management. Designed to counteract contractor greed or sloth, they do little, if anything, to address dutiful compliance of the sort that looks harmless enough but has the effect of eroding the administrative separation of powers and distorting its underlying constitutional values.

Note too that this recasting of the privatization debates may help explain why many federal agencies continue to privatize with great zeal, notwithstanding their failure to show much by way of meaningful cost savings. One recent comprehensive study concluded that Washington generally "pays more when it farms out work" and that, on average, "contractors charged the federal government more than twice the amount it pays federal workers."[18] These additional costs incurred via contracting total billions of dollars annually.[19] Here, perhaps, is some support for the proposition that, when it comes to policymaking and policy-implementing responsibilities, agency heads care more about programmatic loyalty and political expediency than cost savings. That is, contractors may run up bills, within reason of course, so long as they keep championing the agency leadership's policies.

The claims I have been making about compliant contractors and cagey officials are, no doubt, still a little abstract. In what follows, I work out more precisely the nature of these privatization relationships and explain how exactly privatization subverts the administrative separation of powers. Again, my focus is on privatization in policy-laden spaces. I thus leave to the side consideration of privatization relationships that neither call for nor allow contractors to make or implement policy decisions. With respect to those latter, ministerial or custodial contracting relationships, sometimes a cigar is indeed just a cigar.

Deep Service Contracting and the Eluding of Legal Constraints

Recall once again that context matters. Many latter-day critics of *pax administrativa* objected to what they saw as a slow, expensive, and unresponsive civil service. They saw contracting out as a panacea, a way to maintain the services the public insisted upon without the concomitant costs and hassles attributed to the federal bureaucracy.[20] And they presented their arguments in terms of economic efficiency or cost savings.[21]

That politically neutral, technocratic story is all well and good. But, long before privatization came back into vogue, we had given up on the fiction of a purely technocratic approach to American public administration.[22] Such a fiction seems especially incredible when it comes to the politically appointed agency heads chosen to implement the president's partisan, time-sensitive agenda. These agency leaders surely need to worry about budgetary costs and technical excellence. But they need to worry even more about politically independent and sometimes defiant civil servants who threaten to delay, water down, or scuttle the president's initiatives.

Thus, though neoliberal economists and budget hawks no doubt champion outsourcing for the presumed fiscal benefits—and with an eye to shrink government—privatization in the hands of the president's agency heads may well be marshaled for very different ends. In Washington, political dexterity, loyalty, and control are quite often far more precious forms of currency.

Loyal, controllable contractors are important because those with day-to-day responsibilities over researching, designing, and implementing public policy have considerable discretion. They may, if they choose, carefully follow the instructions (or try to anticipate the preferences) of agency leaders. Or they may resist or recast those aims and instructions. Because of how they are paid, how they are regulated, and where they are situated in the political economy, the contractors who replace civil servants are, again, much more likely to be of the compliant, dutiful sort, even to the extent that they would help agency leaders evade burdensome legal constraints and nettlesome public obligations. They are apt to do so for several reasons.

First, Congress, appreciating the unique duties and responsibilities that attach to exercises of sovereign power, specially regulates the conduct of government employees. Such regulations—imposing procedural and substantive constraints on government employee behavior—rarely extend to those in the private sector.[23] Like overly caffeinated day traders, enterprising agency heads are quick to sniff out advantageous opportunities for arbitrage. Hence they privatize, swapping out heavily regulated and duty-bound civil servants for less regulated (and therefore more pliable) private contractors expected to advance the administration's agenda in a far more expeditious fashion.

Lest we think contracting changes just the relationship between agency heads and those tasked with carrying out administrative responsibilities, the turn to contractors also affects the relationship between the agency and the public at large. Specifically, contracting marginalizes public participation in the administrative process. State power passed through private conduits becomes much harder for the rest of civil society to monitor and challenge. The difficulty here is that the public has fewer statutory rights to access those private conduits, and the contractors have fewer statutory obligations to act inclusively, transparently, or rationally. Accordingly, deep service contracting directly sidelines civil servants, while also disempowering otherwise influential and rivalrous segments of civil society. As a result, contracting concentrates administrative power in agency heads, who take advantage of the fact that contractors are generally far less regulated and encumbered than are civil servants and better positioned than their government counterparts to keep civil society at bay.

Second, even where no such arbitraging opportunities exist—that is, where deep service contractors are legally required to abide by all of the procedural requirements and substantive directives government workers already follow—agency leaders may still prefer private actors over civil servants. This is because private actors are more likely than their tenured and politically insulated government counterparts to disregard or short-change those procedural and substantive constraints. As I discussed in Chapter 3, civil servants resemble judges in a dispositional sense. Civil servants have strong institutional and cultural reasons befitting their status as scientists, engineers, policy analysts, social workers, and lawyers for complying with congressional mandates and for insisting agency leaders do the same. Because they are tenured and salaried, civil servants have no monetary and few, if any, persistent political incentives that cut against their commitments to the rule of law and codes of professionalism.[24]

Service contractors are very differently situated. They have financial incentives to carry out their responsibilities more quickly, or at least more superficially. Shortchanging congressionally prescribed procedures and even professional obligations may enable contractors to reduce their operating costs—and increase profits.[25] As a result, contractors' pursuit of profits aligns with agency leaders' interests in evading onerous procedures, limiting extensive public engagement, and generally running their units with as few hassles, challenges, and complaints as possible. After all, agency leaders have a narrow window within which to accomplish their goals and no shortage of rivals who might try to resist or hijack the president's agenda.

Third, let's assume a contractor's pay was not tied to how quickly or effortlessly the firm completed its task. Such a contractor would nevertheless still be susceptible to political pressure to cut corners—certainly more so than tenured civil servants. Absent long-term, no-bid, or especially sticky contracts that effectively limit the degree to which agency heads can control and discipline their private hires,[26] contractors are given a very short leash.[27] Like those government workers hired and fired under the old spoils system (and unlike politically insulated civil servants), contemporary contractors can be readily terminated and easily replaced if they prove resistant or disagreeable.[28] As such, they have strong incentives to fiercely and steadfastly support agency leaders and their preference for political expediency.

All told (and, again, because agency leaders need to rely on *somebody* to help develop, administer, and enforce agency policies), the turn to contracting helps consolidate agency leaders' control. This effective fusion of political and commercial power reflects alliances of mutual convenience. Politically hungry agency heads and profit-driven contractors team up to weaken or altogether bypass the administrative rivalries that otherwise broaden and enrich agency decisionmaking, guard against abuse, and promote compliance with the rule of law and fidelity to the enduring constitutional principles underlying the separation of powers.

Deep Service Contracting and the Eluding of Political Constraints

A similar—indeed, largely overlapping—story can be told about compliant contractors and partisan politics. Contractors are motivated to be hired, anxious to be retained, and eager to be assigned additional, fee-generating responsibilities. They thus have every reason to internalize the agency chiefs' political priorities.[29] Again, civil servants are quite different. Civil servants are protected against politically motivated hiring and firing decisions. Civil servants enjoy such protection notwithstanding the ostensible inefficiencies job tenure invites—and do so precisely because we have long valued the rank-and-file's capacity to assert expertise, resist partisan overreaching, and further the mission of the agency.[30]

In this political context as much as the legal one discussed above, agency leaders' turn to deep contracting constitutes a double windfall. Deep contracting sidelines independent, contentious, and potentially adversarial civil servants, installing far more solicitous contractors in their stead. And deep contracting limits the role civil society can play in challenging agency actions, a consequence, again, of agency leaders shunting regulatory policy design and implementation into private (and thus far less accessible) corridors.

Needless to say, some civil servants invariably participate in the everyday management of government contracts. But we should not expect too much to come from their involvement. After all, agency leaders and their staffs are generally the ones who make the initial privatization decision and specify what tasks they want accomplished (and how). At that point, the civil servants' hands are relatively tied—as monitoring becomes the domain of procurement personnel, not policy analysts, social workers, engineers, or environmental technicians.[31]

These overseers are perhaps best characterized as auditors who are not necessarily well versed in the substantive policy or legal domains within which the contractors are working.[32] Consistent with what I said is the prevailing focus on greedy or corrupt contractors, these overseers are well positioned to ensure that the contractors are not being wasteful or fraudulent.[33] But they are not at all properly situated to detect, let alone confront, compliant contractors highly supportive of the administration's partisan agenda. Indeed, from the perspective of an auditor evaluating costs and customer satisfaction (*where the customer is the agency head*), such compliant contractors are likely viewed as the best, safest contractors.

Deep Service Contracting and Runaway Contractors (Circling Back to the Conventional Account)

What about contractual relationships that happen to fit the traditionally conceived doomsday pattern of runaway, greedy contractors? Frolics and detours surely do occur, notwithstanding the technologies designed to deter and counteract contractor deviations.

Though we understand these frolics and detours principally in terms of waste and fraud, we ought to also look at them as threats to the administrative separation of powers, albeit along a different dimension from the one described immediately above. In instances when agency leaders demonstrate enough strength and guile to oust contentious civil servants *though not enough to control contractors,* it is the contractors who may end up monopolizing administrative power.

Contractors may do any number of things if and when they monopolize administrative power. For instance, they may create extra work for themselves—and thereby extract more funds from the agencies in ways that do not automatically register as fraudulent. They may slack off on the job. Or they may pursue their own substantive policy interests, which is more of a possibility when contractors are not prototypical for-profit firms but rather mission-oriented nonprofits, such as faith-based contractors.[34] Regardless what choices contractors make, my structural claim is substantially the same: deep contracting enables administrative power to be consolidated in ways that limit inclusive, heterogeneous, and rivalrous engagement. And that is true no matter which set of actors amasses, possesses, or wields concentrated power.

Marketization of the Bureaucracy and the Eluding of Legal Constraints

Turning now to the marketization of the bureaucracy, recall that among marketization's chief effects is the stripping of government workers' civil service tenure protections. Marketization thus incapacitates one of the principal counterweights in administrative law's system of checks and balances. Like government contractors, marketized government workers no longer insulated from an incumbent administration's rewards and retributions are likely to be more compliant—anxious (though perhaps far from eager) to help advance the agency leaders' agenda.[35] Such marketized workers might very well be directed to cut legal corners. But even absent explicit pressure from the agency heads to do so, government workers shorn of civil service protections are apt to take a hint. They necessarily, and understandably, see themselves as temporary, vulnerable workers, just one misstep away from being fired.

What's more, the overall quality of the rank-and-file workforce suffers under marketization. Already the relatively modest marketization efforts under way are contributing to a "brain drain."[36] This will only intensify over time. Slowly but surely, the marketized workforce will prove less committed to the once prevailing ethos of bureaucratic professionalism[37]—and less forceful and capable stewards of rational public administration.

Marketization of the Bureaucracy and the Eluding of Political Constraints

To be sure, marketization enables more politicized administration, too. Without job security, marketized government workers seemingly share more in common with those party hacks hired under the old spoils system than they do with the professional, politically insulated civil servants of *pax administrativa*. As Jerry Mashaw reminds us, "In a spoils system both expertise and objectivity are suppressed by the demands of party loyalty and rewards for partisan political service."[38]

Even assuming (perhaps too charitably) that the intellectual architects of marketization are true technocrats who expect agency leaders to promote, demote, and terminate government workers based purely on those workers' competence and efficiency—as would generally be the case in the singularly profit-driven corporate realm—it is almost inevitable that any such technocratic endeavor will be distorted by partisan agency leaders more interested in whether those government workers are "loyalists" on questions of politics and policies. Indeed, in the weeks leading up to his inauguration, then President-Elect Trump requested the names of federal civil servants working on climate change policy. This was no random audit to evaluate the productivity of the federal workforce. Instead, it was a highly political power move. As the *New York Times* reported, that inquiry "on the heels of Mr. Trump's appointment of a climate change denialist to head the Environmental Protection Agency, sowed fears that the Trump administration would purge anyone involved in trying to curb the effects of climate change." True enough, a few days later, the presidential transition team addressed similarly pointed queries to the State Department, seeking information on the work its employees do to "promote gender equality, such as ending gender-based violence."[39] News accounts described tenured civil servants as "freaking out."[40] Imagine their reactions were they marketized, at-will workers.

The effects of marketization thus should be apparent enough, facilitating more politically (specifically, presidentially) dominated, less expert, and overall less rivalrous administrative governance. Quoting once again from Mashaw: "today we view the insertion of partisan politics into the routine administrative operations of government as a formula for inefficiency, administrative favoritism, and, possibly, lawlessness."[41] Yet this is precisely what's happening as marketization opens the door to a neo-patronage era.

Military Contracting and the Separation of Powers

The story of military contractors, briefly told in Chapter 5, in many respects tracks my account of deep domestic contracting. Pentagon leaders turn to contractors to replace and supplement active-duty servicemen and women. Active-duty troops are, of course, not part of the federal civil service. So contracting in this special context does not produce an identical weakening of the administrative separation of powers. Nevertheless, surprising parallels between uniformed military personnel and civil servants are worth considering.

First, like civil servants, U.S. troops are largely and intentionally politically aloof from the senior political leaders who run the Defense Department.[42] Watch the annual State of the Union Address. Amid the partisan posturing on both sides of the political aisle, top military officials, seated in the front row, generally appear stone-faced, more Buckingham Palace guards than administration cheerleaders. When partisan politics manages to trickle into the uniformed ranks, as happens from time to time—including, seemingly today[43]—it is a matter of grave concern for any number of reasons, one of which I address below. Second, like civil servants, most military officers are career officials who watch presidents, defense secretaries, and national security advisors come and go.[44] And, third, like civil servants, the uniformed military has a thick and distinctive professional culture. Indeed, the military's professional culture is far thicker, richer, and more respected than the one domestic career employees generally enjoy. This thick culture binds servicemen and women to their craft, colleagues, and corps. (One may recall the famous World War II studies demonstrating how unit cohesion and fidelity to their platoon mates sustained combat troops far more than did ideological or nationalistic commitments.[45])

No doubt these professional codes and sets of in-group loyalties can and do have the effect of emboldening military officers to stand together to push back on some dubious directives handed down by the civilian political leadership. Thus, the military (again, like the civil service) can be a crucial counterweight to politically appointed agency leaders, especially so-called chicken hawks, or senior civilians keen on combat deployments or air raids. Conventional wisdom has it that military insubordination is highly problematic, especially to the extent that military officers challenge the constitutional and cultural primacy of civilian control. But pushback is qualitatively different from insubordination. It is a far milder form of resistance and hardly poses a bona fide "threat to civilian control."[46]

Quite the contrary, military reservations, even objections, are conversation starters, not preludes to coups. Voicing or signaling misgivings may have the salutary effect of forcing greater deliberation and, ultimately, generating more thoughtful, less politicized policies.[47] Indeed, the biggest pushback the George W. Bush administration received on such questionable practices as "enhanced" interrogations came from the uniformed branches of the military, whose officers claimed that those techniques were abusive and inconsistent with the Army Field Manual and the laws of war. The uniformed military also invoked their own expertise, claiming that those techniques simply did not work well.[48] As Diane Mazur puts it:

> Top military lawyers understood that torture and abuse of prisoners would undermine military effectiveness and be a colossal mistake. Decades of hard-won experience had taught the military that abusive conduct in interrogation hurts the war effort, puts our own service members at risk of retaliation, and most simply, does not work because it produces unreliable information.[49]

By stark contrast, we should expect no such pushback from military contractors hired by the civilian Pentagon leadership. Just like their counterparts in domestic regulatory domains, military contractors are apt to be highly compliant and eager to remain in the good graces of those who pay their fees and decide whether to terminate or renew contracts. These military contractors are also far less stringently regulated than are the active-duty servicemen and women subject to the rather all-encompassing Uniform Code of Military Justice and to the prescriptions and proscriptions stipulated in regulatory codes such as the Army Field Manual.[50] It thus stands to follow that civilian Pentagon and White House officials seeking to push the envelope—recall Vice President Dick Cheney's Vader-esque post-9/11 claim that government needs to tap into its "dark side"—may be especially drawn to contractors with fewer legal and cultural scruples.[51] Indeed, by that logic, we should not have been surprised when contractors were assigned a good deal of rendition, detention, and "enhanced" interrogation work emanating out of the wars in Iraq and Afghanistan.[52]

In some ways, the weakening of the rivalry between civilian defense and military personnel (when compliant contractors replace generally apolitical and independent-minded military officers) seems far less disconcerting than the weakening of the rivalry between domestic agency heads and domestic civil servants. One reason is that, again, the interests of the military community should be subordinate to those of the civilian Pentagon—full stop. Another is that a sizable career civilian staff within the Defense Department is presumably already doing some work checking and counterbalancing the presidentially appointed agency leaders. Yet a third reason is that administrative law does not generally apply with as much force in matters of national defense and foreign affairs.[53] Perhaps, then, we ought not fret over the collapsing of a structure of checks and balances that never possessed legal and normative approbation in the first place.

But in a couple of other respects, the weakening of the civilian–military rivalry is just as bad, maybe worse. One such reason has to do with the very same fact that administrative law has extremely limited force in national security domains. Without the procedural safeguards that regularly apply in domestic regulatory settings, there is even greater need for rivalrous, inclusive deliberation to ensure rigorous, fair, and well-thought-out exercises of State power. Indeed, with a public largely excluded from the formation and implementation of national security policy (and a Congress and judiciary often compelled or choosing to remain on the sidelines), an insulated, expert, and professional bureaucratic military class provides a crucial third dimension of rivalry, reflecting the triangulation, however modest, of civilian political, civilian career, and military interests.

Needless to add, to the extent that the civilian career Pentagon workforce becomes marketized (which is already happening), the existence of an independent and potentially rivalrous uniformed military bureaucracy becomes that much more important.

The second reason why we should worry about a weakening of the civilian–military rivalry sounds more directly in constitutional law and politics. Here's one way domestic civil servants and military servicemen and women are very different. Simply put, everyone loves our troops. (I'll have more to say about this in Chapter 10.) We worry about troops, about their well-being, and about the well-being of the families who must cope with their absence. (Whether we provide adequate care for them and their families is of course another question.) So we—and the media and, to an extent, Congress—dwell on the size of forces deployed overseas, the length and number of tours of duty, and casualty counts. There is thus much for the president and for Pentagon leaders to gain by hiring contractors, even if these contractors weren't also more bureaucratically compliant.

Contractors are not nearly as visible (or seemingly important) to the American people as are active-duty servicemen and women. This matters because the White House and Pentagon can give the impression that our engagements overseas are less substantial than is actually the case. Indeed, we do not usually count contractors when it comes to tallying the size of a deployment. As Charles Tiefer, a member of Congress's Commission on Wartime Contracting in Iraq and Afghanistan, insisted, the Defense Department relied heavily on contractors "to keep the illusion of a low number of troops."[54]

Nor do we include contractors when it comes time to announce casualties.[55] Thus using contractors to lessen reliance on uniformed personnel allows political leaders to lighten the statistical and literal load otherwise placed on the politically salient class of servicemen and women. And this ability to redistribute and ultimately conceal the costs of war redound specifically to the benefit of Pentagon leaders and the White House. Simply put, public concern about the prosecution of a given war is dampened by, again in Tiefer's words, "the illusion" of a smaller, less expensive, and less risky engagement.

Accordingly, military contracting weakens a quasi-administrative separation of powers. And it weakens the constitutional separation of powers insofar as Congress is marginalized both in terms of the occlusion of information provided to the legislature and in terms of the circumvention of otherwise fully applicable military–specific laws such as the Uniform Code of Military Justice that Congress enacts to regulate troop behavior.

Privatization and Constitutional Structure

To treat the privatization of policymaking and policy-implementing responsibilities as a purely neutral, technocratic endeavor is to downplay history, law, and even the fundamentals of political psychology. Notwithstanding the anodyne labeling—be it efficiency enhancing or smarter government— the fact remains that privatization is a tool of great normative consequence. Agency heads cannot help but recognize the political and legal differences between, on the one hand, civil servants and, on the other, contractors and marketized employees. What's more, those agency heads have occasion to favor contractors and, again, marketized employees. They have occasion to do so in order to bypass independent, rivalrous civil servants otherwise poised to challenge, complicate, or directly undermine the president's agenda.

All in all, there is every reason to believe that political expediency, rather than discounted service provision, remains the coin of the policymaking realm. As such, we need to understand privatization for what it is or, at least, can be: a political power grab that has heretofore been largely concealed or overlooked by the balladeers of businesslike government who have sung privatization's praises as a decidedly technical undertaking that, if anything, weakens and shrinks rather than fortifies and enlarges the State.

Lest there be any doubt, privatization consolidates administrative and, by extension, constitutional power—and does so by supplanting, marginalizing, and obscuring would-be institutional counterweights. Specifically, agency leaders commingle State and market power, teaming up with politically compliant private (or privatized) actors; sidelining or defanging rivalrous civil servants; and co-opting or disenfranchising potentially rivalrous segments of civil society. As frustrating as those bureaucratic and popular rivals may be to agency leaders, we must remember that it is the contentious interplay among agency heads, civil servants, and the public writ large that has long legitimated the modern administrative state.

To be sure, one might respond by saying that privatization's proponents are doing precisely what the architects of administrative governance did a century ago—nothing more and nothing less. Administrative governance supplanted the all-too-clunky constitutional separation of powers. It did so by concentrating previously disaggregated legislative, executive, and judicial power. Today, privatization is following that very same blueprint, breaking free from what critics see as an administrative infrastructure that has itself grown too sclerotic and is now unable to respond to the instant demands for more immediate, responsive government than the administrative separation of powers allows.

But unlike the first go around, when the emerging administrative state responded to a clear societal need for broader and more powerful governing platforms to confront the demands and strains of modernity (and when we were able to use public legal architecture to redeem the framers' commitment to checking and balancing State power), the nascently privatized State seems far less necessary or coherent—and far more resistant to constitutional domestication. It will be the work of subsequent discussions to underscore the incoherence and incompatibility of a retooled, commercialized, marketized, or generally privatized State that is effectively run like a highly politicized business.

PART III

ESTABLISHING A SECOND
PAX ADMINISTRATIVA

So far I have explained the constitutional and normative virtues of the administrative separation of powers and addressed the strong and possibly existential threat contemporary privatization poses to our liberal republic. What's next? Where do we go from here? This part of the book maps a path forward, one that seeks to restore a well-functioning administrative separation of powers for the twenty-first century. It assigns responsibilities to scholars, judges, policymakers, and concerned citizens, calling upon all of us to help rebuild and support a second *pax administrativa*. This second *pax administrativa* is not a reflexive, nostalgic reversion to the good old days of the New Deal and Great Society. Like those who cobbled together the original administrative separation of powers, we too need to refashion as much as reproduce.

The work that remains ranges from the theoretical and abstract to the practical and concrete. I begin with a twenty-first-century defense of the separation of powers. This is my point of entry for the simple reason that I do not—and cannot—take it for granted that we *should* rededicate ourselves to a system of separated and checked power. I do not take it for granted because so much has changed since the framers constructed that original tripartite edifice. The threat of dictatorship, so palpable in the late-eighteenth century, may seem equal parts quaint and absurd today. In addition, the advent of the party system and the sharpening of the rivalry between the dominant political parties may at times appear to supplant the institutional rivalries that animate the separation of powers. Lastly, the demands for a far more powerful, nimble, and rapidly responsive government (than the one the framers envisioned) surely invite more concentrated amalgams of State power. Given these reasons to question the continuing relevance and utility of separation of powers, Chapter 7 serves as an apologia, explaining why the tripartite architecture remains viable and desirable.

Having presented the case for a twenty-first-century separation of powers, I turn in Chapter 8 to recast the relationship between and among the constitutional and administrative rivals. Here I show that there is considerable room for improvement over the first *pax administrativa*. For much of the twentieth century, the constitutional branches were expected to intervene regularly and forcefully in the administrative arena. Perhaps such aggressive interventions reflected a lack of appreciation for the administrative separation of powers as a self-regulating ecosystem unto itself. Or perhaps such interventions reflected a concerted effort on the part of legislators and presidents alike to unilaterally direct administrative power. Whatever the explanation, such exercises of aggressive, top-down control were and remain unnecessary; even worse, they were and remain destabilizing. Like when adults take sides in what had previously been an evenly matched kids' game, these top-down interventions frustrate and skew administrative rivalries, generally pulling administrative policy in the direction of the most powerful constitutional meddler. Knowing this, a precondition of a second *pax administrativa* must be that the constitutional branches act—or are made to act— custodially rather than opportunistically, working to ensure a healthy, well-functioning administrative separation of powers that is both normatively and constitutionally legitimate.

Such a reconceptualization of the old (the framers') and new (the administrative) separation of powers must be supported by jurisprudential and legislative measures that give meaning and effect to this custodial relationship. Chapter 9 urges jurisprudential reforms, emphasizing how existing and newly proposed legal doctrines can do more to recognize, support, and reinforce a well-functioning administrative separation of powers.

Chapter 10, in turn, takes up the even harder legislative task. Here I argue that it is incumbent upon the political branches to participate in efforts to strengthen the administrative partisans and sharpen administrative rivalries. I adumbrate a list of policy reforms—undertaken, quite possibly, only because the newly custodially oriented courts so direct—to enrich the civil service, expand and facilitate public participation, and reduce opportunities for bad-faith engagement that delays and subverts administrative governance. The goal, again, is to recommit to and improve upon the first *pax administrativa*; reinforce the intellectual, architectural, and constitutional foundations of the administrative separation of powers; and steel this regime against future threats from would-be putschists.

7

The Separations of Powers in the
Twenty-First Century

Notwithstanding my claims that the administrative separation of powers is what describes and helps legitimate the modern administrative state, one might query whether the very model of separating and checking still makes sense, if it ever did. This chapter defends the separating and checking of State power at a time when scholars and policymakers alike have been thinking long and hard about the relevance, efficacy, and normative underpinnings of such arrangments. In what follows, I make the case for embracing and indeed fortifying multiple lines of constitutionally resonant checks and balances. Precisely because I will be addressing both the constitutional separation of powers and the administrative separation of powers—and, on occasion, looping in additional lines of separation—I employ the perhaps infelicitous shorthand "separations" to refer to multiple systems of disaggregated powers.

My account here is divided into two sections. First, I consider the necessity, propriety, and desirability of separating and checking State power today. This section responds to claims that we no longer need to worry about State tyranny; that the constitutional separation of powers has proven too effective—that is, too readily enabling of gridlock; that rivalrous parties, rather than rivalrous institutions, define the terms of political and legal contestation; and that the collapsing of the constitutional and administrative separations of powers is in keeping with broader consolidating trends practiced at home and overseas.

Second, I consider challenges from the other direction: whether we should do even more by way of checking, balancing, and disaggregating State power; or whether we should construct a tertiary system of separation of powers to give shape and constitutional legitimacy to a highly privatized, marketized State.

Resisting Calls to Abandon the Separations of Powers

The Banality of Twenty-first Century Administrative Tyranny. Some will no doubt contend that consolidated government today does not raise the same specter of tyranny—that is, *real, literal, dictatorial tyranny*—that animated a revolutionary generation traumatized by monarchism yet also wary of mob rule.[1] There is much force to this argument. Scholars such as Eric Posner and Adrian Vermeule claim that the contemporary American fear of government abuse—what they label "tyrannophobia"—is overwrought.[2] Vermeule goes further, insisting that we should abandon what he calls precautionary constitutionalism, a constitutional mindset innately distrustful of State power and moved to "[ward] off the worst case." We should do so in favor of a less risk-averse theory of optimizing constitutionalism.[3]

President Obama seemed to agree. Dismayed by exaggerated, almost paranoid, fears of State tyranny, Obama worried that such fears compromised the governing process.[4] Specifically, the president lamented the frequency with which ordinary policymaking decisions would get "wrapped up in broader debates" and "conspiracy theories" about whether "the federal government is oppressive."[5] But just because fears of real, literal, dictatorial tyranny seem misplaced in the United States today—and, to be clear, seem so even after the election of a new president who has at times shown a blatant disregard for the rule of law—it does not follow that the need for the separation or separations of powers has therefore diminished. It does not follow precisely because State power is exponentially greater in modern times than it had ever been in the eighteenth and nineteenth centuries—and individuals' reliance on the State for legal protections, legal rights (such as government licenses, permits, and contracts), and welfare benefits is likewise exponentially greater.[6]

Though there is now no credible threat of a military coup, there remain compelling reasons to fret over the altogether matter-of-fact power of the State to act arbitrarily and abusively in countless ways, often at the touch of a button, and often against those already most marginalized by society. Consider the wrongful denial of life-sustaining welfare or disability payments; disclosure of sensitive personal, health, and financial records; termination of a government-issued license to practice a profession or operate a business; designation as too dangerous to live in public housing; and assignment to the Kafka-esque No-Fly List. Consider too the panoptic surveillance of individuals' whereabouts, commercial transactions, and electronic and telephonic communications; the opportunistic exercise of eminent domain power; and the decision to exact civil forfeitures (rather than initiate more procedurally robust and transparent criminal prosecutions).

We find ourselves in a time and place where tyranny no longer threatens to storm the city walls. Rather what we have are more prosaic forms of abuse. Oz-like officials—petty, often apologetic, and even well intentioned—may hide behind the machinery of Big Data to classify individuals as unworthy, unimportant, menacing, or deviant.[7] With a nod to Hannah Arendt, today's threats come from any number of officious, overburdened, or ideologically reckless administrators of high and low rank. The very *banality* of administrative abuse, perhaps even more so than a cabalistic junta commanding a tank division, demands continued vigilance (from both the Right[8] and Left[9]) of the sort *pax administrativa*'s architectural scheme promotes.

These claims are no doubt apt to be unsatisfying to those who think we suffer from tyrannophobia. Return once more to Vermeule. Vermeule doesn't deny the possibility of tyranny, let alone government abuse. Yet he nevertheless urges us not to go overboard in taking preventive, precautionary measures, particularly if such measures either preclude us from realizing the benefits of "vigorous government action"[10] or perversely invite tyranny insofar as "the separation of powers gridlocks the lawmaking system and thus create[s] pent-up public demand for strong extraconstitutional action."[11]

Recall, however, that the separations of powers are more than simply tools to guard against tyranny. They also promote and enable democratic pluralism.[12] Specifically, constitutional and administrative tripartitism helps accommodate and even harmonize the many different voices and values that the American political and legal community comprises. Constitutional optimization characterized by "vigorous government action" must therefore stand up not just against the remote threat of tyranny but also against the far greater and more immediate danger that inclusive, rivalrous forms of deliberation and contestation are undercut. Here then we can see how my constitutional harmonization (via the separations of powers) approach differs from constitutional optimization (via, presumably, the streamlining and consolidating of government power): the former prizes the inputs of pluralistic, multipolar government rather than the policy outputs. This *voice and value harmonization* component of the constitutional and administrative separations of powers—again, something I introduced in Chapter 3—further informs much of what follows.

Gridlock, Governing, and Culture. There are other reasons why some might view today as a particularly imprudent time to reinforce the separations of powers. In recent years, budgets haven't passed. Outdated laws haven't been repealed or revised. Judicial nominees haven't been accorded hearings. And executive offices requiring Senate confirmation have long remained vacant. Given the intense level of so-called gridlock afflicting the relations between the political branches during good chunks of the Clinton, George W. Bush, and Obama presidencies, shouldn't we welcome any opportunity to start anew—and scrap rather than reinforce an edifice that, at the very least, does not seem to comport well with contemporary political customs and imperatives? Those who have struck such notes of skepticism, including Sanford Levinson, Louis Michael Seidman, and Juan Linz,[13] would seemingly be quick to question my valorization of *pax administrativa*. Perhaps these skeptics would wonder whether it was the initial architects of the modern administrative state who got it right when they first consolidated legislative, executive, and judicial power. Or perhaps these skeptics would conclude that the system of administrative separation of powers (which later generations of administrative lawyers constructed) worked for a while—but no longer.

To some extent, I already answered this challenge in Chapter 3. But let me elaborate further and respond directly to the suggestion that the likelihood of government gridlock undermines the case for a second, twenty-first-century *pax administrativa*.

For starters, gridlock, in the broad sense of the term, is frustrating but not necessarily pathological. Inaction need not be a bad or disreputable thing. Gridlock may instead, as Josh Chafetz argues, be the natural state of affairs when a polity, such as ours, is still working through difficult choices: "[w]e may simply declare the absence of legislative action to be 'gridlock,' but without some evidence that a widespread public consensus around a particular course of action has failed to result in action, we should hesitate to describe it as democratically dysfunctional."[14] We are, after all, a political and legal community that has generally valued (and not just paid lip service to) diversity along many dimensions. If so, gridlock is a necessary byproduct of our cautious approach to governing and of our reluctance to regulate or legislate unless and until broad-based buy-in is secured.[15]

That said, perhaps an even more defiant response is warranted. That is, perhaps I am too quick to concede the pervasiveness of gridlock, which, as economist Tyler Cowen suggests, may be more illusory than real. Cowen contends that what we call gridlock are quite natural periods of retrenchment that arise only after moments of great and often frenetic legislative activity. Cowen points to the construction of the post-9/11 national security state, the economic bailouts of 2008 and 2009, the passage of the landmark Dodd-Frank Act of 2010, and the enactment of the monumental Affordable Care Act of 2010—and notes an almost hangover-like sense of uncertainty and reappraisal that comes hard on the heels of those transformative assertions of federal power.[16] Political scientist R. Shep Melnick concurs. Melnick argues that the legislative achievements of the first few years of the Obama presidency rival that of "the famed 89th Congress of 1965–66"[17]—the Congress that put into effect many of President Lyndon Johnson's Great Society programs. It is a legislative pace that simply cannot be sustained, if not because the nation's politics call for moderation and reassessment then because of the pressures these programs put on the federal fisc.

Moreover, where gridlock exists, persists, and turns pathological—and thus no longer reflects a transitional phase, yet-unresolved debate, lingering uncertainty, or simply good-faith disagreement—it is unlikely solely or even primarily attributable to some latent structural constitutional infirmity that took two centuries to reveal itself. Rather, the pathology seemingly reflects some sort of cultural malady, a desire on the part of elected officials to no longer work for the public good but instead to subvert the process of governing. If so, the answer lies not in scrapping the remarkably resilient (and, as I have been arguing, supple) systems of seperation. Instead, it is to reinvigorate what has often been a very healthy, civil, and productively contentious political culture—a culture that, I hasten to add, has survived other periods of episodic dysfunction and, yes, seemingly impassable gridlock and come out the other side.[18] (President James Madison, Mr. Separation of Powers himself, no doubt appreciated the irony in the following note from his treasury secretary: "Measures of vital importance have been and are defeated [in Congress]" and there is no way "to produce the requisite union of views and action between the several branches of government."[19])

But let's go further. Even conceding that bad-faith gridlock between the political branches is here to stay, it does not follow that such gridlock will seep into the administrative domain—the very domain I am focused on. Full-blown civil wars between agency leaders and civil servants have shown themselves to be exceptionally rare, even when there are wide partisan or programmatic chasms between the president's appointees and the career staffs. Thus the pitched battles that seemingly tie the legislative process up in knots do not appear to readily spill into (and similarly bottle up) the administrative arena. To the extent that intra-administrative disagreements arise, as they certainly do, they tend to be resolved more constructively—and with far less political grandstanding—engendering more moderate expressions of administrative power that are the result of compromise between political leaders and expert staffs.

Thus, the existence (for argument's sake) of pathological gridlock at the constitutional level only underscores the need for a robust administrative separation of powers. After all, during legislative impasses, more—and more serious—federal responsibilities are routed through administrative agencies.[20] President Obama, for one, was quite explicit and unapologetic in his use of agencies to carry out tasks ordinarily entrusted to Congress. For example, Obama directed agencies to implement his Clean Power Plan, to more fully regulate gun ownership, and to follow his "deferred action" plan regarding the nondeportation of undocumented children and families.[21] In all three instances, the president cited congressional obstinacy as grounds for acting through administrative channels:[22] "if Congress won't act soon . . . I will. I will direct my Cabinet to come up with executive actions we can take, now and in the future, to reduce pollution, prepare our communities for the consequences of climate change, and speed the transition to more sustainable sources of energy."[23]

Where a president attempts to bypass a hostile, lumbering, or simply indecisive Congress, the existence of an administrative separation of powers stands as an especially prized safeguard—a check against unfettered presidential power and another means of preserving and promoting multipolar and contentious policy formulation and implementation. Simply stated, the administrative separation of powers ensures that when the president channels legislative-like responsibilities into the administrative domain, inclusive, rivalrous, and heterogeneous governance perdures—and checks and balances are preserved notwithstanding the apparent circumvention of the constitutional separation of powers.[24] This is true regardless whether the president wants to ramp up or scale down federal regulatory power. Indeed, the ease with which President Trump has been able to reverse many key Obama directives is a testament to the robustness of the administrative separation of powers and to the pitfalls of proceeding without administrative consensus. Because Obama did not—and perhaps could not—secure administraive consensus on key policy questions, his directives regularly took the form of policy memos rather than legally binding rules, which new presidents cannot readily rescind.

Powers over Parties (Still). Exacerbating what I am suggesting is a cultural, not structural, problem with respect to the constitutional separation of powers is the way in which party loyalties are seemingly supplanting institutional ones. Some careful political commentators and legal scholars, including Daryl Levinson and Richard Pildes, insist that contemporary American political and legal contestation is defined by a "separation of parties, not powers."[25]

What this means is that we experience moments when Congress and the executive are insufficiently rivalrous.[26] They are insufficiently rivalrous when the president and the majority of Senate and House members are all from the same political party—and they all privilege their party affiliations over their institutional ones. Recall the almost complete absence of congressional investigations into allegations of executive overreaching in the George W. Bush administration—an absence widely attributed to Senate and House oversight committees being run most of the time by Republican chairpersons loyal to the sitting president.

We also experience other moments when the rivalries are preternaturally ferocious. These moments arise when divided government reigns. In light of this claim that party rather than institutional affiliation represents the chief dividing line in American political and legal culture, perhaps it no longer makes sense to recommit to the already weakened separation-of-powers scaffolding.

But here too I think worries about the constitutional separation of powers being outmoded or of ancillary importance are somewhat overstated. It is true that Madison and his fellow framers did not take much stock in political parties.[27] But parties became an important fixture in the Republic's infancy and have remained so ever since. For much of those now two hundred-plus years, the separations of powers *and parties* have coexisted in a more or less consonant fashion.[28]

Moreover, such critiques about party identities supplanting institutional ones generally zero in on Congress. Even if members of Congress seem more tethered to their party than to their institution, it isn't clear that presidents feel the same way. Recent presidents, Republican and Democratic alike, tend to advance distinctly presidentialist interests—specifically, that of an *imperial president.*[29] Indeed there is no better example of such a presidentialist than President Obama. As a senator and presidential candidate, Obama fiercely criticized President George W. Bush, specifically attacking Bush's penchant for exercising unilateral authority when it came to war powers and regulatory matters.[30] But as president, Obama seemingly embraced many of those imperial tendencies[31]—at some cost to his standing in liberal circles.[32]

In any event, even assuming that the "separation of parties, not powers" crowd is right with respect to what happens on the constitutional stage,[33] its argument nevertheless seems to have less force in the administrative arena. This is so because civil servants and members of civil society are far less attached to political parties than are members of Congress and even the president. As discussed above, civil servants have strong institutional ties to their agencies and to their colleagues. These tenured employees have less of a need or opportunity to curry favor with political parties. By law, civil servants are not even permitted to engage in partisan politicking. And, in practice, they are at best apolitical and at worst either ideologically diverse (amongst themselves) or contrarian vis-à-vis agency leaders and various segments of civil society. That is to say, administrative rivalries are likely to remain sharp even where there is considerable ideological overlap between civil servants and those running the agency. The administrative separation of powers thus may do more than simply complement or stand in place of the constitutional separation of powers. It may serve as a bit of an improvement, achieving the normative ends that the original constitutional system endeavored but at times has failed to foster.

Let's consider a seemingly unpropitious scenario, one in which we might expect the administrative separation of powers to (likewise) fall by the wayside. Assume, for example, a progressive Democrat wins the presidency and appoints a like-minded administrator to run the EPA. Assume too that the EPA's rank-and-file tend to be progressive, pro-environment types. Notwithstanding the seemingly shared affinities between the political leadership and the civil servants, the administrator is likely to encounter significant pushback from the true-believer civil servants. This is because the White House will from time to time prefer any number of other fiscal, diplomatic, or political objectives to environmental ones—and the appointed agency head will have to fall in line and accept the president's decision. As a matter of fact, any EPA administrator, including this hypothetical one, is likely to be a political heavyweight in her own right and quite attuned to the multiplicity of demands placed on the White House, any one of which might push environmental initiatives onto the back burner.

By contrast, the civil servants within the EPA are not privy to the president's grand strategic machinations; nor are they bound to endorse them. They will continue to insist that *their* mission is of central, even overriding, importance and ought to be furthered irrespective of the competing political demands that concern the president and, by extension, her loyal EPA head. Accordingly, whether because they are apolitical, politically diverse, provincially minded, or simply have different institutional demands and commitments than their ostensibly like-minded agency heads, the large and critically tenured workforce is unlikely to align perfectly with agency leaders or with the public writ large—and thus remains well positioned to push and pull on administrative policies.

Turning to civil society, this third member of the administrative triumvirate is itself ideologically diverse, less committed to parties than to particular causes, and far less hierarchical than Congress. Compared to Congress, the general public is much less partisan. A whopping 43 percent of Americans are political independents, with Democrats (30 percent) and Republicans (26 percent) trailing the unaffiliated by a good margin.[34] (One suspects the number of independents will only rise in the wake of the heterodox presidential campaigns mounted by Bernie Sanders and Donald Trump in 2016.) Thus we ought not expect party affiliations to be as relevant when individuals and groups constituting civil society participate directly in the administrative domain, especially when public administrative engagement—unlike public political engagement via elections—entails weighing in on single, discrete issues (rather than a unified slate of issues).

What's more, those public participants in administrative governance who align themselves with one of the main political parties are nevertheless subject to many fewer and much weaker party-disciplining mechanisms of the sort that bind members of the House and Senate.[35] We can therefore conclude that some and perhaps a large segment of the broad-ranging public has an interest in opposing (and, importantly, has license and authority to oppose) practically every action agency leaders or civil servants take. Accordingly, it is difficult to imagine party politics supplanting administrative rivalries as they sometimes appear to do on the constitutional stage.

The Consolidation of Powers. We're not out of the woods quite yet. Critics may contend that the political and epistemological demands placed on the modern American welfare state are much more consistent with (and possibly dependent upon) concentrated, consolidated State power. These critics may push further, emphasizing that we are already concentrating, consolidating, and centralizing State power along several important and historically relevant dividing lines. Viewed from that perspective, administrative fragmentation of the sort I'm endorsing is a step in the wrong direction.

As a descriptive matter, these critics are right. Donald Kettl describes the United States as a "tectonic nation," in which federal–state, public–private, and national–international roles and responsibilities are crashing into one another.[36] Indeed, there is seemingly inexorable pressure to concentrate State power in both national security and domestic regulatory domains—to overcome what many see as the once quaint but now frustrating lines of separation that have long marked us as a presidential, federal, and liberal State (with an ample and robust private sector).

Consider the national security landscape before and after 9/11. If only there weren't so many lines of separation—or so the pro-consolidation account goes; if only there had been better communication between and among siloed intelligence agencies; if only there hadn't been a "wall" separating the FBI officials conducting national security investigations from those working on ordinary criminal investigations; if only the states and the feds had done more in the way of coordination and cooperation; if only the private sector had been more fully mobilized and deputized to help detect terrorist plots; and if only agency heads had possessed the authority to summarily fire mediocre or apathetic career personnel.

In response to this litany of *if only*s, government officials have narrowed the divide across agencies and within agencies. They have also narrowed the federal–state and public–private divides. For example, the national security landscape now boasts a consolidated Department of Homeland Security, which integrates twenty-two legacy departments and units from across the federal administrative expanse,[37] and a far more centralized intelligence network.[38] Fusion centers and Joint Terrorism Task Forces link local, state, and federal counterterrorism work.[39] A more unified investigatory framework enables ready collaboration across what previously had been considered the national security/law enforcement "wall."[40] Internally streamlined—a euphemism, perhaps, for marketized—agencies have converted their civil servants into at-will employees. And countless collaborations invite, if not obligate, private involvement in military, counterterrorism, intelligence, and emergency disaster relief operations.[41]

The apparent imperative to consolidate—to ease or erase separations—extends beyond national security domains. As we have explored, marketization of the bureaucracy reduces intra-agency rivalries and concentrates control over regulatory and welfare programs in the hands of agency leaders. Pervasive use of government contracting and broad reliance on private deputies fuse public and private power. And efforts to combine energy and environmental policy[42] as well as to coordinate the activities of nearly a dozen financial regulatory departments suggest an uptick in inter-agency consolidation.[43]

Those championing the consolidation of historically separated powers are aiming to expand and extend the State's reach and to streamline the governing process. Obviously, there is some overlap between the instant arguments in favor of consolidation and those discussed earlier vis-á-vis overcoming gridlock. But the arguments in favor of consolidation are not nearly as dependent on fears of bad faith or obstructionism. Rather, the drive to consolidate seems more in keeping with Vermeule's optimizing constitutionalism insofar as it reflects frustration with the ordinary transaction costs associated with having to work across jurisdictional boundaries. Furthermore, this drive to consolidate seems to signal a concomitant desire to build on common strengths, combine distinct specialties, and minimize the possibility that things or people fall through the cracks of an otherwise disaggregated (but not necessarily pathologically divisive) State.[44]

Clearly, evidence of consolidation, concentration, and centralization of State power abounds. But, if anything, that evidence renders my project all the more urgent. Our constitutional system is undeniably one of multidimensional separations of powers—or, perhaps, as Robert Cover called it, "complex concurrency."[45] These multidimensional separations of powers are readily gleaned not only from our unmistakable textual commitment to tripartitism and federalism but also from the structural disaggregation of public and private power, church and State power, civilian and military power, and—as this book argues—intra-agency administrative power. Our system is therefore not just one of belts and suspenders, as if our only safeguards were the constitutional separation of powers and federalism. It is also one of Velcro, elastic waistbands, bungee cords, and safety pins.[46]

Again, our separations of powers do not, and need not, rest entirely on anti-tyranny grounds. There is also the constitutional harmonization imperative: our multidimensional separations of powers amplify numerous and varied voices—and sponsor (or safeguard) numerous and varied participatory platforms and venues, including town halls, courtrooms, voting booths, soap boxes, engineering labs, newsrooms, military barracks, church pulpits, and, yes, markets.

Thus, precisely because we find ourselves today at a critical moment when multiple lines of separation are simultaneously being collapsed, we surely better cling to whatever separation remains. My claim here is twofold. For starters, it isn't altogether clear that there is much comprehensive thought or analysis given to the simultaneous collapsing of multiple lines of separation. Those seeking to consolidate power may well be focusing on only one particular dimension. If so, they are considering the pros and cons of public–private, federal–state, intra-agency, *or* inter-agency consolidation against what they presume to be an otherwise static and still quite fragmented backdrop.

Thinking that other thick webs of checks and balances remain operational elsewhere (that is, that there still are suspenders and Velcro in place), these engineers of consolidation are especially emboldened to aggressively streamline. Against that presumptively static and still quite fragmented backdrop, any such collapsing of a single line of separation represents little more than a minor incursion on a constitutional system that does indeed prize separation.

But the truth of the matter may well be that these engineers are all very much like characters in an O. Henry story: each streamlining along a single line of constitutionally resonant separation—and unaware that others are doing similar things elsewhere. This perverse *Gift of the Magi* or, more literally, this example of micro-rationality in a world of macro-chaos, produces a number of discrete, individually modest (at least for argument's sake) incursions on only private, local, civilian, or religious autonomy. Altogether, however, these modest incursions add up to a major one as the president and her agency heads accumulate power along multiple dimensions, picking up bits and pieces from co-opted states and municipalities, from dragooned corporations, and from a marketized, defanged federal workforce now effectively serving at the pleasure of the presidential administration. Accordingly, the urgency to preserve some rivalrous separation, rather than go with the (consolidating) flow, is quite acute once we realize the aggregate, reinforcing effects of parallel efforts to dismantle many of the major lines of separation undergirding our constitutional architecture.[47]

The claims made immediately above presuppose an unwitting overinvestment in consolidation, a *tragedy of the separations' commons* as it were. But even if that presupposition is wrong—that is, even if multidimensional consolidation is part of a grand, comprehensively conceived agenda to indeed invest heavily in consolidation—the case for insisting on an administrative separation of powers remains a strong one. It remains strong if for no other reason than we need to nurture heterogeneous, rivalrous engagement consistent with our constitutional and normative commitments to pluralistic, inclusive, and limited government. More to the point, the administrative separation of powers is, perhaps, the most valuable form of separation. If only one of these lines of separation is to perdure, it very well ought to be the intra-administrative one.

Given the overarching themes of the book, my answer here may seem altogether self-serving. So I want to be clear on the reasoning: Unlike other forms of separation, such as inter-agency and federal–state separation, the administrative separation of powers is the last line of defense. A giant consolidated agency—a product of inter-agency consolidation and federal–state consolidation—is not necessarily problematic if that giant agency remains internally fragmented, with power triangulated among agency heads, civil servants, and the public writ large. In such circumstances, the exercises of State power will still reflect the meaningful participation of a range of democratic and countermajoritarian actors, preserving and promoting the fundamentally rivalrous and inclusive design of our constitutional Republic.

But a small agency that has succumbed to intra-administrative consolidation, while successfully resisting inter-agency and federal–state consolidation, is still a problematic one. It is still problematic for the simple reason that it is internally unitary and thus dangerously imbalanced in ways that allow politicized agency heads, insulated mandarins, or selfish interest groups to monopolize the exercise of State power. Thus, at least in a world such as ours in which State power runs primarily through administrative agencies, the most basic safeguards of pluralism, democratic accountability, and compliance with the rule of law operate at the sub-atomic level—*within* triangulated agencies. This assures rivalrous, contentious, and heterogeneous checking and balancing regardless of the size, shape, and jurisdictional sweep of the agency itself.

American Exceptionalism. The last objection to twenty-first-century separations of powers relies less on what's happening at home than on what's happening abroad. There the questions are straightforward, even impatient: Why cling to the constitutional separation of powers? Why remain faithful to this specific structural arrangement? And why, in particular, recommit to a seemingly easily forgotten administrative separation of powers when so many constitutional theorists and drafters around the world have recognized separation and fragmentation as unstable and undesirable?[48] This line of critique picks up on the writings of scholars who endorse parliamentary forms of government[49] and whose empirical work documents the declining popularity of American-style, presidentialist systems in favor of more unitary ones characterized by strong legislative control over a prime minister and cabinet.[50]

Given recent events, perhaps such pro-parliamentary arguments suddenly seem less compelling, here and elsewhere. The stunning Trump victory at home—and the surprising electoral showings of, among others, France's National Front, the United Kingdom's Independence Party, and Austria's Freedom Party[51]—may serve in fact as a cautionary tale, chastening those who've been so eager to discard old-fashioned checks and balances as a relic of more perilous times.

But even assuming that the instant pivot to a populist, authoritarian Right isn't dramatic or serious enough to shatter the faith of pro-parliamentary advocates (and leaving aside the practically insurmountable logistical and constitutional obstacles associated with converting the

United States into a parliamentary republic), there are still compelling reasons for holding tight to our separations of powers. Consider four:

First, we are government skeptics, particularly when it comes to the power of Washington. We have always been and perhaps always will be. There are unhealthy and healthy forms of such skepticism. Unhealthy forms surface from time to time in certain strains of anti-government rhetoric and action: odious conspiracy theories, campaigns of delegitimation, separatist movements, and survivalist militias. Healthy forms, by contrast, permeate and inform our structural architecture: the many dimensions of separation of powers. Here too we see the virtues of tripartite government beyond the simple anti-tyranny principle. It is much harder to reject a government when it is clear that this government's actions reflect sufficiently broad and deep support to overcome our constitutional system's many vetogates.

Second, we are government pluralists. This is, perhaps, a nicer way of saying that we are, now as much as ever before, truly divided about the type of government we want. Our multiple systems of separating and checking enable us to remain a pantheistic people when it comes to our political religion. Like Olympus or Valhalla, the American political pantheon is a crowded one, with notions of liberty, equality, democracy, and expertise jostling with one another and vying for supremacy. The constitutional and administrative separations of powers accommodate this pluralism, allowing various values to compete with one another in fluid, dynamic arenas. The end result of such competition is a good deal of compromise, some stalemates, and a cycling among values. There are no big winners or losers, and everyone lives to fight another day. In short, because of the multiple separations of powers, we can govern ourselves without having to definitely and permanently answer the central question of what kind of State we want—and concomitantly without having to lock in a strong form of majoritarianism, mandarinism, or the like. As a result, we minimize the risk of unlawful or extraconstitutional contestation, guard against permanent disaffection, and keep most of the unhealthier forms of skepticism at bay.

Third, and related, we are a highly diverse political community. This diversity, along regional, religious, ethnic, and racial lines, may partially explain why there is so much political disagreement and even skepticism. Such diversity isn't necessarily as apparent or accounted for in many other parts of the democratic or developed world.[52] In no small part because of our separations of powers, the United States is by and large able to honor and protect this diversity.

To be clear, I'm not saying America is free from discrimination or that the separations of powers are a cure-all. But such discrimination hasn't been part of our national constitutional project for some time—and, again, our commitment to separating and checking stands in the way of any one particular faction, however ascendant, giving great legal effect to resurgent nativist, racist, or misogynistic tendencies. Compared to Westminster-style parliamentary systems and unitary systems, a federal, presidential system such as ours provides, at least in theory, greater opportunities for different and varied voices to find their way into the corridors of State power—*if for no other reason than that there are more corridors.*

Perhaps the best way to appreciate American exceptionalism is by recognizing how fundamentally different the United States is from many other Western, liberal nation-states—including along the three dimensions just described: State skepticism, value pluralism, and demographic diversity. These differences help explain why the United States, law and logistics aside, isn't readily comparable to many parliamentary-style governments.

Indeed, if anything, it is more sensible to compare the United States with the European Union (EU). In terms of size, economic power, and philosophical and demographic diversity, the United States is more like the EU than it is like any of the latter's member states. The comparison goes further. EU skepticism is common, and the political culture of Europe is necessarily pluralistic, sweeping in the values, customs, and identities of Poles, Swedes, Spaniards, Croats, and Cypriots. Tellingly, the EU is far from a streamlined parliamentary system. Rather, as observers such as Francis Fukuyama note, the EU suffers from an American-like affliction of overlapping, checking, and separated powers.[53]

Some find such checking and separating frustrating. Yet, all things considered, the EU architecture makes much sense. The EU's extra and cross-cutting layers of institutional rivalries and procedural constraints serve as an important, and possibly necessary, concession to the realities of a broad and complex twenty-odd-nation confederation. This confederation is, again, more like the American Republic than it is like most of its constituent (and largely parliamentary) nation-states. And it is precisely because of its many structural vetogates that the EU, like the United States, can be trusted to exercise considerable power in the name of a demographically, culturally, and politically diverse public that harbors residual skepticism about a European State.

Fourth, there is the issue of a distinctively American administrative pluralism and the need to carry the constitutional separation of powers *all the way forward* into the administrative realm. I attribute this American administrative pluralism in part to the relatively late arrival of public administration in the United States. Unlike the bureaucracies of many continental European nations, notably France and Germany,[54] and others like Japan and China,[55] public administration in the United States post-dates constitutional democracy. The late arrival of public administration frames our understanding of it. We are seemingly more likely to focus on the artificiality and foreignness of bureaucracy—and to consider administrative governance an intrusion on our democracy (rather than, no doubt, the other way around). For that reason, we labor to ensure that public administration comports well with our underlying republican commitments, not the least of which is a decidedly messy democratic pluralism that allows popular input into the machinery of expert bureaucracy.[56]

Were we to unify federal administrative power—as has been done elsewhere and which, as I have been describing, many are clamoring to do in the United States—we would be giving up on a good deal of this normative pluralism. What we would have instead is one of the following: We would have a mandarin administrative state given over to unelected technocrats, which would please those prizing efficient government while troubling those who champion more democratically inflected versions of public administration. Or we would have a State run by the inmates as it were, with the most passionate or well-heeled public participants driving administrative policy in self-interested, myopic, and not necessarily democratic ways. Most likely, we would have an administrative state led by unrivaled presidential appointees, worrying those who question political leaders' commitment to the rule of law, their relative lack of sophistication and expertise, and the partisan volatility of agency rules and practices from one White House to the next.

Note too that once we start incorporating administrative systems into our constitutional analyses (as we most definitely should), we have occasion to see many overseas parliamentary regimes in a different light. In practice, largely unitary parliamentary governments may be combined with similarly unitary, *but unitarily mandarin,* bureaucracies, thus fostering rivalrous engagement between the democratic parliament and the apolitical bureaucracy. Anyone familiar with the popular British television program *Yes Minister* should immediately recognize this dynamic and perhaps see it as an alternative, bilateral form of separating State power that plays off the tension between parliamentary sovereignty and fiercely independent administration. If so, perhaps the presidential–parliamentary divides aren't as great or as important as they appear at first blush, at least not in an era when so much governing takes place at the subconstitutional levels of public administration.

At the end of the day, we need not rely on any critique of the purity or efficacy of parliamentary systems to make the affirmative case for constitutional and administrative separations of powers. Unless we are going to paper over or definitively resolve the deep-seated tensions in American political and legal culture—between liberty and equality, between populism and the rule of law, between regional and national identities, and between expertise and extensive public participation—we need to work within architectural frameworks that provide constructive and dynamic outlets for debating and structuring those durable conflicts. There are, of course, many definitions of American exceptionalism, some positive and increasingly many that are pejorative. The one I am using here reflects the fact that we have a particularly rich, textured, and resilient commitment to pluralism, one deeply ingrained in our constitutional and administrative architecture and informed by our inherent skepticism of State power and our remarkable and generally honored demographic diversity. Separations of powers give meaning and effect to that pluralism and all that undergirds it.

Resisting Calls to Go Further

Complete Pluralism? I recognize that I might receive pushback from the other side—that is, not just from those decrying the sluggishness and obsolescence of the separations of powers but also from those who might chide me for not going further in the quest for even more inclusive and rivalrous engagement. If some of my arguments in favor of the separations of powers sound in pluralism—as they surely do—why not commit to an even more inclusive, dynamic framework that recognizes and elevates any number of actors excluded, herded together, or relegated to second-class status by my tripartite administrative separation of powers?

Certainly there are additional actors and institutions besides the three central administrative rivals that enrich, moderate, and challenge regulatory and welfare policy. International organizations, foreign governments, other federal agencies, state governments and municipalities, political parties, private regulators,[57] and the media all occupy what Aziz Huq and I have elsewhere termed "the thick political surround."[58] These various actors and organizations assuredly can and often do push and pull on any one agency's appointed leaders, civil servants, and public participants.

Nevertheless, I do not give top billing to this broader, perhaps boundless, constellation of actors and institutions. And I do not privilege administrative pluralism over administrative tripartitism as a matter of theory or institutional design. I do not do so for four reasons. First, having an entirely pluralistic view of administrative engagement—that is, accommodating the thick political surround on its own terms—is likely too chaotic to serve as a framework for governing. It would be constitutional functionalism without a filter. As I see it, the civil society pillar of the administrative separation of powers serves as such a filter, channeling participation and regulating (via the APA and doctrinal glosses) the time, place, and manner of pluralistic participation. Forcing most of the denizens of the thick political surround into the civil society rubric structures, rationalizes, and democratizes public engagement, transforming something otherwise as unruly and frenetic as the Cantina on Mos Eisley into something as rigorous, substantive, and orderly as a New England town meeting.

Second, it is not clear that the rule of law would fare very well in a pluralistic free-for-all. By preserving a large share of administrative governance to an unelected, insulated, and technocratic bureaucracy—rather than turning the project in toto over to the broadly conceived thick political surround—we are acting consistently with a constitutional commitment to a republican form of government that takes seriously countermajoritarian interventions in furtherance of preserving liberty, safeguarding against abuse, and promoting rational, reasoned decisionmaking. This is an argument for a strong, independent judiciary in the constitutional arena. And this is an argument for a similarly strong, independent civil service in the administrative arena.

Third, even if we were not to go so far as boundless pluralism, there would be great difficulty determining which segments of the thick political surround should be given a seat at the grown-ups' table—and which segments should be relegated to the kids' table or altogether excluded. Should organized labor be given its own seat? Should our close trading and military partners, such as Canada, Japan, or the United Kingdom, be given seats? If so, what about the likes of Saudi Arabia or Egypt? Here too the channeling, constraining effects of the tripartite administrative separation of powers pay large dividends. We avoid having to make difficult, undiplomatic, and often arbitrary choices about who or what merits inclusion. Instead, the capacious civil society pillar of administrative governance allows practically all to attempt to influence administrative policy through the public participatory prong of the tripartite scheme. Influence turns on participants' ability to marshal cogent, persuasive arguments in support of their interests or causes. After all, civil servants and agency leaders have no choice but to reckon with any such cogent, persuasive argument, irrespective of the participants' identity, wealth, clout, and even numerical strength.

Fourth, to the extent that the administrative separation of powers is an artificial constraint on pluralism, it finds itself in good company. Our constitutional system does precisely the same thing, with the understanding and expectation that the pluralistic public's participation is to be mediated by Congress and, to a lesser extent, by the president. In short, pluralism is accounted for in the administrative and constitutional separations of powers; and the civil society dimension of the tripartite administrative scheme imposes some order on the thick political surround, structuring broad-ranging participation to minimize chaos and cacophony and limiting the degree to which an otherwise unruly public can overwhelm or simply crowd out other cherished values such as the rule of law, expertise, and liberty.

Note therefore that my tripartite administrative separation of powers represents a sort of synthesis, if not transcendence, of formalist and functionalist constitutional thought. It is playfully functionalist insofar as I recognize and endorse governing paradigms quite different from, but operationally analogous to, the framers' constitutional scheme. And it is doggedly formalist insofar as I insist upon fidelity to the framers' fundamental trinitarian framework and privilege the rough reproduction of the framers' institutional rivalries.

Such a synthesis may well disappoint both camps. But we must remember that neither a purely formalist or functionalist approach can be readily squared with the basic jurisprudential contours of contemporary constitutional and administrative law. For example, the Supreme Court is highly functionalist in orientation when it permits wholesale delegations of legislative-like power to federal agencies. Yet it is highly formalist in rejecting compensating mechanisms such as legislative and line-item vetoes. For this and other reasons, Huq and I advocate jettisoning the formalist–functionalist labeling altogether when discussing the separations of powers, eschewing the terminology as descriptively inaccurate, conceptually hobbling, and normatively undesirable.[59]

A Privatized, Tertiary Separation of Powers? Another challenge from those embracing fragmentation (but quibbling with my version of an administrative separation of powers) might take the following form: given that the administrative separation of powers arose somewhat serendipitously, why shouldn't we expect a privatized separation of powers to do the same? That is to say, given that I was willing to countenance the collapsing of the constitutional separation of powers and to accept the subsequent and admittedly haphazard construction of a tripartite administrative regime, shouldn't I also be open to the possibility that the Privatization Revolution will likewise right itself—a prodigal grandson, returning to the constitutional fold?

I am skeptical for two reasons. The first reason is that I am doubtful lightning will strike twice. Our constitutional structure by and large arrived prêt-à-porter—with a fully articulated political philosophy and corresponding architectural blueprint. By contrast, modern agencies arrived on the scene in an almost feral state. It then took generations of lawyers, jurists, scholars, and policymakers to domesticate administrative power. These nursemaids of *pax administrativa* cobbled together a patchwork edifice of constraints. Only after considerable time and tinkering (and no small amount of good fortune) did they arrive at something that resembles the framers' very intentional scheme. We cannot bet on future generations likewise stumbling upon a way to subject privatized State power to checks and balances, particularly given the antipathy that many of privatization's proponents have to the constitutional order.

The second reason pertains to what I see as a fundamental incompatibility between modern American corporate governance and the separation of powers. Let us assume that State power is indeed allowed to flow through private conduits. Let us further assume that a broad recognition of our enduring commitment to checks and balances inspires attempts to empower new classes of private sector counterweights. Our best-case scenario would seemingly be one in which we spark a privatization "reformation" similar to the one Richard Stewart identified as having occurred within the twentieth-century administrative state as that realm became more rivalrous and democratically inclusive.[60] Such a privatization reformation would likely require the engendering of institutional rivalries among corporate employees, consumers, townspeople, and firm managers and directors.

From a public law perspective, this engendering of private sector rivalries is intriguing. Nevertheless, such a tertiary system of checks and balances—a *pax privatizata*—would appear to conflict with orthodox understandings of American corporate governance. These understandings privilege homogenous organizational control.[61] Firms are understood to work well when—and because—there aren't rivalrous stakeholders gumming up the works.[62] (Even where corporate control is disaggregated, it is disaggregated among stakeholders all more or less striving for the same thing.) For this reason, any proposal requiring the empowerment of, say, multiple classes of employees, consumers, and community members would likely be viewed as anathema to modern American corporations singularly focused on the maximization of profits.[63]

To be sure, we do have examples of more pluralistic corporations, including those not altogether driven by a profit-maximizing imperative. But those atypical businesses are hardly the ones that the pro-privatization—"let's run government like a business"—crowd eyes with envy. The pro-privatization crowd is looking to Monsanto, not Mom-and-Pop shops; to Microsoft, not Mondragon or any other continental European worker cooperative; and to Honeywell, not Hobby Lobby or Chick-fil-A, outfits seemingly willing to sacrifice profits in order to satisfy parochial or partisan interests.

Thus even if we could cordon off special rules that apply only to corporations carrying out State functions, those special rules—effectively designed to make the private more public, less singularly profit focused, and more open to a multiplicity of rivalrous governing voices—would prove self-defeating.[64] Special rules would instantiate the types of constraints and encumbrances that privatization hawks find so frustrating. These hawks would quickly sour on any such domesticated forms of privatization and feel compelled, like Huck Finn, to light out for new possibilities ahead of the Aunt Sallys among us who would attempt to restrict and regulate that which is desirable only because it is free and unhindered. Running business like a government is, so it seems, just as foolhardy as running government like a business.

Besides the mechanical and philosophical differences between engineering a *pax administrativa* and engineering a *pax privatizata,* there are prudential reasons for preserving both the public and private realms as separate and distinct. Governments and corporations are very different and quite possibly necessarily different animals. They have different goals, carry out different responsibilities, and exercise different powers. They are, moreover, subject to different legal, fiscal, cultural, and popular constraints.[65] At the same time, there is a vital, symbiotic relationship between the two institutions—and welfare capitalism of the sort that describes the modern American political economy relies on a strong State and a strong Market, each playing complementary and reinforcing roles in the lives of individuals and communities. Indeed, it is not at all clear that businesses themselves would benefit from a more privatized, businesslike government, regardless whether such a privatized regime were led by an autocratic CEO or cut from the mold of a European workplace democracy.

Recall President Obama's "you didn't build that" speech. The president exclaimed that successful businessmen and women "didn't get there on [their] own." Rather, he insisted, they received plenty of help from the State along the way. "Somebody helped to create this unbelievable

American system that we have that allowed you to thrive. Somebody invested in roads and bridges. If you've got a business—you didn't build that. Somebody else made that happen."[66]

Obama was crushed for giving voice to such sentiment.[67] But political delicacies aside, the president was essentially right. As much as America's captains of industry might like to think that government only gets in their way, it is government's decidedly unbusinesslike modus operandi that ensures that the State is ready and able to fund and fix infrastructure, to underwrite entrepreneurism, to regulate impartially, to ease the burdens associated with starting a business, and to make sure the people running and employed by firms that fail land on their feet.

In effect, the government is business's designated driver. Like many designated drivers, the State might well be tempted to join in the revelry. But despite that temptation, the State must abjure. It must refrain from acting like a business for its own good. And it must do so for the good of the market economy, whose experimentation, risk-taking, creativity, and rational callousness are supported by the government's abstemiousness.[68]

For these reasons, too, we ought to be wary of suggestions to simply wait for—or actively try to bring about—a third-generation separation of powers as a corollary to privatized governance. Such a *pax privatizata* is apt to be insufficiently public-regarding to satisfy either kumbaya neo-New Dealers or wolfish entrepreneurs savvy enough to appreciate the virtues of a welfare state. By the same token, a privatized separation of powers is apt to be insufficiently efficient for privatization hawks and equity investors alike. We thus may find ourselves in a position not too different from Arthur Miller's when supposedly propositioned by Marilyn Monroe to start a family. Dampening Monroe's enthusiasm for a child she envisioned as blessed with the playwright's brains and her starlet looks, the bookish Miller reminded her of the very real possibility that the baby would get her brains and his looks. That's about the best we could hope for when it comes to any such *pax privatizata*.

8

Recalibrating the Relationship between and among the Constitutional and Administrative Rivals

The first *pax administrativa* was, and still is, a remarkable achievement. It is also one that has remained incomplete, underappreciated, and politically vulnerable. I have already explained how the first *pax administrativa* suffered at the hands of those rejecting the big government infrastructure of the New Deal and Great Society. But those opponents—the Chicago-school economists, the Chamber of Commerce types, and the Reagan Democrats—do not deserve all of the blame. They received help from self-professed champions of the modern welfare state. Through a combination of neglect, misunderstanding, and their own exploitative efforts, they too hastened the demise of the twentieth-century administrative separation of powers. These Neros didn't just fiddle while Rome burned. They joined in the pillaging.

What follows is, in many respects, the late-arriving answer to the Powell Memo. Recall the future Supreme Court Justice's cri de coeur. Powell roused the business community, urging corporate leaders to awaken from their slumber and, in effect, tear down the first *pax administrativa*. It is now time to reverse the script: to commit to legitimating and valorizing twenty-first-century administrative governance. In order to do so, we need to take off the rose-colored glasses and diagnose where the initial *pax administrativa* project fell short and why. This chapter and the two that follow engage in the conceptual, jurisprudential, and programmatic work required to reconstruct and refashion a second, sturdier *pax administrativa*.

First, the conceptual. This chapter emphasizes the need to rethink the often unhealthy relationship between and among constitutional and administrative rivals. For too long, Congress and the president have intervened aggressively and opportunistically in administrative affairs, ostensibly to control illegitimate or wayward agency personnel but no doubt often simply to influence, even dictate, agency outcomes. In effect, if not intent, these top-down interventions destabilized, compromised, obscured, and discredited the administrative separation of powers. It is hard to defend, let alone celebrate, a system that has been routinely debased. Thus what we need now is a recalibration of that relationship. We need the political branches to act custodially, nurturing rather than exploiting the administrative separation of powers.

Second, the jurisprudential. Chapter 9 focuses on the judiciary, the constitutional branch most likely to promote a richer, thicker conception of the administrative separation of powers. Here I explain that the courts are already implicitly supportive of a custodial approach to administrative governance. Now, newly cognizant of and emboldened by the explicit constitutional project of an administrative separation of powers, courts should, I argue, look askance at agency actions that are the product of a compromised or subverted administrative separation of powers. Scrutinizing these procedurally deficient agency actions, courts would be well advised to push, if not compel, the political branches to take the administrative separation of powers—and their own corresponding custodial duties—seriously. It is with this in mind that I furnish a doctrinal roadmap in service of what I call reinforcing rivalrous administration.

And, third, the programmatic. Left to their own devices, Congress and the White House are unlikely to embrace custodialism. After all, the political branches have much to gain by continuing to destabilize the administrative separation of powers. But once pressured by the courts, the political branches may be obligated to design and implement custodial strategies. Chapter 10 thus proffers a legislative blueprint for sharpening and strengthening administrative rivalries and for enhancing the reputation and standing of those rivals in the broader political and legal worlds.

Constitutional Control (and Exploitation) during the First *Pax Administrativa*

So long as administrative agencies have existed, it has simply been understood that the constitutional branches would—and should—assert top-down control. And assert top-down control they have. This urge to exert control has been especially powerful during modern times, when agencies emerged as truly dominant players; when the common law and even statutory law started to be eclipsed by administrative rules, guidance documents, and orders;[1] and when members of Congress and the president (and their coteries of aides) began feeling outgunned and outclassed by the far more numerous and expert agency personnel.[2]

It no doubt goes without saying but presidents view control over the administrative state as crucial. Presidents are, after all, constitutionally authorized and required to take care that the laws are faithfully executed.[3] And they are under intense political pressure to advance their respective parties' programmatic goals in short order. Such pressure is only heightened during times of divided government, when securing congressional support is more difficult and policymaking via agency regulation thus becomes a greater imperative.[4] Control surely matters to Congress as well. Congress has abiding constitutional, institutional, and political interests in how delegated powers and appropriated funds are put to use, and its members are, of course, eager to put their stamp on administrative policies.

Such efforts to control administrative power have long been deemed so obviously appropriate and necessary that consideration of their propriety has rarely been debated. (Scholarly and wonkish conversations pivot instead to operational strategies regarding how best to intervene and exert control.) But why? Recall once more the all-too-commonly-held belief that agencies are constitutionally suspect or simply problematic entities, too far removed from direct elections and too fully under the spell of powerful special interests or Svengali-like mandarins. Strong involvement by the political branches thus might well legitimate otherwise questionable administrative activity.

Let's dig in a little deeper. We're apt to view agencies as unruly in part because we generally assume those entities to be unitary.[5] It is here where the descriptive informs the normative: Scholars, policymakers, and judges who fail to appreciate that agencies are internally fragmented and rivalrous might well conclude that such agencies are troublingly and perhaps unconstitutionally *imbalanced*—and thus in need of control.

A truly unitary agency may be singularly dominated by presidential appointees quick to defy congressional directives, to "exploit ambiguous laws as license for their own prerogative," and to play politics in adjudicating disputes.[6] For many, including seemingly our newest justice, that is a problem.[7] As a federal circuit judge, Neil Gorsuch worried about highly politicized agencies "seeking to pursue whatever policy whim may rule the day."[8] Characterizing agencies in this fashion, he objected to the high degree of deference courts accord to agency decisions and interpretations. In essence, then Judge Gorsuch was calling for greater top-down control.

A truly unitary agency may instead be puppeteered by gadflies, regulated parties, or program beneficiaries who capture the agency.[9] For many, capture by special interests is just as big of a problem—and likewise calls for more intensive supervision and intervention by the constitutional branches.

Lastly, a truly unitary agency may be monopolized by civil servants indifferent, if not altogether hostile, to the president's popular mandate and to lay public input. This third permutation of an imbalanced agency poses perhaps the most politically salient and constitutionally visible problems of all.[10] Certainly it is this mandarins-on-top formulation that troubles Chief Justice John Roberts. "One can," the chief has written, "have a government that functions without being ruled by functionaries, and a government that benefits from expertise without being ruled by experts."[11] Here too impressions of imbalanced agencies seemingly prompt calls for more forceful political interventions.

All told, presumptively unitary agencies have been generally perceived as one of two things: insufficiently attentive to the broad range of democratic, technocratic, and rule-of-law values expected to inform and balance State power—as exercised by constitutional, administrative, or any other set of actors; or, on a baser, more self-interested level, simply insufficiently attentive to one's own favored grouping or value. Thus for those worried about the illegitimacy, unfairness, or unconstitutionality of unitary (and hence imbalanced) administrative power, strong, top-down control by the constitutional branches has been welcomed[12]—just as foreign interventions may be encouraged and justified in cases involving purportedly *failed* or otherwise illegitimately governed nation-states.[13]

Of course, no such constitutional imperative exists. This justification for strong, top-down constitutional control rests on a persistent but mistaken premise: that agencies are insufficiently balanced. Yet, as we now know, the existence of an administrative separation of powers generates the very balance too readily assumed to be lacking. Administrative power that is internally fragmented, heterogeneous, and rivalrous necessarily accommodates the interplay of legalistic, technocratic, majoritarian, and broader public interests—in ways that tethered twentieth-century American public administration to the fragmented, heterogeneous, and rivalrous enterprise of American constitutional governance. And just as we generally trust and respect exercises of State power that emerge from the inclusive and contentious domain known as the constitutional separation of powers, so too should we trust and respect those exercises of State power that emerge from the similarly inclusive and contentious domain that I have been calling the administrative separation of powers.

Once the administrative separation of powers is recognized, strong, asymmetric interventions by constitutional actors can no longer be justified as a constitutional or normative corrective legitimating otherwise imbalanced or overly concentrated forms of administrative authority. Such interventions must instead be seen for what they are (and have long been): political power grabs that threaten a largely self-regulating, constitutionally sound administrative ecosystem. This is, after all, an ecosystem capable of eliciting, ventilating, amplifying, and ultimately harmonizing populist sentiments, presidential priorities, legislative interests, expert opinions, and legal obligations. And it is an ecosystem whose claim of constitutional legitimacy rests to a substantial degree on the existence of heterogeneous, rivalrous administrative stakeholders who individually and collectively channel many of the institutional, dispositional, and cultural characteristics of the constitutional branches.

Consider then, briefly, the likely destabilizing effects of strong constitutional interventions on already triangulated administrative agencies. At least since the mid-twentieth century, agency power has not been concentrated in defiance of the framers' tripartite scheme. To the contrary, administrative design has been faithful, its powers disaggregated. Thus whatever top-down control has been exerted by the political branches, it has not been exerted on an undifferentiated administrative mass in need of greater constitutional legitimacy or plain old Aristotelian balancing. Instead, such vertical interventions have operated on top of a fragmented, internally rivalrous administrative domain—and thus have compromised the integrity and efficacy of administrative checks and balances.

Two basic strategic patterns of top-down control merit discussion. My sketches below are not meant to be comprehensive or exhaustive. Nor are they intended to take the place of formal modeling or historiographic case studies. Rather, they serve a far more modest but nevertheless foundational purpose: to suggest how ambitious constitutional actors may exert influence over—and ultimately destabilize and delegitimate—the otherwise largely self-regulating administrative ecosystem.

The Proxy War Approach. Picture, first, a constitutional branch entering into a long-term, durable alliance with one of the administrative rivals. The constitutional branch fortifies and then uses this administrative partner as a proxy—a vehicle through which to exercise ongoing control over administrative decisions. The agency actor in such a proxy relationship would be expected to help advance its constitutional partner's programmatic and institutional interests in the administrative arena. That administrative satrap would also be well positioned to help resist countervailing initiatives championed by rival constitutional–administrative duos.[14]

To be clear, this isn't just about constitutional actors making their preferences known. Nor is it about constitutional actors simply leaning a bit on their particular administrative allies. It runs deeper. It is about constitutional actors altering the administrative balance of power. For instance, we might see the president teaming up with her most obvious and controllable ally—namely, agency leaders—to help subordinate contentious civil servants and to limit public engagement, all in service of ensuring that the White House's interests are prioritized, advanced expeditiously and with minimal resistance from dissenting administrative stakeholders. The president might do so by reclassifying career personnel as at-will employees or by directing agency heads to outsource tasks. Both measures enable the circumvention of formidable civil servants and concomitantly concentrate administrative power in agency leaders who are themselves loyal to the White House. Or, the president might instruct agency leaders to engage in less transparent or less participatory forms of administrative action, thus using procedural shortcuts to cabin the role that civil society can play.[15]

The Realpolitik Approach. Picture, second, a more fluid, but no less destabilizing, approach. Here the constitutional branches prioritize (or settle for) shifting, rather than long-term, alliances. They selectively partner with one or more of the administrative rivals as opportunities arise, circumstances change, and allegiances wax and wane. The actual instruments of influence are substantially the same as those deployed during proxy wars. The only differences are the volatility of such relationships and the greater number and frequency of partnership permutations. This strategy looks like another international relations practice: *realpolitik*.[16]

Congress is rightly considered a "they" rather than an "it."[17] Different factions, caucuses, and committees in the House and Senate might find common ground with different administrative groupings, often at the same time. Hence there is good reason to assume that Congress is the constitutional branch most drawn to realpolitik, as various legislative cohorts partner with and pressure various combinations of agency leaders, members of civil society, and even civil servants to advance partisan, institutional, regional, or programmatic interests.

Given these two strategies, the constitutional practitioners of proxy wars and realpolitik can treat the administrative domain as a chessboard to be controlled and dominated in the manner of a Kissinger or Metternich. Yet herein lies the problem. The failure or unwillingness to recognize and respect the administrative domain as disaggregated—or, more precisely, as *disaggregated in a constitutionally meaningful fashion*—has been harmful in the following three ways:

First, it has resulted in the waste of considerable time and energy. As shown, the twentieth-century administrative state was already fragmented and triangulated in ways that largely preempted the need for aggressive remedial interventions by the constitutional actors. The administrative state was conceived in part to spare the constitutional branches, particularly Congress, from much of the day-to-day grind of federal governing.[18] Any requirement or expectation for the political branches to then aggressively and pervasively intervene in administrative matters beyond delegating authority, appropriating funds, and appointing and confirming responsible and accountable officials would defeat much of the purpose of an administrative state, let alone a decidedly balanced, rivalrous administrative state.

Indeed, we are regularly reminded that Congress delegated massive legislative power to agencies because the legislators were themselves overburdened, understaffed, technically unsophisticated, and politically indecisive. Knowing all of that, wouldn't it be incongruous to expect those on Capitol Hill to have the resources, aptitude, and appetite for closely overseeing the everyday operations of administrative governance[19]—particularly when Congress can instead delegate that charge, too, to someone or something more willing and able? Consider, for example, congressional "fire alarms." Political scientists Mathew McCubbins and Thomas Schwartz famously posit that Congress installs fire alarms for concerned citizens to pull, thereby relieving legislators of primary responsibility for monitoring agencies. Like firefighters, members of the House and Senate are obligated to swing into action if and only if alarms are sounded.[20] In reality, it seems as if Congress as a collective body had—and still has—reason to prefer a *fire brigade* to a fire alarm, empowering those concerned citizens to do the actual work of putting out the proverbial fire. More to the point, it seems as if Congress has already given effect to that preference—prescribing, as it has, a robust, self-executing role for civil society to play in nearly all facets of administrative governance.[21]

For those tempted to discount as trifling any consideration of the costs associated with (unnecessary or redundant) constitutional supervision and micromanagement of the administrative sphere, do bear in mind that a goodly number of *pax administrativa*'s harshest critics harp on the wastefulness and costliness of federal public administration. One cannot, it seems to me, have it both ways.

Second, this disregard for the administrative separation of powers lends credence to those attacking the constitutional bona fides of the administrative state. So long as the administrative separation of powers is overlooked, unacknowledged, or asymmetrically exploited by one or both of the political branches, would-be defenders remain poorly positioned to fend off the barrage of constitutional challenges leveled against the administrative state.

Third, and most importantly, this failure has seemingly done great violence to the actual workings of the administrative separation of powers. Either Congress or the president jumps the gun, scheming early on to fortify an administrative ally or disable one or more administrative rivals; or they parachute in at the last minute, disrupting whatever *balanced* policy decision was (or was about to be) forged in the crucible of truly rivalrous administrative separation of powers.

These interventions from above aren't random. Nor can we expect them to cancel each other out. Instead, they consistently advantage those administrative rivals most naturally aligned with the meddling political branches. Thus constitutional intrusions of this sort seemingly engender relatively fixed power imbalances within the administrative sphere, with punctilious, independent civil servants regularly passed over—like the class hall monitor come prom season—when the time comes to build alliances. The end result is a systematic skewing of administrative law and policy in a more partisan, political direction and correspondingly away from expertise and fidelity to the rule of law.

Any such systematic skewing of administrative law and policy provides further reason for critics and even the marginalized participants themselves to dismiss the administrative separation of powers. And, fair enough: All the blood, sweat, and tears of battling in the administrative arena might go for naught if, at the last moment, the president or a powerful congressional committee chair swoops in, weakens or marginalizes one of the administrative rivals, and ends up altering the terms of a hard-fought administrative settlement. What's more, even if a constitutional meddler were thwarted in her attempts to dictate administrative outcomes— thwarted, say, by the combined efforts of the two unaligned administrative rivals—any such "administrative" victory would be a Pyrrhic one. The collusive, horizontal intra-administrative alliance (forged quite sensibly to stop the powerful constitutional–administrative duo) would preserve administrative sovereignty but blunt the important institutional frictions that are expected to exist between and among all three of the administrative rivals.

A Custodial Approach for a Second *Pax Administrativa*

Now that we see what compromised the first *pax administrativa,* we can begin to construct a new, improved second *pax administrativa.* For starters, we need to restructure the relationship between the constitutional and administrative rivals. Constitutional branches must resist the urge to treat the administrative domain as deficient and in need of rescuing. Instead, they should respect the administrative realm as a legitimate and virtuous one—and adopt a more custodial approach to constitutional–administrative relations. Under this approach, the constitutional actors promote a well-functioning administrative separation of powers, supporting and sharpening truly rivalrous engagement even at the expense of advancing their own parochial objectives.

In keeping with this chapter's international relations leitmotif, a custodial model could be likened to the old balance-of-power geostrategic arrangements. Constitutional actors work together—again, at times contrary to their particular institutional self-interests—to create and maintain rough parity among administrative actors and work to prevent the rise of administrative hegemons that threaten the stability or order of that increasingly important realm. In our case, the hegemon to be feared would be whatever rival—agency heads, civil servants, or special interests—is given too much help, grows too strong, and ultimately threatens to throw the administrative separation of powers out of whack.

Generally speaking, expressions of administrative policymaking that take place outside of the strictures of the administrative separation of powers ought to be considered no more legitimate than expressions of congressional or presidential policymaking that take place outside of the strictures of the constitutional separation of powers. Hence in *INS v. Chadha,* the Supreme Court invalidated legislative vetoes by Congress that had the effect of overturning administrative immigration determinations.[22] And, in *Clinton v. City of New York,* the Court held unconstitutional the president's line-item veto authority to cancel specific provisions of already enacted spending bills.[23] The Court did so because each of these exercises was the product of one branch acting unilaterally in contexts demanding broader, interbranch engagement.

Clinton is particularly instructive. In a sharply worded dissent, Justice Antonin Scalia voiced surprise at the Court's invalidation: Why didn't the majority treat the line-item veto like any other run-of-the-mill delegation of lawmaking authority to the executive? Scalia's question was, and remains, a good one. After all, the Court's doctrinal touchstone for delegations is the very forgiving "intelligible principle" standard. That generous standard was surely met here, as Congress prescribed exactly when and how the president could exercise the veto.[24]

Most observers understand *Clinton* as a case in which the Court distinguished between Congress, on the one hand, delegating discretionary authority to the executive to make rules that further the goals of already enacted statutes and, on the other, delegating discretionary authority to the executive to cancel or revise already enacted statutes. Yet Justice Scalia found this distinction unimportant. Conceding that the line-item veto was "technically different" from ordinary delegations, Scalia nevertheless insisted that "the doctrine of unconstitutional delegation . . . is preeminently *not* a doctrine of technicalities."[25]

Perhaps, then, the better way to make sense of *Clinton* is to recognize that delegations to the president are fundamentally (and not just technically) different from run-of-the-mill delegations to agencies—and far more dangerous. A delegation to the president is a naked delegation. The president is, after all, above the administrative fray, exempt from much of the APA, and unburdened by administrative checks and balances.

By contrast, a delegation to agency leaders is a delegation to actors enmeshed in thick webs of rivalries and constraints. Agency leaders entrusted with lawmaking power must necessarily work with civil servants and members of civil society. Thus the line-item veto authorizes unilateral and unitary lawmaking (by the president), whereas ordinary administrative delegations preserve rivalrous, encumbered lawmaking consistent with the spirit of the framers' separation of powers.[26]

Administrative hegemons silence competing voices and marginalize alternative perspectives. Those voices and perspectives matter. They matter because agency decisions that are not the product of the contentious interplay of three sharp administrative rivals are generally less sound on the merits. By *sound on the merits*, I do not mean the objectively best, or optimal, policy outcome. That is not our test and, in truth, really can't be anyone's objective test. Instead, I mean the outcome that best—that is, most faithfully—reflects our distinctive admixture of populism, legalism, establishment politics (mediated through the president), and bureaucratic expertise.

No doubt any such commitment to a custodial approach will distress unitary executive theorists as well as those pundits and consultants who insist that government should be run like a business, with a CEO-style executive calling the shots. It will seem jarring too to those who bristle at the political branches being refereed according to Queensberry rules, and who thus would prefer granting Congress and the president leave to tussle more freely with one another and with the administrative rivals.[27] Yet for the administrative separation of powers and, with it, the modern American welfare state to warrant constitutional respect and claim constitutional authority, Congress and the president must limit their disruptive interventions. They must suppress (or be forced to suppress) the urge to exploit and try to dominate the administrative sphere. And they must embrace (or, again, be forced to embrace) their underlying custodial responsibilities to preserve and nurture a roughly balanced administrative ecosystem. After all, it isn't at all clear that such asymmetric, exploitative interference represents a constitutionally legitimate alternative to the administrative separation of powers—any more than the legislative veto or line-item veto constitutes a valid substitute for bicameralism and presentment. Nor is it at all clear that asymmetric, exploitative interference, even by the democratically accountable political branches, advances the prudential goals of American public administration.

Custodialism will be a tough pill for the political branches to swallow. As such, just as I associate the president with proxy wars and Congress with realpolitik, I view the courts as most inclined to adopt a balance-of-power approach. What makes judges different? Why should we expect them to be the custodians of a rivalrous administrative realm?[28] Unlike the political branches, judges have relatively little, if any, institutional incentive to disable deliberation-enhancing procedures or to subvert or bypass any of the administrative rivals. Judges do not, for instance, face the same external pressure to deliver a specific package of regulations and public benefits, let alone to do so before an impending election.

More to the point, courts seemingly have intrinsic and self-interested reasons for affirmatively supporting a custodial model of the sort I am sketching. The more work the administrative separation of powers does, the less the courts will need to do in terms of reviewing agency actions. This is because a well-functioning administrative separation of powers helps ensure that agency officials are acting in compliance with congressional dictates, are not abusing their discretion, and are crafting sound, reasoned policies informed by a diversity of viewpoints. If courts know that agency actions reflect the meaningful engagement of civil servants, political appointees, and members of the public, they can be more comfortable deferring to agencies. After all, most of the battles over the content and design of agency actions will have already been fought within capacious and inclusive decisionmaking venues characteristic of a healthy, rivalrous administrative separation of powers.[29]

In addition, the judiciary is an institution generally committed to the rule of law. For this reason alone, we might expect the courts to chart a different course from that of Congress and the president: to endorse and enforce a custodial approach that helps maintain a self-governing (and constraining) system of checks and balances, again very much reminiscent of what we find at the constitutional level. It is therefore quite possible that the courts, just as they do with the constitutional separation of powers, can and will police as much as participate in the proper workings of the administrative separation of powers.

Of course, judges are hardly saints and, at times, may be tempted to act on their own political biases. But notwithstanding that temptation, judges surely realize that their efforts to game the administrative process are uniquely suspect. Unlike meddling members of the political branches vigorously attempting to advance constituent and institutional interests, similarly intrusive, disruptive judges would be acting principally out of private self-interest and personal predilection. In other words, among the three constitutional branches, judges alone would be meddling in ways that conflict, rather than comport, with their professional and institutional responsibilities—and thus only judges ought to appreciate their *prima facie* obligation to act custodially.

9

Judicial Custodialism

The previous chapter defined and defended constitutional custodialism and explained why the judiciary is the branch most likely to take its custodial responsibilities seriously. This chapter fashions the courts' custodial responsibilities into a workable jurisprudence—a jurisprudence that nudges and, if necessary, compels the coordinate branches to foster a well-functioning administrative separation of powers.

In some respects, the exact contours of such a jurisprudence are less important than the mere fact that the courts demonstrate a willingness to regularly invalidate agency actions that reflect something short of a well-functioning administrative separation of powers. This is because Congress and the president—no doubt frustrated by custodially minded judges' invariably disjointed, piecemeal, and fact-sensitive holdings—will be spurred to act preemptively, constructing a thicker, richer, and more transsubstantive framework for supporting and sharpening administrative rivalries than anything the courts could incrementally cobble together.

The discussion that follows necessarily takes us into the doctrinal weeds. For those with a healthy aversion to administrative case law (or simply eager to turn to Chapter 10's legislative reform proposals), the gist of this chapter is, again, that the courts can—and should—deter and punish efforts to circumvent or weaken the administrative separation of powers. Courts can do so in ways that demand a greater commitment on everyone's part to a healthy, vibrant form of rivalrous administrative engagement.

Reinforcing Rivalrous Administration

Courts have limited tools. But they can use them to great effect. What I envision here is for custodially minded judges to propound an administrative jurisprudence somewhat akin to what constitutional theorists call "reinforcing representative democracy."[1]

Reinforcing representative democracy requires judges to invalidate legislation only to the extent that they conclude that the political process has broken down, has been circumvented or compromised, or has been systematically disadvantaging discrete and insular minorities.[2] This theory, which has its doctrinal roots in a memorable footnote to a New Deal case titled *United States v. Carolene Products Co.*,[3] is most closely associated with John Hart Ely. In his magisterial *Democracy and Distrust,* Ely compares judges to antitrust regulators. Unlike in many other public regulatory domains in which agency officials prescribe substantive outcomes—think EPA emissions standards or FDA food purity rules—antitrust regulators focus on inputs. Antitrust personnel monitor and police the fairness of market competition and, generally speaking, are content with whatever outcome fair competition generates.[4] Ely further compares his judges to sports referees who enforce compliance with the rules of the game but do not dictate, correct, or negate substantive outcomes absent some showing that a match was rigged.

We can piggyback on the powerful but not uncontroversial *Carolene Products*/Ely approach and retool it for use in the administrative arena. When thinking about republican government in an administrative rather than legislative domain, reinforcing representative democracy becomes *reinforcing rivalrous administration.* Under reinforcing rivalrous administration, judges consider whether a fair, inclusive administrative process has been short-circuited, disabled, or unduly interfered with in a manner that precludes or limits meaningful participation by all three administrative rivals.[5] If the administrative process is basically sound—and the resulting rule, order, or decision reflects robust participation by empowered civil servants, agency leaders, and members of civil society—then courts ought to look quite skeptically (and possibly not at all) at claims challenging the substance of agency actions and legal interpretations. After all, those agency actions and interpretations are the end result of multipolar administrative engagement. They thus have already been carefully scrutinized, contested, and finessed by the relevant—and representative—administrative stakeholders.[6] But if instead the administrative process appears compromised by the effective disregard for, exclusion, or debilitation of one or more of the rivals, then the courts would necessarily intercede.

Of course, identification and verification problems abound. The difference between well-functioning and dysfunctional administrative engagement is not always apparent and is open to subjective interpretation. There will surely be close and controversial cases where the line between a constitutional actor simply supporting an administrative stakeholder and that constitutional actor undermining the administrative separation of powers proves difficult to draw; or where it isn't abundantly clear whether sparse public participation is the product of some structural or legal impediment—or simply a reflection of informed and voluntary decisions not to participate.

This is surely challenging work. But remember: judges engage in line-drawing exercises of this sort all the time, including when policing the constitutional separation of powers. Is, for example, a constitutional branch acting zealously to promote its own institutional interests; or is that branch crossing the line and compromising a well-functioning constitutional separation of powers? Remember too that line-drawing exercises surrounding the administrative separation of powers may not be any more difficult or disruptive than what judges are currently tasked with doing in administrative domains—that is, evaluating the substantive merits of, say, that new emissions standard or food purity rule.

Constructing a Jurisprudence for Reinforcing Rivalrous Administration

Courts carrying out their custodial responsibilities can surely draw upon their existing tools and doctrines. But they may want to consider a complete doctrinal overhaul. In what follows, I first describe an off-the-shelf approach to constitutional custodialism. I then proffer a more ambitious approach, one that is at odds with current administrative law doctrines but that more squarely addresses impediments to a well-functioning administrative separation of powers. Under either approach, my aim is the same: to induce the political branches to act custodially and in a comprehensive fashion, ultimately obviating the need for courts to do the hard and messy work of policing the administrative separation of powers on a case-by-case basis.[7]

Reinforcing Rivalrous Administration through Merits Review. Courts can employ their longstanding tools to support the administrative separation of powers. Specifically, they can increase or decrease the deference accorded to agency actions or interpretations depending on the degree to which those actions or interpretations were arrived at through a truly rivalrous, heterogeneous, and inclusive administrative process.

Lest one think otherwise, judicial deference to agencies matters a whole lot. Agency actions and interpretations accorded deference are far more likely to survive judicial scrutiny. Rather than needing to convince a court of, say, the propriety of an agency action based on the *preponderance of the evidence,*[8] an agency granted deference may have to show only that its position is supported by *some evidence*[9] or isn't *arbitrary or capricious.*[10] Deference, particularly strong deference, means agencies enjoy considerable leeway to interpret laws and design policies. Needless to say, the stakes at the judicial review stage are quite high: judicial invalidation can set a given program back several years.[11] For agency personnel, the president, affected interest groups, and the courts themselves (which no doubt will be asked to review the next, revised iteration of said program), judicial invalidation represents a colossal waste of labor, money, time, and political capital and often constitutes a personal and professional affront to those most closely associated with the rejected legal interpretation or policy design.

How specifically could granting, withholding, or titrating deference respond to—and ultimately affect—the administrative separation of powers? Consider, for example, a court that suspects civil servants weren't given their due in an administrative proceeding. That court, troubled by the breakdown or shortchanging of the administrative separation of powers, may apply a particularly demanding version of arbitrariness review—or altogether withhold deference. Withholding or limiting deference punishes agencies that either never delved especially deeply into, among other things, the science, sociology, or economics of a given rule or disregarded those expert findings.

Agency leaders who've grown accustomed to receiving considerable deference would thus be wise to ensure that career personnel—those often best positioned and qualified to employ technocratic expertise—play a large role going forward.[12] We have actually seen judicial nudges of this sort in the Court's landmark *Massachusetts v. EPA* and *Motor Vehicles Manufacturers Association v. State Farm* cases.[13] In both instances, the Court expressed concern that agency leaders were making decisions not clearly supported by the best scientific evidence (but instead seemed motivated largely by political considerations). Thus Jody Freeman and Adrian Vermeule cite these cases as examples of the Court demanding that agency leaders pay more attention to the findings of the expert technocrats.[14] Canvassing administrative law cases more broadly, Gillian Metzger adds: "evidence that decisions were made over the objections of career staff and agency professionals triggers more rigorous [judicial] review."[15]

Similarly, following another seminal case, *United States v. Mead Corp.*, the courts are likely to give less deference to unilaterally arrived at agency legal interpretations (rendered either by agency heads or civil servants) than to interpretations reflecting the robust participation of agency leaders, civil servants, and members of the public.[16] *Mead* itself involved the Court withholding the most agency-friendly form of judicial deference (called *Chevron* deference) on the ground that career agency personnel formulated their own legal interpretations outside of the democratically inclusive and rigorous rulemaking process—and without apparent input from agency leaders or the public writ large.[17] *Mead* has thus created a strong incentive for agency leaders and career staffers alike to eschew quicker, less inclusive decisionmaking in favor of more intensive, multipolar forms of deliberative rulemaking.[18]

Empirical evidence suggests that the incentive for agency leaders and civil servants to engage more broadly and more fully with each other and with civil society is indeed significant. In an important new study, Kent Barnett and Christopher Walker canvass over 1500 administrative law cases from the federal courts of appeals. According to their findings, the circuit courts are far more likely to uphold agency interpretations subject to *Chevron* deference (77.3 percent affirmance rate) than when *Mead* applies (56 percent affirmance rate).[19]

Reinforcing Rivalrous Administration through Process-Perfecting Review. The focus on agency outputs—that is, reviewing the substantive merits of an agency's legal, factual, and policy determinations—has been the jurisprudential standby for decades.[20] During this time, courts have resisted the urge to expressly obligate agencies to undertake more robust policymaking procedures. Hence *Mead* instructs courts to more vigorously scrutinize the merits of an agency official's unilateral legal interpretations. But there is no insistence that agencies actually engage in more rigorous, inclusive deliberative processes.

This emphasis on merits review may seem puzzling.[21] After all, judges are generally understood to be well equipped to assess the adequacy of procedures[22] and are often out of their element when it comes to evaluating substantive agency findings regarding the dangers of petrochemicals in the workplace or the toxicity of a new cancer drug.[23] Speaking decades ago to this puzzling emphasis was David Bazelon, who at the time was Chief Judge of the D.C. Circuit: "I am convinced that in highly technical areas, where judges are institutionally incompetent to weigh evidence for themselves, a focus on agency procedures will prove less intrusive, and more likely to improve the quality of decisionmaking, than judges steeping themselves in technical matters to determine whether the agency has exercised a reasoned discretion."[24] But Bazelon's stance on the relative advantages of process-based judicial review has not carried the day.[25]

Instead, for the past forty years, we've been wandering in the wilderness of substantive, merits-based judicial review. Now, however, once we acknowledge the administrative separation of powers as a self-regulating ecosystem capable of generating reasonable, rational outcomes that reflect a balancing of technical imperatives, legal obligations, presidential priorities, and the sundry concerns of the public writ large, we should consider retiring our hiking boots. That is to say, we may want to jettison our heavy reliance on merits review (and corresponding deference doctrines) in favor of policing the administrative process itself. Were we to pivot in that direction, judges would be called upon to investigate whether the administrative checks and balances were operational—summarily affirming agency actions that reflect robust participation by all three administrative rivals and categorically rejecting those actions that came about through a compromised or subverted administrative framework.

The benefits of this pivot to process-perfecting review are numerous. First, the courts would be directly addressing the specific and constitutionally relevant problem that I am identifying. Today courts dangle promises of more or less deference, implicitly enticing agency officials to adopt more robust, inclusive administrative procedures, especially notice-and-comment rulemaking.[26] But, it isn't necessarily the case that agency officials are so readily nudged. Notwithstanding extant promises of more permissive judicial scrutiny, agencies have not gone on a rulemaking binge. Rather than commit to more fully inclusive, robust agency procedures and deliberations, agency officials may roll the dice and subject themselves to more searching judicial review.

If indeed agencies are not so readily nudged, those agency officials continuing to act outside of the strictures of the administrative separation of powers—by, for instance, shortchanging the involvement of civil servants or the public at large—may nevertheless expect many of their decisions to be affirmed. This is because agency actions can survive even ratcheted-up, rigorous merits review and yet still be relatively impoverished (*if not technically unreasonable*): the policies arrived at were, after all, not the product of truly rivalrous, heterogeneously inclusive engagement. Robust participation by all three administrative rivals ensures that agency actions are constitutionally legitimate—not just technically reasonable.

Second, even if agencies can be nudged, it isn't necessarily clear that minimal compliance with notice-and-comment rulemaking procedures ensures meaningful participation, or even the opportunity for meaningful participation by all three sets of administrative rivals. This argument will be developed more fully in Chapter 10, where I consider the shortcomings of the contemporary notice-and-comment process.

Third, process-perfecting review plays to the judiciary's strengths: Chief Judge Bazelon was surely right in suggesting that courts are more adept at identifying shoddy procedures than they are at assessing suspect substantive policy decisions, particularly in cases involving heavy reliance on sophisticated scientific, sociological, or economic analysis. Here again the analogy to reinforcing representative democracy is a useful one. Under Ely's theory, courts are not supposed to consider (or second guess) whether legislation is sensible or misguided. They are, instead, obligated to affirm those acts that reflect open, fair, and inclusive legislative engagement and reject those that do not.

Fourth, a commitment to process-perfecting review will minimize some unnecessary and easily gamed forms of judicial interference. Administrative policies that arise from robust, rivalrous administrative proceedings ought not be waylaid by the courts. Assuming agency officials can readily show that the actions under review are the product of a well-fuctioning administrative separation of powers, the courts should quickly dispense with merits challenges leveled by those whose substantive policy preferences did not prevail in the administrative arena. Rather than engage in the judicial equivalent of Monday morning quarterbacking, judges would simply conclude that robust administrative procedures necessarily generate nonarbitrary, noncapricious substantive outcomes.

Fifth, there is a judicial and political economy story to tell. The judicial pivot to process-perfecting review will slow agencies down at the beginning stages of rulemaking and policy development. This is because ensuring robust, rigorous engagement and meaningful participation takes time and resources. But that will be time and money well spent if subsequent judicial challenges, which otherwise would take years to resolve and might result in the invalidation of years of past agency work, are summarily rejected.

Of course, some will see this pivot to process-perfecting review as nothing more than a shell game, enabling politically motivated judges to hide behind the ostensible neutrality of administrative procedure while still dictating substantive outcomes. Indeed, this was one of the more trenchant critiques of Chief Judge Bazelon's jurisprudence forty years ago. (A version of this critique was also employed in response to Ely's reinforcing representative democracy.) Though the critique remains salient to this day, it is readily answerable.

There is surely a politics to reinforcing rivalrous administration, just as there is a politics to reinforcing representative democracy. The politics, though, is not of the partisan, dickering sort that plays out in squabbles over the scope of a financial or auto-safety regulation. Rather the politics is of a philosophical sort: a devotion to the liberal republican principles that motivate inclusive, multipolar, and rivalrous engagement.[27]

But besides conceding while reframing the "shell game" critique, there is further reason not to yield to those criticizing process-perfecting review. As Cass Sunstein and Adrian Vermeule recently argued, the D.C. Circuit has long been using conventional merits review to dictate libertarian regulatory outcomes.[28] Similar observations have been made with great frequency about the Supreme Court—not surprisingly, given that many of the most prominent administrative law cases in recent years have been decided 5–4, with the Court dividing along highly predictable ideological lines. Thus it isn't as if our current, merits-based review is immune to the machinations of politically motivated judges.

What's more, I harbor hope that judges newly sensitized to the constitutional foundations of the administrative separation of powers will find themselves drawn to a principled process-perfecting review. But even if judges fall off the custodial wagon once in a while, there is a silver lining when it comes to judicial flakiness and process-perfecting review. Fear that the courts won't fairly (or simply ably) referee administrative procedure ought to provide even greater impetus for Congress and the president to act preemptively and comprehensively. Specifically, the political branches can prescribe richer, transsubstantive suites of measures, the effects of which scream out rivalrous, vigorous administrative governance and obviate the need for further judicially prescribed remediation that is, at best, piecemeal and disjointed and, at worst, tainted by the judges' political predilections. The APA of course did a good deal of this back in 1946. But, as I alluded to above and will argue more fully in the following chapter, what the APA prescribes may at times fall short of ensuring a well-functioning administrative separation of powers.

Judicial partisanship and piecemeal remediation are not the only concerns with a pivot to process-perfecting review. Some, particularly those less enamored with the virtues of the administrative separation of powers, might find a judicial retreat from reviewing the merits of agency rules and orders troubling. Specifically, critics may worry that process-perfecting courts will not be able to correct clear substantive errors apt to arise from time to time notwithstanding the meaningful participation of all three administrative rivals. Thus, for them, the availability of a judicial backstop is a source of great comfort.

Yet it is far from certain that the administrative triumvirate is collectively any less sensitive to the imperatives of administrative law and sound public policy than are judges, likely to apply some form of arbitrary and capricious review, apt to be over their heads when it comes to evaluating technocratic challenges, and not entirely free from political bias. Indeed, judges might introduce as many substantive errors as they correct.[29]

One is therefore reminded of Justice Robert Jackson's wry admonishment not to put too much stock in the accuracy or wisdom of judges—something we are conditioned to do, Justice Jackson surmised, simply because courts usually enjoy the last word. Throwing shade on his own venerated court, the justice cautioned: "We are not final because we are infallible, but we are infallible only because we are final."[30] By adopting process-perfecting review, courts will be the final word far less frequently. This seemingly suits some long-time observers like Jerry Mashaw well, for he too has been known to strike a skeptical note about the much-ballyhooed wonders of judicial review. For Mashaw, "[j]udicial review controls administrative action in the same way that tornadoes control the rice crop in Arkansas: they appear unpredictably, wreak havoc, and then depart."[31]

Beyond these sundry objections to process-perfecting review lies one more: a doctrinal one. Some may insist that the courts have already committed themselves to a hands-off approach to administrative process. In *Vermont Yankee Nuclear Power Corp. v. Natural Resources Defense Council,* the Supreme Court seemed to have done exactly that. Writing for a unanimous Court, then Justice William Rehnquist found process-based review (of the David Bazelon variety) to be inconsistent with the dictates of the APA.[32] Yet a return today to process-based review would not directly conflict with the *Vermont Yankee* precedent. My custodial imperative is grounded in theories of constitutional structure and turns less on agency conformity to statutory procedures than on an understanding of administrative law as coextensive with constitutional law.[33] Simply stated, the APA by itself may not do enough to ensure the constitutional legitimacy of administrative governance. It therefore cannot be the final word on administrative procedure.

Reinforcing Rivalrous Administration in Action: Judicial Review Where the Administrative Separation of Powers Is Disabled

Before taking up legislative solutions to address the constitutional vulnerabilities of the first *pax administrativa*—the work of Chapter 10—let us dig even deeper in the doctrinal weeds. Let us apply this custodial theory of reinforcing rivalrous administration, employing both merits and process-perfecting forms of review to address some real-world examples where the administrative separation of powers appears to be disabled.

One of the virtues of the administrative separation of powers as an explanatory and normative phenomenon is its broad, transsubstantive reach. Despite or, quite possibly, because of its broad, transsubstantive reach, the tripartite system is susceptible to being thwarted in several ways and across any number of locations. The administrative separation of powers can be expressly violated, quietly or even accidently subverted, or legally cabined through duly authorized acts of Congress.

In what follows, I identify three classes of cases. First, I take up the easiest of cases. Here the letter of the law is flouted in ways that marginalize, defang, or circumvent one or two administrative rivals. Second, I confront more challenging cases in which technically lawful practices nevertheless have the effect of marginalizing, defanging, or circumventing one or two administrative rivals. Lastly, I tackle especially hard cases in which the constitutional branches legally and collectively subvert the administrative separation of powers. In the course of discussing easy, moderate, and difficult cases, I consider whether and with what force courts should intervene to reinforce rivalrous administration—and quite possibly spur comprehensive legislative reform.

A quick note before proceeding: The examples below tend to cast the president and agency heads as our story's chief villains. This is true-to-life casting, reflecting contemporary administrative power imbalances. Modern presidents have shown great eagerness and dexterity in their efforts to dominate the administrative domain. As discussed, outsourcing and marketization have done much to incapacitate the civil service—and the various privatization initiatives have had the further effect of sapping the strength and capacity of civil society. Indeed, the entire businesslike government movement envisions a CEO-style agency head with far more authority and control than exists within a well-functioning system of administrative checks and balances. Surely we can conceive of the civil service or civil society acting subversively on a regular basis. But, for the moment at least, it is implausible to think of either of them out-Heroding Herod.

Easy Cases. Easy cases involve violations of the letter of the law—that is, when some statutorily guaranteed component of the administrative separation of powers is supposed to apply in full but does not because of an unauthorized act, omission, or indulgence by administrative or constitutional actors. Imagine, for instance, that the White House or an agency head directs the promulgation of a rule without first providing the public with notice or an opportunity to comment. In this example, the constitutional branches have not collectively acted to suspend or reconfigure the default framework that engendered the first *pax administrativa*'s administrative separation of powers. Quite the contrary, the presumption, however implicit, is the converse one—that rivalrous, inclusive administrative governance is intended and expected to operate in full.

The judicial remedy here is fairly intuitive: a rejection of whatever substantive action the agency arrives at through these impoverished, imbalanced, and statutorily deficient administrative processes. This remedy, moreover, ought to be perceived as uncontroversial. After all, judicial invalidation does not rely on my new constitutional theory of public administration. Courts already reject agency actions that arise out of statutorily deficient processes. That is, they insist on compliance with congressionally prescribed procedures regardless whether the judges recognize those procedures as an essential part of the constitutional scaffolding that supports the administrative separation of powers. (To be clear, this doesn't mean that statutory violations of this sort are necessarily *mala in se*. They may seem so, but only because we've already internalized the constitutional norms motivating the statutory prohibitions.)

Moderately Challenging Cases. Moderately challenging cases present themselves when the spirit of the administrative separation of powers is violated—that is, when neither constitutional nor administrative actors expressly violate specific statutory laws or judicial orders but nevertheless act in ways that undercut the tripartite architecture of administrative power. Consider a few examples.

First, agency leaders may hire contractors to draft rules or to determine whether those seeking disability benefits or welfare support are indeed eligible. Though no specific law is violated,[34] the outsourcing of these discretionary responsibilities endangers our enduring, evolving separation of powers, for reasons explained in Chapter 6.

When confronted with agency actions that reflect engagement by contractors rather than civil servants, courts can and should restore a well-functioning administrative separation of powers. Judges committed to existing tools and doctrines may provide agencies with a choice: accept a nudge in favor of reinforcing rivalrous administration or disregard that nudge and suffer, as a consequence, more searching—that is, less deferential—merits review. Alternatively, process-perfecting courts may categorically reject agency actions arising out of compromised procedures, thereby conditioning judicial approval on the agency's fidelity to the administrative separation of powers. This latter, process-perfecting approach would, quite possibly, obligate agency officials to abandon the use of contractors, at least those who carry out policymaking or policy-implementing responsibilities.

Second, Congress may empower select segments of civil society, by granting interest groups special advisory roles, funding their activities, or even giving them veto authority over administrative rules.[35] Supporting segments of civil society in these ways may not be unlawful. But, when viewed through the lens of the administrative separation of powers, such group-specific congressional support—unless, perhaps, its effect is unmistakably remedial or redistributive—appears to disrupt the democratic inclusivity and heterogeneity of civil society. Courts distressed by such moves may apply greater scrutiny when reviewing agency actions on the merits; or they may invalidate said actions on process grounds alone.

Third, we might classify some of the more novel forms of new millennial privatization—among them, deputization and backdoor regulation—as presenting moderately difficult cases. Recall that deputization involves private actors serving as informal and voluntary counterterrorism agents. Deputization is appealing because of its force-multiplying effects: We need more eyes and ears helping to detect and neutralize terrorist attacks. But the feds turn to deputies for another reason, too: Those deputies are at times better situated to conduct surveillance and acquire and analyze intelligence.

The deputies' comparative advantage is part legal and part cultural. As a matter of constitutional and statutory law, deputies are generally less stringently regulated than are government officials. They thus can reach further and deeper than their public sector counterparts. And, as a cultural matter, suspects or targets are more likely to let their guard down when interacting with someone they believe is serving in a helpful, purely commercial capacity—think delivery guys, bank employees, telecom technicians, and the like—than when they are interacting with government officials whom they see as powerful and adversarial.

How should courts respond when agencies deploy deputies? Most straightforwardly, courts may drop the longstanding (and regularly accorded) presumption of regularity in those contexts heavily influenced by the work of deputies.[36] Deputies stand in, and do the dirty work, for civil servants whose expertise, bureaucratic socialization, and special legal obligations make them especially worthy candidates for judicial trust and deference.

Note that here we see the administrative separation of powers serving one of its less heralded functions. The administrative separation of powers is not just engendering rivalrous deliberation but also promoting effective specialization—that is, allocating discrete responsibilities among differently situated rivals. The bottom line is that deputization interferes with the proper allocation of administrative responsibilities. This has a practical component insofar as we understand bureaucratic professionals to be better trained and acculturated (than political appointees or members of the general public) to handle the pressures, challenges, and temptations of counterterrorism work. And it has a legal component insofar as Congress and the courts have set up regulatory structures with the expectation that bureaucratic professionals will be the ones doing the investigating and prosecuting. Transferring counterterrorism assignments from civil servants to private deputies has the undeniable effect of evading those regulatory structures. Thus courts may also consider treating private deputies as de facto *state actors,* subject to both the constitutional limitations imposed by the Fourth Amendment's prohibition on unreasonable searches and seizures and to privacy laws that obligate government officials to take special precautions when acquiring and analyzing personal data.

Turning to backdoor regulation, recall that in the aftermath of the 2008–2009 economic meltdown, the United States took controlling shares of teetering firms. In their capacity as corporate directors, the feds insisted that the firms adopt labor, environmental, and internal corporate governance reforms. How should we think of those reforms?

From a private law perspective, perhaps no problem exists. Deals had to be made to keep failing businesses afloat. Ceding control in exchange for a cash infusion is something struggling firms regularly do. Hence AIG was held up to considerable ridicule when word spread that the once otherwise sure-to-fail insurance giant was suing the federal government for imposing harsh bailout terms and conditions.[37] But from a public law perspective, concerns abound. Regardless how unsympathetic overextended, bailed-out businesses may be, we still need to demand State rectitude and unflinching compliance with the rule of law. One may therefore question the propriety of effectuating public policy reforms using commercial, rather than sovereign tools. We have public, transparent, and rigorous rulemaking and adjudicatory procedures that legitimate the exercise of sovereign force. Such procedures were largely elided here, leaving little room for civil servants and practically no room at all for civil society to participate in the design and implementation of regulatory measures.

The net result of backdoor regulation might seem fair insofar as the backdoor regulation didn't technically injure bailed-out firms, a fact not lost on the federal district court that entertained AIG's suit but awarded the firm no money damages.[38] Indeed, acceding to even the most draconian of government fiats left those firms better off than they would have been absent the bailout. The ghosts of Lehman Brothers can attest to that. But the very fact that the government purchased compliance should matter. It should matter insofar as the terms of that compliance were not subject to the type of rivalrous, deliberative input we've come to expect and demand whenever the State legislates or regulates.[39]

So, what to do? When it comes to reviewing commercially fashioned, backdoor regulations, judges may once again ratchet up the level of substantive scrutiny. Or they may simply invalidate such backdoor regulations as inconsistent with the democratic and bureaucratic imperatives of American public law. Note too that backdoor regulation of this sort puts federal officials in both an entirely enviable and altogether unwinnable situation—enviable because the officials had lawmaking and commercial tools at their disposal, and could use either or both as circumstances dictated; and unwinnable because the feds owed seemingly conflicting duties as corporate fiduciary and sovereign regulator. Perhaps this is yet another reason why courts should look askance at whatever policies derive from the fusion of sovereign–commercial relationships.

Fourth, and no doubt controversially, our study of the administrative separation of powers (and the constitutional custodialism that I say supports it) invites a reassessment of the role played by the powerful Office of Information and Regulatory Affairs (OIRA) in the federal rulemaking process. Through a series of executive orders, modern-day presidents have tasked OIRA with, among other things, ensuring all-but-finalized agency rules mesh well with White House priorities.[40] As a practical matter, when it comes to the promulgation of major rules, OIRA often enjoys something approximating the final say, determining whether those rules are indeed approved, reshaped, or scuttled.

There is no doubt that OIRA advances many important and salutary goals. But we may nevertheless question whether OIRA contributes positively to a well-functioning administrative separation of powers. OIRA, which is classified as part of the Executive Office of the President, seemingly offers the White House a major thumb on the scale at the last possible minute—after the administrative rivals have duked it out, collaborated, compromised, and ultimately arrived at a ready-to-promulgate rule. As Steven Croley puts it, "[t]here is a sense, after all, in which agencies and the White House occupy antagonistic positions, for the agency sends the White House a rule that the agency believes already responds to all implicated issues in the best possible way."[41] From this perspective, it seems as if OIRA's late-stage intervention gives the president a potentially destabilizing second bite of the apple. The first bite comes, we know, when the White House indirectly participates in the triangulated administrative scrum via its chosen, like-minded, and loyal agency leaders. Now, the second bite occurs when OIRA swoops in and alters that which was already forged in the administrative arena.

Note that some view OIRA as having a very different institutional valence. Some see OIRA as dominated by its civil servants, rather than by its presidentially appointed administrator.[42] But even if that were true, the problem is substantially the same: either way, one of the administrative rivals, be it presidential loyalists or independent civil servants, gets an eleventh-hour, second bite of the apple.

Thus as much as OIRA is a fixture, we may want to reconsider its role in light of its capacity to destabilize tripartite administrative governance. Here, too, courts committed to reinforcing rivalrous administration may do one of two things. Courts may look highly skeptically at agency actions altered by *ex post* OIRA involvement—and thus withhold or reduce the amount of deference accorded when conducting merits review. Or, instead, courts may simply invalidate any and all actions that reflect noninclusive, after-the-fact alterations by OIRA. The latter, process-perfecting approach would seemingly force the president and Congress to rethink the way OIRA bridges line agencies and the White House. Perhaps a better, more constitutionally compatible role for OIRA would be for it to participate directly in the notice-and-comment process, articulating presidential (or expert bureaucratic) interests and concerns like any other party or entity in an effort to persuade and shape rather than dictate substantive outcomes.[43]

One might, of course, wonder what if OIRA were fragmented in ways quite similar to how the line agencies themselves are disaggregated. That is, what if presidential appointees, civil servants, and members of the public all participated in OIRA's review of rules? Such a triangulated OIRA wouldn't raise the same concerns identified immediately above. To the contrary, the OIRA process would then constitute another iteration of separation of powers all the way forward. Still, there would be questions of necessity and utility: what work would a triangulated OIRA be doing above and beyond what the first set of administrative rivals had already accomplished?

Hard Cases. Hard cases arise when the constitutional branches have collectively and legally disabled the administrative separation of powers. Here I include federal legislative efforts to marketize the bureaucracy, to create independent agencies, and to exempt national security agencies and government corporations from many of administrative law's routine procedural and personnel protocols. Because I discussed marketization at length in Chapters 5 and 6, the practice warrants no further elaboration here. As such, I turn straightaway to the other three examples.

Independent Agencies. This book has concentrated on executive agencies, largely to the exclusion of independent agencies such as the FTC, the SEC, and the NLRB. (Roughly speaking and tracking how the Supreme Court treats the distinction, executive agencies are those whose presidentially appointed leaders are subject to summary dismissal; independent agencies are those whose presidentially appointed leaders—often called commissioners—may be fired only upon a "for cause" showing.) Now, however, it is worth taking a step back to consider how independent agencies fit within my account of the administrative separation of powers. The short answer is not well.

This might be surprising. At first blush, independent agencies seem to pose no special problem. Doctrinally, the constitutional pedigree of independent agencies is long and largely beyond question.[44] And, as a structural matter, the architecture of independent agency power is triangulated among agency leaders, members of civil society, and civil servants.

But independent agency tripartism and executive agency tripartism differ. They differ in two significant ways. First, as suggested above, independent agency heads are not as tightly tethered to the president. Congress insulates those running independent agencies from summary removal, subjecting them instead to presidential termination only upon a showing of some sort of dereliction of duty.[45] Congress further reduces presidential control over most independent agencies by obligating the president to make bipartisan appointments.[46] Thus some high-ranking appointees to independent agencies must be drawn from outside of the president's political party (and, quite likely, her circle of trusted aides and allies). Combined, these restrictions on presidential appointments and removal mean that a fair number of independent agency leaders are unlikely to fully share the president's ideological vision or programmatic objectives—and that none of the agency leaders can be readily dismissed simply for deviating from or resisting the White House's agenda.[47]

The president—and all that she stands for in our constitutional system—is thus systematically underrepresented in the administrative architecture of independent agencies. The corollary is also true: independent agency commissioners cannot claim an especially close connection or kinship to *any* of the constitutional branches—a connection that executive agency heads, civil servants, and members of civil society can each assert to demonstrate their own constitutional and administrative bona fides.

Second, independent agency commissioners are not only too distant from the president but also perhaps not distant enough from the civil service. After all, both independent agency heads and civil servants enjoy protection against summary removal and are generally expected to operate in a relatively apolitical fashion across presidential administrations.[48] Of course, this isn't always the case. Independent agency heads may very well act politically and, in any event, they are not completely insulated from subtle yet still powerful forms of presidential persuasion.[49] But to the extent that independent agency design serves its intended purpose—and thus succeeds in blunting presidential influence and control—we should expect to see some shared and overlapping traits between independent agency heads and civil servants. If so, the two groups may well be insufficiently rivalrous with one another in ways that overly homogenize administrative governance and thus threaten a well-functioning, tripartite administrative separation of powers.

In sum, independent agencies lack one of the isomorphic connections to the three great constitutional branches, with independent agency leaders at least somewhat disconnected from the president and thus less committed to championing the political interests of the nationally elected president. And independent agencies may well lack internal balance because two of the ostensible rivals are a lot alike: politically insulated, effectively tenured, and nominally nonpartisan experts.

I should add that my concerns with independent agencies are not the same as those usually raised by unitary executive theorists. Unitary executive theorists understand independent agencies as constitutionally suspect for the sole and, by their lights, sufficient reason that independent agency leaders are too disconnected from the president.[50] The existence of independent agencies may indeed have some limiting effects on the president's ability to carry out her constitutional duty to take care that the laws are faithfully executed.

My position differs from that of the unitary executive theorists, however, in the following way: I am just as troubled by an overly presidentialist administrative agency too closely tethered to the White House (perhaps as a result of civil servants and members of the public being bypassed, marginalized, or co-opted) as I am by an insufficiently presidentialist administrative agency largely insulated from the Oval Office. When it comes to agencies that do more than simply enforce or execute federal law, satisfying the Constitution's Take Care Clause is not, on its own, enough. An enduring, evolving separation of powers that carries forward into the administrative arena requires more. It requires a presidential standard bearer among the three administrative rivals, and that such a standard bearer is neither too dominant nor too dominated. Accordingly, assuming that independent agency heads and career civil servants are themselves too similar and thus insufficiently heterogeneous or rivalrous, the problem with independent agencies is a counterintuitive one: they are too unitary and therefore imbalanced—albeit not unitary and imbalanced in ways unitary executive theorists might welcome. And if they are imbalanced, then they are constitutionally suspect.

National Security Agencies. I plead guilty to a second material omission. I have largely bracketed the work of national security and foreign affairs agencies, even though those agencies play vital roles in the creation and expression of American law and policy.[51]

I am, however, hardly alone in treating national security and foreign affairs agencies differently: Congress and the courts certainly do. Congress exempts those agencies from many of administrative law's core obligations.[52] For example, the Pentagon, CIA, and State Department often need not go through the procedural requirements associated with notice-and-comment rulemaking.[53] And exemptions to the Freedom of Information Act permit those agencies to withhold from the public documents pertaining to the national defense.[54] In addition, the civil service is not nearly as strong in at least some of the national security agencies[55]—rendering the in-house workforces less independent and internally rivalrous. Lastly, both Congress and the courts have limited the public's ability to bring suits challenging administrative actions of a national security variety.[56] As such, much of what is conducted in the name of American national security policy occurs outside of the framework of the administrative separation of powers.[57]

Government Corporations. Over the years, Congress has delegated an increasing number of federal responsibilities to government corporations.[58] These corporations likewise—and by design—routinely operate outside of the ambit of ordinary federal domestic administrative law. For instance, Amtrak, the U.S. Postal Service, and In-Q-Tel (the CIA's venture capital firm), are each led by officials relatively insulated from the president. What's more, many corporations are staffed by at-will employees. (The Postal Service is a notable and telling exception. In fact, the businesslike government crowd harshly criticizes the Postal Service precisely because its rank-and-file employees are insufficiently marketized—and instead receive better compensation than their commercial counterparts at UPS and FedEx and enjoy greater job security.) And most government corporations are far less open than federal domestic agencies to the full range of opportunities for public participation.[59] Such differential treatment of government corporations prompted none other than Justice Scalia to gripe that Congress could "evade the most solemn obligations imposed by the Constitution by simply resorting to the corporate form."[60] For all the reasons just described, the administrative separation of powers as we know it is largely disabled in this space as well.

Remember that in all three of these contexts—really, four, once we loop marketization back in—the subversion of the administrative separation of powers is technically lawful and duly authorized. It isn't as if the rules of the game are violated by one constitutional or administrative actor mid-match. Marketized bureaucracies, independent agencies, national security agencies, and government corporations do not come about by one administrative rival marginalizing the others; nor do they come about by one constitutional actor, on its own, intervening when and how it sees fit in a blatant attempt to dominate the administrative chessboard. Rather, the rules of the game are changed *ex ante* and by consensus. And they are changed in a way that reflects a formal, procedurally sound, and collective, if still tacit, disavowal of an otherwise operable system of administrative separation of powers.

In deciding how courts ought to respond, we should begin by querying whether the curtailing or preemption of the administrative separation of powers in these particular contexts tracks what we encounter—*and accept*—on the constitutional playing field. In other words, is it possible that these departures from the administrative separation of powers make sense because the special powers exercised by a marketized bureaucracy, independent agencies, national security agencies, and government corporations are ones the Constitution assigns to one and only one branch (or doesn't even worry about)?

Let us start with marketization. Marketization isn't a targeted, surgical tool employed only in narrow domains. Instead, marketization sweeps widely across much of the federal expanse, converting many policymaking and policy-implementing civil servants into at-will employees. Policymaking and policy-implementing responsibilities are, as I have been stressing, quintessential functions of the liberal democratic State—and, generally speaking, must submit to the logic and discipline of our separations of powers, constitutional and administrative alike.

All of this is to say that any claim that marketized bureaucacies are sound because the powers they exercise are ones not traditionally subsumed within constitutional checks and balances would be a fatuous one. Marketization enables the consolidation and greater politicization (and presidentialization) of administrative power in a manner that we would find offensive if concentrated at the constitutional level. While marketization merits some respect, if only because the practice arises out of duly enacted legislation and duly promulgated regulations, we cannot ignore the fact that it undercuts a vital administrative rivalry and does so broadly and largely indiscriminately. Insofar as entire categories of civil servants are identified for reclassification, marketization jeopardizes the entire *pax administrativa* project.

The basis for challenging marketization laws and regulations is therefore the same one we would use to dispute acts of Congress authorizing legislative and line-item vetoes. Recall that legislative veto provisions permitted Congress, or even a single house of Congress, to unilaterally invalidate agency rules or orders.[61] The line-item veto, in turn, empowered the president to unilaterally cancel specific spending provisions already signed into law.[62] The Court found both types of vetoes constitutionally anathema, largely because they each concentrated constitutional powers that should have remained disaggregated—shared among the three great branches. The Court did so notwithstanding the procedurally impeccable pedigrees of those laws authorizing legislative and line-item vetoes in the first place.

Judicial reaction to marketized bureaucracy should be similarly strong. Courts may withhold deference in an attempt to encourage the political branches to engender more rivalrous deliberation (ideally, by reinstating a politically insulated civil service). Or courts may simply reject any decision, interpretation, or action that arises out of this compromised, marketized administrative process, effectively obligating Congress to reinstate the civil service.

Moving beyond marketization, perhaps it is true that the constitutional separation of powers isn't supposed to fully apply when it comes to the specific responsibilities entrusted to independent agencies, national security agencies, and government corporations. If, say, Congress tasked independent agencies only with adjudicatory responsibilities, we might then be comfortable with aspects of the administrative separation of powers being disabled. Because we do not expect—or, indeed, usually permit—the president to involve herself in the resolution of disputes before the federal courts, it should not be surprising to likewise deny the president's appointed and readily removable agency leaders a role in administrative adjudications.[63]

Turning to national security and foreign affairs, some surely argue that the courts and Congress should yield to the president on questions of defense, diplomacy, and intelligence. Following that logic, most forcefully expressed by Justice George Sutherland in *United States v. Curtiss-Wright Export Corp.*,[64] when it comes to the delegation of national security-related responsibilities to administrative agencies, perhaps it is only sensible for civil servants and civil society to similarly stand down. In other words, maybe the administrative separation of powers should be relaxed, just as the constitutional separation of powers purportedly is.

And, to the extent that government corporations perform only commercial—and not sovereign—functions, we might not be so bothered by the disabling of the administrative separation of powers. After all, the Supreme Court has identified a range of "market participant" exceptions that limit the reach or applicability of constitutional proscriptions and prescriptions to government entities acting in a decidedly commercial capacity.[65]

There is, however, a major problem. Each of these arguments is highly contestable, if not objectively wrong. Independent agencies do far more than simply adjudicate disputes. They also promulgate rules that look and operate a lot like the laws that Congress passes. The SEC, for instance, is a prodigious promulgator of such rules. Furthermore, independent agencies exercise executive power when they investigate and prosecute perceived wrongdoers. Again, the SEC is a case in point but hardly alone. In short, most of our independent agencies cannot claim to be exclusively adjudicating in ways that might warrant or justify categorical insulation from the president. Likewise, national security and foreign affairs agencies carry out responsibilities far broader than those few that the Constitution vests in the president alone. From raising a navy, to regulating the gathering of intelligence, to ratifying treaties, Congress (*pace* Justice Sutherland) is frequently the president's co-equal and potentially rivalrous partner.[66] Hence just as big-picture national security policies reflect the combined efforts of the constitutional branches, so too should the associated administrative responsibilities reflect, wherever possible, the full and hearty engagement of all of our administrative rivals. Lastly, government corporations exercise any number of sovereign powers, including rulemaking and rate setting, that cannot be characterized as mere market transactions or as proprietary interventions entirely peripheral to the task of democratic governance.[67] As such, claims that there is no need for government corporations to submit to checks and balances similarly fall wide of the mark.

So, mindful of both the legally sound processes that engendered these administrative carve-outs and the constitutional problems these carve-outs pose (insofar as they disable the administrative separation of powers), judges may consider applying a rebuttable presumption against said carve-outs. It would be the responsibility of the political branches to justify any such subversion of the administrative separation of powers. Specifically, they would have to explain why some aspect of the administrative separation of powers is particularly injurious or simply unnecessary. The Federal Reserve, the independent body that sets national macroeconomic policy, may well be such a case where everyone agrees that populist and presidentialist involvement would be ill advised and incongruous. But if no such reason is proffered, or if the reasons proffered are unpersuasive, then courts may ratchet up their merits-based scrutiny. That is to say, the courts may more stringently police administrative outcomes that do not reflect the internal balancing of diverse, rivalrous interests that the administrative separation of powers tries to ensure. Alternatively, the courts may employ their new, process-perfecting tools and insist upon an administrative decisionmaking framework that is more rivalrous, heterogeneous, and inclusive.

Potemkin Administrative Separation of Powers

The pages immediately above contain my suggestions for countering express and apparent (if not always witting) challenges to a well-functioning administrative separation of powers. But the effects of outsourcing, marketization, and other privatization initiatives are more broadly and subtly felt. In fact, they are felt even in places that haven't (yet) been marketized or outsourced.

Specifically, the effects are felt in departments and offices where the remaining civil servants are hanging on by a thread. These civil servants may well be demoralized and battered from years and years of anti-bureaucracy rhetoric—and now act compliantly if only because they know that any showing of resistance or defiance might result in their jobs being outsourced or marketized. Worse still, these surviving civil servants run the risk of being even less respected going forward precisely because they are perceived as meek and overly accommodating. Note too that some of those with an acute instinct for self-preservation have already marketized themselves. As a RAND report from 2000 notes, one way that government employees keep privatization and marketization hawks at bay is by voluntarily and preemptively downgrading their employment positions—that is, accepting lower pay and more limited benefits in exchange for retaining their jobs.[68]

It would be wrong, therefore, to assume that those departments and offices technically and nominally untouched by outsourcing or marketization are oases of the administrative separation of powers. They may well be mirages. We have what appears to be the proper ingredients for vibrant, heterogeneous, and rivalrous administrative engagement. But, upon closer inspection, it is apparent that what we really have is a very troubled, hollowed-out enterprise.

Distinguishing these Potemkin administrative villages from the real thing presents a major challenge. And bolstering the former is an even bigger challenge. How, after all, are courts supposed to counter unspoken but palpable threats to the administrative separation of powers? Here especially the courts need an assist from the political branches to take affirmative, comprehensive steps to rebuild the civil service and enrich civil society. It is to that political project that I now turn.

10

Legislative Custodialism

B elieve it or not, articulating a jurisprudence of constitutional custodialism is the simple part. By intuition, disposition, and practice, courts
are already inclined to act in ways that promote a well-functioning administrative separation of powers. My goal in the previous chapter was to turn
that judicial inclination into a full-blown doctrinal commitment, to provide a philosophical and legal blueprint that gives effect to that commitment, and to identify a range of contexts in which the courts may be called
upon to reinforce rivalrous administration.

Now to the really heavy lifting: persuading or compelling Congress and
the president to turn their swords into ploughshares—and dedicate themselves to strengthening administrative checks and balances. It is heavy lifting
because it requires the political branches to undertake measures likely to be
unpopular, expensive, and at odds with their own self-interests.

What's more, this lifting needs to begin soon. Time is short. The administrative separation of powers has been foundering for decades. Absent an
imminent revival, the modern constitutional project of *pax administrativa*
will most certainly fail.

What we need now is a set of legislative reforms to reverse the privatization agenda and to embolden, harden, and inspire the administrative partisans such that they are not readily deterred or disheartened notwithstanding any procedural, political, or institutional hurdles placed before
them. And we need to telegraph the purpose behind these reforms, making

sure the electorate (and the rivals themselves) understand what we're doing and why it is worth the time, effort, and expense to bring about a twenty-first-century bureaucratic renaissance.

Thus accompanying and reinforcing the various proposals must be some sort of anti-Powell Memo, a better-late-than-never rejoinder to Lewis Powell's deeply influential 1971 manifesto. Recall again that Powell urged corporate titans to take the reins of government—and to do so by spending money, drumming up grassroots support, lobbying and litigating, and preaching the virtues of markets and the corresponding depravities of government regulation. Today, that script needs to be flipped, alerting the rest of us to the perversity and unconstitutionality of the Privatization Revolution and trailblazing a way out of our current morass.

Reinforcing Rivalrous Administration through Legislation

If custodially minded courts signal a willingness to routinely strike down agency actions, or even just withhold deference, because one or more administrative rival is excluded, marginalized, or subordinated, the political branches will likely be compelled to respond. Under such circumstances, the primary way Congress and the president should respond is by enacting laws that reinstate excluded rivals and strengthen those rivals who were nominally present but effectively marginalized.

Of course, there is always the possibility of a *Eureka!* moment, with the political branches acting the part of Christmas morning Ebenezer Scrooge, who awakens to the error of his ways and is quick to make amends. Short of the president and members of Congress being visited by the ghost of *pax administrativa* past or the ghost of privatization yet to come, I don't think we should hold our breath. Old habits die hard, particularly if those old habits are as rational as trying to dominate the administrative sphere for programmatic, institutional, or partisan gain. So nudging and obligating it is, with the courts essentially requiring the political branches to act custodially.

The political branches may, at first, be inclined to patch up whatever discrete tear the courts locate in the increasingly shopworn fabric of the administrative separation of powers. But case-by-case fixes are tedious and unreliable. Whatever marginal advantage the political branches might obtain by proceeding incrementally—and minimally compliantly—is apt to be offset by the costs incurred when still unsatisfied courts continue invalidating agency actions in other, still unpatched parts of the administrative state. Thus, as I have been suggesting, it would behoove the political branches to act preemptively and comprehensively, boosting the entire class of civil servants and enriching civil society writ large. Here we might draw an analogy to structural litigation and to the forward-looking reforms that arise out of judgments or consent decrees imposed on, say, municipal police departments, county school boards, or state prison systems. Specifically, when government units are found to be acting in an unconstitutional fashion, they are expected to work with the courts to cure past infirmities and guard against future wrongdoing. With that analogy in mind, I turn here to discuss systemic reforms that the political branches should and, perhaps, must take to promote a healthy, vibrant administrative sphere.

I focus first on the civil service—the most battered and beleaguered of the three administrative branches. This book has repeatedly shown the many ways in which outsourcing, marketization, and the overall commercialization and politicization of the executive branch weaken the federal civil service. It has also shown that the general public is itself wary, and generally unsupportive, of the mandarin institution.

I then turn to civil society. In addition to being marginalized or co-opted by the forces of privatization, civil society is also becoming more and more internally imbalanced and unequal. The concern here is that rising economic and political inequalities are spilling over into the administrative sphere and affecting—in truth, skewing—public participation in the administrative process. Accordingly, work needs to be done to ensure that more than just well-heeled lobbyists, campaign bundlers, assorted one-percenters, and the occasional (and exceptionally dogged) gadfly are heard on matters of regulation and public benefits.

A few notes before proceeding. First, agency leaders are notably absent from my list of rivals needing fortification. Again, this is because agency leaders have shown themselves to be the principal beneficiaries of privatization's fusion of political and commercial power.

Second, we must remain mindful of this exercise's constitutional dimensions. The policy proposals and prescriptions that follow are necessary to reestablish the American administrative state's constitutional bona fides. One can quibble with some of the policy choices I make, question certain omissions, and suggest ready alternatives. But though opportunities certainly exist for revisions, additions, and improvements, there are certain features of a second *pax administrativa* that are nonnegotiable. Specifically, there is little room for concession or compromise when it comes to ensuring that the rank-and-file administrative workforce remains meaningfully politically independent, legally empowered, and professionally competent. Likewise, there is little room for concession or compromise when it comes to ensuring that all members of civil society are meaningfully empowered to participate vigorously in practically all facets of administrative governance.

Third, I am well aware that today's political climate may be especially inhospitable to the proposals that follow. But this is precisely the time to lay out a blueprint for reform and present it as a stark and urgent alternative to a Trumpist vision of public administration. As of the time of this writing, President Trump continues to push a businesslike government agenda—and does so in ways that are especially easy to cast as corrupt and denounce as dangerous. I may go so far as to suggest that Trump's intemperate attacks on bureaucracy, his appointment of glaringly unqualified cabinet officials and presidential aides, and the torrent of conflicts of interest surrounding him, his family members, and his inner circle of advisors may prompt even those most dismissive of the first *pax administrativa* to give the civil service and civil society a second chance. Paraphrasing John F. Kennedy, a crisis brings danger but also great opportunity.[1] If—or, rather, when—opportunity knocks, this should be our answer.

Rebuilding the Civil Service

Support for the civil service in the administrative arena is critical in the same way support for the courts is critical in the constitutional arena. In both settings, space must be preserved for reasoned research and deliberation detached from the hurly-burly, coarseness, and occasional bullying tactics of majoritarian politics. In what follows, I propose several ways the political branches can improve the quality of the civil service, its standing in political, legal, and cultural milieus, and, ultimately, its capacity to hold its own among administrative rivals. Doing so is a necessary precondition for achieving a constitutionally sound second *pax administrativa*.

Increasing the quality and the standing of the civil service are two distinct goals. Yet they go hand-in-hand. A newly and objectively improved but still poorly regarded civil service will be saddled with the burden of continually having to fend off popular outsourcing, marketizing, and politicizing efforts. If anything, those attacks will intensify; a still disliked but now more powerful civil service will be viewed as an even bigger threat. What's more, the civil servants themselves will grow weary of the constant defensive struggle. Recruitment, retention, and on-the-job morale will no doubt continue to suffer[2]—thus jeopardizing whatever work is done to improve the quality of American bureaucracy.

By the same token, a weak, hollowed-out, Potemkin civil service that the public (mistakenly) holds in high regard is likewise fated to fail. Either we will quickly see through the facade or we will foolishly buy in, believing that the administrative separation of powers is working when in fact the bureaucracy is getting outmaneuvered and outclassed at every turn.

So, again, we need both. We need an esteemed *and* formidable civil service. A highly regarded civil service is likely to attract even stronger personnel, whose quality work will further increase the bureaucracy's stature and its effectiveness in the administrative domain.

The Five *R*s

We may frame our comprehensive civil service reclamation project around five *R*s: renationalization, reinstatement, recruitment, retention, and reputation building. I begin with the need to reverse the privatization movement—specifically, to *renationalize* outsourced work and *reinstate* civil service protections for those government employees recently converted into at-will workers. Simply stated, an independent civil service—as opposed to highly dependent cadres of contractors and marketized government workers—centrally involved in administrative policymaking and policy-implementation responsibilities is a necessary step in the constitutional reconstruction of the American administrative state.

Still, this is only the first step. Without more, a renationalized, reinstated civil service remains a relatively weak institutional counterweight. The perception of a dysfunctional, unimportant bureaucracy enabled the outsourcing and marketization movements of the late twentieth and early twenty-first centuries. And, completing the vicious circle, the popularity of those movements further degraded and demoralized the contingent of civil servants still standing. Those still standing civil servants are, as discussed, highly vulnerable. They may fear, with justification, that unless they act compliantly, they too will be replaced by contractors.

Thus supplementation in the form of civil service recruitment, retention, and reputation building is needed to strengthen the appearance and reality of the federal civil service. It is only then that we can make an especially forceful claim that the administrative separation of powers is (again) worthy of constitutional and, ideally, popular approbation.

With regard to advancing the quality and standing of the civil service, I confess that many of the proposals detailed below are taken straight from the pages of the military's playbook. This shouldn't be too surprising. The military is, after all, a large bureaucracy—and a bureaucracy that succeeds where the civil service seemingly fails (or fails to play): in higher education, on Madison Avenue, and in the hearts and minds of the American people.

Renationalizing and Reinstating

Most urgently, Congress and the president need to reverse the outsourcing craze, at least where contractors or other privatized deputies play a substantial policymaking or policy-implementing role. In calling for the political branches to reverse course, I am intentionally leaving to the side consideration of private actors assigned purely ministerial, nondiscretionary responsibilities. I am also leaving to the side the contracting out of largely commercial jobs that have no particular relation to the State *qua* State—for example, secretarial, catering, gardening, clerical, IT, and janitorial work. There might be good reasons to insource those jobs, too. Perhaps we worry about contractor corruption. Or perhaps we value nonmarketized, well-paying government employment as a form of economic empowerment and security—a gateway to the middle class as it historically has been. But those reasons sound in something other than fidelity to separating and checking State power and thus are beyond the scope of this project of constitutional reconstruction and redemption.

Any commitment to insource even just the discretion-laden privatized government jobs would constitute a monumental shift in the theory and practice of contemporary American public administration. Such insourcing surely couldn't be realized overnight. President Obama came into office signaling interest in insourcing and directed his agency heads accordingly.[3] But Obama soon realized that the United States lacked the public infrastructure and, perhaps, political will to make good on this pledge.[4] So did his first secretary of state. As a senator, Hillary Clinton cosponsored legislation (with Senator Bernie Sanders, of all people) limiting reliance on private military contractors, with the ultimate goal of banning contractors from combat and security roles.[5] Within a year's time, once she moved across town to Foggy Bottom, she found herself relying heavily on military contractors, including the notorious Blackwater[6]—already identified by the governments we installed in Baghdad[7] and Kabul[8] as well as by Congress and the Justice Department as disreputable, if not criminal.[9] All of this is to say that the difficulty of unwinding existing contractual relationships, coupled with the fact that the government sector is currently short on personnel and in-house expertise, suggests a need for a phased transition.

Perhaps a realistic plan of attack would take the following form: First, Congress imposes an immediate moratorium on all new contracts involving the outsourcing of discretionary sovereign responsibilities. Second, all federal agencies promptly review all existing contracts (and other deputization arrangements). For those contracts (and arrangements) involving the outsourcing of discretionary sovereign responsibilities, agencies have two years to insource—that is, to unwind the private sector relationships and build up the necessary in-house capacity. Third, Congress fully finances, and slightly subsidizes, renationalization. Thus agencies committed to insourcing automatically receive additional government FTEs—that is, funding to hire, say, 1.25 full-time government employees for every full-time contractor or private deputy that is let go. John DiIulio has recently called on the feds to hire one million new government workers.[10] That number strikes me as about right, if not a little low.

To be sure, overseeing the agency review process presents a major problem. Agency officials are already generally supposed to refrain from outsourcing "inherently governmental responsibilities." Yet, as we know from Chapters 5 and 6, these officials routinely outsource some of the most sensitive and discretionary federal responsibilities.[11]

In fairness to the agency officials, they've been receiving mixed signals. Notwithstanding the general prohibition on privatizing inherently governmental responsibilities, the default position has long been to contract out whenever and wherever possible. Clearly, we need to switch the default. There should now be a rebuttable presumption against outsourcing—such that officials bear the burden of justifying why they are not insourcing a given task. Coupled with that reversal of default positions ought to be an expansion of the universe of agency personnel involved in the insourcing review process. Specifically, insourcing decisions should be entrusted to a panel comprised of an equal number of agency leaders and career personnel, the latter of whom ought to be reliably far less favorably disposed to contractors.

At the same time as we are renationalizing, we also have to reinstate the civil service. The government workforce that stands to assume many of the heretofore outsourced tasks and responsibilities needs to be a politically insulated and professional workforce. This means that the marketization script must likewise be flipped, again at least with respect to jobs that call for the exercise of discretionary State power. Marketization is not nearly as pronounced a practice as outsourcing. Nor is it a trend that is as hard to reverse as outsourcing. Therefore, a commitment to restore civil service protections could and should begin right away, through legislation reversing the marketization practices of the new millennium.

Major reforms are always expensive. But let's remember a couple of things. First, outsourcing hasn't proven to be nearly as cost-effective as promised. There are, to be sure, plenty of fiscal illusions—that is, accounting tricks suggestive of cost savings. But there is very little tangible evidence.

Recall the data we have suggesting that contracting is more expensive, even in the absence of allegations of fraud or abuse. (Such evidence further supports my claim that contracting is often more about political power and political expediency than dollars and cents).

Second, there is likewise reason to suspect that the cost savings from marketizing the bureaucracy look bigger on paper than they actually are. Under a neo-spoils system, there are real and appreciable costs associated with declining wages, higher turnover, more bureaucratic amateurism, lower-quality work, and a greater incidence of judicial intervention and invalidation as a result of said lower-quality work.

Thus, while the expenditures associated with insourcing and reinstating the civil service—that is, the unwinding of contracts, the staffing up of the civil service, the reallocation of responsibilities, workspaces, and the like—will no doubt be high in the short term, it is far from certain that the long-term costs of a truly demarketized government workforce will be considerably higher than they would be were we to continue privatizing from within and without. But, again, the costs are beside the point. Demarketization isn't just a good idea under the right circumstances. It is also a constitutional imperative.

Recruitment

Renationalizing government jobs and reinstating government workers into the civil service would nominally restore the administrative separation of powers. I say nominally because, if nothing else were done, the administrative separation of powers would remain a precarious proposition. After all, formal restoration of the civil service would do little to address the fact that its members remain vulnerable, weak from years of attrition and demoralization, and susceptible to future incursions of the sort that helped undermine the first *pax administrativa*. Accordingly, in order for the administrative separation of powers to merit constitutional valorization, the reinstated civil service needs to be substantially fortified along a number of dimensions. What follows are some proposals.

Elite Training: A National Government Service Academy. The U.S. military boasts West Point, Annapolis, and the Air Force Academy. Their pageantry, history, and cultural and professional cachet are unrivaled. When we think of these academies, we think of sacrifice, excellence, and valor—and quickly associate these schools with their staggering rosters of graduates: Dwight Eisenhower, Ulysses S. Grant, Douglas MacArthur, William Tecumseh Sherman, George Patton, John J. Pershing, Omar Bradley, Matthew Ridgway, Chester Nimitz, and Senator John McCain. Darlings of the Confederacy, including Jefferson Davis, Robert E. Lee, Thomas "Stonewall" Jackson, and J.E.B. Stuart were themselves once West Point standouts.

The highly selective admissions process—requiring congressional sponsorship, academic distinction, and physical prowess—sparks interest, fuels ambition, and no doubt breeds envy. The perception of student and institutional excellence is reflected in, among other things, the academies' outsized success in securing prestigious Rhodes Scholarships. West Point boasts ninety-one Rhodes Scholars. That is the fifth most, behind only Harvard, Princeton, Yale, and Stanford, each of which enrolls a much larger academic class. The Naval and Air Force academies have forty-six and thirty-eight scholars, respectively; the Air Force's number is particularly impressive given that the school wasn't founded until 1954, just about fifty years after the scholarships to Oxford were first awarded. For comparison's sake, Columbia students have won only twenty-seven such scholarships and Berkeley's only twenty-four. Even the Virginia Military Institute, a considerably less selective or academically esteemed state military academy, has won more Rhodes Scholarships than the likes of Carnegie Mellon, Cal Tech, Georgia Tech, USC, and William & Mary.[12]

Education at all of the national military academies is free, and students commit themselves to a certain number of years of postgraduate service.[13] Successful graduates receive their choice of plum postings. For example, "more than nine out of ten midshipmen get their first or second choice." And most are then primed to be fast-tracked up the chain of command.[14]

We of course have no such national collegiate academy for civilian government service. We should.[15] Other nations do. France's École nationale d'administration (ENA) is perhaps the gold standard. The ENA reflects—and in turn helps validate—the high esteem the French civil service and its *haut fonctionnaries* have long enjoyed.[16] Creating a similar academy in the United States would go a long way in making clear the prominence and importance of the American civil service. It would encourage young men and women to aspire to careers in the civil service and would make those careers more affordable, accessible, enriching, and influential.[17]

The *affordability* point is straightforward. College tuition is expensive, and increasingly so, rising at what many see as unsustainable rates.[18] Federal government pay is fine but not exceptional. An academy that provided full scholarships and assured graduates of their choice of civil service postings would go a long way in attracting top students.[19]

The *accessibility* point is just as critical. In an absurdist inversion of the old Groucho Marx line, securing membership in this currently beleaguered, seemingly undesirable club is actually quite difficult. The exam process is notoriously inflexible, and the timing and likelihood of hires uncertain.[20] The unpredictable hiring process discourages capable, committed would-be public servants from applying. Rather than wait around for the possibility of a job opening in some department at some time in the future, they instead choose alternative careers.[21] Thus the very best of our civically minded young college and professional school graduates are likely to seek a more direct, though still extremely competitive, political appointment, serving as the special assistant to the special assistant to the assistant secretary of whatever.

This preference to serve the agency leadership is doubly consequential. Like when LeBron James chose the Miami Heat over the New York Knicks in free agency, the decision of top graduates to work as political aides to agency leaders rather than join the civil service affects both "teams" and the relative competitiveness of the two. The agency leadership is fortified by this infusion of talent. The civil service is correspondingly weakened. And, perhaps most importantly, the administrative separation of powers— just like the Eastern Conference of the NBA—becomes that much less balanced, lopsided in favor of agency leaders. For this reason, guaranteed civil service commissions in the agency of graduates' choice would make the path to service easier to navigate,[22] strengthen the civil service, and make the administrative arena a more competitively balanced one as impressive academy graduates operate as formidable counterweights to the agency politicos.

The *enriching and influential* claim is a social and cultural one. As noted, military academies portray the profession in the best light. If anything needs a beacon of excellence and a font of pride, it is our embattled civil service. But the civil service academy would also provide a profound intrinsic payoff, engendering what Paul Light calls a strong "spirit of service."[23] Students would, in effect, grow up as civil servants. Just as the Battle of Waterloo was, according to the Duke of Wellington, won on the pitches of Eton, future struggles to fix Social Security, combat climate change, and end homelessness may well be won on the intramural fields of America's civil service academy.

What's more, these students would, upon graduation, rise through the ranks together, building important and lifelong bridges within and across agencies and within and across professions. After all, liberal arts classes at the academy would be populated with aspiring Department of Transportation engineers, HHS social workers, Commerce Department economists, and

FDA lawyers, all learning, living, and playing together. This professional bonding and bridging—already so common among military officers—would help create (and revive) a thick, proud bureaucratic culture that is, on one hand, duly respectful and solicitous of agency leaders and members of civil society—and, on the other, fully prepared to resist those rivals' unsound or hyperpartisan proposals.

Agency leaders across the federal administrative state already know each other, if not socially then at the very least through their tight and often clubby political circles. It would be beneficial for talented civil servants to forge similar bonds of solidarity. And, like graduates of any other school, members of an academy class would be able to support one another, celebrate each other's accomplishments, and work extra hard to one up their old classmates as bureaucratic leaders and innovators. (Such tight-knit groups of civil servants might also apply healthy doses of peer pressure, thereby dissuading their classmates from "selling out" in favor of more remunerative jobs in the private sector.)

Lastly, the cohort of teachers staffing such an academy would serve as cheerleaders, critics, professional matchmakers, and, in many respects, the conscience of the civil service, lauding successes, documenting failures, and examing the ethics of bureaucracy—not a small or uninteresting topic given the various responsibilities imposed on civil servants by Congress, agency leaders, judges, their professional communities, and the public at large. Just like at the military academies, at least some of the instructors could be pulled from the upper ranks of the civil service and assigned a "tour" teaching a class or two at the civil service academy. Such a teaching assignment would no doubt be a mark of distinction—and thus would have a secondary effect of rewarding excellent mid-career work, fostering intergenerational mentorship, and strengthening the overall culture and morale of the civil service.

While a new and shiny public service academy should no doubt be the centerpiece of any strategy to infuse new talent into the civil service, space in such an academy would no doubt be limited. For this reason, among others, some civilian version of ROTC should be established at many of our leading colleges and universities. Like ROTC, a civilian government officers training corps—call it *GOTC*—would offer enrolled students supplemental academic and field work, cultural immersion, tuition assistance, and guaranteed civil service commissions upon graduation.

Retention

A Mid-Career Civil Service Leadership Academy. We should not stop with entry-level training, nor with the concomitant commitment to entry-level mentoring, morale-boosting, and bureaucratic socialization. There should also be several mid-career academies, again modeled on what the U.S. military does exceedingly well. Consider the Army War College, the Naval War College, the Marine Corps War College, and the Air War College. These elite, competitive "staff colleges" train promising mid-career military personnel to assume the mantle of leadership. Alumni listings of the war colleges read like yet another *Who's Who*. They include the aforementioned Eisenhower, Patton, Bradley, Pershing, Ridgway, and Nimitz, as well as Colin Powell, Leslie Groves, the director of the Manhattan Project, and astronaut Alan Shepard. The current presidents of Bulgaria, Egypt, and Nigeria, and a former president of Lebanon, also trained at U.S. war colleges.

Establishing analogous mid-career elite civil service academies would encourage and reward excellence among those working their way up the ranks. Among other things, these academies would teach substantive skills, offer leadership training, and provide opportunities for the next generation of top-flight civil servants to connect with one another as well as with officials in Congress, in the White House, and in the professional communities.

Establishing such mid-career academies for the civil service would also send important signals to the rest of government: that there is true star power in the civil service; that the civil service can and does incubate new ideas and approaches—quieting those quick to accuse the bureaucracy of stagnation and torpor; and that fast-rising civil servants are deserving of the same respect within agencies and on Capitol Hill as is commonly accorded to similarly fast-rising Army colonels and Navy captains.

Lastly, mid-career service academies would support and supplement the work of a collegiate civil service academy. Even if an undergraduate academy proved itself to be highly successful from the get-go, it would still take years, and probably decades, before its graduates assumed positions of considerable influence. The simultaneous founding of mid-career institutes would hasten the process of improving the quality and stature of the civil service.

I recognize that civil servants already have numerous opportunities to pursue further study. Top-notch, mid-career training can be found at Princeton's Woodrow Wilson School, Harvard's Kennedy School, and Texas A&M's Bush School of Government, to name just a few. Those certainly are great programs, and federal monies should be set aside to support civil servants wishing to do postgraduate work there. But—and this is also true at the undergraduate level—there is something special about creating, staffing, and populating mid-career civil service academies dedicated exclusively to the improvement of the bureaucracy's brand, capabilities, and morale. Indeed, currently the top schools of "government" are breeding grounds for future management consultants, bankers, and assorted entrepreneurs and businessmen and women. The culture of those schools is decidedly and intentionally eclectic.[24] There is, of course, plenty to celebrate about such eclecticism. But if the goal is to foster a distinctive, rich, and somewhat priestly government service culture—such that civil servants can hold their own in the administrative arena—some distance from those pursuing different (and often more enticingly lucrative) careers in the private sector is desirable.

Note too that it should be groups of senior civil servants—themselves nominated by their colleagues—who select candidates for elite, mid-career study. First, giving this responsibility to civil servants cabins the influence of agency heads. Were agency heads in charge of selection, they could exert subtle political and managerial influence over key civil servants in precisely the ways I worry about most. And, second, allowing career employees to make these selections provides yet another opportunity to boost on-the-job morale and to signal to anyone paying attention the importance of a merits-based civil service free from the taint of presidential and party politics.

Of course, better pay never hurts. But, lest we worry about runaway costs, a little salary bump can go a long way. It is important to remember that many of our best and most accomplished civil servants work for a fraction of what they'd make on Wall Street or K Street. In fact, some of the most competitive, desirable, and prestigious government positions—think Treasury financial analysts, Justice Department lawyers, CDC doctors, and NASA rocket scientists—are ones where the public–private pay disparity is greatest.

This is what the businesslike government crowd fails to grasp. Throughout the twentieth century, very talented people were willing to work for the government for relatively modest pay. What's different now is not the pay but rather the work. A consequence, no doubt, of the Privatization Revolution, civil service work is no longer as prestigious and often not as meaningful. Reviving the civil service and restoring it to its place of prestige and influence should go far in making the bureaucracy a once again proud, vibrant organization—one where the traditionally high esprit de corps of the underpaid (by market standards) Foreign Service diplomats and Forest Service rangers is renewed and becomes altogether unremarkable and where the phrase "good enough for government work" ceases to be a punchline. (Further aiding this reversal will be the very act of insourcing. As contracting jobs dry up, there will be fewer immediate substitutes for civil service employment. Insourcing will thus deepen the government talent pool and liberate agencies from the perverse effects of having to compete against themselves for labor.)

Reputation Building

When it comes to boosting the public as well as the inside-the-Beltway image of American bureaucracy—so the civil service is given its due—once again the military is as good a place as any to look for guidance. Public confidence in the military (72 percent) is higher than it is for any other major U.S. institution, far outpacing the likes of organized religion (42 percent), the presidency (33 percent), the Supreme Court (32 percent), the criminal justice system (23 percent), and Congress (8 percent).[25] Even more impressive, the reputation of the military has risen steadily during times of increased disillusionment with government writ large. And the military's reputation has remained high even when the armed services have not shown themselves to be entirely effective, successful, or trustworthy.

To be sure, the military generally does great work—and its personnel and their families make incredible sacrifices in service of the State. But even if the military floundered, many of us would be hesitant to say so. This is precisely my point: saluting the troops has become de rigueur. The military in that regard is almost the polar opposite of the almost reflexively derided domestic civil service.

It is important to realize, however, that none of this military adoration has happened by accident. Corporate America has nothing on the Pentagon, which spends oodles of money on recruiting, advertising, and self-promotion. Estimates from earlier this decade pegged the military's annual advertising budget to be around $667 million.[26] To put that number in perspective, the military spends in advertising roughly the same amount as Taco Bell, Burger King, Starbucks, and Dunkin' Donuts spend *combined*.[27] The military spends $100 million more in advertising than the Occupational Safety and Health Administration (OSHA) spends in total—that is, on *all* of its programs to develop safety rules, inspect workplaces, and prosecute and adjudicate wrongdoing.[28] And the Pentagon's advertising allotment is about twice as large as the entire budget for the Department of Labor's

Wage and Hour Division, a critical unit entrusted with administering and enforcing, among other things, the Fair Labor Standards Act, the Family and Medical Leave Act, and the Davis-Bacon Act.[29] Perhaps most alarmingly, the Pentagon spends four times more on advertising than Congress appropriates in total to the National Highway Traffic Safety Administration,[30] the federal government's chief but perennially understaffed and underfunded auto safety unit that has been harshly criticized for its slow and tepid response to acts of industry negligence and malfeasance involving defective brakes, airbags, ignition switches, and fuel tanks.[31]

What is the military doing with all this money? Funds are being spent on memorable advertising campaigns. Over the years, we've grown accustomed to Uncle Sam's *I Want You; Be All You Can Be,* and *The Few. The Proud. The Marines.* Military slogans and jingles are permanently imprinted on our minds, branded as strongly as KFC's classic *Finger lickin' good* or M&M's evocative *Melts in your mouth, not in your hands.*

Funds are also being spent to shore up partnerships with Hollywood. Today the Pentagon fuses its "brands" with those of Superman, X-Men, and other comic book superheroes.[32] The military participates in the crafting of movie and TV scripts that venerate military culture and show off the latest military hardware.[33] Most memorably, the Navy collaborated on *Top Gun,* the blockbuster Tom Cruise production that is perhaps less of a fully realized movie than a two-hour advertisement for Navy Flight School.[34] Indeed, cashing in on *Top Gun's* box office success, the Navy went so far as to set up recruitment tables in the lobbies of those movie theaters showing Maverick and Iceman dogfighting over the Indian Ocean.[35]

Yet another strategic partnership existed for some time between the Defense Department and professional sports leagues. Here too the military seemed alarmingly obsessive in its efforts to manage and promote its image. In a move of orchestration equal parts West Egg and Pyongyang, the Pentagon paid professional football and baseball teams to stage ostensibly impromptu celebrations honoring America's fighting men and women. Ultimately exposed as events prompted, paid for, and choreographed by Pentagon PR flacks, for years these tributes were presented to unsuspecting audiences as organic, grassroots outpourings of patriotic community support.[36]

I do not mean to belabor the point, nor to suggest that the civil service should go quite to such lengths. Some of these strategic partnerships are, after all, versions of the problematically deceptive practice of State ventriloquism, which I adverted to in Chapter 5. But we need to appreciate that considerable effort, creativity, and money go into cultivating the type of support the military enjoys. (In yet another form of outsourcing, the Army contracts with advertising heavyweight McCann Erickson,[37] the same powerhouse firm used by Coca-Cola, countless other Fortune 500 companies, and even Generalissimo Franco, when he wanted to burnish his dictatorship's image in the United States.[38])

My claim is simply, first, that when the government wants—and needs— to promote its work, it knows how to do so. And, second, support for even the vaunted military does not come easy or cheap. This should give us a sense of what the civil service is up against, of what is achievable, and why we need funding to make plain the constitutional and everyday instrumental value of bureaucratic work. (Believe it or not, there are actually legal obstacles, on top of the very apparent political and fiscal ones, associated with the expenditure of funds in furtherance of agency cheerleading. I'll address those legal obstacles later in the chapter.)

Of course, we should also appreciate that the military has long been a much easier sell. The civil service is more Clark Kent than Superman. And like Lois Lane, the American public is naturally drawn to the latter. With or without intensive Pentagon public relations campaigns, we would be a country that loves adventurism and, seemingly, violence, as evidenced by our choice in TV shows, movies, and books, both fiction and nonfiction. When popular culture fixes its gaze on civilian government, the focus is on do-gooder politics (*The West Wing*; *Madam Secretary*), satire (*Veep*), corruption and intrigue (*House of Cards*), or sex and scandals (*Scandal*). It is rarely on bureaucracy. To the extent that bureaucracy is shown, it is generally as a foil, an obstacle in the way of real public servants doing their jobs— consider the recent film *Sully*'s characterization of the National Transportation Safety Board as petty and villainous; or as farce—consider such indolent characters as *Cheers*' Cliff Claven, *Seinfeld*'s Newman, and *The Simpsons*' Patty and Selma. Even a likable, admirable character, *Parks and Recreation*'s bubbly bureaucrat Leslie, is surrounded at work by slackers, yokels, and crackpots. And Leslie herself spends years aspiring to something greater— namely, elected office—as intensely as a frog wants to turn into a prince.

The fact that Hollywood isn't churning out movies or serials about civil servants makes the case for a strong and creative public relations campaign all the more imperative. Sure, there is plenty of drudgery in the civilian civil service. But tell that to the new Army enlistee recruited by the promise of action yet tasked with peeling potatoes or digging latrines. There is also a lot of rewarding and challenging civil service work that can and should be celebrated: enabling new medical treatments, improving vehicle and workplace safety, providing clean water, safeguarding our ports, and managing our glorious national parks. Right now, all we hear about are the scandals and failures, but never the great successes or, even better, the simple, small, and routine things that we take for granted but that keep people safe and secure. As Donald Kettl reminds us, "Newspapers never headline . . . 'Social Security Checks Arrive by the Millions'"—yet that gigantic, remarkable system runs like clockwork.[39]

If domestic agency officials spent even a fraction of what the military spends, their departments could make clear the good and valuable work they do and remind us how well that work is generally carried out.[40] In short, the bureaucracy needs to make obvious—though perhaps more gently package—the truth of President Obama's "you didn't build that" speech.

Strengthening Civil Society

Civil society likewise requires a shot in the arm. There is, as an initial matter, privatization's effective marginalization of civil society. As discussed in Chapter 6, the outsourcing of government responsibilities sidelines much of civil society. The renationalization strategies mentioned above thus serve not only to reinstate the civil service but also to reopen channels for public participation in the administrative process.

Still left unaddressed, however, is the problem of unequal, spotty, and structurally skewed civic engagement. That is, even when the channels for public participation are formally open, not everyone is capable of accessing, let alone properly navigating, them. By my lights, a nominally equal opportunity to participate is not enough, at least not in a society such as ours marked by major social, economic, and educational inequalities. Indeed, why should we ascribe legal and normative value to public administrative engagement—the third prong of the administrative separation of powers— when the likes of Big Pharma, Wall Street, and environmental elites monopolize civic proceedings?[41]

The answer to such troublingly unequal public participation isn't, however, to throw the baby out with the bathwater—that is, to give up on civil society; nor is it to stand pat and hope for some exogenous force to narrow the American inequality gap writ large. Instead, the answer—as it was for a demoralized, desiccated civil service—is to double down: We must enrich civil society, lower barriers to knowledge and access, and affirmatively support broader and more democratic forms of administrative engagement.

We are quick to celebrate administrative law's democratic inclusiveness, applauding in particular the iconic notice-and-comment regime. But it isn't clear that the notice-and-comment requirements specified in the APA produce real and meaningful opportunities for public participation. Indeed, our present-day regime seems to fall short along the following dimensions:

First, the current statutory forms of notice are laughably limited. Congress does not, Justice Scalia memorably insisted, hide elephants in mouse holes.[42] But that's pretty much what agencies do when they perform their statutorily required duty: to post notice of a proposed new rule (or change to an existing rule) in the little-known *Federal Register*. Second, even if the *Federal Register* actually reached a sizable segment of civil society, many of us couldn't make heads or tails out of the notices themselves. These jargon-ridden announcements tend to confuse, discourage, and ultimately alienate even well-educated audiences, clearing the field for only the most sophisticated and affluent of individuals and groups to participate. And, third, our civic culture looks very different from what it once was (or aspired to be). Americans today are not regularly attending civic meetings, discussing politics at local union halls, or even kibitzing by the water coolers at work. Thus, opportunities for ready conversations about democratic governance seem in woefully short supply.

To make good on the constitutional promise of a second *pax administrativa*, we need to do more to boost public participation in the administrative process. In what follows, I propose a series of reforms, oriented around achieving effective public notice; lay comprehension of administrative rules and procedures; and dynamic dialogue between the broadly conceived public and agency officials.

Virtual Civil Society

An overhaul of the sort I am proposing is never a simple undertaking. But it is much simpler today than it would have been a couple of decades ago. This is because technologies—and concomitant cultural shifts attendant to those technologies—furnish ready solutions to the problems and shortcomings just identified.[43]

Let's start with the basics. We might, as Robert Putnam famously told us, be *bowling alone*.[44] But we're now Facebook friends with half the country, quick to join in impromptu political discussions on Twitter, Instagram, and Reddit, and eager to comment on articles and editorials in national and local online periodicals. Physically cocooned, we are nonetheless virtual civic butterflies, regularly reflecting, advocating, and bonding over social media. The existence of virtual platforms lowers the real and psychic costs of public outreach and participation; accommodates and even encourages greater (and more democratic) forms of peer-to-peer education, engagement, and mobilization; and invites sustained interactions with agency programs and officials.[45]

Again, it is these technologies and technologically inflected cultural shifts that will enable us to flatten, deepen, and broaden public participation in the administrative process.

Effective Public Notice

The APA requires agencies proposing new rules to give notice to the public, via publication in the *Federal Register*.[46] You will be forgiven if you have let your subscription lapse. As suggested, many Americans have never heard of the *Federal Register*, and most have never seen it, let alone read from it. Yet despite the rather limited reach of the *Federal Register* and its almost inescapable obscurantism, judges and lawmakers hold true to the conceit that this government publication has a true public audience.

To be clear, this was a conceit in 1946, too, when Congress specified the terms of public notice. Indeed, just a few years later, the Supreme Court in its celebrated *Mullane* case insisted on a far more capacious understanding of public notice in federal civil litigation proceedings.[47] Not unlike the *Mullane* justices, I see a more expansive commitment to administrative public notice to be a constitutional imperative. If the goal is a well-functioning administrative separation of powers, then agency officials need to do much more to keep civil society clued in. Fortunately, opportunities to better notify the public—and thus to facilitate broader and deeper civic engagement—are bountiful and inexpensive today.

Mainstream Media. Virtually every major newspaper and magazine has an online presence. For a nominal fee, the feds could pay these publications to post a link, connecting their site with an official government webpage cataloging the daily list of newly proposed rules. But that would be just a start. After all, a daily listing of proposed rules would be long, dense, and tedious, covering lots of issues that do not interest even the most civically minded of readers. Such ubiquitously posted links would indeed provide greater nominal notice. But they'd be the furthest thing from juicy clickbait. Thus, by themselves, these posted links would do little to increase effective public notice—that is, meaningfully register with a wider, more diverse public audience.

We should therefore insist upon, as a necessary supplement, dreaded *banner ads.* The accuracy and precision of targeted online advertising today is often astonishing. We read an article about a natural disaster and—lo and behold!—the article is accompanied by a banner ad soliciting Red Cross donations. We check a weather site's local pollen count and—presto!—are bombarded with ads for antihistamines. Why not use targeted advertising to highlight proposed federal regulations? A *New York Times* article about climate change could easily generate a corresponding advertisement alerting readers to a pending EPA rule on greenhouse gases.

Consider too *sponsored links*. Web users rely heavily on smart search engines and personalized news feeds to help them process the world's information. We could imagine a scenario in which those who run, say, a Google search for "food safety" might be drawn to sponsored links, including ones that connect readers directly to the Department of Agriculture's food safety webpage. These sponsored links thus represent another way to pull already moderately engaged, mildly interested members of civil society—namely, those at least willing to read up on matters of federal regulatory policy—into the administrative process.

Social Media. At the same time, agencies should maximize their use of social media. A social media campaign would proceed as follows. Agency officials post their announcements on Facebook, Twitter, Instagram, and other such platforms. Michael Herz, who has studied how federal agencies use social media, reports that there are currently 10,000 or so "federal government social media accounts across dozens of different platforms."[48] The EPA is particularly prodigious. Its staggering number of social media accounts is enough to make a Kardashian blush.

The problem right now is that agency social media campaigns are often viewed as unseemly if not altogether unlawful—veering into the realm of propaganda. Most congressional appropriations expressly ban the use of funds for "publicity or propaganda purposes,"[49] and the EPA, among others, has been heavily criticized for allegedly drumming up support for its initiatives.[50] Here, as elsewhere, our seemingly instinctive fears of imperious domestic agencies sharply contrast with our willingness to indulge the far more licentious military propagandists. This differential treatment—worrying more about bureaucracy than bayonets—is further evidence both of the special place the vaunted military occupies and of the changing perception of American tyranny.

The ubiquity of such bans on agency publicity or propaganda limits, constrains, and blunts administrative messaging. If anything, it puts agency officials at a comparative disadvantage insofar as critics are entirely free to use any and all resources and technologies to discredit agency programs, policies, or personnel.[51] At the very least, the congressional restrictions on agency publicity need to be lifted, and the definition of propaganda needs to be narrowed, proscribing only misleading representations.

Pressing further, Congress should directly finance agency publicity campaigns, just as it funds Pentagon media buys. Doing so strengthens the civil service and civil society in one fell swoop. Agencies get to promote their brands, policies, and personnel, *and* civil society receives more meaningful notice and encouragement to comment on specific programs and initiatives.

Specifically, a more comprehensive, legally sound messaging campaign allows agencies to reach more people—and reach them more effectively. Already engaged members of the public will have more opportunities to "follow" or "friend" an agency—and will thus more readily learn that a new rule is being considered. The followers and friends can then be invited, and perhaps expected, to distribute those announcements to all of their friends, colleagues, and acquaintances in typical Facebook style. All of this reposting, retweeting, and "liking" of agency announcements help disseminate agency news in a truly viral fashion.

Note too that peer-to-peer, viral distribution of the sort just described does more than simply spread the word rapidly. It also spreads it organically, largely unmediated by the State (and, more specifically, agency officials). Peer-to-peer distribution helps engender and solidify networks of concerned citizens who can then use those very same social media platforms to discuss, strategize, and conduct collective research in ways that broaden and thicken civic engagement. The trick, as Herz recognizes, is to ensure that agencies are not just "pushing" their agenda but also are subjecting themselves to "pulling" forces—that is, resistance by civil society demanding that agency officials rethink and recalibrate their programs and policies.[52] Again, the constitutional imperative to support public outreach strategies presupposes that public participation will be hearty and rivalrous.

Real and Virtual Community Outreach. Agency officials should, moreover, increase the frequency with which they venture into communities, of both the physical and virtual variety. They should speak at town gatherings, schools, libraries, unions, Chamber of Commerce meetings, and the like. And they should host online chats that serve substantially the same functions. The goal here is primarily to educate the public about the importance of administrative governance, to advise them of new developments, to encourage and facilitate participation, including adversarial participation, and to lay the foundation for ongoing or sustained engagement. Among other things, community outreach allows the public to put actual faces (or, at the very least, digital avatars) to the otherwise faceless bureaucracy, shrink the seeming distance between Washington and cities and counties across the United States, and enlarge the agency's list of contacts who sign up to receive electronic newsletters and alerts, follow Twitter feeds, and become Facebook pals. (Just think how campaigns prize the email lists maintained by movement politicians such as Senators Bernie Sanders and Elizabeth Warren. Those digital rolodexes are the Comstock Lode of contemporary political mobilization efforts, and agencies might well be advised to start compiling their own.) A more engaged public will then be better positioned to learn of new rules and, one hopes, more inclined to comment on those rules—and even draw friends, neighbors, and co-workers into the process.

My call for greater agency outreach may trouble those who worry that such outreach amounts to de facto State lobbying, galvanizing support for agency policies and thereby co-opting rather than empowering civil society. After all, agency officials have broad discretion in shaping their message, may be selective in what audiences they target, and may receive more favorable press now that they're purchasing ad blocs with news outlets such as CNN and news aggregators such as Google.

Such message-shaping critiques seem overblown. We certainly want agencies to explain and justify their positions. It only follows that agency officials who do a good job of explaining and justifying their positions will indeed drum up support for said positions. I'm further comforted by the fact that the American public is not an easy mark. As I have shown, the American public is highly wary of administrative governance—and thus agencies regularly find themselves shouldering the initial burden of persuasion. Viewed from that perspective, and again keeping in mind that the military is given free rein (and plenty of funding) to promote its endeavors, agency personnel should be given similar opportunities to convince a skeptical civil society.

The selective-outreach critique likewise seems much ado about nothing. The practically costless nature of digital publishing and dissemination should reduce the effects of even the most brazen forms of selective advertising. It takes only a small group of bloggers, journalists, and activists—not to mention members of the House and Senate, state and local officials, and celebrity tweeters—opposed to a new agency rule to mobilize their followers and fellow travelers to submit comments attacking the merits of the proposed rule. But even assuming that the selective-outreach concern is serious enough, Congress or the courts could mandate that agencies reach out to broad and diverse segments of civil society. Failure to do so might well constitute a violation of the administrative separation of powers, particularly if the failure forecloses or impedes meaningful and inclusive civic engagement.

Lastly, fears of media co-optation seem similarly far-fetched. Agencies will not be taking out major full-page glossy ads like the ones found in the print edition of the Sunday *New York Times*. (Even if they did, media news and business departments have long been segregated to avoid such conflicts of interest.) Instead, agencies will be procuring low-cost banner ads that barely register in the revenue tallies of content providers, content compilers, and search engines. It is thus inconceivable that government advertising will influence editorial choices. Critical news reporting and commentary will, no doubt, continue apace.

Lay Comprehension

Above I referenced the public's unfamiliarity with the *Federal Register*. But the problem is more than just one of low circulation and limited readership. It is also a problem of comprehension. The average American may struggle mightily to parse the notices agencies publish,[53] many of which seem to have been ghostwritten by the clerks staffing *Little Dorrit*'s Circumlocution Office. In drafting recondite notices, agencies seem to be defying the spirit, if not also the letter, of the APA—while simultaneously endangering a well-functioning administrative separation of powers. In short, regardless how much work we do to better distribute and draw attention to newly proposed rules, we will not get very far unless and until those rules are written with lay audiences in mind.

"Really" Plain English Synopsis. Agencies ought to be required to do more—perhaps considerably more—to explain in crisp, clear, and concise language:

1. the current state of federal regulations or public benefits. For example, the agency might, by way of background, write that there is currently no protection against environmental toxin X or that the current regulations categorically ban the use of toxin X for commercial purposes;
2. the proposed change;
3. the circumstances motivating today's proposed change. For example, the agency might write that there are new scientific findings, new

statutory authorities granting more or less power, or new reports revealing why current regulations are insufficiently protective, easily evaded, or unnecessarily stifling; and

4. how the proposed change is likely to affect the public at large as well as specific groups of regulated parties and beneficiaries.

We might liken this "really" plain English synopsis to an eminently readable executive summary—and task each agency with hiring additional professional writers to convert legalese, policy esoterica, and technical mumbo jumbo into conversational English.

Lest this "really" plain English requirement seem too high a burden, take note that many other professional entities regularly employ teams of such writers. Apple writers play the part of Cupertino translators, simplifying engineer-speak into something that iPhone-addicted art history majors can readily understand. The Supreme Court's Reporter of Decisions condenses extremely complex, lengthy, and often painstakingly and necessarily precisely worded opinions, distilling them for journalists, who then further (and rapidly) repackage for lay audiences.

Such translation work is challenging and ought to be recognized and prized as such. To date and despite congressional prodding—consider the aptly named Plain Writing Act of 2010—most agency efforts in this regard have failed to make their announcements appreciably more accessible to ordinary Americans,[54] who (to make matters worse) are increasingly accustomed to being spoon-fed all of their other news in small, digestible bites. Major print and online media are masterful at concocting plainly written, often dumbed-down news reports, placing bulleted "story highlights" in the margins of their already simplified prose. And news tickers or crawlers scroll endless streams of vacuous sound bites across the bottom of our TV screens. Part of this failure is a function of the rather weak imperative—notwithstanding the Plain Writing Act—to write for the median citizen. And part of this failure is, again, a function of there being little value placed on cogent, accessible writing. After all, such administrative writing tasks are rather thankless ones—and quick to fall by the wayside whenever government personnel are inundated with more pressing, more quantifiable responsibilities.

Perhaps, then, the use of professional, creative, and dedicated writers (not just regular personnel pulled away from their other substantive projects) will improve the quality of public engagement. Perhaps modest forms of recognition, such as periodic awards given to agency writers judged by their peers to be composing the clearest, most informative public notices, would also have a meaningful effect.[55]

Links to the Rule and Supplemental Materials. Appended to the "really" plain English synopses ought to be Internet hyperlinks, which readers could effortlessly click to access the official, unabridged proposed rule, the authorizing legislation, the old rule (if one exists), and any other relevant materials that agency officials are relying on. This digital dossier allows for one-stop researching, making it easy for particularly interested parties, journalists, and members of the public to quickly educate themselves about the laws, policies, and scientific findings informing the proposed rule. Moreover, peer-to-peer circulation of these widely available documents will provide additional opportunities for engaged participants to put their own editorial glosses on proposed rules, further fueling the project of more accessible, comprehensible notice (both because agencies will have even greater incentive to make sure their aims and intentions are clear and won't be misconstrued and because the proposed rules themselves will invariably be dissected, explained, and critiqued in the course of peer-to-peer texting, posting to Facebook, or tweeting).

Dynamic Dialogue

Once we are satisfied that notice is indeed widespread and comprehensible, the challenge is to convert all of this enhanced public notice into serious and constructive civic engagement. The answer is *dynamic dialogue,* which can be broken down into four components: education, interactivity, multimedia correspondence, and feedback.

Education. Facility with democratic governance cannot be taken for granted. Justice David Souter, for one, has written and spoken movingly about his early, hands-on experience attending honest-to-goodness New England town meetings as a child.[56] Few of us have been as fortunate to observe real, functioning democracy in action. Instead, we have cobbled together a rudimentary understanding of civics from the brittle pages of high school textbooks, grainy YouTube clips of *Schoolhouse Rock!,* and the cacophony of talking heads on the Sunday morning news shows. Such limited familiarity is even on display in law schools, where otherwise quite strong students confess never having had occasion before to grapple with the basics of our system of government. This all needs to change, if not for the overall well-being of our society then at least for the instrumental realization of a legitimate administrative state that takes seriously its democratic commitment to public engagement.

We cannot, alas, give every kid the equivalent of David Souter's seemingly Rockwellian Weare, New Hampshire. But we can certainly intensively teach civics—which, again, has intrinsic and instrumental payoffs. Such a project happens to be the driving passion of one of Justice Souter's old colleagues, Sandra Day O'Connor. Since retiring from the Court, Justice O'Connor has labored to help reverse the secular decline in Americans' understanding of public affairs and their participation in government. To that end, O'Connor launched the highly celebrated *iCivics* program, which provides schools and families with extensive and, by all accounts, *fun* lesson plans, literature, and video games to inform and excite today's youth and encourage political engagement.[57] Creating additional *iCivics* units on regulatory governance would make clear the importance of administrative governance and encourage a greater sense of connection and obligation to the administrative state. That is to say, administrative engagement should be treated as a privilege and a duty no different from voting or jury service.

To be sure, the traditional must supplement the trendy. Complementing *iCivics* should be old-fashioned social studies coursework for students of all ages. Here specifically I'm calling for a direct reversal of what the business community engineered in the 1970s, when it began pressing schools to deemphasize the study (and, as they saw it, the glorification) of government. That fateful pivot away from government studies became even more pronounced in the opening decades of the twenty-first century, amid the frenetic rush to train Americans to be globally competitive in the so-called STEM subjects. Math and science are surely important. But we must not lose sight of our basic responsibilities as a self-governing people. Accordingly, public funds should be recommitted to civics education. For a fraction of what it costs to upgrade engineering labs, purchase biology textbooks replete with expensive-to-publish photographs, and acquire chemistry equipment, we could teach students about government, its importance, and how ordinary Americans can make a difference through electoral and regulatory engagement.

It is in this respect that John Adams got things spectacularly wrong. Writing to his wife from Paris, Adams explained that it was his duty to study the "Science of Government," and the "Art of Legislation and Administration" so that his sons would be free to study math and philosophy, which in turn would enable his grandchildren to study the fine arts.[58] It is a beautiful sentiment, one in keeping with those who foresee an end to history. But it isn't our reality. Our reality is more in keeping with that envisioned by Adams's fellow revolutionary-turned-statesman, Benjamin

Franklin, whose "a republic, if you can keep it" commands us never to take the "Science of Government" for granted. Clearly, we've been taking civics for granted for too long, endangering our ongoing republican project in the process.

Interactivity. As mentioned above, agencies from time to time convene public meetings and hold information sessions to discuss newly proposed rules and to hear from interested parties. Such meetings are, today, quite limited. They are expensive to host, rarely statutorily guaranteed, and tend to favor those already blessed with financial resources, a facility with public speaking, and familiarity with parliamentary procedure. In some ways, therefore, the meetings serve primarily to reinforce existing socio-economic inequalities: the well-heeled and highly educated excel in these public fora, just as they do when crafting and submitting written comments pursuant to the requirements of the first *pax administrativa.*

For this reason, I propose a less demanding, less expensive, and far more accessible and inclusive complement to public meetings—one modeled on something as simple but powerful as Reddit's popular AMAs, short for "ask me anything." (Lest one think Reddit is too coarse a venue for federal engagement, President Obama hosted a very well-received AMA in 2012. Other politicians have, not surprisingly, rushed to follow suit.) Agency officials could host, say, two AMAs per week during the pendency of a rulemaking comment period, and these sessions would allow the officials to interact with the public, field questions, offer clarifications, and share technical and legal insights. Transcripts of such sessions would be entered into the public record for the benefit of those who could not participate.

Multimedia Correspondence. Submitting comments on rules takes some work. This is true even where e-rulemaking is already an option. Still, we can make commenting easier and faster. All of the viral alerts, digital notifications, and synopses discussed above should include a prominently displayed "SEND A COMMENT" hyperlink. Clicking on that hyperlink would result in the opening of a new browser window (or a pop-up box) offering ample space for members of the public to share their particular thoughts with the agency. And all paper-based notifications, mailings, and the like should include already addressed, postage-paid envelopes such that the recipients of these materials can quickly write down and mail in their reactions. Lastly, both electronic and paper-based notifications should include a pair of prominently displayed telephone numbers. One such number should route callers to a voicemail system, allowing members of the public to record an oral comment. Computer software is sufficiently sophisticated today such that the contents of telephonic comments can be quickly and inexpensively transcribed, cataloged, and entered into the digital administrative record for all to see and scrutinize. The second such number should be a rulemaking hotline, staffed by government officials who may speak to the nuts and bolts of comment drafting. (Again, agencies already do all sorts of outreach. On one extreme, we have the Internal Revenue Service providing extensive over-the-phone counseling services to taxpaying individuals and businesses. And, on the other, we have NORAD—the North American Aerospace Defense Command—devoting time and resources every Christmas Eve to fielding hundreds of thousands of calls from children wishing to be apprised of Santa's flight trajectory.[59])

Needless to say, such easy-to-access conduits for commentary may encourage mostly superficial participation. Yet perhaps it is unfair to single out comments solicited via social media platforms for their superficiality: Many, perhaps most, old-school paper comments have proven to be nothing more than mass-generated, prepackaged form letters written and delivered by powerful special interest groups. Those letters may look sophisticated, but everyone knows that they reflect minimal public engagement.

More to the point, there is no reason to believe comments solicited through social media won't be serious and thoughtful, especially in due time. We should think of the current social media platforms as welcoming, low-cost points of entry—easy, painless ways for members of the public to get involved. Over time, some of these newcomers will start caring more. They'll study the issues. They'll share their thoughts and reactions with friends near and far. And, perhaps most importantly, they'll come to the realization that they need more than 140 characters to influence public policy.

Feedback. And that's where feedback comes in. Rulemaking should be gratifying and edifying. People should feel as if their comments matter. Such gratification is important both to increase public support for the rulemaking process and to encourage continued, ongoing, and ultimately deeper engagement. Simple tokens of recognition—akin, perhaps, to the ubiquitous "I Voted!" stickers worn on election days—and pro forma letters of receipt and thanks from agency officials might go a long way in maintaining and encouraging sustained civic engagement.

In addition, participants should be specially notified if and when an agency's rulemaking process fails, is delayed, or spawns a final rule—and venues should be created (perhaps, more AMAs) to allow discussion of the reasons underlying the agency's decision or delay and to field questions about drafting persuasive comments. All such correspondence should include invitations and reminders to continue the conversation.

This menagerie of measures is hardly perfect. There are plenty of challenging details and specifics to work out. Still, these measures aim to make the civil society component of administrative governance far more open, knowing, and accessible than it currently is. Such work is absolutely necessary for, again, without a truly engaged and democratic civil society, the case for a well-functioning and constitutionally sound administrative separation of powers remains a hopeless one.

*   *   *

Ultimately, the construction of a second *pax administrativa* will require a lot of money, moxie, and patience. It is, quite frankly, nothing short of an administrative moon shot. But lest we throw up our hands, this is a task for Hercules, not Sisyphus. It is achievable and redemptive. We are not torturing ourselves, haunted by the demons of the first *pax administrativa* and now stubbornly rolling the same old rock up the hill again and again.

We are instead constructing a newer, better administrative separation of powers, improving the relationship between and among the constitutional and administrative rivals, restoring the administrative state's normative currency, and reinforcing its constitutional foundation. We are, furthermore, doing so in a way that, though surely expensive, represents a tremendous investment in human, democratic, and regulatory capital, an investment that will pay considerable dividends in many pockets of our complex political economy. These measures and others like them will, I hope, recast the public's understanding of government, its special purposes, and its special architecture—and steel the second *pax administrativa* for whatever challenges await it going forward.

Epilogue

The commitment I seek is not to outworn views but to old values
that will never wear out.

—SEN. EDWARD M. KENNEDY, DEMOCRATIC
NATIONAL CONVENTION (1980).

In this book, I have documented the constitutional infirmities with
outsourced and marketized American public administration. I have
explained how the dynamics underlying the contracting out of State
responsibilities and the hollowing out of the government itself have greatly
damaged the twentieth-century *pax administrativa*. And I have suggested
a rationale, vocabulary, and blueprint for redeeming the administrative
separation of powers and constructing a second, sturdier *pax administrativa* for the twenty-first century.

Yet privatization is nothing if not resilient. Throughout U.S. history,
privatization has adopted various guises and forms and has done so in
service of various ends. Privatization has surfaced, resurfaced, and will
surely surface again. Accordingly, this book's concluding message is as
much one last parting shot at the instant and, to be sure, still existential
constitutional threat new millennial privatization poses as it is a preemptive, anticipatory shot across the bow of whatever new forms of businesslike government may be waiting to take its place.

My concluding message is simple: government cannot and ought not be
run like a business in any meaningful sense of the term. To understand
why, we must remember that government and businesses have very different powers and responsibilities; that government and businesses
answer to very different constituencies; and that these differences in
powers, responsibilities, and constituencies make good, practical sense, are
normatively desirable, and are mutually reinforcing. Indeed, these differences enable an important symbiosis that would largely be lost were we to
collapse or ignore them in an effort to make the State more businesslike
(or, possibly, businesses more Statelike).

Until that message is heard, until government's intrinsic, albeit idiosyncratic, worth is recognized on its own terms, American public administration will continue to look inadequate—a sickly, inexplicably inefficient enterprise in need of rescuing by, quite literally, corporate raiders intent on restructuring and possibly liquidating government as if it were a failing business. This is, in many respects, the credo of privatization.

Recall one last time Dr. Franklin's reminder that we have been deeded a *conditional* republic. It is ours . . . *if we can keep it*. Keeping it today—that is, preserving the spirit of constitutional republicanism as we accommodate the institutional and programmatic demands of modernity—means not succumbing to the lures of the Market but instead celebrating government's clunky contentiousness as constitutionally necessary and appropriate given the special obligations under which the State operates. Such clunky contentiousness is a feature, not a bug, of our rivalrous public administration, which not only prizes but also needs pluralism, which accepts encumbrances as legitimating the exercise of sovereign, coercive powers, and which understands that its responsibilities are best satisfied by preserving rather than eliminating checks and balances. This is, in many respects, the credo of Our Republic.

Notes

Acknowledgments

Index

NOTES

Introduction

Epigraph: *The Federalist,* No. 51 (Madison); James M. Landis, *The Administrative Process,* 46 (New Haven: Yale University Press, 1938); Martin Gottlieb, *Who Can Fix Wollman Rink Faster? City and Trump Agree It's Trump,* N.Y. Times, Jun. 6, 1986, http://www.nytimes.com/1986/06/06/nyregion/who-can-fix-the -wollman-rink-faster-city-and-trump-agree-it-s-trump.html.

1. Ronald Reagan, *The President's News Conference,* Aug. 12, 1986, https:// ml.reaganfoundation.org/pdf/SQP081286.pdf.

2. John F. Kennedy, *Inaugural Address,* Jan. 20, 1961, http://www.jfklibrary .org/Research/Research-Aids/Ready-Reference/JFK-Quotations/Inaugural -Address.aspx.

3. Kevin R. Kosar, *Privatization and the Federal Government: An Introduction,* Cong. Res. Serv., Dec. 26, 2006, at 6–7, 17, http://www.fas.org/sgp/crs/misc /RL33777.pdf. For discussions of such contractors, see P. W. Singer, *Corporate Warriors: The Rise of the Privatized Military Industry* (Ithaca, NY: Cornell University Press, 2003); Jon D. Michaels, *Beyond Accountability: The Constitutional, Democratic, and Strategic Problems with Privatizing War,* 82 Wash. U.L.Q. 1001 (2004); Martha Minow, *Outsourcing Power: How Privatizing Military Efforts Challenges Accountability, Professionalism, and Democracy,* 46 B.C. L. Rev. 989 (2005); Sharon Dolovich, *State Punishment and Private Prisons,* 55 Duke L.J. 437, 457–462 (2005); William Rodgers, 4 *Environmental Law* § 8.9, at 619 n. 139 (St. Paul, MN: West Pub., 2009); Matthew Diller, *The Revolution in Welfare Administration: Rules, Discretion,*

and Entrepreneurial Government, 75 N.Y.U. L. Rev. 1121 (2000); Miriam Seifter, *Rent-a-Regulator: Design and Innovation in Privatized Governmental Decisionmaking,* 33 Ecology L.Q. 1091, 1118–1125 (2006).

4. For discussions of such enterprises, see Kevin R. Kosar, *The Quasi Government: Hybrid Organizations with Both Government and Private Sector Legal Characteristics,* Cong. Res. Serv., Jun. 22, 2011, at 28–31, https://fas.org/sgp/crs/misc/RL30533.pdf; Dale Russakoff, *The Prize* (New York: Houghton Mifflin Harcourt, 2015); Robinson Meyer, *Obama's Tech Reforms Are Now Permanent,* Atlantic, May 5, 2016, https://www.theatlantic.com/technology/archive/2016/05/18f-becomes-a-permanent-part-of-the-government/481260/; Eric Berkowitz, *Is Justice Served?,* L.A. Times W. Mag., Oct. 22, 2006, at 20, 22.

5. *The Federalist,* No. 51 (Madison).

6. When discussing legitimacy in this project, I am almost invariably referring to normative legitimacy rather than popular or sociological legitimacy. Compare John Rawls, *Political Liberalism,* 217 (New York: Columbia University Press, 1993) ("[O]ur exercise of political power is proper and hence justifiable only when it is exercised in accordance with a constitution the essentials of which all citizens may reasonably be expected to endorse in the light of principles and ideals acceptable to them as reasonable and rational."). See also Richard H. Fallon, Jr., *Legitimacy and the Constitution,* 118 Harv. L. Rev. 1787, 1796–1797 (2005). To the extent I use *legitimacy* or *legitimation* to refer to anything other than normative legitimacy or legitimation, I will make clear any such alternative formulation.

7. *FTC v. Ruberoid Co.,* 343 U.S. 470, 487 (1952) (Jackson, J., dissenting); see also Landis, *Administrative Process*; Robert M. Cooper, *Administrative Justice and the Role of Discretion,* 47 Yale L.J. 577, 577 (1938) (describing critics of agencies as invoking such terms as *tyranny* and *despotism*).

8. Lisa Schultz Bressman, *Beyond Accountability: Arbitrariness and Legitimacy in the Administrative State,* 78 N.Y.U. L. Rev. 461, 462 (2003). See generally Jacob E. Gersen, *Unbundled Powers,* 96 Va. L. Rev. 301, 305 (2010); Jeremy K. Kessler, *The Struggle for Administrative Legitimacy,* 129 Harv. L. Rev. 718, 718 (2016).

9. Philip Hamburger, *Is Administrative Law Unlawful?* (Chicago: University of Chicago Press, 2014).

10. Gary Lawson, *The Rise and Rise of the Administrative State,* 107 Harv. L. Rev. 1231, 1248 (1994).

11. Ibid.

12. Some, of course, are not particularly troubled. See, for example, Eric A. Posner & Adrian Vermeule, *Interring the Nondelegation Doctrine,* 69 U. Chi. L. Rev. 1721 (2002); Bruce A. Ackerman, 1 *We the People: Foundations,* 105–130 (Cambridge: Harvard University Press, 1991); Bruce A. Ackerman, 2 *We the People: Transformations,* 279–311, 359–382 (Cambridge: Harvard University Press, 1998). For Ackerman, the New Deal amounted to a "constitutional moment;" as such, the "People" effectively amended the

Constitution to accommodate and legitimate otherwise quite probably unconstitutional actors and powers.

13. Harold H. Bruff, *Presidential Power and Administrative Lawmaking*, 88 Yale L.J. 451, 451 (1979) ("The increasing sprawl of the federal agencies has challenged the effectiveness of the checks and balances designed by the Constitution."); *INS v. Chadha*, 462 U.S. 919, 986–997 (1983) (White, J., dissenting) (describing the courts' tolerance of Congress delegating "lawmaking power to independent and Executive agencies," which then use that power to "issue regulations having the force of law without bicameral approval and without the President's signature").

14. Douglas H. Ginsburg, *On Constitutionalism*, 2002–2003 Cato Sup. Ct. Rev. 7, 15; see also Daniel R. Ernst, *Tocqueville's Nightmare: The Administrative State Emerges in America, 1900–1940*, at 7 (New York: Oxford University Press, 2014) (describing the popularity of the belief that the New Deal administrative state marked a "decisive wrong turn in the nation's history").

15. Douglas H. Ginsburg, *Delegation Running Riot*, 18 Reg. 83, 84 (1995).

16. See, for example, Cynthia R. Farina, *The Consent of the Governed: Against Simple Rules for a Complex World*, 72 Chi.-Kent L. Rev. 987, 1019–1020, 1020 n. 137 (1997) (suggesting that the Madisonian system of separation of powers may reflect a broader, deeper commitment to establishing "multiple opportunities for people to 'speak' and be heard in the regulatory process").

17. Ronald Coase, *The Nature of the Firm*, 4 Economica 386 (1937).

18. William J. Clinton, *State of the Union Address*, Jan. 23, 1996, https://clinton2.nara.gov/WH/New/other/sotu.html.

19. For U.S. government investigations and prosecutions of Blackwater, see Katherine Zoepf & Atheer Kakan, *U.S. Prosecutor Goes to Iraq to Work on Blackwater Case*, N.Y. Times, Dec. 7, 2008, http://www.nytimes.com/2008/12/08/world/middleeast/08iraq.html; Mark Mazzetti & James Risen, *Blackwater Said to Pursue Bribes to Iraq After 17 Died*, N.Y. Times, Nov. 11, 2009, http://www.nytimes.com/2009/11/11/world/middleeast/11blackwater.html?pagewanted=all. For local opposition, see *Iraq: "Blackwater Must Go,"* CNN, Oct. 17, 2007, http://www.cnn.com/2007/WORLD/meast/10/16/iraq.blackwater/index.html; Joshua Partlow, *Karzai Wants Private Security Firms out of Afghanistan*, Wash. Post, Aug. 17, 2010, http://www.washingtonpost.com/wpdyn/content/article/2010/08/16/AR2010081602041.html?sid=ST2010081700028. For an account expressing some surprise that the United States continues to contract with Blackwater, see Mark Landler & Mark Mazzetti, *U.S. Still Using Security Firm It Broke With*, N.Y. Times, Aug. 21, 2009, http://www.nytimes.com/2009/08/22/us/22intel.html.

20. Donald F. Kettl, *The Next Government of the United States*, 9, 30 (New York: W. W. Norton & Co., 2009) (describing a paradoxical state of affairs where people rely heavily on government services but do not realize those services are truly governmental, in large part because those services are processed and administered through private intermediaries).

21. Barack Obama, *Remarks by the President at a Campaign Event in Roanoke, Virginia*, Jul. 13, 2012, https://www.whitehouse.gov/the-press-office/2012/07/13/remarks-president-campaign-event-roanoke-virginia.

22. See, for example, *Can Obama Defuse the "You Didn't Build That" Attacks?*, The Week, Jul. 25, 2012, http://theweek.com/articles/473613/obama-defuse-didnt-build-that-attacks; Amy Gardner, *Obama Facing Mounting Questions over "You Didn't Build That" Remark*, Wash. Post, Sept. 2, 2012, http://www.Washingtonpost.Com/Politics/Obama-Facing-Mounting-Questions-Over-You-Didnt-Build-That-Remark/2012/09/02/C409F90C-F52B-11E1–86A5-1F5431D87DFD_STORY.HTML.

23. Kimberly A. Strassel, *Four Little Words: Why the Obama Campaign Is Suddenly So Worried*, Wall St. J., Jul. 26, 2012, http://www.wsj.com/articles/SB10000872396390443931404577551344018773450.

24. Jacob S. Hacker & Paul Pierson, *American Amnesia: How the War on Government Led Us to Forget What Made America Prosper* (New York: Simon & Schuster, 2016).

1. Historic Privatization

1. Privateers were often backed by "the leading merchants of a seaport." Nicholas R. Parrillo, *Against the Profit Motive: The Salary Revolution in American Government*, 316 (New Haven: Yale University Press, 2014). But leading merchants were not the only investors. Estimates from the city of Baltimore indicate that some 10,000 people had an interest in privateering operations during the War of 1812. Jerome R. Garitee, *The Republic's Private Navy: The American Privateering Business as Practiced by Baltimore during the War of 1812*, at 43 (Middletown, CT: Wesleyan University Press, 1977).

2. Edgar Stanton Maclay, *A History of American Privateers*, at viii (New York: D. Appelton & Co., 1899).

3. Parrillo, *Profit Motive*, 316.

4. U.S. Const. art. I, sec. 8, cl. 11. These Letters of Marque were seen as an incident of Congress's Declare War power. See Joseph Story, 3 *Commentaries on the Constitution of the United States*, §1170 (Boston: Hillard, Gray, 1833).

5. Parrillo, *Profit Motive*, 317.

6. Daniel Walker Howe, *What Hath God Wrought: The Transformation of America, 1815–1848*, at 67, 81 (New York: Oxford University Press, 2007).

7. 83 U.S. 366, 372 (1873).

8. David A. Sklansky, *The Private Police*, 46 UCLA L. Rev. 1165, 1205 (1999) (internal quotations omitted).

9. Ibid., 1206 n. 226.

10. New York City's professional police department dates back to 1853. Eric Monkkonen, *Crime, Justice, History*, 31 (Columbus, OH: Ohio State University Press, 2002). Most smaller cities constituted their metropolitan police forces in the latter part of the nineteenth century. Ibid., 177 ("Uniformed

police spread across the United States to most cities in the three decades between 1850 and 1880."); ibid., 57 (describing smaller cities such as Auburn, New York, Lynn, Massachusetts, and Saint Joseph, Missouri as adopting public police forces by the 1890s).

11. Frank Morn, *The Eye That Never Sleeps: A History of the Pinkerton National Detective Agency,* 22, 40–41, 43, 54, 63, 69, 180 (Bloomington, IN: Indiana University Press, 1982).

12. Ibid., 58, 94.

13. Sklansky, *Private Police,* 1211. Note that some such private police forces still exist. See, for example, Jon D. Michaels, *All the President's Spies: Private–Public Intelligence Partnerships in the War on Terror,* 96 Cal. L. Rev. 901, 915 (2008) (describing FedEx's extraordinary policing license granted by the state of Tennessee); Ron Nixon, *Complaints Rise against Nation's Railroad Police,* N.Y. Times, May 28, 2015, https://www.nytimes.com/2015/05/29/us /complaints-rise-against-nations-railroad-police.html?_r=0 (describing powerful and at times abusive private railroad police forces, licensed by states "to make arrests, issue warrants and perform undercover work").

14. Robert P. Weiss, *Private Detective Agencies and Labour Discipline in the United States, 1855–1946,* 29 Historical J. 87, 90–92 (1986).

15. Ibid., 93–95.

16. Jerry L. Mashaw, *Creating the Administrative Constitution: The Lost One Hundred Years of American Administrative Law,* 59 (New Haven: Yale University Press, 2012); Leonard D. White, *The Federalists: A Study in Administrative History,* 182–187 (New York: Macmillan, 1948).

17. This is, of course, the postal motto, https://about.usps.com/who-we-are /postal-history/mission-motto.pdf.

18. Discussions of private conveyance date back to the very early days of the Republic, occupying the attention of America's leading statesmen. For instance, George Washington and John Jay corresponded about the utility of using commercial stagecoaches to transport the federal mails. See *Letter from George Washington to John Jay,* Jul. 18, 1788, http://founders.archives.gov /documents/Washington/04-06-02-0349.

19. Parrillo, *Profit Motive,* 191–193 ("[T]ax ferrets received the approval of the legislature in ten states and were employed by at least some localities (often the biggest ones) in ten others. The ten states giving legislative approval included 30 percent of the national population as of 1900, while the other ten included 21 percent."). See also Report No. 559, House Committee on Ways and Means, *Discovery and Collection of Monies Withheld from the Government,* May 4, 1874 (Rep. Foster), http://www.taxhistory.org/thp /readings.nsf/cf7c9c870b600b9585256df80075b9dd/cfdfd7ecba8d6fba85256 f1e0065e427?OpenDocument.

20. John E. Brindley, *History of Taxation in Iowa,* 327 (Iowa City: State Historical Society of Iowa, 1911).

21. For qui tam suits in the nineteenth century, see Charles Doyle, *Qui Tam: The False Claims Act and Related Federal Statutes,* Cong. Res. Serv., Aug. 6, 2009, at 3–6, https://www.fas.org/sgp/crs/misc/R40785.pdf.

22. See, for example, *Filarsky v. Delia,* 132 S. Ct. 1657, 1663 (2012); Allen Steinberg, *The Transformation of Criminal Justice: Philadelphia, 1800–1880,* part II (Chapel Hill, NC: University of North Carolina Press, 1989); Roger A. Fairfax, Jr., *Delegation of the Criminal Prosecution Function to Private Actors,* 43 U.C. Davis L. Rev. 411 (2009).

23. *Filarsky,* 132 S. Ct. at 1663.

24. Howe, *What Hath God Wrought,* 441.

25. Parrillo, *Profit Motive,* 296–300; Byron Eugene Price, *Merchandizing Prisoners: Who Really Pays for Prison Privatization,* 2–3 (Westport, CT: Prager, 2006) (describing private prison arrangements in nineteenth-century Mississippi, Texas, Louisiana, and New York). There was also the contracting out of prison labor. Beverly A. Smith & Frank T. Morn, The History of Privatization in Criminal Justice, in *Privatization in Criminal Justice: Past, Present, and Future,* 3, 15 (David Shichor & Michael Gilbert, eds.) (London: Routledge, 2001).

26. Other seemingly central services, including those pertaining to customs and land grants, were also at least partially privatized. See Mashaw, *Creating the Administrative Constitution,* 26, 295.

27. Ibid., 119–143, 187–208. See also Brian Balough, *A Government Out of Sight: The Mystery of National Authority in Nineteenth-Century America* (New York: Cambridge University Press, 2009); William J. Novak, *The People's Welfare: Law and Regulation in Nineteenth-Century America* (Chapel Hill, NC: University of North Carolina Press, 1996).

28. Gerald Gunderson, *Privatization and the 19th-Century Turnpike,* 9 Cato J. 193 (1989).

29. James T. Patterson, *America's Struggle against Poverty in the Twentieth Century,* 55 (Cambridge: Harvard University Press, 2000) (describing historical reliance on private charities to support America's poor and dispossessed).

30. Alexis de Tocqueville, *Democracy in America,* 280 (Phillips Bradley, ed.) (New York: A. A. Knopf, 1945) (1835).

31. Stephen Skowronek, *Building a New American State: The Expansion of National Administrative Capacities, 1877–1920,* at 25 (New York: Cambridge University Press, 1982) (calling the early American Republic a "state of courts and parties").

32. *Hayburn's Case,* 2 U.S. (2 Dall.) 409 (1792).

33. William Novak emphasizes the fear of public corruption as being pervasive in the early American Republic. William J. Novak, Public–Private Governance: A Historical Introduction, in *Government by Contract: Outsourcing and American Democracy,* 23, 31, 33 (Jody Freeman & Martha Minow, eds.) (Cambridge: Harvard University Press, 2009). But that's a different claim from an outright and affirmative embrace of the Market *qua* Market.

34. See Parrillo, *Profit Motive,* 184, 202, 284, 290.

35. See Patricia Wallace Ingraham, *The Foundation of Merit: Public Service in American Democracy,* 21 (Baltimore: Johns Hopkins University Press, 1995); Jerry L. Mashaw, *Administration and "The Democracy": Administrative Law from Jackson to Lincoln, 1829–1861,* 117 Yale L.J. 1568, 1615, 1624 (2008).

36. But see Jerry L. Mashaw, *Foreword: The American Model of Federal Administrative Law*, 78 Geo. Wash. L. Rev. 975, 986–987 (2010) (arguing that "the spoils system did not necessarily destroy competence in the public service" because "the party was responsible for the performance of the officers that it selected").

37. Parrillo, *Profit Motive*, 183.

38. Mashaw, *Creating the Administrative Constitution*, 53–64.

39. Frederic P. Lee, *The Origins of Judicial Control of Federal Executive Action*, 36 Geo. L.J. 287, 295 (1948) (describing the thinness of judicial review of nineteenth-century administrative actions); Thomas W. Merrill, *Article III, Agency Adjudication, and the Origins of the Appellate Review Model of Administrative Law*, 111 Colum. L. Rev. 939, 947–949 (2011); Mashaw, *American Model*, 987 ("Where review was by mandamus or injunction, courts were unwilling to review to the extent that the statute provided the administrative officer any discretion."); see also *United States v. Mead Corp.*, 533 U.S. 218, 241–242 (2001) (characterizing common law writs challenging agency action as highly circumscribed vehicles of remediation).

40. See Ann Woolhandler, *Judicial Deference to Administrative Action—A Revisionist History*, 43 Admin. L. Rev. 197, 204 (1991). Woolhandler writes:

> Historically, citizen-initiated suits against governmental officials were brought as private law actions. If his invasion of the citizen's interests were not justified by statutory authority, the official was treated as a private person who had committed a tort or other legal wrong. Threatened governmental invasions that might lead to irreparable harms similarly gave rise to actions in equity for injunctions, or at law for mandamus. In such citizen-against-officer actions for injunctive relief, as well as in actions for damages, the court treated the officer as a private party if he acted without authority.

> Ibid.

41. Robert L. Rabin, *Federal Regulation in Historical Perspective*, 38 Stan. L. Rev. 1189, 1189 (1986) (suggesting that the New Deal represented "a commitment to permanent market stabilization activity by the federal government" as part of a "market-corrective model of economic regulation.").

42. *Address by President Eisenhower*, White House, Jan. 17, 1961, https://www.eisenhower.archives.gov/research/online_documents/farewell_address/1961_01_17_Press_Release.pdf.

43. See, for example, John J. Harrigan, *Political Change in the Metropolis* (5th ed.) (New York: Harper Collins, 1993); Samuel P. Hays, *The Politics of Reform in Municipal Government in the Progressive Era*, 55 Pac. Nw. Q. 157 (1964).

44. Sklansky, *Private Police*, 1213.

45. See Act of Mar. 3, 1893, ch. 208, 27 Stat. 572, 591 (codified at 5 U.S.C. § 3108).

46. Parrillo, *Profit Motive*, 125–127.

47. See, for example, Ari Arthur Hoogenboom, *Outlawing the Spoils: A History of the Civil Service Reform Movement, 1865–1883* (Westport, CT: Greenwood

Press, 1982); Paul P. Van Riper, *History of the United States Civil Service* (Evanston, IL: Row, Peterson & Co., 1958).

48. Jon D. Michaels, *An Enduring, Evolving Separation of Powers,* 115 Colum. L. Rev. 515, 540–547 (2015).

49. Harry S. Truman, *Address at the 70th Anniversary Meeting of the National Civil Service League,* May 2, 1952, http://www.trumanlibrary.org/publicpapers /index.php?pid=1284&st=&st1; see also David E. Lewis & Jennifer L. Selin, Admin. Conference of the U.S., *Sourcebook of United States Executive Agencies,* 69, fig. 1 (2012), http://permanent.access.gpo.gov/gpo37402 /Sourcebook-2012-Final_12-Dec_Online.pdf.

50. Daniel Guttman, *Public Purpose and Private Service: The Twentieth Century Culture of Contracting Out and the Evolving Law of Diffused Sovereignty,* 52 Admin. L. Rev. 859, 867–868 (2000).

51. Ibid., 868–869.

52. See Kim Phillips-Fein, *Invisible Hands: The Businessmen's Crusade against the New Deal,* 9 (New York: W. W. Norton, 2010).

53. Paul C. Light, *The True Size of Government* (Washington, DC: Brookings Institution Press, 1999).

54. Alexander Keyssar, *The Right to Vote: The Contested History of Democracy in the United States* (New York: Basic Books, 2000).

55. Gregory Sisk, *The Continuing Drift of Federal Sovereign Immunity Jurisprudence,* 50 Wm. & Mary L. Rev. 517, 531–532 (2008). Sisk explains that no federal waiver of sovereign immunities existed until 1855, when the United States allowed contractual claims to be brought against it. The court entrusted to handle such challenges was, however, not truly operational until 1863. What's more, Sisk adds that "the right to bring tort claims against the federal government was delayed another 80 years." Ibid.

56. Civil Rights Act, ch. 22, 17 Stat. 13 (1871) (codified as amended at 42 U.S.C. § 1983).

57. Federal Tort Claims Act, ch. 753, 60 Stat. 812 (1946) (codified as amended at 28 U.S.C. § 1346(b)).

58. *Bivens v. Six Unknown Named Agents of Federal Bureau of Narcotics,* 403 U.S. 388 (1971).

59. 397 U.S. 150 (1970).

60. *Goldberg v. Kelly,* 397 U.S. 254 (1970); Charles A. Reich, *The New Property,* 73 Yale L.J. 733 (1964).

61. But see Mashaw, *Creating the Administrative Constitution* (emphasizing the robustness and thoroughness of nineteenth-century administrative governance).

62. Novak, *Public–Private Governance,* 28–31; Novak, *The People's Welfare,* 106; Adolph A. Berle & Gardiner C. Means, *The Modern Corporation and Private Property,* 11 (New York: Harcourt, Brace & World, 1968).

63. Robert Britt Horwitz, *The Irony of Regulatory Reform,* 49 (New York: Oxford University Press, 1989) ("Early corporations essentially were special development projects, chartered by legislatures to benefit the community as a whole. As such, early corporations embodied a clear public interest."). Only

more recently did the "link between corporations and the public interest" become "unbundled." Ibid.

64. Kent Greenfield, *Ultra Vires Lives! A Stakeholder Analysis of Corporate Illegality (with Notes on How Corporate Law Could Reinforce International Law Norms)*, 87 Va. L. Rev. 1279, 1303–1304 (2001).

65. *Citizens United v. FEC*, 558 U.S. 310, 427 (2010) (Stevens, J., dissenting) (quoting Oscar Handlin & Mary F. Handlin, *Origins of the American Business Corporation*, 5 J. Econ. Hist. 1, 22 (1945)). Of course, not everyone agrees with Justice Stevens's treatment of early American corporations. See, for example, *Citizens United*, 558 U.S. at 386–389 (Scalia, J., concurring).

2. The Rise and Reign of *Pax Administrativa*

1. U.S. Census Bureau, *U.S. Statistical Abstract*, 164 (1929).

2. U.S. Census Bureau, *U.S. Statistical Abstract*, 154 (1937).

3. U.S. Census Bureau, *U.S. Statistical Abstract*, 208 (1949).

4. U.S. Office of Personnel Mgmt., *Historical Federal Workforce Tables*, https://archive.opm.gov/feddata/HistoricalTables/TotalGovernmentSince1962.asp.

5. See U.S. Government Publishing Office, *U.S. Government Manual 2015 Edition* (public handbook, *Federal Register*, 2015), https://www.gpo.gov/fdsys/pkg/GOVMAN-2015-07-01/xml/GOVMAN-2015-07-01.xml; David E. Lewis & Jennifer L. Selin, Admin. Conference of the U.S., *Sourcebook of United States Executive Agencies*, 69, fig. 1 (2012), https://www.acus.gov/sites/default/files/documents/Sourcebook-2012-Final_12-Dec_Online.pdf.

6. Randall G. Holcombe, *The Growth of the Federal Government in the 1920s*, 16 Cato J. 175 (Fall 1996), http://object.cato.org/sites/cato.org/files/serials/files/cato-journal/1996/11/cj16n2-2.pdf.

7. Ibid., 182; see also Thomas A. Garrett & Russell M. Rhine, *On the Size and Growth of Government*, 88 Fed. Res. Bank of St. Louis Rev., 13, 14 (Jan./Feb. 2006).

8. Sam Peltzman, *The Growth of Government*, 23 J. L. & Econ. 209 (1980); Budget of the U.S. Government, *Historical Tables, FY 2016*, Tbl. 1.2.

9. See *Historical Federal Workforce Tables*; see also Garrett & Rhine, *Size and Growth*.

10. See, for example, Patricia Wallace Ingraham, *The Foundation of Merit: Public Service in American Democracy*, 34–36 (Baltimore: Johns Hopkins University Press, 1995).

11. The landmark Pendleton Act of 1883 was, in itself, a quite modest act, and tenure protections became a reality for most federal employees only decades later. See Stephen Skowronek, *Building a New Administrative State: The Expansion of National Administrative Capacities, 1877–1920*, at 64–80 (New York: Cambridge University Press, 1982); Jerry L. Mashaw, *Federal Administration and Administrative Law in the Gilded Age*, 119 Yale L.J. 1362, 1390–1391 (2010). See Lewis & Selin, *Executive Agencies*, 69, fig. 1.

12. Jon D. Michaels, *An Enduring, Evolving Separation of Powers*, 115 Colum. L. Rev. 515, 542–547 (2015).

13. Nicholas R. Parrillo, *Against the Profit Motive: The Salary Revolution in American Government* (New Haven: Yale University Press, 2014).

14. See, for example, Hatch Act, Pub. L. No. 76–252, 53 Stat. 1147 (1939) (codified in Chapter 5 of the U.S. Code); Leon D. Epstein, *Political Sterilization of Civil Servants: The United States and Great Britain*, 10 Pub. Adm. Rev. 281 (1950).

15. *Civil Service Comm'n v. Letter Carriers*, 413 U.S. 548, 566 (1973).

16. Ibid.

17. Ibid., 565.

18. I thank Steven Schooner of George Washington University Law School for our correspondence on this point.

19. Jerry L. Mashaw, *Creating the Administrative Constitution: The Lost One Hundred Years of American Administrative Law*, 84 (New Haven: Yale University Press, 2012) (noting that though contemporary audiences "see judicial review as a relatively unified and statutorily prescribed practice of holding government accountable to law, Federalist Congresses, administrators, and courts accepted and adapted a variegated set of highly particularized common law actions . . . [and] concocted a mixture of positive and negative incentives—political, economic, and social—to manage federal officials").

20. *Wong Yang Sung v. McGrath*, 339 US 33, 41 (1950); see also *Univ. Camera Corp. v. NLRB*, 340 U.S. 474, 489 (1951) (characterizing the APA as promoting uniform standards of judicial review of administrative actions).

21. Letter from Tom Clark, Attorney General to Senator Pat McCarran, Oct. 19, 1945, Admin Conference of the U.S., *Fed Admin. Proc. Sourcebook*, 189–191 (1992).

22. Richard E. Levy & Robert L. Glicksman, *Agency-Specific Precedents*, 89 Tex. L. Rev. 499, 505 (2011); see also Kenneth Culp Davis & Richard J. Pierce, 1 *Administrative Law*, 1.1, at 2 (3d ed.) (Boston: Little, Brown, and Co., 1994); Jerry L. Mashaw, *Foreword: The American Model of Federal Administrative Law*, 78 Geo. Wash. L. Rev. 975, 979–981 (2010) (describing the APA as regularizing and harmonizing rulemaking and adjudicatory protocols); McNollgast, *The Political Origins of the Administrative Procedure Act*, 15 J. L. Econ & Org. 180, 184–185 (1999) (characterizing the APA as standardizing federal administrative procedure).

23. See, for example, *SEC v. Chenery Corp.* (*Chenery I*), 318 U.S. 80 (1943); *Crowell v. Benson*, 285 U.S. 22 (1932); *Bi-Metallic Investment Co. v. State Board of Equalization*, 239 U.S. 441 (1915); *Londoner v. City of Denver*, 29 U.S. 373 (1908); see also Mashaw, *American Model*, 991 ("Our contemporary transsubstantive administrative law is built on the foundation of administration practices that long antedate the APA's codification.").

24. *Motor Vehicles Mfrs. Ass'n v. State Farm Mut. Auto. Ins. Co.*, 463 U.S. 29 (1983); *Ass'n of Data Processing Serv. Orgs. v. Camp*, 397 U.S. 150 (1970); *Goldberg v. Kelly*, 397 U.S. 254 (1970).

25. Antonin Scalia, *Vermont Yankee: The APA, the D.C. Circuit, and the Supreme Court,* 1978 Sup. Ct. Rev. 345, 363 (noting that the Supreme Court regards "the APA as a sort of superstatute, or subconstitution"); see also Kathryn E. Kovacs, *Superstatute Theory and Administrative Common Law,* 90 Ind. L.J. 1207, 1223–1237 (2015).

26. See Arthur E. Bonfield, *The Federal APA and State Administrative Law,* 72 Va. L. Rev. 297 (1986).

27. See 5 U.S.C. § 553; see also *Chocolate Manu. Ass'n v. Block,* 755 F.2d 1098 (4th Cir. 1985); *United States v. Nova Scotia Food Prods. Corp.,* 568 F.2d 240 (2d Cir. 1977).

28. See 5 U.S.C. §§ 701–706. For a brief discussion of the availability of judicial challenges against agency actions, see Ronald A. Cass, et al., *Administrative Law: Cases and Materials,* 232–236 (6th ed.) (New York: Wolters Kluwer Law & Business, 2011).

29. See, for example, Theodore J. Lowi, *The End of Liberalism: The Second Republic of the United States* (New York: W. W. Norton, 1979).

30. See *NLRB v. Wyman-Gordon,* 394 U.S. 759, 778 (1969) (Douglas, J., dissenting) ("Public airing of problems through rule making makes the bureaucracy more responsive to public needs").

31. Kenneth Culp Davis, *Administrative Law Treatise,* 6.15, p. 283 (1970 supp.) (St. Paul, MN: West, 1971); see also J. Skelly Wright, *The Courts and the Rulemaking Process,* 59 Cornell L. Rev. 375 (1974).

32. Tom Fox, *Cass Sunstein on the Virtue of Anxious Leaders,* Wash. Post, Jun. 10, 2015, https://www.washingtonpost.com/news/on-leadership/wp/2015/06 /10/cass-sunstein-on-the-virtue-of-anxious-leaders.

33. 5 U.S.C. §§ 556–557; see also Henry J. Friendly, *Some Kind of Hearing,* 123 U. Pa. L. Rev. 1267 (1975).

34. *Goldberg,* 397 U.S. at 254.

35. *Univ. Camera Corp.,* 340 U.S. at 474.

36. See, for example, *CFTC v. Schor,* 478 U.S. 833 (1986) (Brennan, J., dissenting) (emphasizing that litigants will almost invariably choose administrative over judicial fora for reasons of convenience and efficiency). Currently, there are nearly 1,600 administrative law judges, who hear roughly 250,000 cases annually. *Free Enter. Fund v. PCAOB,* 561 U.S. 477, 542–543 (2010) (Breyer, J., dissenting); Kent Barnett, *Resolving the ALJ Quandary,* 66 Vand. L. Rev. 797, 799 (2013).

37. See Bruce A. Ackerman, 1 *We the People: Foundations,* 134–135 (Cambridge: Harvard University Press, 1991). Jacob S. Hacker & Paul Pierson, *American Amnesia: How the War on Government Led Us to Forget What Made America Prosper,* 146–151 (New York: Simon & Schuster, 2016).

38. Hacker & Pierson, *American Amnesia,* 153.

39. James R. Kurth, A History of Inherent Contradictions: The Origins and End of American Conservatism, in *American Conservatism: NOMOS LVI,* at 27 (Sanford V. Levinson, et al., eds.) (New York: New York University Press, 2016).

40. Robert E. Ellickson, *Order Without Law: How Neighbors Settle Disputes* (Cambridge: Harvard University Press, 1991).
41. James M. Acheson, *The Lobster Gangs of Maine* (Hanover, NH: University Press of New England, 1988).
42. *Williamson v. Lee Optical Co.*, 348 U.S. 483 (1955); *West Coast Hotel Co. v. Parrish*, 300 U.S. 379 (1937).
43. See generally Guido Calabresi, *A Common Law for the Age of Statutes*, 1 (Cambridge: Harvard University Press, 1982) (referring to twentieth-century American law as "[c]hoking on [s]tatutes").
44. James M. Landis, *The Administrative Process*, 8, 36 (New Haven: Yale University Press, 1938); Cass R. Sunstein, *Constitutionalism After the New Deal*, 101 Harv. L. Rev. 421, 437–438 (1987). Both Landis and Sunstein emphasize that the common law courts were apt to, in Sunstein's words, give priority to "the rights of private property" over "the interests of the poor, consumers of dangerous food and drugs, the elderly, traders on security markets, and victims of unfair trade practices." Sunstein, *Constitutionalism*, 438.
45. See, generally, Ackerman, *Foundations*, 105–130; Bruce A. Ackerman, 2 *We the People: Transformations*, 279–311, 359–382 (Cambridge: Harvard University Press, 1998).

3. The Constitutional and Normative Underpinnings of the Twentieth-Century Administrative State

1. William O. Douglas, *Administrative Government in Action,* Speech to the Lotos Club, New York, Nov. 1938, http://www.sechistorical.org/collection /papers/1930/1938_1100_Douglas_AdmGov.pdf.
2. See Richard A. Posner, *The Rise and Fall of Administrative Law,* 72 Chi.-Kent L. Rev. 953, 953 (1997).
3. See Kenneth A. Shepsle, *Representation and Governance: The Great Legislative Trade-off,* 103 Pol. Sci. Q. 461, 464 (1988) ("[T]he process of passing a bill, much less formulating a coherent policy, is complicated, drawn-out, filled with distractions, and subjected to the whims of veto groups at multiple points."); Roderick Kiewiet & Mathew D. McCubbins, *Parties, Committees, and Policymaking in the U.S. Congress: A Comment on the Role of Transaction Costs as Determinants of the Governance Structure of Political Institutions,* 145 J. Inst. & Theoretical Econ. 676 (1989) (explaining the high costs of securing and maintaining legislative majorities for any one vote).
4. See Zachary S. Price, *Enforcement Discretion and Executive Duty,* 67 Vand. L. Rev. 671 (2014).
5. An equally divided Supreme Court affirmed the decision of the Fifth Circuit, which struck down parts of President Obama's deferred action program. *United States v. Texas,* No. 15–674 (Jun. 23, 2016) (per curiam), aff'g *Texas v. United States,* 809 F.3d 134 (5th Cir. 2015). Had President Obama secured the confirmation of Chief Judge Merrick Garland to the Supreme Court, a majority of the justices would quite likely have voted to uphold the

president's program. See, for example, Jonathan H. Adler, *Tripped Up by a Tie Vote*, Scotusblog, Jun. 24, 2016, http://www.scotusblog.com/2016/06 /symposium-tripped-up-by-a-tie-vote/.

6. See Lawrence M. Friedman, *American Law in the Twentieth Century*, 170 (New Haven: Yale University Press, 2002); Stephen Skowronek, *Building a New Administrative State: The Expansion of National Administrative Capacities, 1877–1920*, at 4, 290 (New York: Cambridge University Press, 1982).

7. Friedman, *American Law*, 170.

8. Neal Devins & David E. Lewis, *Not-So Independent Agencies: Party Polarization and the Limits of Institutional Design*, 88 B.U. L. Rev. 459, 485 (2008) ("When the parties are polarized and the White House and Congress are divided, Presidents have strong incentives to pursue unilateral policymaking through loyal appointees."); Elena Kagan, *Presidential Administration*, 114 Harv. L. Rev. 2245, 2248 (2001) (underscoring how important it is to control the levers of administrative policymaking in times of divided, obstructionist constitutional government); Gillian E. Metzger, *Embracing Administrative Common Law*, 80 Geo. Wash. L. Rev. 1293, 1322–1323 (2012) (explaining how legislative impasses further encourage presidential policymaking through administratvie agencies).

9. Douglas, *Lotos Speech*.

10. Felix Frankfurter, *The Public and Its Government*, 89 (New Haven: Yale University Press, 1930).

11. On the need to strike this compromise, see Joseph Story, 2 *Commentaries on the Constitution of the United States*, §§ 635, 641–642 (Boston: Hillard, Gray, 1833).

12. *The Federalist*, No. 46 (James Madison).

13. *The Federalist*, No. 51 (James Madison). See generally Josh Chafetz, *Congress's Constitution*, 160 U. Pa. L. Rev. 715, 771 (2012) (describing the conflict-enabling virtues of the constitutional separation of powers). Peter L. Strauss, *The Place of Agencies in Government: Separation of Powers and the Fourth Branch*, 84 Colum. L. Rev. 573, 577 (1984) ("The [legislative, executive, and judicial] powers of government are kept radically separate, because if the same body exercised all three of them, or even two, it might no longer be possible to keep it within the constraints of law."). See generally Laurence Claus, *Montesquieu's Mistakes and the True Meaning of Separation*, 25 Oxford J.L.S. 419 (2005) (describing how checks and balances protect liberty and promote the rule of law).

14. *Morrison v. Olson*, 487 U.S. 654, 697 (1988) (Scalia, J., dissenting).

15. See, for example, *Wayman v. Southard*, 23 U.S. (10 Wheat.) 1, 43 (1825) (describing delegations to merely "fill up the details").

16. Kim Phillips-Fein, *The Businessmen's Crusade against the New Deal*, 10–15 (New York: W. W. Norton, 2009); Kenneth Finegold & Theda Skocpol, *State and Party in America's New Deal*, 138 (Madison, WI: University of Wisconsin Press, 1995).

17. See generally James M. Landis, *The Administrative Process* (New Haven: Yale University Press, 1938); Harold H. Bruff, *Presidential Power and*

Administrative Lawmaking, 88 Yale L.J. 451, 451 (1979) ("The increasing sprawl of the federal agencies has challenged the effectiveness of the checks and balances designed by the Constitution."); Robert M. Cooper, *Administrative Justice and the Role of Discretion,* 47 Yale L.J. 577, 577 (1938) (describing critics of administrative governance as invoking the language of "tyranny" and "despotism"); Jerry L. Mashaw, *Creating the Administrative Constitution: The Lost One Hundred Years of American Administrative Law,* 288 (New Haven: Yale University Press, 2012) (noting that "agencies' combination of legislative, executive, and judicial functions struck many as dangerously aggrandizing executive power and creating the potential for bias and prejudgment in administrative determinations").

18. See, for example, *Whitman v. Am. Trucking Ass'ns, Inc.,* 531 U.S. 457, 488–490 (2001) (Stevens, J., concurring) (contending that the majority is engaging in a fiction insofar as it "pretend[s]" that agencies are doing something short of lawmaking).

19. See Cass Sunstein & Adrian Vermeule, *Libertarian Administrative Law,* 82 U. Chi. L. Rev. 393 (2015) (describing longstanding and newly arising constitutional challenges to the administrative state); Jody Freeman, *The Private Role in Public Governance,* 75 N.Y.U. L. Rev. 543, 545 (2000) ("Since the New Deal explosion of government agencies, administrative law has been defined by the crisis of legitimacy.... Agencies can claim, after all, only a dubious constitutional lineage.... The combination of executive, legislative, and adjudicative functions in administrative agencies appears to violate the separation of powers principles embodied in the Constitution.").

20. Philip Hamburger, *Is Administrative Law Unlawful?* (Chicago: University of Chicago Press, 2014).

21. Adrian Vermeule, *No,* 93 Tex. L. Rev. 1547 (2015).

22. *Dep't of Transp. v. Ass'n of Am. R.R.,* 135 S. Ct. 1225, 1242, 1243, 1244 (2015) (Thomas, J., concurring). For Hamburger's immediate influence on federal circuit court jurisprudence, see, for example, *De Niz Robles v. Lynch,* 803 F.3d 1165, 1171 n.5 (10th Cir. 2015); *United States v. Nichols,* 784 F.3d 666, 670 n.2 (10th Cir. 2015) (Gorsush, J., dissenting from the denial of rehearing en banc); *Esquivel-Quintana v. Lynch,* 810 F.3d 1019, 1027 (6th Cir. 2016) (Sutton, J., concurring in part and dissenting in part).

23. *City of Arlington v. FCC,* 133 S. Ct. 1863, 1878 (2013) (Roberts, C. J., dissenting).

24. *Gutierrez-Brizuela v. Lynch,* 834 F.3d 1142, 1149 (10th Cir. 2016) (Gorsuch, J., concurring).

25. Ibid.

26. Stuart Taylor Jr., *Does the President Agree with This Nominee?,* Atlantic, May 2005, http://www.theatlantic.com/magazine/archive/2005/05/does-the-president-agree-with-this-nominee/304012/.

27. *See* Jon D. Michaels, *Running Government Like a Business ... Then and Now,* 128 Harv. L. Rev. 1152, 1176 (2015). Compare Chafetz, *Congress's Constitution,* 769 (describing the conflict among constitutional branches as "features rather than bugs" in our constitutional system).

28. See Lisa Schultz Bressman, *Beyond Accountability: Arbitrariness and Legitimacy in the Administrative State*, 78 N.Y.U. L. Rev. 461, 462 (2003); Jacob E. Gersen, *Unbundled Powers*, 96 Va. L. Rev. 301, 305 (2010). See generally Richard H. Fallon, Jr., *Implementing the Constitution* (Cambridge: Harvard University Press, 2001) (contemplating constitutional compatibility).

29. See, for example, *Yakus v. United States*, 321 U.S. 414, 424–425 (1944); *Whitman*, 488–490 (Stevens, J., concurring).

30. Jack M. Balkin, *Framework Originalism and the Living Constitution*, 103 Nw. U. L. Rev. 549, 560 (2009).

31. Elizabeth Magill & Adrian Vermeule, *Allocating Power Within Agencies*, 120 Yale L.J. 1032 (2011) (describing and critiquing conventional treatments of agencies as monolithic).

32. *See* David E. Lewis, *The Politics of Presidential Appointments: Political Control and Bureaucratic Performance*, 202–204 (Princeton: Princeton University Press, 2008); David Fontana, *The Second American Revolution in the Separation of Powers*, 87 Tex. L. Rev. 1409, 1414 (2009) (observing that "substantial partisan and ideological homogeneity" exists among agency leaders across most presidential administrations); see also Bruce Ackerman, *The Decline and Fall of the American Republic*, 33 (Cambridge: Harvard University Press, 2010) (underscoring the clear expectation that appointed agency leaders are to be loyal to the president and her agenda).

33. Lewis, *Presidential Appointments*, 51–56.

34. Jon D. Michaels, *Of Constitutional Custodians and Regulatory Rivals: An Account of the Old and New Separation of Powers*, 91 N.Y.U. L. Rev. 227, 236 (2016); Kagan, *Presidential Administration*, 2277–2279, 2281–2282, 2331–2333. See generally *Morrison*, 487 U.S. at 706–710 (Scalia, J., dissenting).

35. Bruce Ackerman, *The New Separation of Powers*, 113 Harv. L. Rev. 633, 709, 710 (2000).

36. Cary Coglianese, *The Internet and Citizen Participation in Rulemaking*, 1 J.L. & Pol'y for Info. Soc'y 33, 36 (2005); Strauss, *The Place of Agencies*, 586 ("The President and a few hundred political appointees are at the apex of an enormous bureaucracy. . . ."); David E. Lewis & Jennifer L. Selin, Admin. Conference of the U.S., *Sourcebook of United States Executive Agencies*, 69, fig. 1 (2012), https://www.acus.gov/sites/default/files/documents /Sourcebook-2012-Final_12-Dec_Online.pdf (illustrating the small number of appointed leaders relative to the large number of permanent employees).

37. Lewis & Selin, *Executive Agencies*, 69, fig. 1. The formal federal civil service does not sweep in all permanent, politically insulated government employees. There are, for instance, a few agency-specific and occupation-specific systems that are technically distinct from the formal federal civil service but provide substantially the same privileges and protections. Anne Joseph O'Connell, *Vacant Offices: Delays in Staffing Top Agency Positions*, 82 S. Cal. L. Rev. 913, 925–926 (2008); Lewis, *Presidential Appointments*, 20–25. For my purposes, all such federal employees are effectively civil servants—and I refer to them as such.

38. In addition, federal law prohibits civil servants from engaging in partisan political activities. See, for example, Hatch Act, Pub. L. 76–252, 53 Stat. 1147 (codified in Chapter 5 of the U.S. Code); see also *Civil Service Comm'n v. Letter Carriers*, 413 U.S. 548, 565–566 (1973).

39. The courts deserve some credit for ensuring that civil servants are taken seriously. Among other things, courts have stressed the importance of administrative records and factual findings—responsibilities that almost necessarily fall to the career staff. See, for example, *Citizens to Preserve Overton Park v. Volpe*, 401 U.S. 402 (1971) (demanding the production of the whole agency record and refusing to give credence to *post hoc* justifications proffered by an agency's appellate lawyers); *United States v. Nova Scotia Food Prods. Corp.*, 568 F.2d 240, 249 (2d Cir. 1977) (emphasizing the necessity of an "adequate [administrative] record" to ensure "meaningful [judicial] review"); *Motor Vehicles Mfrs. Ass'n v. State Farm Mut. Auto. Ins. Co.*, 463 U.S. 29 (1983) (insisting an agency give thorough and comprehensive consideration to relevant factual and policy considerations when promulgating or rescinding a rule). See generally Jody Freeman & Adrian Vermeule, *Massachusetts v. EPA: From Politics to Expertise*, 2007 Sup. Ct. Rev. 51, 52 (highlighting recent Supreme Court opinions that "override executive positions . . . found untrustworthy, in the sense that executive expertise had been subordinated to politics").

40. Sanford C. Gordon, *Politicizing Agency Spending Authority: Lessons from a Bush-Era Scandal*, 105 Am. Pol. Sci. Rev. 717 (2011) (stressing the role civil servants play in awarding federal grants); Matthew Diller, *The Revolution in Welfare Administration: Rules, Discretion, and Entrepreneurial Government*, 75 N.Y.U. L. Rev. 1121, 1130 (2000) ("It is difficult to conceive of an area in which the distance between grand policy decisions and ground-level implementation is as vast as in the welfare system. . . . Policies are implemented through the aggregate actions of literally thousands of officials who take actions with respect to individual cases."); David A. Super, *Offering an Invisible Hand: The Rise of the Personal Choice Model for Rationing Public Benefits*, 113 Yale L.J. 815, 836–840 (2004) (explaining how rank-and-file government officials can and do influence welfare policy on the ground); Norma M. Riccucci, *How Management Matters: Street-Level Bureaucrats and Welfare Reform*, 59–76 (Washington, DC: Georgetown University Press, 2005).

41. See, for example, Jon D. Michaels, *An Enduring, Evolving Separation of Powers*, 115 Colum. L. Rev. 515, 543–546 (2015); Alex Hemmer, Note, *Civil Servant Suits*, 124 Yale L.J. 758, 762 (2014); Adam Shinar, *Dissenting from Within: Why and How Public Officials Resist the Law*, 40 Fla. St. U. L. Rev. 601, 622–624, 630 (2013).

42. Lewis, *Presidential Appointments*, 30; see also Gillian E. Metzger, *The Interdependent Relationship between Internal and External Separation of Powers*, 59 Emory L.J. 423, 445 (2009). See generally Charles T. Goodsell, *The Case for Bureaucracy*, 89 (Chatham, NJ: Chatham House Publishers,

1983) (describing findings that corroborate the claim that career government workers embrace their professional and legal duties).

43. Harold H. Bruff, *Balance of Forces: Separation of Powers Law in the Administrative State,* 408 (Durham, NC: Carolina Academic Press, 2006); see also Aaron Wildavsky, *The Beleaguered Presidency,* 165, 179 (New Brunswick, NJ: Transaction Publishers, 1991) (calling independent government employees "an essential part of the balances that guard our liberties").

44. This understanding is different from leading accounts that characterize career civil servants as mere agents of the appointed leaders. That principal–agent characterization is, again, one that seems to gloss over civil servants' legal independence.

45. Strauss, *Place of Agencies,* 586; see also Magill & Vermeule, *Allocating Power,* 1037–1038 ("The conflicts between political appointees and the 'bureaucracy'—usually taken to refer to well-insulated-from termination members of the professional civil service—are legion.").

46. Freedom of Information Act, Pub. L. 89–487, 80 Stat. 250 (1967) (codified at 5 U.S.C. § 552).

47. 5 U.S.C. § 553(e).

48. Miriam Seifter, *Second-Order Participation in Administrative Law,* 63 UCLA L. Rev. 1300 (2016).

49. 5 U.S.C. § 553(c).

50. 5 U.S.C. § 702; *Massachusetts v. EPA,* 549 U.S. 497 (2007) (invalidating an agency's denial of a request for rulemaking as insufficiently reasoned).

51. 5 U.S.C. § 702; *State Farm,* 463 U.S. at 29 (finding unreasonable an agency's failure to consider material comments regarding seatbelt use and safety).

52. 5 U.S.C. § 706(2)(A), (E); see also *Goldberg v. Kelly,* 397 U.S. 254 (1970); *Universal Camera Corp. v. NLRB,* 340 U.S. 474 (1951).

53. Richard Murphy, *Enhancing the Role of Public Interest Organizations in Rulemaking via Pre-Notice Transparency,* 47 Wake Forest L. Rev. 681, 682 (2012); see also Peter M. Shane, *Madison's Nightmare: How Executive Power Threatens American Democracy,* 159–160 (Chicago: University of Chicago Press, 2009) (explaining how administrative procedures enable the public to hold agencies accountable).

54. See Mariano-Florentino Cuellar, *Rethinking Regulatory Democracy,* 57 Admin. L. Rev. 411 (2005); Susan Webb Yackee, *Participant Voice in the Bureaucratic Policymaking Process,* 25 J. Pub. Admin. Res. Theory 427 (2015); William F. West & Connor Raso, *Who Shapes the Rulemaking Agenda? Implications for Bureaucratic Responsiveness and Bureaucratic Control,* 23 J. Pub. Adm. Res. Theory 495 (2013).

55. See, for example, *Nat'l Tour Brokers Ass'n v. United States,* 591 U.S. 896, 902 (D.C. Cir. 1978) (describing the notice-and-comment process as ensuring that an agency "maintains a flexible and open mind about its own rules"); *Small Refiner Lead Phase-Down Task Force v. EPA,* 705 F.2d 506, 547 (D.C. Cir. 1983) (explaining that notice-and-comment rulemaking empowers members of the public to "develop evidence in the [rulemaking] record to support

their objections" upon judicial review); *Portland Cement v. Ruckelshaus*, 486 F.2d 375, 393–394 (D.C. Cir. 1973) (obligating agency officials to address material comments that the public proffers); *Nova Scotia*, 568 F.2d at 252–253 (insisting that agency officials address material comments in the concise general statement that accompanies publication of final rules).

56. Effective public participation can, but need not, reflect majoritarian sentiments. The power of the idea, more so than the number of people endorsing that idea, may well carry the day in reasoned administrative proceedings. As such, civil society may be more majoritarian than a presidential administration, particularly one that eked out a narrow electoral college victory, while losing the popular vote, or one that has simply lost considerable popular support since the last election. But civil society may also be far less majoritarian insofar as a single, highly persuasive comment may prove dispositive in shaping an agency's decision.

57. Ronald N. Johnson & Gary D. Libecap, *The Federal Civil Service System and the Problem of Bureaucracy: The Economics and Politics of Institutional Change*, 51, 68 (Chicago: Chicago University Press, 1994).

58. Harry S. Truman, *Address at the 70th Anniversary Meeting of the National Civil Service League*, May 2, 1952, http://www.trumanlibrary.org/publicpapers/index.php?pid=1284&st=&st1=; see also Lewis & Selin, *Executive Agencies*, 69, fig. 1.

59. Richard B. Stewart, *The Reformation of American Administrative Law*, 88 Harv. L. Rev. 1667 (1975).

60. In a similar vein, Abner Greene contends that the constitutional separation of powers ought to carry over into a post-New Deal era dominated by powerful executive agencies. He and I differ, however, in terms of solutions. Greene prefers to embolden Congress to serve as a more effective check on these executive agencies. Abner S. Greene, *Checks and Balances in an Era of Presidential Lawmaking*, 61 U. Chi. L. Rev. 123, 153–158 (1994).

61. Among those who style themselves biologists or engineers first (and civil servants second), it would nevertheless seem that even if their motivations differed from those of "true-believer" servants of the State, they would arrive at substantially the same place. After all, professional scientists are no less committed to reasoned decisionmaking.

62. See, for example, William M. Landes & Richard A. Posner, *The Independent Judiciary in an Interest Group Perspective*, 18 J.L. & Econ. 875 (1975) (positing that judicial review of agency action serves as a mechanism of contract enforcement, with the courts operating as guarantors of the original deal struck by the Congress that enacted the relevant authorizing legislation).

63. See, for example, Lewis, *Presidential Appointments*, 28–30; Goodsell, *Bureaucracy*; Michaels, *Enduring, Evolving*, 544–545. See generally Max Weber, Bureaucracy, in *From Max Weber: Essays in Sociology*, 196, 220 (H. H. Gerth & C. Mills Wright, trans., eds.) (London: Routledge, 2009) ("[A] system of rationally debatable 'reasons' stands behind every act of bureaucratic administration.").

64. *Youngstown Sheet & Tube Co. v. Sawyer*, 343 U.S. 579 (1952).

65. Compare Joel D. Aberbach & Bert A. Rockman, *In the Web of Politics: Three Decades of the U.S. Federal Executive*, 168 (Washington, DC: Brookings Institution Press, 2000) (characterizing many federal civil servants as politically left-leaning) with Frank B. Cross & Emerson H. Tiller, *Judicial Partisanship and Obedience to Legal Doctrine*, 107 Yale L.J. 2155 (1998) (describing politically and ideologically minded jurists).

66. See generally Ronald J. Krotoszynski, Jr., *The Unitary Executive and the Plural Judiciary: On the Potential Virtues of Decentralized Judicial Power*, 89 Notre Dame L. Rev. 1021 (2014).

67. Jürgen Habermas, *Structural Transformation of the Public Sphere: An Inquiry into a Category of Bourgeois Society*, 141–181 (Cambridge: MIT Press, 1989) (commenting on the decline of the public sphere in the twentieth century); Thomas O. McGarity, *Administrative Law as Blood Sport: Policy Erosion in a Highly Partisan Age*, 61 Duke L.J. 1671 (2012) (describing the domination and thus skewing of civil society by powerful interest groups).

68. *Citizens United v. FEC*, 558 U.S. 310, 427 (2010) (Stevens, J., dissenting); Lawrence Lessig, *Republic, Lost: How Money Corrupts Congress—And a Plan to Stop It* (New York: Twelve Books, 2011).

69. 488 U.S. 366, 372 (1989).

70. See David A. Strauss, *The Living Constitution*, 120–122 (New York: Oxford University Press, 2010). See generally James O. Freedman, *Crisis and Legitimacy*, 125–126, 259–264 (New York: Cambridge University Press, 1978).

71. See Mashaw, *Creating the Administrative Constitution*; Daniel R. Ernst, *Tocqueville's Nightmare: The Administrative State Emerges in America, 1900–1940* (New York, Oxford University Press, 2014); Jeremy K. Kessler, *The Struggle for Administrative Legitimacy*, 129 Harv. L. Rev. 718, 719 (2016) (taking note of scholarly work "redescribing the formation of the American administrative state as a centuries-long process of doctrinal development, intellectual adjustment, and political bargaining rather than a constitutional rupture").

72. Bruce Ackerman assigns constitutional status to the administrative state in large part because it represents the culmination of a bona fide "constitutional moment," a self-consciously revolutionary period of popular support, bipartisan acceptance, and de facto constitutional ratification of the New Deal agenda. *See* Bruce A. Ackerman, 1 *We the People: Foundations* (Cambridge: Harvard University Press, 1991); Bruce A. Ackerman, 2 *We the People: Transformations* (Cambridge: Harvard University Press, 1998).

73. See Jack M. Balkin, *Living Originalism*, 138–139, 179 (Cambridge: Harvard University Press, 2011).

74. Balkin, *Framework Originalism*, 559. See generally Keith E. Whittington, *Constitutional Construction: Divided Powers and Constitutional Meaning* (Cambridge: Harvard University Press, 1999).

75. Balkin, *Framework Originalism*, 560.

76. Thomas W. Merrill, *The Constitutional Principle of Separation of Powers*, 1991 Sup. Ct. Rev. 225, 225.

77. No one, seemingly, realized the importance of administrative restaging better than New Deal official and Harvard Law Dean James Landis. Landis stressed intra-administrative balancing as a means of preserving the framers' commitment to the separation of powers. Writing almost a decade before Congress enacted the APA, Landis suggested that the practices and instruments of State power may evolve beyond those contemplated in the 1787 Constitution *provided* that the new practices and instruments are themselves subject to a similarly robust system of checks and balances. Landis, *Administrative Process*, 46.

78. Compare Charles L. Black, Jr., *Structure and Relationship in Constitutional Law*, 7, 11 (Baton Rouge, LA: Louisiana State University Press, 1969). Some, of course, reject such structural constitutional readings. See, for example, John F. Manning, *Separation of Powers as Ordinary Interpretation*, 124 Harv. L. Rev. 1939, 1971–2005 (2011) (contesting interpretations grounded in "freestanding principles of separation of powers"). For a critique of those critiques, see Gillian E. Metzger, *The Constitutional Legitimacy of Freestanding Federalism*, 122 Harv. L. Rev. F. 98, 103–105 (2009), http://cdn.harvardlawreview.org/wp-content/uploads/pdfs/Forum_Vol_122_metzger.pdf (arguing that many of the Court's decisions seem to be "fundamentally animated by general visions of the meaning of constitutional separation of powers").

79. William N. Eskridge, Jr. & John Ferejohn, *Super-statutes*, 50 Duke L.J. 1215, 1215 (2000).

80. William N. Eskridge, Jr. & John Ferejohn, *A Republic of Statutes: The New American Constitution*, 6–8, 26, 214–16 (New Haven: Yale University Press, 2010).

81. Eskridge & Ferejohn, *Super-statutes*, 1227.

82. Adrian Vermeule, among others, has expressed surprise that Eskridge and Ferejohn mention the APA "only in passing." Adrian Vermeule, *Superstatutes*, New Republic, Oct. 25, 2010, https://newrepublic.com/article/78604/superstatutes. Vermeule posits that most scholars would include the APA on their list of superstatutes, and, seemingly, we may count Cass Sunstein and Antonin Scalia among those others who have. Antonin Scalia, *Vermont Yankee: The APA, the D.C. Circuit, and the Supreme Court*, 1978 Sup. Ct. Rev. 345, 363 (suggesting that the Supreme Court regards "the APA as a sort of superstatute, or subconstitution"); Sunstein & Vermeule, *Libertarian Administrative Law*, 466 (referring to the APA as "a super-statute"); see also Kathryn E. Kovacs, *Superstatute Theory and Administrative Common Law*, 90 Ind. L.J. 1207, 1223–1237 (2015).

83. Sunstein & Vermeule, *Libertarian Administrative Law*, 466.

84. See, for example, Skowronek, *Building a New American State*, 47–50, 58–65.

85. Ibid., 65–67.

86. See, for example, Tom C. Clark, *Attorney General's Manual on the Administrative Procedure Act*, 5–6 (1947), https://archive.org/stream/AttorneyGeneralsManualOnTheAdministrativeProcedureActOf1947#page/n1/mode/2up; Report of the President's Committee on Administrative

Management, in *Basic Documents of American Public Administration: 1776–1950*, at 110 (Frederick C. Mosher, ed.) (New York: Holmes & Meier, 1976) ("Brownlow Committee"). See generally Walter Gellhorn, *The Administrative Procedure Act: The Beginnings*, 72 Va. L. Rev. 219 (1986) (describing administrative reform commissions working throughout the 1930s and 1940s).

87. Skowronek, *Building a New American State*, 70–84.
88. Charles A. Beard, *American Government and Politics*, 72 (New York: Macmillan, 1917).
89. U.S. Const. art. II, sec. 2, cl. 2.
90. See, for example, Landis, *Administrative Process*, 10–17, 46–47.
91. See, for example, Bressman, *Beyond Accountability*, 461 (positing that administrative legitimacy is largely a function of reasonable, non-arbitrary public administration).
92. See, for example, Jodi L. Short, *The Political Turn in American Administrative Law: Power, Rationality, and Reasons*, 61 Duke L.J. 1811, 1820–1823 (2011).
93. See, for example, Adrian Vermeule, *The Constitution of Risk* (New York, Cambridge University Press, 2013).
94. See, for example, Mark Seidenfeld, *A Civic Republican Justification for the Bureaucratic State*, 105 Harv. L. Rev. 1511, 1563–64 (1992).
95. See, for example, Stewart, *Reformation*, 1670.
96. See, for example, Jerry L. Mashaw, *Prodelegation: Why Administrators Should Make Political Decisions*, 1 J.L. Econ. & Org. 81 (1985).
97. Compare Gerald E. Frug, *The Ideology of Bureaucracy in American Law*, 97 Harv. L. Rev. 1276 (1984); Aberbach & Rockman, *Web of Politics*, 606; Robert B. Reich, *Public Administration and Public Deliberation: An Interpretive Essay*, 94 Yale L.J. 1617, 1624 (1985); Stewart, *Reformation*, 1669.
98. Robert W. Hamilton, *Procedures for the Adoption of Rules of General Applicability: The Need for Procedural Innovation in Administrative Rulemaking*, 60 Cal. L. Rev. 1276, 1287–1288 (1972).
99. See Aberbach & Rockman, *Web of Politics*, 608. Aberbach and Rockman focus on two conflicting values—political accountability and expert administration. But they draw roughly the same conclusion as I do. For them, and largely for me, "[t]he problem for government and . . . the public interest is not to have one of these values completely dominate the other, but to provide a creative dialogue or synthesis between the two." Ibid.
100. Compare Josh Chafetz, *Multiplicity in Federalism and the Separation of Powers*, 120 Yale L.J. 1084, 1112–1113 (2011) (describing his theory of "multiplicity" in the constitutional separation of powers). Chafetz explains "that there is sometimes affirmative value in promoting the means for inter-branch tension and conflict without any sort of superior body that can articulate a global, principled, final, and binding decision on the matter." Ibid. Like the constitutional separation of powers, the administrative separation of powers provides a framework for structuring conflict over substantive values,

enabling that conflict to play out in an indeterminate, contestable, and sometimes politically charged fashion.

101. Guido Calabresi & Philip Bobbitt, *Tragic Choices,* 41, 195–196 (New York: W. W. Norton, 1978).

102. Heather K. Gerken, *Second-Order Diversity,* 118 Harv. L. Rev. 1099, 1174 (2005).

103. Compare Heather K. Gerken, *Foreword: Federalism All the Way Down,* 124 Harv. L. Rev. 4 (2010).

104. See Michaels, *Running Government,* 1175–1177.

4. The Beginning of the End

1. See, for example, Reuel E. Schiller, *Rulemaking's Promise: Administrative Law and Legal Culture in the 1960s and 1970s,* 53 Admin. L. Rev. 1139, 1146–1147 (2011).

2. Kim Phillips-Fein, *Invisible Hands: The Businessmen's Crusade against the New Deal,* 23 (New York: W. W. Norton, 2009); Jeffrey R. Henig, *Privatization in the United States: Theory and Practice,* 104 Pol. Sci. Q. 649, 652 (1989).

3. Phillips-Fein, *Invisible Hands,* 42.

4. Jacob S. Hacker & Paul Pierson, *American Amnesia: How the War on Government Led Us to Forget What Made America Prosper,* 146–153, 239 (New York: Simon & Schuster, 2016).

5. James Reston, *What Goldwater Lost,* N.Y. Times, Nov. 4, 1964, at 23.

6. Henig, *Privatization,* 652.

7. Phillips-Fein, *Invisible Hands,* 138–139.

8. Hacker & Pierson, *American Amnesia,* 137–145; Phillips-Fein, *Invisible Hands,* 31.

9. Hacker & Pierson, *American Amnesia,* 137–138, 140–142.

10. See, for example, James M. Buchanan, Rent Seeking and Profit Seeking, in *Toward a Theory of the Rent-Seeking Society,* 3, 8–15 (James M. Buchanan, et al., eds.) (College Station, TX: Texas A&M University Press, 1980); Gordon Tullock, *Private Wants, Public Means,* 35–38, 51–54 (New York: Basic Books, 1970); Milton Friedman & Rose Friedman, *Free to Choose,* 117–118 (New York: Harcourt Brace Jovanovich, 1980). The Friedmans write "[t]he temptation [for government workers] to engage in corruption, to cheat, is strong and will not always be resisted or frustrated. People who resist the temptation to cheat will use legitimate means to direct the money to themselves. They will lobby for legislation favorable to themselves, for rules from which they can benefit. The bureaucrats administering the programs will press for better pay and perquisites for themselves—an outcome that larger programs facilitate." Ibid.

11. See William A. Niskanen, Jr., *Bureaucracy and Representative Government* (Chicago: Aldine, Atherton, 1971).

12. Francis Fukuyama, *Political Order and Political Decay,* 164, 472 (New York: Farrar, Straus and Giroux, 2014).

13. Pew Research Center, *Public Trust in Government: 1958–2014*, Nov. 13, 2014, http://www.people-press.org/2014/11/13/public-trust-in-government/.

14. Ibid.

15. Ibid.

16. Phillips-Fein, *Invisible Hands*, 69, 77–81.

17. Jules Witcover, *Party of the People: A History of the Democrats*, 534–535 (New York: Random House, 2003); Jerry F. Hough, *Changing Party Coalitions: The Mystery of Red State-Blue State Alignment*, 201 (New York: Agathon, 2006); Hacker & Pierson, *American Amnesia*, 197.

18. Ruth H. DeHoog, *Contracting Out for Human Services: Economic, Political, and Organizational Perspectives*, 1 (Albany, NY: State University of New York Press, 1984).

19. Henig, *Privatization*, 656; Hacker & Pierson, *American Amnesia*, 197.

20. *Goldberg v. Kelly*, 397 U.S. 254 (1970).

21. Ibid., 278–79 (Black, J., dissenting).

22. William E. Simon, Foreword to James T. Bennett & Manuel H. Johnson, *Better Government at Half the Price: Private Production of Public Services*, at vii (Ottawa, IL: Caroline House, 1981).

23. Nicholas Lemann, *The Unfinished War*, Atlantic, Dec. 1988, https://www.theatlantic.com/past/politics/poverty/lemunf1.htm.

24. Sean Wilentz, *The Age of Reagan: A History, 1974–2008*, at 35–36 (New York: Harper, 2008).

25. Ralph Blumenthal, *Recalling New York at the Brink of Bankruptcy*, N.Y. Times, Dec. 5, 2002, http://www.nytimes.com/2002/12/05/nyregion/recalling-new-york-at-the-brink-of-bankruptcy.html; Davita Silfen Glasberg, *The Political Economic Power of Financial Capital and Urban Fiscal Crisis: Cleveland's Default, 1978*, 10 J. Urb. Aff., 219 (Oct. 1988).

26. Daniel Yergin, *The Prize: The Epic Quest for Oil, Money & Power*, 598–599 (New York: Simon & Schuster, 1991).

27. Josef Joffe, *The Myth of America's Decline: Politics, Economics, and a Half Century of False Prophets*, 23 (New York: W. W. Norton, 2011).

28. James W. Hughes & Joseph J. Seneca, Introduction: The Demographic Trajectory and Public Policy, in *America's Demographic Tapestry: Baseline for the New Millennium*, 9 (James W. Hughes & Joseph J. Seneca, eds.) (New Brunswick, NJ: Rutgers University Press, 1999); Robert Gilpin, *Global Political Economy: Understanding the International Economic Order*, 175 (Princeton: Princeton University Press, 2001).

29. David O. Sears & Jack Citrin, *Tax Revolt: Something for Nothing in California*, 40 (Cambridge: Harvard University Press, 1982).

30. Ibid., 19–42 (describing the state referendum movement to pass Proposition 13, which drastically reduced California property taxes).

31. For recognition of the importance of the deregulatory movement to the Reagan coalition, see *Republican Party Platform of 1980*, Jul. 15, 1980, http://www.presidency.ucsb.edu/ws/?pid=25844; see also Andrew E. Busch, *Ronald Reagan and the Politics of Freedom*, 88 (Lanham, MD: Rowman & Littlefield, 2001); Jacob S. Hacker & Paul Pierson, *Winner-Take-All Politics:*

How Washington Made the Rich Richer—and Turned Its Back on the Middle Class, 184 (New York: Simon & Schuster, 2010) (emphasizing that the deregulation movement began in earnest in the late 1970s and carried some bipartisan support).

32. Hugh Heclo, Ronald Reagan and the American Public Philosophy, in *The Reagan Presidency: Pragmatic Conservatism and Its Legacy*, 27–29 (W. Elliot Brownlee & Hugh Davis Graham, eds.) (Lawrence, KS: University Press of Kansas, 2003) (describing President Reagan's anti-government ideology and rhetoric and explaining how Reagan managed to maintain an anti-government, outsider image notwithstanding the fact that he was a two-term governor of California).

33. Carl Bernstein & Bob Woodward, *All the President's Men* (New York: Simon & Schuster, 1974).

34. Todd Belt, Nixon, Watergate, and the Attempt to Sway Public Opinion, in *Watergate Remembered: The Legacy for American Politics*, 147, 163 (Michael A. Genovese & Iwan W. Morgan, eds.) (New York: Palgrave Macmillan, 2012).

35. See generally Robert S. McNamara, *In Retrospect: The Tragedy and Lessons of Vietnam* (New York: Vintage Books, 1995).

36. Anthony Campagna, *The Economic Consequences of the Vietnam War*, 108, 135 (New York: Praeger, 1991).

37. Neil Sheehan, *Pentagon Study Traces 3 Decades of Growing U. S. Involvement*, N.Y. Times, Jun. 13, 1971, at A1; John Hart Ely, *War and Responsibility: Constitutional Lessons of Vietnam and Its Aftermath*, 30–32, 34–46, 68–104 (Princeton: Princeton University Press, 1993).

38. Seymour M. Hersh, *Huge C.I.A. Operation Reported in U.S. against Antiwar Forces, Other Dissidents in Nixon Years*, N.Y. Times, Dec. 22, 1974, at A1.

39. Jimmy Carter, *"Crisis of Confidence" Speech*, Jul 15, 1979, http://millercenter.org/president/speeches/speech-3402.

40. Jimmy Carter, *1978 State of the Union Address*, Jan. 19, 1978, http://www.jimmycarterlibrary.gov/documents/speeches/su78jec.phtml.

41. Memo from Lewis F. Powell, Jr. to Eugene B. Sydnor, Jr., *Attack on American Free Enterprise System*, Aug. 23, 1971, http://law2.wlu.edu/deptimages/Powell%20Archives/PowellMemorandumTypescript.pdf.

42. Ibid.

43. Phillips-Fein, *Invisible Hands*, 158–165; John B. Judis, *The Paradox of American Democracy: Elites, Special Interests, and the Betrayal of Public Trust*, 116–117 (New York: Pantheon Books, 2000).

44. Mark Schmitt, *The Legend of the Powell Memo*, Am. Prospect, Apr. 27, 2005, http://prospect.org/article/legend-powell-memo.

45. Phillips-Fein, *Invisible Hands*, 167.

46. Gregg Easterbrook, *Ideas Move Nations*, Atlantic, Jan. 1986, http://www.theatlantic.com/past/politics/polibig/eastidea.htm.

47. Phillips-Fein, *Invisible Hands*, 162.

48. Pacific Legal Foundation, *Issues and Cases: PLF in the Supreme Court*, http://

www.pacificlegal.org/SupremeCourt. See generally Steven M. Teles, *The Rise of the Conservative Legal Movement: The Battle for Control of the Law,* 67–88 (Princeton, Princeton University Press, 2008).

49. See John J. Miller, *A Gift of Freedom: How the John M. Olin Foundation Changed America* (San Francisco: Encounter Books, 2001).

50. Phillips-Fein, *Invisible Hands,* 186.

51. Ibid., 188.

52. David Vogel, *Fluctuating Fortunes: The Political Power of Business in America,* 207 (New York: Basic Books, 1989).

53. For discussions of business lobbying, see Lee Drutman, *The Business of America Is Lobbying: How Corporations Became Politicized and Politics Became More Corporate* (New York: Oxford University Press, 2015); Vogel, *Fluctuating Fortunes,* 197–198; Robert B. Reich, *Regulation by Confrontation or Negotiation,* 59 Harv. Bus. Rev. 82, 86 (1981). For discussions of anti-regulatory business litigation, see Hacker & Pierson, *American Amnesia,* 201–227; Phillips-Fein, *Invisible Hands,* 192–212.

54. *The Guardian: Origins of the EPA,* Historical Publication-1 (Spring 1992), https://www.epa.gov/aboutepa/guardian-origins-epa; *EPA Reorganization Plan No. 3 of 1970,* https://www.epa.gov/aboutepa/reorganization-plan-no-3-1970; Consumer Product Safety Act, Pub. L. 92–573, 86 Stat. 1207 (1972) (codified at 15 U.S.C. §§ 2051–2089); Williams-Steiger Occupational Safety and Health Act of 1970, Pub. L. 91–596, 84 Stat. 1590 (1970) (codified as amended at 29 U.S.C. §§ 651–678).

55. Richard Nixon, *Address to the Nation on Domestic Programs,* Aug. 8, 1969, http://www.presidency.ucsb.edu/ws/?pid=2191.

56. See Exec. Order 11,615, 36 Fed. Reg. 15727 (Aug. 17, 1971).

57. Hacker & Pierson, *American Amnesia,* 153.

58. Alfred E. Kahn, *Deregulation: Looking Backward and Looking Forward,* 7 Yale J. Reg. 325, 325–326 (1990) ("In this attempt to place deregulation in historical perspective, I feel compelled to emphasize, in contradiction of the widespread popular impression that President Reagan deserves most of the credit—or blame—how much of it occurred between 1978 and 1980."); Curtis W. Copeland, *Federal Rulemaking: The Role of the Office of Information and Regulatory Affairs,* Cong. Res. Serv., Jun. 9, 2009, at 5–6, http://fas.org/sgp/crs/misc/RL32397.pdf (describing Carter's regulatory review initiatives); see also Donald F. Kettl, *The Next Government of the United States: Why Our Institutions Fail and How to Fix Them,* 169–170 (New York: W. W. Norton, 2009) (describing Carter's commitment as Georgia's governor to zero-base budgeting involving department heads having "to make a fresh case for each new infusion of money instead of taking for granted that a program, once funded, would last forever").

59. Rowland Evans Jr. & Robert D. Novak, *The Reagan Revolution,* 84 (New York: Dutton, 1981); James T. Patterson, Afterword: The Legacies of the Reagan Years, in *The Reagan Presidency: Pragmatic Conservatism and Its Legacy,* 361–365 (W. Elliot Brownlee & Hugh Davis Graham, eds.) (Lawrence, KS: University Press of Kansas, 2003).

60. See generally Michael Laurie Tingle, *Privatization and the Reagan Administration: Ideology and Application*, 6 Yale L. & Pol'y Rev. 229, 229–230 (1988). For discussions of how relatively small groups with particularly strong interests in an issue or a program may dominate larger groups opposed to the issue or program, see Mancur Olson, *The Logic of Collective Action: Public Goods and the Theory of Groups*, 60–65 (Cambridge: Harvard University Press, 1971); Anthony Downs, *An Economic Theory of Democracy*, 265–274 (New York: Harper, 1957). For a discussion of how administrators and other indirect beneficiaries resist program cuts, see, for example, David A. Super, *Privatization, Policy Paralysis, and the Poor*, 96 Cal. L. Rev. 393, 462–463 (2008).

61. Barry D. Friedman, *Regulation in the Reagan-Bush Era: The Eruption of Presidential Influence*, 155–156 (Pittsburgh: University of Pittsburgh Press, 1995); Kettl, *Next Government*, 114 (noting that in the 1980s Americans wanted both to retain all of the social welfare and regulatory programs of the New Deal and Great Society—"and [pay] lower taxes").

62. Henry Waxman with Joshua Green, *The Waxman Report: How Congress Really Works*, 75–102 (New York, Twelve Books, 2009).

63. Miller Center, *Ronald Reagan Domestic Affairs*, https://millercenter.org /president/reagan/domestic-affairs.

64. Alex Park, *These Charts Show How Ronald Reagan Actually Expanded the Federal Government*, Mother Jones, Dec. 30, 2014, www.motherjones.com /mojo/2014/12/ronald-reagan-big-government-legacy.

65. U.S. Office of Personnel Mgmt., *Historical Federal Workforce Tables*, https:// archive.opm.gov/feddata/HistoricalTables/TotalGovernmentSince1962.asp.

66. *Commercial-Industrial Activities of the Government Providing Products or Services for Governmental Use*, Executive Office of the President, Bureau of the Budget, Bulletin No. 55-4, Jan. 15, 1955, http://www.governmentcompetition .org/uploads/Bureau_of_the_Budget_Bulletin_55-4_January_15_1955.pdf. But see Daniel Guttman, *Public Purpose and Private Service: The Twentieth Century Culture of Contracting Out and the Evolving Law of Diffused Sovereignty*, 52 Admin. L. Rev. 859 (2000) (highlighting the emergence of a class of highly skilled contractors working in the realms of national defense, energy, and systems analysis).

67. Daniel Yergin & Joseph Stanislaw, *The Commanding Heights: The Battle between Government and the Marketplace That Is Remaking the Modern World*, 359 (New York: Simon & Schuster, 1998); Philip E. Fixler, Jr. & Robert W. Poole, Jr., Status of State and Local Privatization, in *Prospects for Privatization*, 164 (Steve H. Hanke, ed.) (New York: Academy of Political Science, 1987); DeHoog, *Contracting Out*, 2.

68. Fixler, Jr. & Poole, Jr., *State and Local Privatization*, 165 (noting that from 1973 to 1982 "the percentage growth [in contracting out] ranged from 43% for refuse collection to 3,644% for data processing (record keeping)").

69. Kevin Lavery, *Smart Contracting for Local Government Services: Processes and Experience*, 98–123 (Westport, CT: Praeger, 1999).

70. Oliver D. Cooke, *Rethinking Municipal Privatization*, 13, 14 (New York: Routledge, 2008); Ray Suarez, *The Old Neighborhood: What We Lost in the Great Suburban Migration: 1966–1999* (New York: Free Press, 2009); Jan Blakeslee, *"White Flight" to the Suburbs: A Demographic Approach,* Institute for Research on Poverty Newsletter, Vol. 3, No. 2 (1978–1979), http://www.irp.wisc.edu/publications/focus/pdfs/foc32a.pdf.

71. Henig, *Privatization*, 658.

72. William E. Simon, Foreword, in *Cutting Back City Hall*, 9 (Robert W. Poole, Jr., ed.) (New York: Universe Books, 1980).

73. Thomas Meehan, *Moynihan of the Moynihan Report*, N.Y. Times, Jul. 31, 1966, http://www.nytimes.com/books/98/10/04/specials/moynihan-report.html.

74. Ibid.; Jon D. Michaels, *Privatization's Progeny*, 101 Geo. L.J. 1023, 1068 (2013).

75. *The President's Private Sector Survey on Cost Control, Report on Privatization*, at i (1983), https://babel.hathitrust.org/cgi/pt?id=uiug.30112105134347;view=1up;seq=21. The report underscores that privatization need not entail "an abdication of Government services, but presents a more cost-effective way for the Government to deploy its limited resources." Ibid.

76. Curriculum vitae of Professor E. S. Savas, http://www.baruch.cuny.edu/spa/faculty-and-staff/documents/cv_savas.pdf. I am indebted to Professor Savas for an illuminating conversation in which he recounted some of his experiences in the Reagan administration.

77. E. S. Savas, *Municipal Monopoly*, Harper's, Dec. 1971, at 55–60.

78. E. S. Savas, *Privatizing the Public Sector* (Chatham, NJ: Chatham House Publishers, 1982).

79. Philip E. Fixler & Robert W. Poole, Jr., *The Privatization Revolution: What Washington Can Learn from State and Local Government*, Pol'y Rev. 68 (Summer 1986).

80. Margaret Thatcher, *Airey Neave Memorial Lecture*, Mar. 3, 1980, http://www.margaretthatcher.org/document/104318.

81. Ibid.

82. See John Vickers & George Yarrow, *Privatization: An Economic Analysis* (Cambridge: MIT Press, 1988).

83. For a similar argument, see Donald F. Kettl, *Escaping Jurassic Government* (Washington, DC: Brookings Institution Press, 2016).

84. Kevin R. Kosar, *Privatization and the Federal Government: An Introduction*, Cong. Res. Serv. 14, Dec. 28, 2006, at 13, http://www.fas.org/sgp/crs/misc/RL33777.pdf.

85. Yergin & Stanislaw, *Commanding Heights*, 358.

86. Henig, *Privatization*, 661.

87. Kettl, *Next Government*, 44–49 (describing contracting as a smart political strategy, one that allowed officials to "preach[] the gospel of small government" while maintaining and even increasing the range of services offered).

88. Easterbrook, *Ideas*.

89. For discussion of the political influence of the Heritage Foundation's first *Mandate* (*Mandate I*) and the second (*Mandate II*), see Lee Edwards, *Leading the Way: The Story of Ed Feulner and the Heritage Foundation,* 27 (New York: Crown Forum, 2013); Molly Ball, *The Fall of the Heritage Foundation and the Death of Republican Ideas,* Atlantic, Sept. 25, 2013, http://www .theatlantic.com/politics/archive/2013/09/the-fall-of-the-heritage-foundation -and-the-death-of-republican-ideas/279955/; Brad Knickerbocker, *Heritage Foundation's Ideas Permeate Reagan Administration,* Christian Sci. Monitor, Dec. 7, 1984, http://www.csmonitor.com/1984/1207/120768.html.

90. *Mandate for Leadership II: Continuing the Conservative Revolution* (Stuart M. Butler, et al., eds.) (Washington, DC: Heritage Foundation, 1984).

91. David F. Linowes, et al., *Privatization: Toward More Effective Government: Report of the President's Commission on Privatization,* 1 (1988), https:// babel.hathitrust.org/cgi/pt?id=mdp.39015017633325;view=1up;seq=25 ("The United States is experiencing a renewed interest in the systematic examination of the boundary between public and private delivery of goods and services. The interest has been stimulated in part by concern that the federal government has become too large, too expensive, and too intrusive in our lives.").

92. See, for example, *Office of Federal Procurement Policy to the Heads of Executive Agencies and Departments,* Pol'y Letter 92–1 (Sept. 23, 1992), https://www.whitehouse.gov/sites/default/files/omb/procurement/policy _letters/92-01_092392.html.

93. Al Gore, *From Red Tape to Results: Creating a Government That Works Better & Costs Less, Report of the National Performance Review* (1993), http://files.eric.ed.gov/fulltext/ED384294.pdf (underscoring the Clinton administration's quest for "a government that works for people, cleared of useless bureaucracy and waste and freed from red tape and senseless rules").

94. Al Gore, *Common Sense Government: Works Better and Costs Less, Third Report of the National Performance Review,* 9 (1995), http://files.eric.ed.gov /fulltext/ED387065.pdf (calling for a better managed—but still programmat- ically robust—federal government).

5. The Mainstreaming of Privatization

1. John D. Donahue, *Privatization and Public Employment,* 28 Fordham Urb. L.J. 1693, 1703 (2001).

2. Memorandum from Douglas W. Elmendorf to Representative Chris Van Hollen, *Federal Contracts and the Contracted Workforce,* Mar. 11, 2015, https://www.cbo.gov/sites/default/files/114th-congress-2015-2016/reports /49931-FederalContracts.pdf.

3. See, for example, Chris Isidore, *Uncle Sam's Outsourcing Tab: $517 Billion,* CNN, Jun. 13, 2013, http://money.cnn.com/2013/06/10/news/economy /outsourced-federal-government/.

4. Paul C. Light, *The True Size of Government,* 16 (Washington, DC: Brookings Institution Press, 1999). Perhaps the most relevant study accounts for the

growth of the federal nondefense contractor population, which did indeed rise from 668,000 in 1990 to 1,088,000 in 2002; Paul C. Light, *Fact Sheet on the New True Size of Government*, 7 tbl. 4 (2003), http://www.brookings.edu /~/media/research/files/articles/2003/9/05politics-light/light20030905.pdf.

5. Project on Gov't Oversight, *Bad Business: Billions of Taxpayer Dollars Wasted on Hiring Contractors*, 5 (2011), http://www.pogo.org/our-work /reports/2011/co-gp-20110913.html?referrer=https://www.google.com/.

6. Light, *True Size*, 41–44; Steve Cohen & William Eimicke, Contracting Out, in *The SAGE Handbook of Governance*, 237 (Mark Bevir, ed.) (London: SAGE, 2010); Gillian E. Metzger, *Privatization as Delegation*, 103 Colum. L. Rev. 1367, 1369 (2003); Jody Freeman, *Extending Public Law Norms Through Privatization*, 116 Harv. L. Rev. 1285, 1289 (2003); Jacques S. Gansler, *Moving Toward Market-Based Government: The Changing Role of Government as the Provider*, IBM Endowment for The Business of Government, Jun. 2003, at 8, http://www.businessofgovernment.org/sites /default/files/MarketBasedGovernment.pdf. For state and local trends, see, for example, Deborah A. Auger, *Privatization, Contracting, and the States: Lessons from the State Government Experience*, 22 Pub. Productivity & Mgmt Rev. 435 (1999); Report to the Chairman, House Republican Task Force on Privatization, *Privatization: Lessons Learned by State and Local Governments*, Gen. Accounting Office, Mar. 1997, http://govinfo.library .unt.edu/npr/library/gao/gg97048.pdf.

7. Federal Activities Inventory Reform Act of 1998, Pub. L. 105–270, 112 Stat. 2382 (codified at 31 U.S.C. § 501 note); Federal Acquisition Reform Act of 1996, Pub. L. No. 104–106, 110 Stat. 186 (codified at 41 U.S.C. § 423); OMB A-76 Circular, rev. 1999, 64 Fed. Reg. 121, 33927–33935 (Jun. 24, 1999); Presidential Memorandum for Heads of Departments and Agencies, *Streamlining the Bureaucracy*, Sept. 11, 1993, http://govinfo.library.unt.edu /npr/library/direct/memos/230a.html; Al Gore, *From Red Tape to Results: Creating a Government That Works Better & Costs Less, Report of the National Performance Review* (1993), http://files.eric.ed.gov/fulltext /ED384294.pdf; Al Gore, *Common Sense Government: Works Better and Costs Less, Third Report of the National Performance Review*, 9 (1995), http://files.eric.ed.gov/fulltext/ED387065.pdf.

8. Bill Clinton, *1996 State of the Union Address*, Jan. 23, 1996, http://clinton4 .nara.gov/WH/New/other/sotu.html; Jacob S. Hacker & Paul Pierson, *Winner-Take-All Politics: How Washington Made the Rich Richer—And Turned Its Back on the Middle Class*, 163–169 (New York: Simon & Schuster, 2010).

9. Personal Responsibility and Work Opportunity Reconciliation Act of 1996, Pub. L. No. 104–193, 110 Stat. 2105 (codified as amended in scattered sections of Chapters 7 and 42 of the U.S. Code) (imposing lifetime caps on welfare payments and introducing more stringent work requirements); Telecommunications Act of 1996, Pub. L. No. 104–104, 110 Stat. 56 (codified in scattered sections of Chapter 47 of the U.S. Code) ("To promote competition and reduce regulation . . ."); Gramm-Leach-Bliley Act, Pub. L. No.

106–102, 113 Stat. 1338 (1999) (codified in scattered sections of Chapters 12 and 15 of the U.S. Code); see also Jacob S. Hacker & Paul Pierson, *American Amnesia: How the War on Government Led Us to Forget What Made America Prosper,* 187 (New York: Simon & Schuster, 2016).

10. U.S. Office of Personnel Mgmt., *Historical Federal Workforce Tables, Exec. Branch Civilian Employment Since 1940,* https://www.opm.gov/policy -data-oversight/data-analysis-documentation/federal-employment-reports /historical-tables/executive-branch-civilian-employment-since-1940/.

11. Thomas L. Neff, *Decision Time for the HEU Deal,* Arms Control Ass'n, Jun. 1, 2001, http://www.armscontrol.org/print/864.

12. Jon D. Michaels, *The (Willingly) Fettered Executive: Presidential Spinoffs in National Security Domains and Beyond,* 97 Va. L. Rev. 801, 812–817 (2011).

13. Kevin R. Kosar, *The Quasi Government: Hybrid Organizations with Both Government and Private Sector Legal Characteristics,* Cong. Res. Serv., Jun. 22, 2011, at 29, https://www.fas.org/sgp/crs/misc/RL30533.pdf.

14. Joe Davidson, *Firm That Did Background Check on Snowden Is Under Investigation,* Wash. Post, Jun. 20, 2013, https://www.washingtonpost.com /politics/federal_government/firm-that-did-background-check-on-snowden-is -under-investigation/2013/06/20/1d06c248-d9e1-11e2-a9f2-42ee3912aeoe _story.html.

15. Steven Gillon, *The Pact: Bill Clinton, Newt Gingrich, and the Rivalry That Defined a Generation,* 219–231 (New York: Oxford University Press, 2008).

16. David Maraniss, *First in His Class: A Biography of Bill Clinton* (New York: Simon & Schuster, 1995).

17. The N.J. Privatization Task Force, *Report to Governor Chris Christie,* 3 (2010), http://www.nj.gov/governor/news/reports/pdf/2010709_NJ_Privatization_Task _Force_Final_Report_(May_2010).pdf.

18. Leonard Gilroy, *Local Government Privatization 101,* Reason Foundation Pol'y Br., 89, Mar. 16, 2010, http://reason.org/news/show/local-government -privatization-101 (quoting Mayor Daley).

19. E. S. Savas, *Privatization in the City: Successes, Failures, Lessons,* 3 (Washington, DC: CQ Press, 2005).

20. Ryan Holeywell, *How Weston, Florida, a City of 65,000, Gets By on 9 Employees,* Governing, May 14, 2012, http://www.governing.com/blogs /view/How-.html.

21. *Presidential Election Results, City Data on Weston, Florida,* http://www .city-data.com/city/Weston-Florida.html#b; Broward County Supervisor of Elections, *General Election,* http://enr.electionsfl.org/BRO/1642/Precincts /12755/?view=graphical.

22. Harris Kenny, *Georgia Contract Cities Continue to Evolve,* Reason, May 6, 2013, http://reason.org/news/show/1013361.html.

23. David Segal, *A Georgia Town Takes the People's Business Private,* N.Y. Times, Jun. 23, 2012, http://www.nytimes.com/2012/06/24/business/a -georgia-town-takes-the-peoples-business-private.html.

24. David Osborne & Ted Gaebler, *Reinventing Government: How the Entrepreneurial Spirit Is Transforming the Public Sector* (Reading, MA:

Addison-Wesley Pub., 1993); see also Donald F. Kettl, *Transformation of Governance: Public Administration for the Twenty-First Century*, 21 (Baltimore: Johns Hopkins University Press, 2002) (characterizing Osborne and Gaebler's book as a best seller).

25. Kettl, *Transformation*, 21.

26. Michael Nelson, Foreword, in Brian J. Cook, *Bureaucracy and Self-Government: Reconsidering the Role of Public Administration in American Politics*, at xvi (Baltimore: Johns Hopkins University Press, 2014).

27. B. Guy Peters, *The Future of Governing*, 21 (Lawrence, KS: University Press of Kansas, 1996).

28. David Osborne, *Biography*, http://reason.org/authors/show/david-osborne.

29. Jay M. Shafritz & Albert C. Hyde, From Reagan to Reinvention: The 1980s and 1990s, in *Classics of Public Administration*, 358, 362 (Jay M. Shafritz & Albert C. Hyde, eds.) (8th ed.) (Boston: Wadsworth, 2015).

30. Osborne & Gaebler, *Reinventing Government*, at xxi.

31. Frank Ackerman & Lisa Heinzerling, *Pricing the Priceless: Cost–Benefit Analysis of Environmental Protection*, 150 U. Pa. L. Rev. 1553, 1553–1556 (2002); Alexander Volokh, *Rationality or Rationalism? The Positive and Normative Flaws of Cost–Benefit Analysis*, 48 Hous. L. Rev. 79, 88–89 (2011); see also David M. Driesen, *Is Cost–Benefit Analysis Neutral?*, 77 U. Colo. L. Rev. 335 (2006) (criticizing the notion that cost–benefit analysis is neutral, arguing instead that it is inherently anti-regulatory).

32. For discussions of the 1990s as representing a political and economic turning point, see Francis Fukuyama, *The End of History and the Last Man* (New York: Free Press, 1992); Charles Krathammer, *The Unipolar Moment*, For. Affairs, Winter 1990/1991, at 23.

33. In Japan, the 1990s were a time of economic struggle. Scholars and politicians label the period the "lost decade." For insightful volumes on this period, see *Japan's "Lost Decade": Causes, Legacies, and Issues of Transformative Change* (W. Miles Fletcher III & Peter W. von Staden, eds.) (London: Routledge, 2013); *Examining Japan's Lost Decades* (Yoichi Funabashi & Barak Kushner, eds.) (London: Routledge, 2015). In Germany, economic challenges stemmed principally from the reunification of West and East Germany. Wolfgang Seibel, The Quest for Freedom and Stability: Political Choices and the Economic Transformation of East Germany 1989–1991, in *German Unification: Expectations and Outcomes*, 99 (Peter C. Caldwell & Robert R. Shandley, eds.) (New York: Palgrave Macmillan, 2011).

34. John Baffes et al., *The Great Plunge in Oil Prices*, 9–11, World Bank Group, Mar. 2015, http://www.worldbank.org/content/dam/Worldbank/Research/PRN01_Mar2015_Oil_Prices.pdf; F. Gregory Gause, III, *Sultans of Swing? The Geopolitics of Falling Oil Prices*, Brookings Doha Center, Apr. 2015, at 1, 4, 6–7.

35. Lael Brainard, *Trade Policy in the 1990s*, Brookings, Jun. 29, 2001, http://www.brookings.edu/research/papers/2001/06/29globaleconomics-brainard; Uri Berliner, *Back to the Economy of the '90s? Not So Fast*, NPR, Dec. 25,

2012, http://www.npr.org/2012/12/25/167970805/back-to-the-economy-of
-the-90s-not-so-fast; Nancy Birdsall & Carol Graham, Mobility and Markets:
Conceptual Issues and Policy Questions, in *New Markets, New Opportunities?
Economic and Social Mobility in a Changing World*, 3 (Nancy Birdsall &
Carol Graham, eds.) (Washington, DC: Brookings Institution Press, 2000).

36. Brainard, *Trade Policy.*
37. John M. Berry, *Expansion Is Now Nation's Longest,* Wash. Post, Feb. 1,
2000, at E1.
38. For other, comprehensive treatments of privatization, see Daphne Barak-
Erez, Three Questions of Privatization, in *Comparative Administrative Law,*
493, 494–497 (Susan Rose-Ackerman & Peter L. Lindseth, eds.) (Cheltenham,
UK: Edward Elgar, 2010); Judith Resnik, *Globalization(s), Privatization(s),
Constitutionalization, and Statization: Icons and Experiences of Sovereignty
in the 21st Century,* 11 Int'l J. Const. L. 162 (2010).
39. Peter L. Strauss, *Private Standards Organizations and Public Law,* 22 Wm.
& Mary Bill Rts. J. 497, 502 (2013); Stacy Baird, *The Government at the
Standards Bazaar,* 18 Stan. L. & Pol'y Rev. 35, 55 (2007); Mary F. Donaldson
& Nathalie Rioux, Nat'l Inst. of Standards & Tech., U.S. Dep't of Commerce,
*Fifteenth Annual Report on Federal Agency Use of Voluntary Consensus
Standards and Conformity Assessment,* 1 (2012), https://standards.gov/nttaa
/resources/nttaa_ar_2011.pdf.
40. Jonathan Macey & Caroline Novogrod, *Enforcing Self-Regulatory
Organization's Penalties and the Nature of Self-Regulation,* 40 Hofstra L.
Rev. 963, 969 (2012) (internal citations omitted).
41. Ibid., 969–971.
42. Jon D. Michaels, *All the President's Spies: Private-Public Intelligence
Partnerships in the War on Terror,* 96 Cal. L. Rev. 901 (2008); Glenn
Greenwald & Ewen MacAskill, *NSA Prism Program Taps into User Data of
Apple, Google and Others,* Guardian, Jun. 7, 2013, http://www.theguardian
.com/world/2013/jun/06/us-tech-giants-nsa-data.
43. Office of Inspector General, U.S. Dep't of Justice, *A Review of the Federal Bureau
of Investigation's Use of Exigent Letters and Other Informal Requests for
Telephone Records,* Jan. 2010, http://www.justice.gov/oig/special/s10011.pdf.
44. Jon D. Michaels, *Deputizing Homeland Security,* 88 Tex. L. Rev. 1435
(2010).
45. Tiffany Burlingame, *Lay's Potato Chips Announces Four Finalists for "Do
Us a Flavor" Contest,* Snack Chat Blog, Jul. 15, 2015, http://www.fritolay
.com/blog/blog-post/snack-chat/2015/07/15/lay-s-potato-chips-announces
-four-finalists-for-do-u-a-flavor-contest.
46. Michaels, *Deputizing.*
47. Elaine S. Povich, *Challenge.gov Contests Liberate Labor Department Data,*
Breaking Gov, Sept. 12, 2012, http://breakinggov.com/2012/09/12/challenge
-gov-contests-liberate-labor-department-data/.
48. Ibid.
49. Michael Arnold, *Move Over Words with Friends: DOL Develops Use of
Smartphone Apps,* Soc'y for Human Res. Mgmt, Aug. 2, 2013, http://www

.shrm.org/legalissues/federalresources/pages/dol-smartphone-apps.aspx; Povich, *Challenge.gov Contests*. I am grateful to UCLA Law graduate Matthew Seipel, whose seminar paper first introduced me to the federal government's experimentation with these particular social media–mediated partnerships. See Matthew B. Seipel, *Partnering Up with the NLRB: The NLRB's Potential Use of Private Actors*, https://papers.ssrn.com/sol3/papers.cfm ?abstract_id=2866497.

50. Ezra Ross & Martin Pritikin, *The Collection Gap: Underenforcement of Corporate and White-Collar Fines and Penalties*, 29 Yale L. & Pol'y Rev. 453 (2011).

51. Kosar, *Quasi Government*, 14–15, 18–19.

52. Felicity Barringer, *Parks Chief Blocked Plan for Grand Canyon Bottle Ban*, N.Y. Times, Nov. 9, 2011, http://www.nytimes.com/2011/11/10 /science/earth/parks-chief-blocked-plan-for-grand-canyon-bottle-ban.html; Jim Hightower, *Op-ed, Sold: National Parks Go to the Highest Corporate Bidder*, Seattle Times, Jul. 31, 2015, http://www.seattletimes.com/opinion/sold -national-parks-go-to-the-highest-corporate-bidder/.

53. Margaret H. Lemos, *Privatizing Public Litigation*, 104 Geo. L.J. 515, 534 n. 103, 537 (2016).

54. Dale Russakoff, *The Prize: Who's in Charge of America's Schools?* (Boston: Houghton Mifflin Harcourt, 2015).

55. Michaels, *(Willingly) Fettered*, 812–817, & n. 50; Peter Eisler, *Government Challenges Firms to Build Better Batteries*, USA Today, Apr. 16, 2009, http:// usatoday30.usatoday.com/tech/news/techinnovations/2009-04-15-batteries _N.htm; Marc Kaufman, *NASA Invests in Its Future with Venture Capital Firm*, Wash. Post, Oct. 31, 2006, http://www.washingtonpost.com/wp-dyn /content/article/2006/10/30/AR2006103001069.html; Matt Richtel, *Tech Investors Cull Start-ups for Pentagon*, N.Y. Times, May 7, 2007, http://www .nytimes.com/2007/05/07/technology/07venture.html.

56. Tim Shorrock, *Spies for Hire: The Secret World of Intelligence Outsourcing*, 145 (New York: Simon & Schuster, 2008).

57. Jon D. Michaels, *Privatization's Progeny*, 101 Geo. L.J. 1023, 1052–1057 (2103).

58. Daniel Forbes, *Propaganda for Dollars*, Salon, Jan. 14, 2000, http://www .salon.com/2000/01/14/payola.

59. Daniel Forbes, *Prime-time Propaganda: How the White House Secretly Hooked Network TV on Its Anti-Drug Message*, Salon, Jan. 13, 2000, http:// www.salon.com/2000/01/13/drugs_6/.

60. Jon D. Michaels, *Running Government Like a Business . . . Then and Now*, 128 Harv. L. Rev. 1152, 1178–1179 (2015) (considering the federal government's use of corporate governance tools to regulate AIG and American automakers). For in-depth treatments of the federal government's equity ownership and use of its ownership shares to influence corporate behavior, see, for example, Andrew Ross Sorkin, *Too Big to Fail: The Inside Story of How Wall Street and Washington Fought to Save the Financial System from Crisis— And Themselves*, 392–408 (New York: Viking, 2010); Benjamin Templin,

The Government Shareholder: Regulating Public Ownership of Private Enterprise, 62 Admin. L. Rev. 1127, 1185–1186 (2010); J. W. Verret, *Treasury Inc.: How the Bailout Reshapes Corporate Theory and Practice*, 27 Yale J. on Reg. 283, 303–305 (2010); Louise Story & Gretchen Morgenson, *In U.S. Bailout of AIG, Extra Forgiveness for Big Banks*, N.Y. Times, Jun. 29, 2010, http://www.nytimes.com/2010/06/30/business/30aig.html.

61. Steven J. Kelman, Contracting, in *The Tools of Government: A Guide to the New Governance*, 282 (Lester M. Salamon, ed.) (New York: Oxford University Press, 2002); Wesley Magat, et al., *Rules in the Making: A Statistical Analysis of Regulatory Agency Behavior*, at 33, 37 (Washington, DC: RFF Press, 2011); U.S. Congress, Office of Tech. Assessment, *Assessing Contractor Use in Superfund—A Background Paper*, OTA-BP-ITE-51, Gov't Printing Office, Jan. 1989, 28–29; Light, *True Size*, 13–14 (describing the central role contractors play in preparing for and participating in agencies' public hearings); Testimony of Scott Amey, *General Counsel of the Project on Government Oversight, before the Congressional Oversight Panel Hearing on Treasury's Use of Emergency Contracting Authority*, Sept. 22, 2010, http://www.pogo.org/our-work/testimony/2010/co-ca-20100922.html.

62. Michele Estrin Gilman, *Legal Accountability in an Era of Privatized Welfare*, 81 Cal. L. Rev. 569 (2001); Jon Michaels, *Deforming Welfare: How the Dominant Narratives of Devolution and Privatization Subverted Federal Welfare Reform*, 34 Seton Hall L. Rev. 543 (2004); David A. Super, *Privatization, Policy Paralysis, and the Poor*, 96 Cal. L. Rev. 393 (2008).

63. Contracting firms are, today, far more likely to tout the sensitive policy-making services they provide. See, for example, Kimberly N. Brown, *Public Laws and Private Lawmakers*, 93 Wash. U. L. Rev. 615, 622–623 (2016).

64. Michael Lipsky, *Street-Level Bureaucracy: Dilemmas of the Individual in Public Services*, 60–70 (New York: Russell Sage, 1980); Matthew Diller, *The Revolution in Welfare Administration: Rules, Discretion, and Entrepreneurial Government*, 75 N.Y.U. L. Rev. 1121, 1132 (2000). Diller asks: "Do case-workers explain the eligibility rules and requirements of the program? If so, how is the explanation provided, and what elements are emphasized? Do caseworkers inform people of other benefits and services to which they may be entitled? Do workers help applicants obtain necessary documents and forms? Do they allow individuals more time or a second chance to obtain necessary documents? Do they return phone calls? Do they convey signals of approval or disapproval to the clients with whom they deal?" Ibid. Rebecca Cook, *Group Decries Tactics To Reduce Welfare Cases*, Seattle Post-Intelligencer, Aug. 23, 2004, http://www.seattlepi.com/local/article/Group-decries-tactics-to-reduce-welfare-cases-1152376.php (describing "rudeness as a tool to discourage needy people from applying for benefits); Bryce Covert, *How States Are Trying to Make Life Harder for the Poor*, Think Progress, May 22, 2015, http://thinkprogress.org/economy/2015/05/22/3662043/welfare-states-restrictions/.

65. *Goldberg v. Kelly*, 397 U.S. 254 (1970); *Mathews v. Eldridge*, 424 U.S. 319, 350 (1976) (Brennan, J., dissenting); Charles A. Reich, *The New Property*, 73 Yale L.J. 733 (1964).

66. See generally Scott Shane & Ron Nixon, *In Washington, Contractors Take on Biggest Role Ever*, N.Y. Times, Feb. 4, 2007, http://www.nytimes.com/2007/02/04/washington/04contract.html.

67. Paul D. Shinkman, *A Slippery Slope for Drone Warfare?*, U.S. News & World Rept, Aug. 21, 2015, http://www.usnews.com/news/articles/2015/08/21/pentagon-opening-drone-missions-to-private-contractors.

68. Steven L. Schooner, *Contractor Atrocities at Abu Ghraib: Compromised Accountability in a Streamlined, Outsourced Government*, 16 Stan. L. & Pol'y Rev. 549 (2005).

69. Kirit Radia, *Controversial Blackwater Security Firm Gets Iraq Contract Extended by State Dept*, ABC News, Sept. 1, 2009, http://abcnews.go.com/Blotter/Blackwater/blackwater-security-firm-iraq-contract-extended-state-dept/story?id=8466369.

70. The most infamous of such patrols led to the so-called Nisour Square massacre, involving Blackwater contractors killing seventeen Iraqis and wounding another twenty-four. James Glanz & Alyssa J. Rubin, *From Errand to Fatal Shot to Hail of Fire to 17 Deaths*, N.Y. Times, Oct. 3, 2007, http://www.nytimes.com/2007/10/03/world/middleeast/03firefight.html.

71. Spencer Ackerman, *More Than 50 Countries Helped the CIA Outsource Torture*, Wired, Feb. 5, 2013, http://www.wired.com/2013/02/54-countries-rendition/; Jane Mayer, *The CIA's Travel Agent*, New Yorker, Oct. 30, 2006, http://www.newyorker.com/magazine/2006/10/30/the-c-i-a-s-travel-agent.

72. James Risen & Mark Mazzetti, *Blackwater Guards Tied to Secret CIA Raids*, N.Y. Times, Dec. 10, 2009, http://www.nytimes.com/2009/12/11/us/politics/11blackwater.html (internal quotations omitted).

73. T. Christian Miller, *Contractors Outnumber Troops in Iraq*, L.A. Times, Jul. 4, 2007, http://articles.latimes.com/2007/jul/04/nation/na-private4; Moshe Schwartz, *Department of Defense Contractors in Iraq and Afghanistan: Background and Analysis*, Cong. Res. Serv., Aug. 13, 2009, at 13, http://www.fas.org/sgp/crs/natsec/R40764.pdf.

74. Nicholas R. Parrillo, *Against the Profit Motive: The Salary Revolution in American Government*, 247–249 (New Haven: Yale University Press, 2014).

75. Janice E. Thomson, *Mercenaries, Pirates and Sovereigns: State-Building and Extraterritorial Violence in Early Modern Europe*, 76, 79–84, 105 (Princeton: Princeton University Press, 1994); *Protocol Additional to the Geneva Conventions of 12 August 1949, and Relating to the Protection of Victims of International Armed Conflicts (Protocol I)*, art. 47, 1125 U.N.T.S., Jun. 8, 1977.

76. The controversial practices during the Civil War of substitution and commutation, in which drafted men could furnish a willing substitute or altogether buy their way out of the service, respectively, suggest forms of grassroots subcontracting.

77. P. W. Singer, *Corporate Warriors: The Rise of the Privatized Military Industry*, 37–38 (Ithaca, NY: Cornell University Press, 2004); Thomson, *Mercenaries*, 88–95.

78. Freeman, *Extending Public Law*, 1300 (calling the privatization of national defense "unfathomable"); Michael J. Trebilcock & Edward M. Iacobucci, *Privatization and Accountability*, 116 Harv. L. Rev. 1422, 1444 (2003)

(treating "the formulation and implementation of a country's foreign or defense policy" as too sensitive to outsource).

79. Micah Zenko, *The New Unknown Soldiers of Afghanistan and Iraq,* For. Pol'y, May 29, 2015, http://foreignpolicy.com/2015/05/29/the-new-unknown -soldiers-of-afghanistan-and-iraq/.

80. Warren Strobel & Phil Stewart, *As U.S. Troops Return to Iraq, More Private Contractors Follow,* Reuters, Dec. 24, 2014, http://www.reuters.com/article /us-usa-iraq-contractors-idUSKBN0K20AW20141224.

81. John D. Donahue, The Ideological Romance of Privatization, in *Morality, Rationality, and Efficiency: New Perspectives on Socio-Economics,* 133, 137 (Richard M. Coughlin, ed.) (Armonk, NY: M. E. Sharpe, 1991).

82. Richard Michael Fischl, *Running the Government Like a Business: Wisconsin and the Assault on Workplace Democracy,* 121 Yale L.J. Online 39, 49–50 (2011), http://www.yalelawjournal.org/forum/running-the-government-like -a-business-wisconsin-and-the-assault-on-workplace-democracy; Donald S. Wasserman, Collective Bargaining Rights in the Public Sector, in *Justice on the Job: Perspectives on the Erosion of Collective Bargaining in the United States,* 62–63 (Richard N. Block et al., eds.) (Kalamazoo, MI: W. E. Upjohn Institute for Employment Research, 2006).

83. Michaels, *Progeny,* 1049.

84. See E. S. Savas, *Privatization: The Key to Better Government,* 4–11 (Chatham, NJ: Chatham House Pub., 1987); Michaels, *Running Government,* 1152, 1154–1155.

85. Michaels, *Progeny,* 1026.

86. Ralph C. Nash, Jr., Karen R. O'Brien-Debakey & Steven L. Schooner, *The Government Contracts Reference Book* (4th ed.) (Chicago: Wolters Kluwer Law & Business, 2013).

87. Steve L. Schooner, *Fear of Oversight: The Fundamental Failure of Businesslike Government,* 50 Am. U. L. Rev. 627 (2001).

88. John D. Donahue, *The Privatization Decision: Public Ends, Private Means,* 109 (New York: Basic Books, 1989); Osborne & Gaebler, *Reinventing Government,* 87. Whether such overhead for contract management is necessary, yet more evidence of bureaucratic red tape, or both is, of course, a separate question.

89. Michaels, *Progeny,* 1041, n. 87; Lisa Colangelo, *In Search of Civil Service Givebacks,* Daily News (NY), Jan. 13, 2010, http://www.nydailynews.com /new-york/civil-service-jobs-envy-private-sector-article-1.462391.

90. Karen Tumulty & Ed O'Keefe, *Public Servants Feeling Sting of Budget Rancor,* Wash. Post, Dec. 21, 2010, http://www.washingtonpost.com/wp-dyn /content/article/2010/12/20/AR2010122005951.html.

91. Joe Davidson, *Federal-Worker Flag Salute Won't Fly,* Wash. Post, Sept. 13, 2011, https://www.washingtonpost.com/politics/column/feddiary/federal -worker-flag-salute-wont-fly/2011/09/13/gIQAHI2mQK_story.html. (quoting Erick Erickson).

92. Michaels, *Progeny,* 1042–1049.

93. Ibid., 1049–1050.

94. Donald F. Kettl, *Scott Walker's Real Legacy,* Wash. Monthly, June/July/

August 2015, http://www.washingtonmonthly.com/magazine/junejulyaugust
_2015/features/scott_walkers_real_legacy055860.php?page=all#.

95. Lisa Rein, *Trump Has a Plan for Government Workers. They're Not Going to Like It,* Wash. Post, Nov. 21, 2016, at https://www.washingtonpost.com/news/powerpost/wp/2016/11/21/trump-republicans-plan-to-target-government-workers-benefits-and-job-security/?utm_term=.ef7d2db790c3.

96. Joe Davidson, *Rubio, Miller Would Take away Employee Rights in Name of Serving Veterans,* Wash. Post, Feb. 20, 2014, https://www.washingtonpost.com/politics/federal_government/rubio-miller-would-take-away-employee-rights-in-name-of-serving-veterans/2014/02/20/5f536b9e-9a5a-11e3-b931-0204122c514b_story.html; Luther F. Carter & Kenneth D. Kitts, Managing Public Personnel: A Turn-of-the-Century Perspective, in *Handbook of Public Administration,* 381, 396 (Jack Rabin et al., eds.) (3d ed.) (Boca Raton, FL: CRC/Taylor & Francis, 2007); Neal Kumar Katyal, *Internal Separation of Powers: Checking Today's Most Dangerous Branch from Within,* 115 Yale L.J. 2314, 2333 (2006); Donald P. Moynihan, *Homeland Security and the U.S. Public Management Policy Agenda,* 18 Governance 171, 172 (2005); Joseph Slater, *Homeland Security vs. Workers' Rights? What the Federal Government Should Learn from History and Experience, and Why,* 6 U. Pa. J. Lab. & Emp. L. 295, 297, 316 (2004); Wasserman, *Collective Bargaining,* 60. For examples of marketization spilling over into matters relating to government speech, see Pauline T. Kim, *Market Norms and Constitutional Values in the Government Workplace,* 94 N.C. L. Rev. 601 (2014).

97. One version of this bill, H.R. 5169, passed the House of Representatives in 2014 on a voice vote. Senior Executive Service Accountability Act, H.R. 5169, 113th Cong. (2013). The bill was again introduced in the House in January 2016 and was quickly reported out of committee. Senior Executive Service Accountability Act, H.R.4358, 114th Cong. (2016). See also Kellie Lunney, *Panel Approves Bill Making It Easier to Suspend and Fire Senior Execs,* Gov. Exec., Jan. 12, 2016, http://www.govexec.com/management/2016/01/house-panel-approves-bill-making-it-easier-suspend-and-fire-senior-executives/125066/.

98. 5 C.F.R. § 1400. This rule may well open the door to high-ranking officials having broad authority over how to classify large segments of the federal workforce. See *Press Release, Gov't Accountability Project, Proposed Rule Could Void Civil Service System for Most Federal Employees,* May 28, 2013, http://www.whistleblower.org/press/proposed-rule-could-void-civil-service-system-for-most-federal-employees.

99. Ibid.

100. Sally Coleman Selden & Gene A. Brewer, *Rolling Back State Civil Service Systems: Assessing the Erosion of Employee Rights and Protections, and Their Impacts,* Aug. 30, 2011, at 8 (unpublished study), http://papers.ssrn.com/sol3/papers.cfm?abstract_id=1919624.

101. Steven W. Hays & Jessica E. Sowa, *A Broader Look at the "Accountability" Movement: Some Grim Realities in State Civil Service Systems,* 26 Rev. Pub. Personnel Admin. 102 (2006).

102. A California state trial court held teacher tenure to be unconstitutional, but that holding was reversed on appeal. *Vergara v. State*, 209 Cal. Rptr. 532, 532–538 (Ct. App. 2016). The California Supreme Court declined to review the appellate court's decision. Ibid., 558–570. North Carolina passed a law in 2013 removing teacher tenure protections. The state courts declared that law unconstitutional, principally because of its retroactive effect. See *N.C. Ass'n of Educators v. State*, 786 S.E. 2d 255 (N.C. 2016). For discussions of the tenure battle in New York, see Jon Campbell, *Group Fights N.Y. Tenure Rules*, Press & Sun-Bulletin, Jun. 24, 2014, http://www.pressconnects.com /story/news/local/new-york/2014/06/24/group-fights-ny-tenure-rules/11336993; Elizabeth A. Harris, *Cuomo Gets Deals on Tenure and Evaluations of Teachers*, N.Y. Times, Mar. 31, 2015, http://www.nytimes.com/2015/04/01 /nyregion/cuomo-gets-deals-on-tenure-and-evaluations-of-teachers.html?_r=0.

103. Erik Kain, *Op-ed, 80% of Michigan Charter Schools Are For-Profits*, Forbes, Sept. 20, 2011, http://www.forbes.com/sites/erikkain/2011/09/29/80-of -michigan-charter-schools-are-for-profits/#34679fc470fd.

104. See, for example, Martha Minow, *Partners, Not Rivals: Privatization and the Public Good* (Boston: Beacon Press, 2002); Samuel E. Abrams, *Education and the Commercial Mindset* (Cambridge: Harvard University Press: 2016).

105. Lyndsey Layton, *With California Tenure Ruling, a Democratic Divide*, Wash. Post, Jun. 12, 2014, https://www.washingtonpost.com/local/education/with -california-tenure-ruling-a-democratic-divide/2014/06/12/1816784c-f267 -11e3-9ebc-2ee6f81ed217_story.html.

106. Dana Goldstein, *The Most Important Figure in School Reform We Never Talk About*, Slate, Sept. 1, 2014, http://www.slate.com/articles/life/education /2014/09/principals_matter_and_teacher_tenure_lawsuits_are_a_sideshow _that_won_t.html.

107. Diane Ravitch, *When Public Goes Private, as Trump Wants: What Happens?*, New York Rev. of Books, Dec. 8, 2016, http://www.nybooks.com/articles /2016/12/08/when-public-goes-private-as-trump-wants-what-happens/; Stephen Sawchuk, *Reactions to the Vergara Teacher-Tenure Case Pour In*, Ed. Week, Jun. 10, 2014, http://blogs.edweek.org/edweek/teacherbeat/2014 /06/reactions_to_the_vergara_teach.html.

108. Molly Ball, *Why Do Liberals Hate Cory Booker?*, Atlantic, Aug. 23, 2013, http://www.theatlantic.com/politics/archive/2013/08/why-do-liberals-hate -cory-booker/278992/.

6. Privatization as a Constitutional— and Constitutionally Fraught—Project

1. E. S. Savas, *Privatizing the Public Sector: How to Shrink Government*, 89–90 (Chatham, NJ: Chatham House Pub., 1982) (characterizing privatization as a most "promising" method to "restrict the size of government" and calling contracting more efficient because it "harnesses competitive forces and brings the pressure of the marketplace to bear on inefficient producers. . . .").

2. John D. Donahue, *The Privatization Decision: Public Ends, Private Means,* 79–80, 109 (New York: Basic Books, 1989); David Osborne & Ted Gaebler, *Reinventing Government: How the Entrepreneurial Spirit Is Transforming the Private Sector,* 87 (Reading, MA: Addison-Wesley Pub., 1993); Steven L. Schooner, *Fear of Oversight: The Fundamental Failure of Businesslike Government,* 50 Am. U. L. Rev. 627 (2001).

3. Ashley Southall, *A Former G.S.A. Official Is Indicted in a Fraud Case,* N.Y. Times, Sept. 25, 2014, https://www.nytimes.com/2014/09/26/us/a-former-gsa -official-is-indicted-in-a-fraud-case.html; Jackie Calmes & Matt Flegenheimer, *Secret Service Agents Accused of Misconduct,* N.Y. Times, Apr. 14, 2012, http://www.nytimes.com/2012/04/14/world/americas/secret-service-agents-in -colombia-accused-of-misconduct.html; Michael S. Schmidt, *Investigator in Secret Service Prostitution Scandal Quits,* N.Y. Times, Oct. 28, 2014, https:// www.nytimes.com/2014/10/29/us/politics/investigator-in-secret-service -prostitution-scandal-resigns-after-being-implicated-in-own-incident.html; Evan Perez, *NSA: Some Used Spying Power to Snoop on Lovers,* CNN, Sept. 27, 2013, http://www.cnn.com/2013/09/27/politics/nsa-snooping/; Rebecca Leung, *Cashing in for Profit?,* CBS News, Jan. 4, 2005, http://www.cbsnews .com/news/cashing-in-for-profit/; Richard A. Oppel, Jr., *Veterans Secretary Ousts Health Care Official amid Criticism,* N.Y. Times, May 16, 2014, https://www.nytimes.com/2014/05/17/us/politics/shinseki-ousts-head-of -health-care-for-veterans-affairs.html.

4. *INS v. Chadha,* 462 U.S. 919, 944 (1983).

5. *Myers v. United States,* 272 U.S. 52, 293 (1926) (Brandeis, J., dissenting).

6. Donahue, *Privatization Decision,* 32.

7. Paul C. Light, *Outsourcing and the True Size of Government,* 33 Pub. Cont. L.J. 311 (2004).

8. Compare William J. Clinton, *State of the Union Address,* Jan. 23, 1996, https://clinton2.nara.gov/WH/New/other/sotu.html ("Today the Federal work force is 200,000 employees smaller than it was the day I took office as President.") with Paul C. Light, *The True Size of Government,* 37–44 (Washington, DC: Brookings Institution Press, 1999) (describing the "shadow government" of millions of contractors and other private actors who more than offset official federal employee downsizing). See also Jon D. Michaels, *Privatization's Pretensions,* 77 U. Chi. L. Rev. 717, 751–756 (2010); Charles Tiefer, *The Iraq Debacle: The Rise and Fall of Procurement-Aided Unilateralism as a Paradigm of Foreign War,* 29 U. Pa. J. Int'l L. 1, 28 (2007).

9. John J. DiIulio Jr., *Bring Back the Bureaucrats: Why More Federal Workers Will Lead to Better (and Smaller!) Government* (West Conshohocken, PA: Templeton Press, 2014).

10. James Risen, *Pay Any Price: Greed, Power, and Endless War* (Boston: Houghton Mifflin Harcourt, 2014) (expanding the traditional understanding of the military-industrial complex into the homeland security context); Eric Schlosser, *The Prison-Industrial Complex,* Atlantic, Dec. 1998, at 51, 64.

11. Paul R. Verkuil, *Outsourcing Sovereignty: Why Privatization of Government Functions Threatens Democracy and What We Can Do about It,* 103 (New

York, Cambridge University Press, 2007). Verkuil does, however, attempt to locate other, less explicit, textual grounds. Ibid., 103–106 (suggesting possible claims under the Appointments Clause); ibid., 123 (indicating the possible relevance of the Subdelegation Act). See also Alfred C. Aman, Jr., *The Democracy Deficit: Taming Globalization through Law Reform*, 136–137 (New York: New York University Press, 2004) (proffering possible statutory challenges to privatization initiatives).

12. Harold J. Krent, *Federal Power, Non-Federal Actors: The Ramifications of Free Enterprise Fund*, 79 Fordham L. Rev. 2425, 2429–2431 (2011) (explaining that "[n]o delegation to private actors after . . . *Schechter* . . . has been invalidated" and that the Court's post-*Schechter* jurisprudence "suggest[s] a wide ambit for the private exercise of delegated authority").

13. Gillian E. Metzger, *Privatization as Delegation*, 103 Colum. L. Rev. 1367, 1410–1437 (2003); Jon D. Michaels, *Deputizing Homeland Security*, 88 Tex. L. Rev. 1435, 1462–1466 (2010).

14. Charles M. Lamb, *Housing Segregation in Suburban America since 1960: Presidential and Judicial Politics*, 110 (New York: Cambridge University Press, 2005).

15. Annie Snider, *Pruitt Allies Exploring Hiring Private Lawyers to Rewrite EPA Rule*, Politico, Apr. 18, 2017, http://www.politico.com/story/2017/04/pruitt -water-rules-private-lawyers-237339.

16. *Richardson v. McKnight*, 521 U.S. 399, 418–419 (1997) (Scalia, J., dissenting).

17. 31 U.S.C. § 3730(d)(2) (2006); Charles Doyle, *Qui Tam: The False Claims Act and Related Federal Statutes*, Cong. Res. Serv., Aug. 6, 2009, at 1–7, https://www.fas.org/sgp/crs/misc/R40785.pdf.

18. Ron Nixon, *Government Pays More in Contracts, Study Finds*, N.Y. Times, Sept. 2, 2011, http://www.nytimes.com/2011/09/13/us/13contractor.html.

19. Paul Chassy & Scott H. Amey, *Bad Business: Billions of Dollars Wasted on Hiring Contractors*, Project on Gov't Oversight, Sept. 13, 2011, http:// pogoarchives.org/m/co/igf/bad-business-report-only-2011.pdf.

20. E. S. Savas, *Privatization: The Key to Better Government*, 5 tbl. 1.1 (Chatham, NJ: Chatham House Pub., 1997); Richard C. Box, *Running Government Like a Business: Implications for Public Administration Theory and Practice*, 29 Am. Rev. Pub. Admin. 19, 19 (1999); James P. Pfiffner, *The First MBA President: George W. Bush as Public Administrator*, 67 Pub. Admin. Rev. 6 (2007).

21. Kevin R. Kosar, *Privatization and the Federal Government*, Cong. Res. Serv., Dec. 28, 2006, at 6–7, 15–17, https://www.fas.org/sgp/crs/misc/RL33777 .pdf; Mark H. Moore, *Introduction to Symposium: Public Values in an Era of Privatization*, 116 Harv. L. Rev. 1212, 1218 (2003); Jon D. Michaels, *Privatization's Progeny*, 101 Geo. L.J. 1023, 1030–1032 (2013).

22. Richard B. Stewart, *The Reformation of American Administrative Law*, 88 Harv. L. Rev. 1669, 1675–1678 (1975).

23. Michaels, *Pretensions*, 738–739; Jack M. Beermann, *Privatization and Political Accountability*, 28 Fordham Urb. L.J. 1507, 1554 (2001); Daniel

Guttman, *Public Purpose and Private Service: The Twentieth Century Culture of Contracting Out and the Evolving Law of Diffused Sovereignty,* 52 Admin. L. Rev. 859, 895 (2000).

24. Matthew Diller, *The Revolution in Welfare Administration: Rules, Discretion, and Entrepreneurial Government,* 75 N.Y.U. L. Rev. 1121, 1186–1202 (2000).

25. Ralph C. Nash, Jr., Karen R. O'Brien-Debakey & Steven L. Schooner, *The Government Contracts Reference Book* (4th ed.) (Chicago: Wolters Kluwer Law & Business, 2013) (explaining flat-fee government contract arrangements that permit contractors to keep as profits whatever portion of the flat payment they did not spend); Dru Stevenson, *Privatization of State Administrative Services,* 68 La. L. Rev. 1285, 1290 (2008) (arguing that government service contractors have "perverse financial motivations . . . to spend as little time as possible" on their assigned tasks "in order to collect higher profits for fewer labor-hours" or to focus only on "the easiest cases," to the neglect of more difficult, resource-intensive ones).

26. David A. Super, *Privatization, Policy Paralysis, and the Poor,* 96 Cal. L. Rev. 393, 414–444 (2008) (explaining how government officials can lose control over those contractors operating pursuant to long-term contracts or serving in contexts where they are unlikely to be replaced).

27. See generally Daniel Guttman & Barry Willner, *The Shadow Government: The Government's Multi-Billion Dollar Giveaway of Its Decision-Making Powers to Private Management Consultants* (New York: Pantheon Books, 1976).

28. Guttman, *Public Purpose,* 917 (describing the process of dismissing government contractors as easier than dismissing civil servants); see also Katherine V. W. Stone, *Revisiting the At-Will Employment Doctrine,* 36 Indus. L.J. 84, 84 (2007) ("In the United States, the dominant form of [private] employment contract is at-will.").

29. Michaels, *Pretensions,* 748–750; Paul R. Verkuil, *Public Law Limitations on Privatization of Government Functions,* 84 N.C. L. Rev. 397, 465 (2006) ("Government officials often feel that they have more control over private contractors than they do over their own employees due to restrictions on hiring or firing permanent employees.").

30. Michaels, *Progeny,* 1036–1037 ("[Civil servants are able to] provide expert, unfiltered advice without fear of being fired for doing so."). See generally Matthew C. Stephenson, *Optimal Political Control of the Bureaucracy,* 107 Mich. L. Rev. 53, 93–95 (2008) (explaining the accountability-enhancing effects of directives that require agency leaders and civil servants to share administrative responsibilities).

31. Schooner, *Fear of Oversight,* 631–671.

32. See ibid.

33. Michaels, *Pretensions,* 762–763.

34. Jon Michaels, *Deforming Welfare: How the Dominant Narratives of Devolution and Privatization Subverted Federal Welfare Reform,* 34 Seton Hall L. Rev. 573, 640–658 (2004).

35. Another component of marketization is a shift in the direction of performance-based pay for government workers. Michaels, *Progeny,* 1048–1049. Where agency leaders also have discretion in awarding performance-based bonuses, they can exert even greater control over an at-will, marketized workforce.

36. Joe Davidson, *Report Shows Federal Workers Are Increasingly Dreary about Their Jobs,* Wash. Post, Nov. 16, 2011, http://www.washingtonpost.com /politics/report-shows-federal-workers-are-increasingly-dreary-about-their-jobs /2011/11/16/gIQAjaIXSN_story.html (citing a federal official explaining that government "[p]ay freezes and reductions in benefits will only exacerbate the coming brain drain" and that reductions in pay and benefits will discourage "the best and brightest [from] public service"); Dan Eggen, *Civil Rights Focus Shift Roils Staff at Justice,* Wash. Post, Nov. 13, 2005, http://www .washingtonpost.com/wp-dyn/content/article/2005/11/12/AR2005111201200 .html (describing efforts to politicize the Justice Department and explaining how such politicization undermined worker morale and prompted a large exodus of career staffers).

37. David E. Lewis, *The Politics of Presidential Appointments: Political Control and Bureaucratic Performance,* 30 (Princeton: Princeton University Press, 2008); Gillian E. Metzger, *The Interdependent Relationship between Internal and External Separation of Powers,* 59 Emory L.J. 423, 430 (2009).

38. Jerry L. Mashaw, *Creating the Administrative Constitution: The Lost One Hundred Years of American Administrative Law,* 178 (New Haven: Yale University Press, 2012).

39. Mark Landler, *Transition Team's Request on Gender Equality Rattles State Dept.,* N.Y. Times, Dec. 22, 2016, https://www.nytimes.com/2016/12/22/us /politics/state-department-gender-equality-trump-transition.html (discussing both the gender equality and climate change inquiries).

40. Tracy Wilkinson, *Trump's Team Singles out State Department Programs for Women for Special Review,* L.A. Times, Dec. 22, 2016, http://www.latimes .com/politics/la-na-trump-state-women-20161222-story.html.

41. Mashaw, *Creating the Administrative Constitution,* 177.

42. Mark Thompson, *An Army Apart: The Widening Military-Civilian Gap,* Time, Nov. 10, 2011, http://nation.time.com/2011/11/10/an-army-apart-the -widening-military-civilian-gap/; Thomas E. Ricks, *The Widening Gap between Military and Society,* Atlantic, Jul. 1997, http://www.theatlantic .com/magazine/archive/1997/07/the-widening-gap-between-military-and -society/306158/.

43. Bruce Ackerman, *The Decline and Fall of the American Republic,* 43–64 (Cambridge: Harvard University Press, 2010).

44. Senior military officers do not become senior overnight: They generally need to have logged years and years of active duty before being promoted to Army colonels or Navy captains. See 10 U.S.C. § 619.

45. Samuel A. Stouffer, et al., *The American Soldier: Combat and Its Aftermath* (Princeton: Princeton University Press, 1949) (reporting that unit cohesion

and loyalty to fellow soldiers were what sustained combat troops during World War II, more so than commitments to ideological, nationalistic, or geopolitical causes); Leonard Wong et. al., *Why They Fight: Combat Motivation in the Iraq War,* Strategic Studies Institute, Jul. 2003, http://www .strategicstudiesinstitute.army.mil/pdffiles/pub179.pdf (reviewing studies from the 1940s to 2000s and concluding that soldiers have historically fought for each other, rather than a normative commitment).

46. Diane H. Mazur, *A Constitutional Bond in Military Professionalism: A Reply to Professor Deborah N. Pearlstein,* 90 Tex. L. Rev. See Also 145, 154 (2012).

47. Ibid.

48. Deborah N. Pearlstein, *The Soldier, the State, and the Separation of Powers,* 90 Tex. L. Rev. 797, 822–824 (2012).

49. Mazur, *Constitutional Bond,* 154.

50. Jon D. Michaels, *Beyond Accountability: The Constitutional, Democratic, and Strategic Problems with Privatizing War,* 82 Wash. U.L.Q. 1001, 1073–1074, 1087–1094 (2004).

51. Compare Jack Goldsmith, *The Terror Presidency: Law and Judgment Inside the Bush Administration* (New York: W. W. Norton, 2007); Jane Mayer, *The Dark Side: The Inside Story of How the War on Terror Turned into a War on American Ideals* (New York: Doubleday, 2009).

52. Steven L. Schooner, *Abu Ghraib: Compromised Accountability in a Streamlined, Outsourced Government,* 16 Stan. L. & Pol'y Rev. 549 (2005); Katherine Eban, *The Psychologists Who Taught the CIA How to Torture (and Charged $180 Million),* Vanity Fair, Dec. 10, 2014, http://www.vanityfair .com/news/daily-news/2014/12/psychologists-cia-torture-report.

53. Oona A. Hathaway, *Presidential Power over International Law: Restoring the Balance,* 119 Yale L.J. 140, 221–224 (2009) (explaining that administrative law's central safeguards do not operate as fully in areas of foreign affairs and national defense); Adrian Vermeule, *Our Schmittian Administrative Law,* 122 Harv. L. Rev. 1095, 1112 (2009).

54. Tiefer, *Iraq Debacle,* 28.

55. Steven Schooner, *Don't Contractors Count When We Calculate the Costs of War?,* Wash. Post, May 25, 2009, at A21; Renae Merle, *Contract Workers Are War's Forgotten: Iraq Deaths Create Subculture of Loss,* Wash. Post, Jul. 31, 2004, at A1.

7. The Separations of Powers in the Twenty-First Century

1. Declaration of Independence (1776); Paul Downes, *Democracy, Revolution, and Monarchism in Early American Literature,* 5 (New York: Cambridge University Press, 2004) ("The American Revolution's defining gesture . . . was its rejection of the English crown and with it the rejection of absolute monarchy in general."); *The Federalist,* No. 10 (James Madison); G. Edward

White, *Reading the Guarantee Clause,* 65 U. Colo. L. Rev. 787, 798 (1994) (describing the Guarantee Clause as ensuring a Republican form of government "not tainted by . . . foreign monarchy and domestic mobocracy").

2. Eric A. Posner & Adrian Vermeule, *The Executive Unbound: After the Madisonian Republic,* 176–205 (New York: Oxford University Press, 2010); see also Jodi L. Short, *The Paranoid Style in Regulatory Reform,* 63 Hastings L.J. 633, 680–681 (2012) (criticizing fear-of-tyranny rhetoric as "devalu[ing] state-directed regulatory tools" and insisting we move beyond narratives about the State that traffic in such fears).

3. Adrian Vermeule, *The Constitution of Risk,* 11–13 (New York: Cambridge University Press, 2014).

4. Barack Obama, *Commencement Speech,* Ohio State University, May 5, 2013, https://www.osu.edu/index.php?q=features/2013/obamacommencement .html.

5. *Guns in America Town Hall with President Obama,* CNN, Jan. 7, 2016, http://www.cnn.com/2016/01/07/politics/transcript-obama-town-hall-guns-in-america/.

6. See, for example, Charles A. Reich, *The New Property,* 73 Yale L.J. 733 (1964).

7. See, for example, Nina Bernstein, *Suit to Seek Food Stamps for Thousands Wrongly Denied Them,* N.Y. Times, Mar. 31, 2002, http://www.nytimes .com/2002/03/31/nyregion/suit-to-seek-food-stamps-for-thousands-wrongly -denied-them.html (documenting the wrongful denial of food stamps to thousands of eligible persons); Mike McIntire, *Ensnared by Error on Growing U.S. Watch List,* N.Y. Times, Apr. 6, 2010, http://www.nytimes.com/2010/04/07 /us/07watch.html ("Every year, thousands of people find themselves caught up in the government's terrorist screening process. Some are legitimate targets of concern, others are victims of errors in judgment or simple mistaken identity."); Stephanie Condon, *22,000 File Appeals with Obamacare Site, Report Says,* CBS News, Feb. 3, 2014, http://www.cbsnews.com/news/22000-waiting-for -obamacare-website-errors-to-be-fixed-report-says/ (bringing to light the fact that tens of thousands of people have been wrongfully denied federal health benefits or were assigned to the wrong federal insurance program).

8. *City of Arlington v. FCC,* 133 S. Ct. 1863, 1878 (2013) (Roberts, C.J., dissenting).

9. See *Wyman v. James,* 400 U.S. 309, 335 & n. 13 (1971) (Douglas, J., dissenting) (referring to the modern American bureaucracy as omnipresent and oppressive, conducting "mass raids upon the homes of welfare recipients"); Jared P. Cole, *Terrorist Databases and the No-Fly List: Procedural Due Process and Hurdles to Litigation,* Cong. Res. Serv., Apr. 2, 2015, http:// www.fas.org/sgp/crs/homesec/R43730.pdf (documenting constitutional challenges to the federal government's No-Fly List designations); David A. Super, *Against Flexibility,* 97 Cornell L. Rev. 1375 (2011) (addressing the dangers and concerns associated with administrative discretion over vulnerable populations); Noah D. Zatz, *Poverty Unmodified?: Critical Reflections on the Deserving/Undeserving Distinction,* 59 UCLA L. Rev. 550, 558 (2012) (explaining how those seeking welfare assistance are "vulnerab[le] to the

discretionary judgment of caseworkers"); Editorial, *At an Immigration Detention Center, Due Process Denied*, N.Y. Times, Aug. 25, 2014, https://www.nytimes.com/2014/08/26/opinion/at-an-immigrant-detention-center-due-process-denied.html?_r=0 (characterizing the truncated asylum process as unfair and unreasonable).

10. Vermeule, *Risk*, 4.

11. Ibid., 80.

12. Abner S. Greene, *Checks and Balances in an Era of Presidential Lawmaking*, 61 U. Chi. L. Rev. 123, 132–53 (1994).

13. Sanford Levinson, *Our Undemocratic Constitution: Where the Constitution Goes Wrong (and How We the People Can Correct It)* (New York: Oxford University Press, 2006); Juan J. Linz, *The Perils of Presidentialism*, 1 J. Dem. 51 (1990); Louis Michael Seidman, *Op-ed, Let's Give Up on the Constitution*, N.Y. Times, Dec. 30, 2012, http://www.nytimes.com/2012/12/31/opinion/lets-give-up-on-the-constitution.html; see also Bruce Ackerman, *The New Separation of Powers*, 113 Harv. L. Rev. 633, 723 (2000) (encouraging scholars and lawyers to step back from our "ritualistic incantations of Madison and Montesquieu").

14. Josh Chafetz, *The Phenomenology of Gridlock*, 88 Notre Dame L. Rev. 2065, 2082 (2013); see also Jason S. Oh, *Diagnosing Gridlock*, 67 Tax L. Rev. 627, 632 (2014) ("If Congress acts in a particular policy sphere and legislator preferences stay the same, then no further legislative action should be expected.").

15. For related discussions on supermajoritarian rules, see, for example, John O. McGinnis & Michael B. Rappaport, *Originalism and the Good Constitution* (Cambridge: Harvard University Press, 2013); Frederic Bloom & Nelson Tebbe, *Countersupermajoritarianism*, 113 Mich. L. Rev. 809 (2013).

16. Tyler Cowen, *No, It Only Looks Like Gridlock*, N.Y. Times, Dec. 22, 2013, http://www.nytimes.com/2013/12/22/business/dont-mistake-this-for-gridlock.html?partner=rss&emc=rss&_r=0.

17. R. Shep Melnick, *The Conventional Misdiagnosis: Why "Gridlock" Is Not Our Central Problem and Constitutional Revision Not the Solution*, 94 B. U. L. Rev. 767, 779 (2014); see Chafetz, *Phenomenology*, 2077.

18. Sarah A. Binder, *Stalemate: Causes and Consequences of Legislative Gridlock* (Washington, DC: Brookings Institution Press, 2003); David Mayhew, *Partisan Balance: Why Political Parties Don't Kill the U.S. Constitutional System*, 190 (Princeton: Princeton University Press, 2011) (recognizing that many periods of perceived legislative dysfunction have proven to be "limited, tolerable, or correctable").

19. Henry Adams, *The Life of Albert Gallatin*, 434 (New York: Peter Smith, 1943).

20. Ackerman, *New Separation of Powers*, 646; Gillian E. Metzger, *Embracing Administrative Common Law*, 80 Geo. Wash. L. Rev. 1293, 1322–1323 (2012).

21. The U.S. Court of Appeals for the Fifth Circuit struck down President Obama's deferred action plan, and that decision was affirmed by an equally

divided, and shorthanded, Supreme Court—one that was missing Obama's nominated but never-confirmed replacement for the late Justice Scalia.

22. *Fact Sheet: New Executive Actions to Reduce Gun Violence and Make Our Communities Safer,* White House, Jan. 4, 2016, https://www.whitehouse .gov/the-press-office/2016/01/04/fact-sheet-new-executive-actions-reduce-gun -violence-and-make-our; Barack Obama, *Remarks by the President in Address to the Nation on Immigration,* Nov. 20, 2014, https://www .whitehouse.gov/the-press-office/2014/11/20/remarks-president-address -nation-immigration.

23. Barack Obama, *2013 State of the Union Address,* Feb. 12, 2013, https:// www.whitehouse.gov/the-press-office/2013/02/12/remarks-president-state -union-address.

24. Ackerman, *New Separation of Powers,* 697 (describing the legitimating effects of American rulemaking in terms of rulemaking's accommodation of various, competing interests and constituencies, populist and bureaucratic alike).

25. Daryl J. Levinson & Richard H. Pildes, *Separation of Parties, Not Powers,* 119 Harv. L. Rev. 2311 (2006).

26. Curtis A. Bradley & Trevor W. Morrison, *Historical Gloss and the Separation of Powers,* 126 Harv. L. Rev. 411, 443 (2012).

27. See, for example, Richard Hofstadter, *The Idea of a Party System: The Rise of Legitimate Opposition in the United States, 1780–1840,* at 53 (Berkeley: University of California Press, 1969).

28. Chafetz, *Phenomenology,* 2076 n. 67 (viewing political parties as having incentives to moderate over time).

29. Harold H. Bruff, *Untrodden Ground: How Presidents Interpret the Constitution* (Chicago: University of Chicago Press, 2015); Arthur M. Schlesinger, Jr., *The Imperial Presidency* (Boston: Houghton Mifflin, 1973); Peter M. Shane, *Madison's Nightmare: How Executive Power Threatens American Democracy* (Chicago: University of Chicago Press, 2009); Charlie Savage, *Power Wars: Inside Obama's Post-9/11 Presidency* (New York: Little, Brown and Co., 2015).

30. See, for example, Jack Goldsmith, *Obama's Breathtaking Expansion of a President's Power to Make War,* Time, Sept. 11, 2014, http://time.com/3326689 /obama-isis-war-powers-bush/. Goldsmith quotes then Senator Obama as insisting that "[h]istory has shown us time and again . . . that military action is most successful when it is authorized and supported by the Legislative branch" and that "[i]t is always preferable to have the informed consent of Congress prior to any military action." Ibid. Goldsmith contends that "[f]uture historians . . . will puzzle over how Barack Obama the prudent war-powers constitutionalist transformed into a matchless war-powers unilateralist." Ibid.

31. See Savage, *Power Wars.*

32. Joan Biskupic & David Ingram, *Once a Beacon, Obama under Fire over Civil Liberties,* Reuters, May 15, 2013, http://www.reuters.com/article /us-usa-obama-liberties-analysis-idUSBRE94E06I20130515; Liz Halloran,

Obama's Year of Disappointing the Liberal Base, NPR, Dec. 17, 2013, http://
www.npr.org/sections/itsallpolitics/2013/12/17/251983136/the-year-of
-disappointing-the-liberal-base-obama-2013.

33. Compare Josh Chafetz, *Congress's Constitution: Legislative Authority and
the Separation of Powers* (New Haven: Yale University Press, 2017); Richard
A. Epstein, *Why Parties and Powers Both Matter: A Separationist Response
to Levinson and Pildes,* 119 Harv. L. Rev. F. 210 (2006).

34. Jeffrey M. Jones, *In U.S., New Record 43% Are Political Independents,*
Gallup, Jan. 7, 2015, http://www.gallup.com/poll/180440/new-record-political
-independents.aspx.

35. For a discussion of party loyalty and organizational discipline within
Congress, see Levinson & Pildes, *Parties,* 2335–2338.

36. Donald F. Kettl, *The Next Government of the United States,* 159–161 (New
York: W. W. Norton, 2009).

37. Dara K. Cohen, Mariano-Florentino Cuellar, & Barry R. Weingast, *Crisis
Bureaucracy: Homeland Security and the Political Design of Legal Mandates,*
59 Stan. L. Rev. 673, 676 (2006).

38. Anne Joseph O'Connell, *The Architecture of Smart Intelligence: Strengthening
and Overseeing Agencies in the Post-9/11 World,* 94 Cal. L. Rev. 1655, 1657
(2006).

39. For discussions touting the benefits of vertical integration of America's intelligence operations, see, for example, Department of Homeland Security, *State
and Major Urban Area Fusion Centers,* http://www.dhs.gov/state-and-major
-urban-area-fusion-centers; *Protecting America Against Terrorist Attack,
Our Joint Terrorism Task Forces,* http://www.fbi.gov/about-us/investigate
/terrorism/terrorism_jttfs; *Ashcroft Memo,* Nov. 13, 2001, www.fas.org/irp
/agency/dojagdirective5.pdf ("[L]aw enforcement officials at all levels of government—federal, state, and local—must work together, sharing information
and resources needed" to deter and punish terrorists); *The 9/11 Commission
Report: Final Report of the National Commission on Terrorist Attacks upon
the United States,* 215–241, 390, 401, 416 (2004), http://www.9-11commission
.gov/report/911Report.pdf.

40. *In re: Sealed Case Nos. 02–001, 02–002,* 310 F.3d 717 (FISC Ct. Rev. 2002).

41. Jon D. Michaels, *Deputizing Homeland Security,* 88 Tex. L. Rev 1435 (2010).

42. Keith Bradley, *The Design of Agency Interactions,* 111 Colum. L. Rev. 745
(2011); Jim Rossi & Jody Freeman, *Agency Coordination in Shared
Regulatory Space,* 125 Harv. L. Rev. 1131 (2012).

43. The multiagency Financial Stability Oversight Council was created pursuant
to Section 112(a)(1)(C) of the Dodd-Frank Wall Street Reform and Consumer
Protection Act, Pub. L. 111–203, 124 Stat. 1376 (2012).

44. Jon D. Michaels, *Separation of Powers and Centripetal Forces: Implications
for the Institutional Design and Constitutionality of Our National-Security
State,* 83 U. Chi. L. Rev. 199 (2016).

45. Robert M. Cover, *The Uses of Jurisdictional Redundancy: Interest, Ideology,
and Innovation,* 22 Wm. & Mary L. Rev. 639, 646 (1981).

46. Michaels, *Centripetal Forces.*

47. For studies of aggregate effects in various legal contexts, see Ariel Porat & Eric A. Posner, *Aggregation and Law*, 122 Yale L.J. 2 (2012); Michael Coenen, *Combining Constitutional Clauses*, 164 U. Penn. L. Rev. 1067 (2016); Michaels, *Centripetal Forces*, 214–219. For aggregate effects analysis in areas of constitutional law, see *United States v. Jones*, 132 S. Ct. 949, 964 (2012) (Alito, J., concurring) (emphasizing a mosaic theory of the Fourth Amendment in which the combination of two or more discrete acts—none of which is, by itself, intrusive enough to rise to the level of a *search*—amounts in toto to a constitutionally relevant search); *Lee v. Keith*, 463 F.3d 763 (7th Cir. 2006) ("In combination . . . the early filing deadline [for those seeking elected office], the 10% signature requirement, and . . . additional . . . restriction[s] . . . operate to unconstitutionally burden the freedom of political association guaranteed by the First and Fourteenth Amendments."); *Free Ent. Fund v. PCAOB*, 561 U.S. 477 (2010) (finding the sum total of two layers of executive officials insulated from presidential control to be unconstitutional).

48. Alfred Stepan & Cindy Skach, *Constitutional Frameworks and Democratic Consolidation*, 46 World Pol. 1, 4 (1993); Scott Mainwaring, *Presidentialism, Multipartism, and Democracy: The Difficult Combination*, 26 Comp. Pol. Stud. 198 (1993); José Antonio Cheibub, *Making Presidential and Semi-Presidential Constitutions Work*, 87 Tex. L. Rev. 1375, 1378 (2009).

49. See, for example, Linz, *Perils*.

50. See, for example, David S. Law & Mila Versteeg, *The Declining Influence of the United States Constitution*, 87 N.Y.U. L. Rev. 762, 791–792 (2012).

51. Jeremy Ashkenas & Gregor Aisch, *European Populism in the Age of Donald Trump*, N.Y. Times, Dec. 5, 2006, http://www.nytimes.com/interactive/2016/12/05/world/europe/populism-in-age-of-trump.html; Josh Lowe, et al., *Why Europe's Populist Revolt Is Spreading*, Newsweek, Nov. 12, 2016, http://www.newsweek.com/2016/12/02/europe-right-wing-nationalism-populist-revolt-trump-putin-524119.html.

52. See, for example, Francis Fukuyama, *Political Order and Political Decay: From the Industrial Revolution to the Globalization of Democracy*, 339–340 (New York: Farrar, Straus and Giroux, 2014) (recognizing that the demographic and cultural homogeneity of some of the more advanced East Asian nation-states makes it easier for those nation-states to engage in state-building).

53. Ibid., 501–502.

54. Ibid., 16–18, 66–80 (describing the well-established bureaucracies of pre-democratic France and Prussia); see also Daniel R. Ernst, *Tocqueville's Nightmare: The Administrative State Emerges in America, 1900–1940*, at 10–27 (New York: Oxford University Press, 2014) (describing *Rechtsstaat* as a continental European understanding of bureaucracy constrained by codes and rules rather than by the public's will).

55. Fukuyama, *Political Order*, 75, 338–343, 354–369.

56. Ernst, *Tocqueville's Nightmare*, 26–27.

57. See, for example Michael P. Vandenberg, *Private Environmental Governance,* 99 Cornell L. Rev. 129 (2013); Daniel A. Farber & Anne Joseph O'Connell, *Agencies as Adversaries,* 105 Cal. L. Rev. __ (forthcoming 2017); Miriam Seifter, *States as Interest Groups in the Administrative Process,* 100 Va. L. Rev. 953 (2014); Daniel Abebe, *The Global Determinants of U.S. Foreign Affairs Law,* 49 Stan. J. Int'l L. 1 (2013); Jessica Bulman-Pozen, *Federalism as a Safeguard of the Separation of Powers,* 112 Colum. L. Rev. 459 (2012).

58. Aziz Z. Huq & Jon D. Michaels, *The Cycles of Separation-of-Powers Jurisprudence,* 126 Yale L.J. 342, 387–403 (2016).

59. Ibid., 350–352; see also Jon D. Michaels, *Of Constitutional Custodians and Regulatory Rivals: An Account of the Old and New Separation of Powers,* 91 N.Y.U. L. Rev. 227, 266–268 (2016).

60. See Richard B. Stewart, *The Reformation of American Administrative Law,* 88 Harv. L. Rev. 1667, 1711–1759 (1975) (explaining that one key element of the "reformation" of American administrative law involves more fully empowering civil society groups to check and enrich the administrative process).

61. Though there is disagreement on the question who should exercise control—shareholders or directors—most American corporate governance scholars conclude that one (and only one) group or constituency should exercise control. See, for example, Henry Hansmann & Reinier Kraakman, *The End of History for Corporate Law,* 89 Geo. L.J. 439, 468 (2001) (stressing a shareholder-focused model of corporate governance); Stephen M. Bainbridge, *Director Primacy and Shareholder Disempowerment,* 119 Harv. L. Rev. 1735 (2006) (emphasizing a director-focused model of corporate governance).

62. Henry Hansmann, *The Ownership of Enterprise,* 39–44 (Cambridge: Harvard University Press, 1996) (underscoring the value of homogeneous corporate control and addressing the costs associated with collective, heterogeneous decisionmaking).

63. Ibid., 44 (remarking on the "nearly complete absence of large firms in which ownership is shared among two or more different types of patrons, such as customers and suppliers or investors and workers").

64. Compare, for example, Jody Freeman, *Extending Public Law Norms Through Privatization,* 116 Harv. L. Rev. 1285 (2003).

65. Jon D. Michaels, *Running Government Like a Business . . . Then and Now,* 128 Harv. L. Rev. 1152, 1154–1155 (2015).

66. Andrew Cline, *What "You Didn't Build That" Really Means—And Why Romney Can't Explain It,* Atlantic, Aug. 10, 2012, http://www.theatlantic .com/politics/archive/2012/08/what-you-didnt-build-that-really-means-and -why-romney-cant-explain-it/260984/.

67. See, for example, *Can Obama Defuse the "You Didn't Build That" Attacks?,* The Week, Jul. 25, 2012, http://theweek.com/articles/473613/obama-defuse -didnt-build-that-attacks; Amy Gardner, *Obama Facing Mounting Questions over "You Didn't Build That" Remark,* Wash. Post, Sept. 2, 2012, https://

www.washingtonpost.com/politics/obama-facing-mounting-questions-over
-you-didnt-build-that-remark/2012/09/02/c409f90c-f52b-11e1-86a5
-1f5431d87dfd_story.html?utm_term=.72454dd92437.

68. Compare William J. Novak, *The Myth of the "Weak" American State,* 113 Am. Hist. Rev. 769 (2008) (describing the ways in which the American State created, shaped, and bolstered the private sector).

8. Recalibrating the Relationship between and among the Constitutional and Administrative Rivals

1. See, for example, Kevin M. Stack, *Interpreting Regulations,* 111 Mich. L. Rev. 355, 356–357 (2012); Christopher J. Walker, *Inside Agency Statutory Interpretation,* 67 Stan. L. Rev. 999, 1000–1001 (2015).

2. Eric Posner, *Imbalance of Power,* EricPosner.com, Feb. 7, 2014, http://ericposner.com/imbalance-of-power/.

3. U.S. Const. art. II, sec. 3; Gillian E. Metzger, *The Constitutional Duty to Supervise,* 124 Yale L.J. 1836 (2015).

4. William Howell, *Power without Persuasion: The Politics of Direct Presidential Action* (Princeton: Princeton University Press: 2003); Neal Devins & David E. Lewis, *Not-So Independent Agencies: Party Polarization and the Limits of Institutional Design,* 88 B.U. L. Rev. 459, 485 (2008) ("When the parties are polarized and the White House and Congress are divided, Presidents have strong incentives to pursue unilateral policymaking through loyal appointees."); Elena Kagan, *Presidential Administration,* 114 Harv. L. Rev. 2245, 2248 (2001) (stressing the importance of policymaking through administrative channels during times of divided or obstructionist constitutional government); Gillian E. Metzger, *Embracing Administrative Common Law,* 80 Geo. Wash. L. Rev. 1293, 1322–1323 (2012) (characterizing legislative impasses as often prompting greater reliance on administrative policymaking).

5. Many leading scholarly accounts describing, modeling, or prescribing pathways of control have treated agencies as monolithic, hierarchical organizations. Though I am obviously generalizing from, and putting a stylized gloss on, a voluminous, nuanced, and multigenerational literature, my characterization of the scholarship matches that of Elizabeth Magill and Adrian Vermeule. Writing several years ago in the *Yale Law Journal,* Magill and Vermeule concluded that in "all of the standard debates" about administrative power and control, "agencies are typically treated as unitary entities." Elizabeth Magill & Adrian Vermeule, *Allocating Power within Agencies,* 120 Yale L.J. 1032, 1035 (2011).

6. *Gutierrez-Brizuela v. Lynch,* 834 F.3d 1142, 1152–1153 (10th Cir. 2016) (Gorsuch, J., concurring).

7. See generally David J. Barron, *From Takeover to Merger: Reforming Administrative Law in an Age of Agency Politicization,* 76 Geo. Wash. L. Rev. 1095 (2008); Peter L. Strauss, *Overseer, or "The Decider"? The President in Administrative Law,* 75 Geo. Wash. L. Rev. 696 (2007).

8. *Gutierrez-Brizuela,* 1153 (Gorsuch, J., concurring).
9. For classic treatments of capture, see Marver H. Bernstein, *Regulating Business by Independent Commission* (Princeton: Princeton University Press, 1955); Samuel P. Huntington, *The Marasmus of the ICC: The Commission, the Railroads, and the Public Interest,* 61 Yale L.J. 467 (1952).
10. *City of Arlington v. FCC,* 133 S. Ct. 1833, 1878 (2013) (Roberts, C.J., dissenting); Theodore J. Lowi, *The End of Liberalism: The Second Republic of the United States,* 121 (New York: W. W. Norton, 1979); Herbert Kaufman, *Fear of Bureaucracy: A Raging Pandemic,* 41 Pub. Adm. Rev. 1 (Jan/Feb 1981).
11. *Free Ent. Fund v. PCAOB,* 561 U.S. 477, 499 (2010).
12. At times, the concern is expressed in terms of insufficient presidential control, see Steven G. Calabresi & Christopher S. Yoo, *The Unitary Executive: Presidential Power from Washington to Bush* (New Haven: Yale University Press, 2008). See also *Myers v. United States,* 272 U.S. 52, 164 (1926); *Morrison v. Olson,* 487 U.S. 654, 706–710 (1988) (Scalia, J., dissenting); *City of Arlington,* 1878 (Roberts, C.J., dissenting). Alternatively, the concern may be framed in terms of the need for greater congressional control. See Terry M. Moe, *The New Economics of Organization,* 28 Am. J. Pol. Sci. 739, 765–769 (1984); Mathew D. McCubbins, Roger G. Noll, & Barry R. Weingast, *Administrative Procedures as Instruments of Political Control,* 3 J.L. Econ. & Org. 243 (1987); Mathew D. McCubbins, *Structure and Process, Politics and Policy: Administrative Arrangements and the Political Control of Agencies,* 75 Va. L. Rev. 431 (1989).
13. U.N. General Assembly member-states have endorsed the concept of "responsibility to protect" vulnerable populations in failing or failed states. *Report of the Secretary-General, Implementing the Responsibility to Protect,* United Nations General Assembly, Jan. 12, 2009, http://www.un.org/en/ga/search /view_doc.asp?symbol=A/63/677; *The Responsibility to Protect,* Office of the Special Adviser on the Prevention of Genocide, http://www.un.org /en/preventgenocide/adviser/responsibility.shtml. Legally and normatively speaking, responsibility to protect is not an unproblematic concept. See, for example, David Chandler, The Responsibility to Protect? Imposing the "Liberal Peace," in *Peace Operation and Global Order,* 59, 74–75 (Alex J. Bellamy & Paul Williams, eds.) (London: Routledge, 2005).
14. See, for example, Ronald E. Powaski, *The Cold War: The United States and the Soviet Union, 1917–1991,* at 87, 90 (New York: Oxford University Press, 1998).
15. See Abbe R. Gluck, Anne Joseph O'Connell, & Rosa Po, *Unorthodox Lawmaking, Unorthodox Rulemaking,* 115 Colum. L. Rev. 1789 (2015); John D. Graham & James W. Broughel, *Stealth Regulation: Addressing Agency Evasions of OIRA and the Administrative Procedure Act,* 1 Harv. J. L. & Pub. Pol'y: Federalist 31 (2014); Connor Raso, *Agency Avoidance of Rulemaking Procedures,* 67 Admin. L. Rev. (2015).
16. See, for example, Henry Kissinger, *Diplomacy,* 137 (New York: Simon & Schuster, 1994) (explaining *realpolitik* and describing a state of affairs in which "the major players of an international system are free to adjust their relations in accordance with changing circumstances").

17. Kenneth A. Shepsle, *Congress Is a "They," Not an "It": Legislative Intent as Oxymoron*, 12 Int'l Rev. L. & Econ. 239 (1992).

18. David Schoenbrod, *Power without Responsibility: How Congress Abuses the People through Delegation*, 13 (New Haven: Yale University Press, 1995).

19. Joshua D. Clinton, David E. Lewis, & Jennifer L. Selin, *Influencing the Bureaucracy: The Irony of Congressional Oversight*, 58 Am. J. Pol. Sci. 387, 389–390 (2014) (discussing Congress's difficulties in staying on top of its oversight responsibilities); Neal Kumar Katyal, *Internal Separation of Powers: Checking Today's Most Dangerous Branch from Within*, 115 Yale L.J. 2314, 2322, 2342 (2006) (suggesting that congressional oversight is intensive only in periods of divided government).

20. Mathew D. McCubbins & Thomas Schwartz, *Congressional Oversight Overlooked: Police Patrols versus Fire Alarms*, 28 Am. J. Pol. Sci. 165 (1984).

21. Jon D. Michaels, *Of Constitutional Custodians and Regulatory Rivals: An Account of the Old and New Separation of Powers*, 91 N.Y.U. L. Rev. 227, 248–249 (2016).

22. 463 U.S. 919 (1983); see also *Metropolitan Wash. Airports Auth. v. Noise Abatement Citizens*, 501 U.S. 252 (1991) (holding unconstitutional a congressional committee's veto over interstate airport authority decisions).

23. 524 U.S. 417 (1998).

24. Ibid., 436. See generally *Whitman v. Am. Trucking Ass'ns*, 531 U.S. 457, 472 (2001) ("[W]e repeatedly have said that when Congress confers decision-making authority upon agencies *Congress* must lay down by legislative act an intelligible principle.") (internal quotation and citation omitted).

25. *Clinton*, 469 (Scalia, J., concurring in part and dissenting in part).

26. For a more thorough treatment of *Clinton*, see Jon D. Michaels, *An Enduring, Evolving Separation of Powers*, 115 Colum. L. Rev. 515, 563–565 (2015).

27. Josh Chafetz, *Multiplicity in Federalism and the Separation of Powers*, 120 Yale L.J. 1084, 1112–1128 (2011) (proffering a "multiplicity-based theory of the separation of powers").

28. See generally Eric A. Posner & Adrian Vermeule, *Inside or Outside the System?*, 80 U. Chi. L. Rev. 1743 (2013).

29. Compare Matthew C. Stephenson, *The Strategic Substitution Effect: Textual Plausibility, Procedural Formality, and Judicial Review of Agency Statutory Interpretations*, 120 Harv. L. Rev. 528, 530 (2006) (positing that courts are likely to give agencies "more substantive latitude" when those agencies employ more "elaborate formal proce[dures]").

9. Judicial Custodialism

1. See John Hart Ely, *Democracy and Distrust* (Cambridge: Harvard University Press, 1980).

2. Ibid., 103.

3. 304 U.S. 144, 152 n.4 (1938).

4. Ely, *Distrust*, 102–103.

5. Compare Anita S. Krishnakumar, *Representation Reinforcement: A Legislative Solution to a Legislative Process Problem*, 46 Harv. J. on Legis. 1, 1–2 (2009) (explaining that "second-generation representation reinforcement scholars" police the process to "ameliorate fundamental representational inequalities in the legislative process").

6. Compare Stephen Breyer, *Breaking the Vicious Circle: Toward Effective Risk Regulation*, 72 (Cambridge: Harvard University Press, 1993) (positing that an interdisciplinary set of administrative officials charged with reviewing agency actions might be "better equipped to investigate general, science-related facts than a court" and might "supplant . . . review by a court").

7. Gillian E. Metzger, *Ordinary Administrative Law as Constitutional Common Law*, 110 Colum. L. Rev. 479 (2010).

8. *Citizens to Preserve Overton Park v. Volpe*, 401 U.S. 402, 416 (1971) (explaining that in reviewing agency actions, a court "is not empowered to substitute its judgment for that of the agency").

9. Ibid. (describing its review of agency determinations of fact or policy as "narrow").

10. Ibid.; see also 5 U.S.C. § 706(2)(A).

11. Empirical studies documenting how long it takes to promulgate federal rules are in scant supply. For one unpublished report, see Stuart Shapiro, *Explaining Ossification: An Examination of the Time to Finish Rulemakings*, Aug. 11, 2009, http://ssrn.com/abstract=1447337.

12. See Elizabeth Magill & Adrian Vermeule, *Allocating Power within Agencies*, 120 Yale L.J. 1032 (2011) (explaining how changes in administrative caselaw empower or marginalize different groups within agencies).

13. *Massachusetts v. EPA*, 549 U.S. 497 (2007); *Motor Vehicle Mfrs. Ass'n v. State Farm Mut. Auto. Ins. Co.*, 463 U.S. 29 (1983).

14. Jody Freeman & Adrian Vermeule, *Massachusetts v. EPA: From Politics to Expertise*, 2007 Sup. Ct. Rev. 51, 52 (describing recent Supreme Court opinions that "override executive positions found untrustworthy, in the sense that executive expertise had been subordinated to politics"); see also Matthew C. Stephenson, *A Costly Signaling Theory of "Hard Look" Judicial Review*, 58 Admin. L. Rev. 753, 758 (2006) (explaining that courts "vary the effort they use and the rigor they apply to hard look review" based on, among other things, the "trustworthiness of the agency involved to provide careful and unbiased analyses").

15. Gillian E. Metzger, *The Interdependent Relationship between Internal and External Separation of Powers*, 59 Emory L.J. 423, 445 (2009).

16. 533 U.S. 218 (2001).

17. See Lisa Schultz Bressman, *Procedures as Politics in Administrative Law*, 107 Colum. L. Rev. 1749, 1791 (2009) (suggesting that *Mead* demands more rigorous scrutiny of informal agency actions rendered without the benefit of public input and deliberation); Jon D. Michaels, *An Enduring, Evolving Separation of Powers*, 115 Colum. L. Rev. 515, 565–566 (2015) (characterizing *Mead* as privileging agency decisions that reflect meaningful participation of agency leaders, civil servants, and members of the public).

18. *Mead,* 533 U.S. at 244–245 (Scalia, J., dissenting) (predicting that agencies will accept the Court's nudge and opt for more robust, inclusive forms of agency decisionmaking to ensure that their decisions and interpretations receive greater judicial deference).

19. Kent Barnett & Christopher J. Walker, *Chevron in the Circuit Courts,* 115 Mich. L. Rev. __ (forthcoming 2017).

20. See *Vermont Yankee Nuclear Power Corp. v. NRDC,* 435 U.S. 519, 524 (1978); Ronald J. Krotoszynski, Jr., *The Bazelon-Leventhal Debate and the Continuing Relevance of the Process/Substance Dichotomy in Judicial Review of Agency Action,* 58 Admin. L. Rev. 995, 996 (2006) (*"Vermont Yankee* . . . definitively rejected process-based review of agency action in favor of substantive 'hard look' review.").

21. See, for example, Richard B. Stewart, *Vermont Yankee and the Evolution of Administrative Procedure,* 91 Harv. L. Rev. 1805, 1819 (1978) (criticizing *Vermont Yankee*'s turn away from process-based review and arguing that "the courts' role in procedural innovation ha[d] been on the whole helpful and constructive").

22. See Ely, *Distrust,* 102.

23. See, for example, Krotoszynski, *Bazelon-Leventhal,* 999–1002.

24. *NRDC v. NRC,* 547 F.2d 633, 657 (D.C. Cir. 1976) (Bazelon, C. J., concurring) (internal citations omitted); *Ethyl Corp. v. EPA,* 541 F.2d 1, 67 (D.C. Cir. 1976) (en banc) (Bazelon, C.J., concurring) ("Because substantive review of mathematical or scientific evidence by technically illiterate judges is dangerously unreliable, I continue to believe we will do more to improve administrative decision-making by concentrating our efforts on strengthening administrative procedures.").

25. Krotoszynski, *Bazelon-Leventhal,* 996–997 (explaining how the Leventhal-Bazelon debate was resolved in favor of those, like Judge Leventhal, preferring a jurisprudence centered on merits-based review).

26. See Matthew C. Stephenson, *The Strategic Substitution Effect: Textual Plausibility, Procedural Formality, and Judicial Review of Agency Statutory Interpretations,* 120 Harv. L. Rev. 528, 558–564 (2006) (explaining how courts can titrate deference to encourage agencies to adopt more rigorous procedures).

27. Compare Laurence H. Tribe, *The Puzzling Persistence of Process-Based Constitutional Theories,* 89 Yale L.J. 1063, 1063–1070 (1980) (critiquing Ely and arguing that process-based theories require grounding in substantive rights or values) with James E. Fleming, *Securing Constitutional Democracy: The Case of Autonomy,* 26–27 (Chicago: University of Chicago Press, 2006) (describing Ely's reinforcing representative democracy as "a process-perfecting theory that perfects process by virtue of its substantive basis in a political theory of representative democracy").

28. Cass R. Sunstein & Adrian Vermeule, *The New Coke: On the Plural Aims of Administrative Law,* 2015 Sup. Ct. Rev. 41.

29. See *Ethyl Corp.,* 541 F.2d at 67 (Bazelon, C.J., concurring) (underscoring the problems with courts reviewing the substance of agency decisions of a technical nature); Lisa Schultz Bressman, *Beyond Accountability: Arbitrariness*

and Legitimacy in the Administrative State, 78 N.Y.U. L. Rev. 461, 548 (2003) (indicating that critics "have characterized the use of hard look doctrine as an excuse for courts to substitute their generalist judgment for the specialized judgment of agencies"); Breyer, *Vicious Circle,* 72.

30. *Brown v. Allen,* 344 U.S. 443, 540 (1953) (Jackson, J., concurring).
31. See Charles W. Tyler & E. Donald Elliot, *Administrative Severability Clauses,* 124 Yale L.J. 1286, 1288 (2015) (paraphrasing a comment often attributed to Jerry Mashaw).
32. *Vermont Yankee,* 435 U.S. at 519.
33. Metzger, *Ordinary Administrative Law,* 508–510 (describing much of what we think of as everyday administrative law and jurisprudence as inflected with overriding "[c]onstitutional concerns with unchecked agency power").
34. Indeed, federal government contracting is generally encouraged. See Competition in Contracting Act of 1984, § 2711, Pub. L. No. 98–366, 98 Stat. 1175, 1175–1181 (codified at 41 U.S.C. § 253); the Federal Activities Inventory Reform Act of 1998 (FAIR Act), § 2(a), Pub. L. No. 105–270, 112 Stat. 2382 (1998) (codified at 31 U.S.C. § 501(2)(a)); Office of Budget and Management, *Circular A-76 (Revised), Performance of Commercial Activities* 1–3, May 29, 2003, http://www.whitehouse.gov/omb/circulars/a076/a76 _ rev2003.pdf. See also Harold J. Krent, *The Private Performing the Public: Delimiting Delegations to Private Parties,* 65 U. Miami L. Rev. 507, 540, 546 (2011) (noting that "[p]ublic and private officials largely exercise functions that are indistinguishable").
35. See, for example, *Currin v. Wallace,* 306 U.S. 1, 6, 15 (1939).
36. See *Hartman v. Moore,* 547 U.S. 250, 263 (2006); *U.S. Postal Serv. v. Gregory,* 534 U.S. 1, 10 (2001) ("[A] presumption of regularity attaches to the actions of Government agencies . . .").
37. Aaron M. Kessler, *Ex-AIG Chief Wins Bailout Suit, but Gets No Damages,* N.Y. Times, Jun. 16, 2015, https://www.nytimes.com/2015/06/16/business /dealbook/judge-sides-with-ex-aig-chief-greenberg-against-us-but-awards-no -money.html.
38. Ibid.
39. Ibid.; Gretchen Morgenson, *Court Casts a New Light on the Bailout,* N.Y. Times, Sept. 27, 2014, http://www.nytimes.com/2014/09/28/business/court -casts-a-new-light-on-a-bailout.html.
40. See, for example, Steven Croley, *White House Review of Agency Rulemaking: An Empirical Investigation,* 70 U. Chi. L. Rev. 821, 877 (2003); William F. West, *The Institutionalization of Regulatory Review: Organizational Stability and Responsive Competence at OIRA,* 35 Pres. Stud. Q. 76 (2005).
41. Croley, *White House Review,* 877.
42. See Stuart Shapiro, *OIRA Inside and Out,* 63 Admin. L. Rev. 135, 141 (2011).
43. See, for example, Lisa Heinzerling, *Inside EPA: A Former Insider's Reflections on the Relationship between the Obama EPA and the Obama White House,* 31 Pace Envtl. L. Rev. 325, 335 (2014) (expressing concerns over interventions by OIRA that "leave no public trail").

44. See *Free Enter. Fund v. PCAOB,* 561 U.S. 477 (2010) (effectively countenancing a single layer of insulation between the president and agency heads); *Morrison v. Olson,* 487 U.S. 654 (1998) (applying a broad and generous test for assessing the constitutionality of independent officials).

45. *Morrison,* 487 U.S. at 706–710 (Scalia, J., dissenting).

46. Aziz Z. Huq, *Removal as a Political Question,* 65 Stan. L. Rev. 1, 27–28 (2013).

47. See, for example, Brian D. Feinstein, *Designing Executive Agencies for Congressional Control,* __ Admin. L. Rev. __ (forthcoming 2017). For scholarship suggesting that the president retains considerable influence over independent agency officials, see Kirti Datla & Richard L. Revesz, *Deconstructing Independent Agencies (and Executive Agencies),* 98 Cornell L. Rev. 769, 772–773 (2013); Neal Devins & David E. Lewis, *Not-So Independent Agencies: Party Polarization and the Limits of Institutional Design,* 88 B.U. L. Rev. 459, 491–492 (2008).

48. See Rachel E. Barkow, *Insulating Agencies: Avoiding Capture through Institutional Design,* 89 Tex. L. Rev. 15, 19, 24 (2010); Lisa Schultz Bressman & Robert B. Thompson, *The Future of Agency Independence,* 63 Vand. L. Rev. 599, 613 (2010).

49. Again, presidents do have some influence over independent commissioners. See Datla & Revesz, *Deconstructing,* 772–773; Devins & Lewis, *Not-So Independent,* 491–492. Moreover, the fact that rank-and-file employees and agency heads have different responsibilities within agencies might well create distance between the two groups and engender rivalry.

50. Steven G. Calabresi & Christopher S. Yoo, *The Unitary Executive: Presidential Power from Washington to Bush* (New Haven: Yale University Press, 2008); *Morrison,* 487 U.S. at 699–711 (1988) (Scalia, J., dissenting); *Myers v. United States,* 272 U.S. 52, 163–164 (1926).

51. Curtis W. Copeland, *The Federal Workforce: Characteristics and Trends,* Cong. Res. Serv., Apr. 19, 2011, http://assets.opencrs.com/rpts/RL34685_20110419.pdf/ (detailing the rapid increases in the size, cost, and influence of national security and foreign affairs agencies).

52. Oona A. Hathaway, *Presidential Power over International Law,* 119 Yale L.J. 140, 221–224 (2009); Adrian Vermeule, *Our Schmittian Administrative Law,* 122 Harv. L. Rev. 1095 (2009).

53. 5 U.S.C. § 553(a)(1).

54. 5 U.S.C. § 552(b)(1).

55. See Neal Kumar Katyal, *Internal Separation of Powers: Checking Today's Most Dangerous Branch from Within,* 115 Yale L.J. 2314, 2333 (2006) (describing the weakening of job protections for many employees in national security agencies).

56. See, for example, Robert M. Chesney, *State Secrets and the Limits of National Security Litigation,* 75 Geo. Wash. L. Rev. 1249 (2007) (emphasizing how difficult it is to sue the United States in matters pertaining to national security).

57. But see Jack L. Goldsmith, *Power and Constraint: The Accountable Presidency after 9/11,* at 209–210 (New York: W. W. Norton, 2012)

(describing the "modern presidential synopticon," with civil society monitoring executive activity on issues of national security); Katyal, *Internal Separation of Powers* (observing and endorsing some modest forms of intra-agency constraints in national security domains).

58. Kevin R. Kosar, *Federal Government Corporations: An Overview*, Cong. Serv. Res., June 8, 2011, http://fas.org/sgp/crs/misc/RL30365.pdf; Anne Joseph O'Connell, *Bureaucracy at the Boundary*, 162 U. Penn. L. Rev. 841 (2015).

59. See Kosar, *Federal Government Corporations* (characterizing government corporations as largely exempt from many of the most critical administrative laws and regulations).

60. *Lebron v. Nat'l R.R. Passenger Corp.*, 513 U.S. 374, 397 (1995).

61. *INS v. Chadha*, 462 U.S. 919 (1983).

62. *Clinton v. City of New York*, 524 U.S. 417, 439–441, 447 (1998).

63. Compare *Wiener v. United States*, 357 U.S. 349, 355–356 (1958) (interpreting the president's power to remove members of the adjudicatory War Claims Commission as circumscribed by a "for cause" requirement); *Myers*, 272 U.S. at 135 (acknowledging that "there may be duties of a quasi-judicial character . . . the discharge of which the President cannot in a particular case properly influence or control").

64. 299 U.S. 304, 319 (1936) (characterizing the president as the "sole organ" of external relations and foreign affairs); see also John Yoo, *The Powers of War and Peace: The Constitution and Foreign Affairs after 9/11* (Chicago: University of Chicago Press, 2008) (insisting on presidential primacy in matters of foreign affairs and national security). Compare Jack L. Goldsmith, *The Terror Presidency: Law and Judgment inside the Bush Administration* (New York: W. W. Norton, 2007) (ascribing unilateral presidentialist views to many of the leading officials in the George W. Bush administration).

65. For instance, the Court has affirmed the practice of states engaging in effectively discriminatory market transactions that favor in-state interests. It has done so notwithstanding the fact that such discriminatory practices would violate the Dormant Commerce Clause if exercised through the tax code or through conventional lawmaking or administrative rulemaking. See, for example, *Reeves, Inc. v. Stake*, 447 U.S. 429, 436–437 (1980); *Hughes v. Alexandria Scrap Corp.*, 426 U.S. 794, 808–810 (1976). Moreover, the Court has relaxed the "strict demands of the one-person, one-vote principle" when it comes to the design of voting rules for government-created water districts. *Ball v. James*, 451 U.S. 355 (1981) (underscoring the commercial nature of a water district's powers).

66. Many such responsibilities correspond to powers the Constitution entrusts principally, or at least in part, to Congress. See U.S. Const. art. I, sec. 8, cl. 3, 11–16 (enumerating military and foreign affairs powers granted to Congress). See also *Hamdi v. Rumsfeld*, 542 U.S. 507, 569 (2004) (Scalia, J., dissenting) ("Except for the actual command of military forces, all authorization for their maintenance and all explicit authorization for their use is placed under the control of Congress under Article I, rather than the President under Article II.").

67. See, for example, *Ass'n of Am. R.Rs v. U.S. Dep't of Trans.*, 821 F.3d 19 (D.C. Cir. 2016) (finding Amtrak's dual status as market participant and market regulator constitutionally problematic); Jon D. Michaels, Government Market Participation as Conflicted Government, in *Administrative Law from the Inside Out: Essays on Themes in the Work of Jerry Mashaw*, 451 (Nicholas Parrillo, ed.) (New York: Cambridge University Press, 2017).

68. Susan M. Gates & Albert A. Robbert, *Personnel Savings in Competitively Sourced DoD Activities*, RAND 42 (2000), https://www.rand.org/content /dam/rand/pubs/monograph_reports/2007/MR1117.pdf.

10. Legislative Custodialism

1. John F. Kennedy, *Remarks at the Convocation of the United Negro College Fund*, Indianapolis, IN, Apr. 12, 1959, https://www.jfklibrary.org/Research /Research-Aids/JFK-Speeches/Indianapolis-IN_19590412.aspx. A version of the Kennedy remark has been popularized by Rahm Emanuel, who quipped: "Never allow a crisis to go to waste. They are opportunities to do big things." Jeff Zeleny, *Obama Weighs Quick Undoing of Bush Policy*, N.Y. Times, Nov. 9, 2008, http://www.nytimes.com/2008/11/10/us/politics/10obama.html.

2. See *Report of the National Commission on the Public Service, Urgent Business for America: Revitalizing the Federal Government for the 21st Century* (2003), http://ourpublicservice.org/publications/viewcontentdetails .php?id=314 (describing the contemporary federal workforce as poorly motivated and explaining that the best federal civil servants are underpaid); *Federal Workforce: Recent Trends in Federal Civilian Employment and Compensation*, Gov't Accountability Office, Jan. 2014, http://www.gao.gov /assets/670/660449.pdf ("[L]arge numbers of retirement-eligible employees in the years ahead may be cause for concern: Their retirement could produce mission critical skills gaps if left unaddressed."); Josh Hicks, *Shrinking Government: Federal Hiring Is Down, Departures Are Up*, Wash. Post, Aug. 20, 2014, https://www.washingtonpost.com/news/federal-eye/wp/2014 /08/20/shrinking-government-federal-hiring-is-down-departures-are-up/; Joe Davidson, *New Report Documents Falling Federal Employee Morale*, Wash. Post, Jul. 15, 2015, https://www.washingtonpost.com/news/federal-eye /wp/2015/07/15/new-report-documents-falling-federal-employee-morale/; Joe Davidson, *Report Shows Federal Workers Are Increasingly Dreary about Their Jobs*, Wash. Post, Nov. 16, 2011, http://www.washingtonpost.com /politics/report-shows-federal-workers-are-increasingly-dreary-about-their -jobs/2011/11/16/gIQAjaIXSN_story.html; Andy Medici, *Federal Innovation Continues to Suffer as Morale Drops*, Fed. Times, Apr. 2, 2015, http://www .federaltimes.com/story/government/management/agency/2015/04/02/federal -innovation/70823306/. Note that employees in the highly marketized Department of Homeland Security experience some of the lowest morale in the federal bureaucracy. See Eric Katz, *No One's Morale Is Dropping Faster Than Homeland Security*, Defense One, Oct. 5, 2015, http://www.defenseone

.com/management/2015/10/no-ones-morale-dropping-faster-homeland
-security/122546/.

3. See *Policy Spotlight: Insourcing: The Pendulum Swing,* Service Contractor,
   Sept. 2009, at 25, 26 ("President Obama has clearly stated his intention to
   reverse this [privatization] trend and to focus on rebuilding and reinvigo-
   rating the civil service."); Memorandum from Deputy Secretary of Defense
   William Lynn, *Insourcing Contracted Services—Implementation Guidance,*
   7, May 28, 2009, http://www.asamra.army.mil/scra/documents/DepSecDef
   %20Memo%2028MAY09%20In-sourcing%20Implementation%20
   Guidance.pdf; see also Loren Thompson, *Pentagon Insourcing Binge Begins
   to Unravel,* Forbes, Mar. 7, 2011, http://www.forbes.com/sites/beltway
   /2011/03/07/pentagon-insourcing-binge-begins-to-unravel/#3a6a16496091
   (citing then Pentagon chief Robert Gates as initially promising to reduce DoD
   reliance on contractors from 39 percent to 26 percent and to hire up to
   30,000 new civil servants).

4. Thompson, *Insourcing* (explaining the difficulties and obstacles associated
   with advancing the insourcing agenda).

5. Hillary Rodham Clinton, *Clinton's Speech on Iraq,* Council on Foreign
   Relations, Mar. 17, 2008, http://www.cfr.org/iraq/clintons-speech-iraq
   -march-2008/p15742; Noah Shachtman, *Clinton, Obama Tussle over
   Blackwater,* Wired, Feb. 29, 2008, http://www.wired.com/2008/02/just-as
   -blackwa/. See generally S. 2398 Stop Outsourcing Security Act, 110th Cong.,
   http://thomas.loc.gov/cgi-bin/bdquery/z?d110:s.02398.

6. See Spencer Ackerman, *Despite Clinton Pledge, State Dept. to Pay Out
   Billions More to Mercs,* Wired, Sept. 29, 2010, https://www.wired.com
   /2010/09/despite-clinton-pledge-state-department-ready-to-pay-mercs-billions/;
   Mark Landler & Mark Mazzetti, *U.S. Still Using Security Firm It Broke
   With,* N.Y. Times, Aug. 21, 2009, http://www.nytimes.com/2009/08/22/us
   /22intel.html.

7. *Iraq: "Blackwater Must Go,"* CNN, Oct. 17, 2007, http://www.cnn
   .com/2007/WORLD/meast/10/16/iraq.blackwater/index.html; *U.S. Dep't of
   State, Information Memorandum: Blackwater Contractor Performance in
   Iraq,* N.Y. Times, Aug. 31, 2007, http://www.nytimes.com/interactive/2014
   /06/30/us/30blackwater-documents.html.

8. Joshua Partlow, *Karzai Wants Private Security Firms Out of Afghanistan,*
   Wash. Post, Aug. 17, 2010, http://www.washingtonpost.com/wpdyn/content
   /article/2010/08/ 16/AR2010081602041.html?sid=ST2010081700028.

9. *Blackwater Most Often Shoots First, Congressional Report Says,* CNN,
   Oct. 2, 2007, http://www.cnn.com/2007/WORLD/meast/10/01/blackwater
   .report/; Katherine Zoepf & Atheer Kakan, *U.S. Prosecutor Goes to Iraq to
   Work on Blackwater Case,* N.Y. Times, Dec. 7, 2008, http://www.nytimes
   .com/2008/12/08/world/middleeast/08iraq.html; Mark Mazzetti & James
   Risen, *Blackwater Said to Pursue Bribes to Iraq after 17 Died,* N.Y. Times,
   Nov. 10, 2009, http://www.nytimes.com/2009/11/11/world/middleeast
   /11blackwater.html?pagewanted=all.

10. John J. DiIulio, Jr., *Bring Back the Bureaucrats: Why More Federal Workers*

Will Lead to Better (and Smaller!) Government (West Conshohocken, PA: Templeton Press, 2014).

11. See, for example, Alon Harel & Ariel Porat, *Commensurability and Agency: Two Yet-to-Be-Met Challenges for Law and Economics,* 96 Cornell L. Rev. 749, 772 (2011) (commenting on the federal prohibition on outsourcing "inherently governmental functions," remarking on the vagueness of the prohibition, and underscoring how "federal agencies use different definitions and interpretations"); Paul R. Verkuil, *Public Law Limitations on Privatization of Government Functions,* 84 N.C. L Rev. 397, 401–402, 457 (2006) ("[The] pro-privatization environment erodes whatever limits [the inherently governmental functions] phrase implies.").

12. Rhodes Scholarships, *Number of Winners by Institution,* The Rhodes Trust (2016), http://www.rhodesscholar.org/assets/uploads/RS_Number%20of% 20Winners%20by%20Institution_1_15_16.pdf. In 2016, Virginia Military School tied (with eight other schools) for 82 on *U.S. News & World Report*'s annual rankings of American liberal arts colleges. *National Liberal Arts Colleges Rankings,* U.S. News & World Rept. (2016), http://colleges .usnews.rankingsandreviews.com/best-colleges/rankings/national-liberal-arts -colleges/data/page+4.

13. 10 U.S.C. §§ 4360, 6979, 9360 (prohibiting charges or fees for tuition, room, or board at the military service academies); 10 U.S.C. §§ 4348, 6959, 9348 (requiring graduating students at the military academies to serve five years as active duty officers).

14. Ian Duncan, *Mids Get Their Career Assignments,* Balt. Sun, Nov. 21, 2014, http://www.baltimoresun.com/news/maryland/anne-arundel/annapolis/bs-md -naval-academy-service-assignments-20141120-story.html; Kathy Eastwood, *West Point Class of 2012 Cadets Select First Duty Assignment,* Army News, Feb. 13, 2012, http://www.army.mil/article/73653/West_Point_Class_of _2012_cadets_select_first_duty_assignments/; see also Ben Fox Rubin, *At West Point, "Goats" Are an Exclusive Bunch,* Wall St. J. Nov. 26, 2012, http://www.wsj.com/articles/SB10001424127887324352004578131262893 535452 (describing the successful careers of West Point graduates who performed poorly as students).

15. I am indebted to UCLA Law graduate Anthony Resnick for his seminar paper on what he called a "Public Service Academy."

16. See Michael Duggett with Manueline Desbouvries, The Civil Service in France: Contested Complacency? in *International Handbook on Civil Service Systems,* 327, 330–333 (Andrew Massey, ed.) (Cheltenham, UK: Edward Elgar, 2011); Marie-Christine Meininger, The Development and Current Features of the French Civil Service System, in *Civil Service Systems in Western Europe,* 188, 191 (Hans A. G. M. Bekke & Frits M. van der Meer, eds.) (Cheltenham, UK: Edward Elgar, 2000) ("[T]he French civil service is among the most powerful in the world. High-ranking civil servants enjoy a social prestige comparable to that of federal judges in the United States."); *A Civil Self-Service,* Economist, Apr. 29, 1999, http://www.economist.com /node/202515 ("[U]nlike public servants in many other countries, French bureaucrats are on the whole liked by their compatriots."). See generally

Francis Fukuyama, *Political Order and Political Decay,* 71 (New York: Farrar, Straus and Giroux, 2014) (describing elite training academies in France, in what was Prussia, and in Japan after the Meiji Restoration).

17. Donald F. Kettl, *The Next Government of the United States: Why Our Institutions Fail Us and How to Fix Them,* 266–267 (New York: W. W. Norton, 2009) (decrying the federal government's inability and unwillingness to train the next generation of government leaders).

18. *College Tuition Costs Soar: Chart of the Day,* Bloomberg News, Aug. 18, 2014, http://www.bloomberg.com/news/articles/2014-08-18/college-tuition -costs-soar-chart-of-the-day (reporting on the dramatic rise in college costs, far outpacing the increases in the cost of housing, medicine, food, and in the overall consumer price index); Annalyn Censky, *Surging College Costs Price Out Middle Class,* CNN, Jun. 13, 2011, http://money.cnn.com/2011/06/13 /news/economy/college_tuition_middle_class/; Jim Puzzanghera, *Soaring Student Loan Debt Poses Risks to Nation's Future Economic Growth,* L.A. Times, Sept. 5, 2015, http://www.latimes.com/business/la-fi-student-debt -20150906-story.html.

19. Paul C. Light, *A Government Ill Executed: The Decline of the Federal Service and How to Reverse It,* 136, 145 (Cambridge: Harvard University Press, 2008).

20. Lisa Rein, *For Federal-Worker Hopefuls, the Civil Service Exam Is Making a Comeback,* Wash. Post, Apr. 2, 2015, https://www.washingtonpost.com /news/federal-eye/wp/2015/04/02/for-federal-worker-hopefuls-the-civil-service -exam-is-making-a-comeback/ (noting that the federal government is "over- whelmed" by the number of applicants, with "some vacancies attracting hun- dreds of applicants" and with some applicants waiting "more than six months . . . [to] receive a form letter telling them they didn't get the job").

21. Light, *Government Ill Executed,* 131.

22. Ibid., 132–133.

23. Ibid., 131.

24. See Zaid Jilani, *The Privatization of Public Service,* Billmoyers.com, Nov. 21, 2013, http://billmoyers.com/2013/11/21/the-privatization-of-public-service/ (documenting the high incidence of students seeking and securing private sector employment upon being graduated from "government" schools of public policy and public administration).

25. *Confidence in Institutions,* Gallup (2015), http://www.gallup.com/poll/1597 /confidence-institutions.aspx.

26. Derek Thompson, *War and Peace in 30 Seconds,* Atlantic, Jan. 30, 2012, http://www.theatlantic.com/business/archive/2012/01/war-and-peace-in-30 -seconds-how-much-does-the-military-spend-on-ads/252222/.

27. *Fast Food Marketing Ranking Tables, 2012–2013,* Yale Rudd Center for Food Policy and Obesity (2013), http://www.fastfoodmarketing.org/media /fastfoodfacts_marketingrankings.pdf.

28. Office of Mgmt. & Budget, *Exec. Office of the President, Table 32–1, Federal Budget by Agency & Account,* 249–250 (2013), https://www.whitehouse .gov/sites/default/files/omb/budget/fy2014/assets/32_1.pdf.

29. U.S. Dep't of Labor, *Wage & Hour Division, Congressional Budget*

Justification, Fiscal Year 2012 (2011), https://www.dol.gov/dol/budget/2012 /PDF/CBJ-2012-V2-03.pdf.

30. U.S. Dep't of Transportation, Office of the Assistant Secretary for Research & Technology, *National Highway Traffic Safety Administration, Fiscal Year 2012* (2011), http://www.rita.dot.gov/sites/default/files/publications/annual _funding/2012_house_subcommittee/html/nhtsa.html.

31. Danielle Ivory, *Federal Auditor Finds Broad Failures at N.H.T.S.A.*, N.Y. Times, Jun. 19, 2015, http://www.nytimes.com/2015/06/20/business/federal -auditor-finds-broad-failures-at-nhtsa.html?_r=0.

32. Stuart Elliott, *Army Seeks Recruits in Social Media*, N.Y. Times, May 24, 2011, http://www.nytimes.com/2011/05/25/business/media/25adco.html?_r=0.

33. David Sirota, *How the '80s Programmed Us for War*, Salon, Mar. 15, 2011, http://www.salon.com/2011/03/15/sirota_excerpt_back_to_our_future/ (describing General Alexander Haig's involvement with the script to *Red Dawn*); Reed Beebe, *"Super-Soldiers": The U.S. Military's Controversial Sponsorship of Superhero Films*, Nothing but Comics, Dec. 9, 2014, http:// nothingbutcomics.net/2014/12/09/militarysponsorssuperherofilms/.

34. Robert Lindsey, *"Top Gun:" Ingenious Dogfights*, N.Y. Times, May. 27, 1986, http://www.nytimes.com/1986/05/27/movies/top-gun-ingenious-dogfights .html; Sirota, *'80s* (reporting that the Top Gun "script was shaped by Pentagon brass in exchange for full access to all sorts of [Navy] hardware").

35. Sirota, *'80s*.

36. Emmarie Huetteman, *Senate Report Says Pentagon Paid Sports Leagues for Patriotic Events*, N.Y. Times, Nov. 4, 2015, https://www.nytimes.com /politics/first-draft/2015/11/04/senate-report-says-pentagon-paid-sports -leagues-for-patriotic-events/.

37. Stuart Elliott, *Army's New Battle Cry Aims at Potential Recruits*, N.Y. Times, Nov. 9, 2006, http://www.nytimes.com/2006/11/09/business/media/09adco .html.

38. Stanley G. Payne, *The Franco Regime: 1939–1975*, at 530 (Madison, WI: University of Wisconsin Press, 1987).

39. Kettl, *Next Government*, 33.

40. Ibid.

41. *See* Wendy Wagner, et al., *Rulemaking in the Shade: An Empirical Study of EPA's Toxic Emission Standards*, 63 Admin. L. Rev. 99 (2011); Jason Webb Yackee & Susan Webb Yackee, *A Bias towards Business? Assessing Interest Group Influence on the U.S. Bureaucracy*, 68 J. Pol. 128 (2006); Kimberly D. Krawiec, *Don't "Screw Joe the Plumber": The Sausage-Making of Financial Reform*, 55 Ariz. L. Rev. 53 (2013).

42. *Whitman v. Am Trucking Ass'ns, Inc.*, 531 U.S. 457, 468 (2001).

43. Already other scholars and legal reformers are moving in this direction. See, for example, Michael Herz, *Using Social Media in Rulemaking: Possibilities and Barriers, Final Rept. to the Admin. Conf. of the United States*, Nov 21, 2013, https://www.acus.gov/sites/default/files/documents/Herz%20Social%20Media %20Final%20Report.pdf; Cynthia R. Farina, *Achieving the Potential: The Future of Federal E-Rulemaking, Committee on the Status and Future of*

Federal e-Rulemaking (2008), http://scholarship.law.cornell.edu/cgi/viewcontent .cgi?article=2505&context=facpub; Cynthia R. Farina, et al., *Rulemaking 2.0*, 65 U. Miami L. Rev. 395 (2011); Cary Coglianese, *Citizen Participation in Rulemaking: Past, Present, and Future*, 55 Duke L.J. 943 (2006); Jeffrey S. Lubbers, *The Transformation of the U.S. Rulemaking Process—For Better or Worse*, 34 Ohio N.U. L. Rev. 469 (2008); Elizabeth G. Porter & Kathryn A. Watts, *Visual Rulemaking*, 91 N.Y.U. L. Rev. 1183 (2016).

44. Robert D. Putnam, *Bowling Alone: The Collapse and Revival of American Community* (New York: Simon & Schuster, 2000).

45. To be clear, for years now, we have had e-rulemaking initiatives, which enable individuals and groups to file and review comments electronically.

46. 5 U.S.C. § 553(b).

47. *Mullane v. Central Hanover Bank & Trust Co.*, 339 U.S. 306 (1950).

48. Michael Herz, *We Are All Publicists Now*, Regulatory Rev., May 3, 2016, https://www.theregreview.org/2016/05/03/herz-we-are-all-publicists-now/.

49. Ibid.

50. Environmental Protection Agency, *Application of Publicity or Propaganda and Anti-Lobbying Provisions*, Gov't Accountability Office, Dec. 14, 2015, http://www.gao.gov/assets/680/674163.pdf.

51. Herz, *Publicists Now*.

52. Herz, *Using Social Media in Rulemaking*.

53. Cynthia R. Farina, et al., *The Problem with Words: Plain Language and Public Participation in Rulemaking*, 83 Geo. Wash. L. Rev. 1358 (2015).

54. See, for example, Rachel Stabler, *"What We've Got Here Is Failure to Communicate:" The Plain Writing Act of 2010*, 40 J. Legis. 280 (2013–2014).

55. One possible model is something akin to the legal periodical *Green Bag*'s "Almanac & Reader," which celebrates the year's best written judicial opinions, legal scholarship, and motions and briefs filed by practicing lawyers in federal and state courts. See http://greenbag.org/green_bag_press/almanacs /almanacs.html.

56. David Souter, *Remarks by Justice Souter*, 99 Geo. L.J. 157, 157 (2010).

57. Natasha Singer, *A Supreme Court Pioneer, Now Making Her Mark on Video Games*, N.Y. Times, Mar. 27, 2016, https://www.nytimes.com/2016/03/28 /technology/sandra-day-oconnor-supreme-court-video-games.html?_r=0.

58. *Letter from John Adams to Abigail Adams*, May 12, 1780, https://www .masshist.org/digitaladams/archive/doc?id=L17800512jasecond.

59. Yoni Appelbaum, *Yes, Virginia, There Is a NORAD*, Atlantic, Dec. 24, 2015, http://www.theatlantic.com/national/archive/2015/12/yes-virginia-there-is-a -norad/421161/.

Epilogue

Edward M. Kennedy, *Democratic National Convention*, Aug. 12, 1980, http://www.tedkennedy.org/ownwords/event/1980_convention.

ACKNOWLEDGMENTS

Eighty percent of life, so the saying goes, is just showing up. I've been fortunate to show up in all the right places. From Massapequa to Williamstown to Oxford to New Haven to Washington to Los Angeles, I have been supported, challenged, inspired, and loved. This book reflects my good fortune in being greeted with nothing but generosity every step of the way.

For incredibly helpful conversations, correspondence, and comments on this project at its various stages of development, thanks are owed to Bruce Ackerman, Frederic Bloom, Samuel Bray, Josh Chafetz, Conor Clarke, Kristen Eichensehr, Blake Emerson, David Fontana, Stephen Gardbaum, Heather Gerken, Abbe Gluck, Dan Guttman, Oona Hathaway, Aziz Huq, Harold Koh, Randy Kozel, Douglas Lichtman, Brian Lipshutz, Jerry Mashaw, Gillian Metzger, Anneliese Michaels, Toni Michaels, Hiroshi Motomura, Douglas NeJaime, Anne Joseph O'Connell, James Park, Nicholas Parrillo, Jeffrey Pojanowski, Robert Post, David Pozen, Sabeel Rahman, Richard Re, Judith Resnik, Cristina Rodriguez, Susan Rose-Ackerman, E.S. Savas, Steven Schooner, Reva Siegel, Kevin Stack, David Super, Paul Verkuil, Andrew Verstein, Alexander Volokh, Adam Winkler, and Noah Zatz.

Special thanks for their extraordinary support and encouragement belong to Bruce Ackerman, Frederic Bloom, Guido Calabresi, Ann Carlson, David Fontana, Aziz Huq, Jerry Mashaw, Toni Michaels, Martha Minow, Jennifer Mnookin, Hiroshi Motomura, Susan Rose-Ackerman, Steven Schooner, Nikhil Shanbhag, Reva Siegel, Alexander Slater, Jeffrey H. Smith, David Souter, and David Super.

This project benefited immeasurably from provocative and generative discussions at workshops, symposia, and conferences at the Cardozo School of Law, University of Chicago Law School, Duke Law School, University of Illinois College of Law, University of Maryland School of Law, Michigan State University College of Law, University of San Diego Law School, University of Southern California School of Law, UCLA School of Law, Vanderbilt Law School, University of Virginia School of Law, University of Wisconsin School of Law, and Yale Law School. It has likewise benefited from discussions, presentations, and conversations at the Administrative Conference of the United States, several annual meetings of the Association of American Law Schools, and a couple of American Constitution Society national conventions. I am grateful to the hosts and participants at all of these gatherings.

I have had the further privilege of developing, testing, and sharpening many of the ideas in this book in articles and essays published over the last several years. Though this book reaches further and deeper than those prior works—and includes a richer theoretical synthesis, greater historical contextualization, and an entirely new prescriptive blueprint—I would be remiss if I failed to mention that some of the project's central insights, conceptual building blocks, and foundational case studies first appeared on the pages of law reviews. Specifically, both my theory of an "administrative separation of powers" and my contention that privatization threatens this tripartite scheme originated in *An Enduring, Evolving Separation of Powers*, 115 Colum. L. Rev. 515 (2015); similarly, my efforts to work through the relationships between and among the constitutional and administrative rivals began in *Of Constitutional Custodians and Regulatory Rivals: An Account of the Old and New Separation of Powers*, 91 N.Y.U. L. Rev. 227 (2016). I analyzed the State-aggrandizing (and executive-enabling) effects of government contracting in *Privatization's Pretensions*, 77 U. Chi. L. Rev. 717 (2010); and I explored the parallels between government contracting and the "marketization of the bureaucracy" in *Privatization's Progeny*, 101 Geo. L.J. 1023 (2013). Ideas about specific forms of privatization and consideration of specific cases derive from the aforementioned *Privatization's Progeny* as well as from *The (Willingly) Fettered Executive: Presidential Spinoffs in National Security Domains and Beyond*, 97 Va. L. Rev. 801 (2011), and *Deputizing Homeland Security*, 88 Tex. L. Rev. 1435 (2010). I thank the staffs of those law reviews for their editorial guidance, substantive insights, and permissions.

I am particularly indebted to Deans Jennifer Mnookin, Rachel Moran, and Robert Post for their invaluable intellectual and institutional support; to the UCLA Faculty Senate for its generous research funding; to the UCLA Law librarians, especially Linda Karr O'Connor and Scott Dewey, for their expert and cheerful assistance; to Sydney Truong of the UCLA Law Faculty Support Group for keeping me afloat at work; to Elizabeth Knoll and Thomas LeBien, my editors at Harvard University Press, for championing my project and shepherding me through the publication process; and to my amazingly talented battalion of research assistants, Artin Afkhami, Claire Chung, Conor Clarke, Michael Grimaldi, Brian Lipshutz, Quinn Nguyen, Tyler O'Brien, Giovanni Saarman, Sina Safvati, Samuel Siegel, and Christian Vanderhooft, whose contributions high in the clouds of constitutional theory and deep in the weeds of regulatory minutiae strengthened not only this book but also my conviction that the future of the legal profession is in good hands.

Most importantly, for their unstinting love and patience, the biggest thanks of all are owed to my parents, Ellen and Larry; to my brother, Craig; and to Toni, Anneliese, Sammy, and Isabelle, the best sleuth a bear could ask for.

INDEX

Ackerman, Bruce, 50, 60, 69
Adams, John, 227
ADAPSO v. Camp, 36
Administrative agencies: constitutional
control over, 168–178; critiques of,
54–56, 85–86, 169–170; delegations to,
8, 16, 41, 46–47, 49, 52, 55, 150, 163,
173, 175–176, 199; fragmentation
within, 59–63, 73–75, 170; *pax
administrativa* and, 42–50. *See also*
Administrative separation of powers;
Administrative state, modern; Administrative state, premodern; Businesslike
government; Government contracting;
Marketization of the bureaucracy;
specific agencies
Administrative era. *See* Administrative
state, modern; New Deal; *Pax
administrativa*
Administrative Procedure Act (APA):
adjudication and, 47–48; administrative
separation of powers and, 62–63,
70–72, 162, 186; concerns with,
186–187, 218–226; informal rulemaking
and, 46–47; origins of, 46, 71;
quasi-constitutional (superstatute) status
of, 46, 65, 71–72; standardizing effects
of, 46, 71

Administrative separation of powers:
administrative theory and, 72–75;
agency leadership and, 59–60, 66;
analogies to constitutional separation of
powers (isomorphism) and, 65–68;
analogies to corporate governance
structures and, 164–165; "balanced"
agencies and, 170–171; constitutional
foundations of, 68–70; civil service and,
60–61, 66–68; civil society and, 61–62,
68; criticisms of, 85–91; deviations and
exemptions from, 188–201; formalism
and functionalism in, 9, 58, 123,
125–126, 161–163; privatization and,
11–13, 17, 126–141; reinforcing
rivalrous administration and, 175–230;
military analogs, 136–139, 196, 199;
serendipity of, 8, 58, 163–164; structure
and mechanics of, 59–63; superstatute
theory of, 70–72. *See also* Administrative
state, modern; Businesslike government;
Pax administrativa; *Pax administrativa,
second*; Privatization
Administrative state, modern: constitutional
defenses of, 50, 63–75; constitutional
criticisms of, 8–9, 55–57; deregulation
and, 89–93, 101–102; disillusionment
with, 84–91; displacement of private